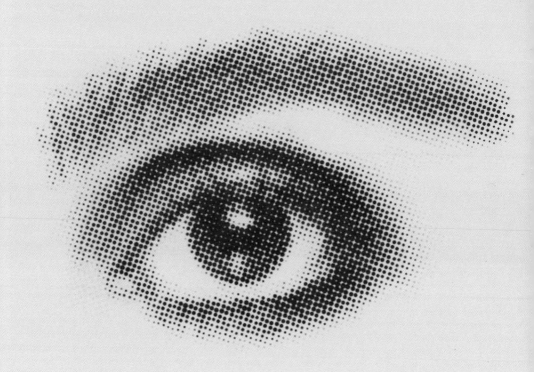

*Cher*

the memoir

# PART ONE

○
○
○

**DEY**ST.

*An Imprint of* WILLIAM MORROW

"You Haven't Seen the Last of Me," written by Diane Warren.
Used by permission of the songwriter.

All insert photographs are courtesy of the author, except insert 1: page 7,
*top left and right:* © Ray Avery/Getty Images; *bottom right:* © Silver Screen
Collection/Getty Images; page 8: © Fred Mott/Getty Images; insert 2: page 1:
Cher, Hollywood, California, September 28, 1966 (contact print). Photograph
by Richard Avedon, © The Richard Avedon Foundation; page 2, *top right:*
© Bettmann/Getty Images; page 3, *top left:* © Gunther/mptvimages.com;
page 5, *bottom:* © Ron Galella/Getty Images; insert 3: page 4, *top left:*
© Everett Collection; *top right:* © MediaPunch Inc/Alamy;
page 5, *top:* © Barry Feinstein Photography

HarperCollins books may be purchased for educational, business, or
sales promotional use. For information, please email the Special Markets
Department at SPsales@harpercollins.com.

FIRST EDITION

*Designed by Renata De Oliveira*

*Endpaper images:* butterfly illustration © Muhammad Zulfan / Adobe Stock;
eyes: © Album/Alamy Stock Photo

Library of Congress Cataloging-in-Publication Data has been applied for.

ISBN 978-0-06-286310-2

24 25 26 27 28 LBC 5 4 3 2 1

this book is dedicated to:

mom~georgia

......................

gee~georganne

......................

chaz

......................

elijah

......................

*Feeling broken*
*Barely holding on*
*But there's just something so strong*
*Somewhere inside me*
*And I am down but I'll get up again*
*Don't count me out just yet*

*I've been brought down to my knees*
*And I've been pushed way past the point of breaking*
*But I can take it*
*I'll be back*
*Back on my feet*
*This is far from over*
*You haven't seen the last of me*
*You haven't seen the last of me*

*They can say that*
*I won't stay around*
*But I'm gonna stand my ground*
*You're not gonna stop me*
*You don't know me*
*You don't know who I am*
*Don't count me out so fast*

*I've been brought down to my knees*
*And I've been pushed way past the point of breaking*
*But I can take it*
*I'll be back*
*Back on my feet*
*This is far from over*
*You haven't seen the last of me . . .*

—"YOU HAVEN'T SEEN THE LAST OF ME"
*(song by Cher)*

# contents

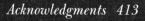

# author's note

This memoir is based on my (sometimes imperfect) memory.

In this memoir, I refer to my son Chaz as Chas, the name he went by during the years covered in this book. Chaz has granted his blessing for this usage. In the next volume, at the appropriate point, I will refer to my son as Chaz.

# preface

*Los Angeles, Summer 1956*

S taring at the television open-mouthed, I let my peanut butter and jelly sandwich drop onto the plate in my lap as chills ran up and down my body.

Home alone after school, I was sitting cross-legged (my favorite position, still) on the floor in front of the TV enjoying the peace and quiet and watching my favorite show, *American Bandstand.* "And now, ladies and gentlemen, Ray Charles," Dick Clark announced as the camera panned to a handsome man in sunglasses sitting at a piano.

"*Georgia, Georgia . . . ,*" he began, and I burst into tears. I couldn't believe he was singing a song about my mom. As tears dripped onto my sandwich, I'd never felt more connected to anything in my life. Ray Charles's voice and the melody seemed to express exactly how I felt.

It took me weeks to get over seeing him sing, and in some ways, I never did, but then someone whose songs I first heard on the radio blew a hole in my understanding of the world and I was never, ever the same. As I stared at the TV with my mom watching *The Ed Sullivan Show,* a popular young singer named Elvis Presley filled the screen. Mom and I were two of the sixty million Americans who witnessed that historic performance in September 1956.

Even though Elvis was dressed quite traditionally that Sunday night, he looked and moved differently than any performer I'd ever seen. He began by singing "Don't Be Cruel," and by the time he broke into "Love Me Tender," I felt as if he was singing only to me. I wanted to jump right into the TV and *be* Elvis.

When I heard a year later that he was giving a concert at the Pan-Pacific Auditorium in Los Angeles, I rushed home with stars in my eleven-year-old eyes. "Mom, Mom! Elvis is going to be at the Pan-Pacific! Can we go? . . . Please?" I was convinced that I had to be there. Secretly, I thought that he would spot me in the crowd and pick me, although I'm sure that's what every girl thought.

Luckily for me, my thirty-one-year-old mother was as crazy about Elvis as I was, a fact that impressed my friends because their moms didn't approve of his raw sexuality. To this day I don't know where she found the money, but somehow Georgia did. Mom and I dressed up and made our way into town, more like sisters than mother and daughter. Feeling the tension grow the closer we got to the Fairfax District, we soon found ourselves caught up in a pulsing mob of nine thousand noisy girls.

We were swept inside the auditorium on a wave of pure adrenaline. Our folding seats were about halfway back in the audience, but that was fine by me. Looking around at all the girls gazing in anticipation at the darkened stage, I could feel my heart pounding inside my flat little chest—a sensation I was to become all too familiar with later in life.

The stage was dark, but when the spotlights hit him, Elvis was there and he was magic. There was a roar from the crowd that was like nothing I had ever heard. An explosion of flashbulbs went off. I only wished I'd brought our little Kodak Brownie. Elvis was standing there in his famous gold suit, which was shimmering and changing color in the spotlights.

He was so handsome with that amazing smile and lustrous black hair, exactly the same color as mine. Everyone around us jumped to their feet and started screaming so hysterically that we could hardly hear a word of "Heartbreak Hotel." But, boy, we could see his moves—the way he gyrated his hips and shook his legs so that they quivered. Not content with making as much noise as they could, the girls began jumping up onto their chairs for a better view, which meant that from then on, we could only see Elvis's head and shoulders.

Being in the middle of that shrieking crowd was like being caught up in a massive swivel-hipped tidal wave, swept along with the hysteria toward the stage. I had no idea why everyone was acting so insane. I was too young to get that part of it, truthfully (but if I had been three years older and my mom had been three years younger, we would have fainted). It was the most exciting experience I'd ever had because I knew that I wanted to be on that stage in the spotlight one day too.

When I looked over at my mother, she was down for the count. We were both mesmerized. She looked so beautiful dressed in some amazing outfit that of all the girls in the place, including me, I felt sure that Elvis would have picked her.

Pressing my mouth to her ear so that she could hear, I cupped my hand over it and yelled, "Mom, can we stand on our seats and scream, too?"

"Yes," she replied, grinning like a teenager and taking off her high heels. "Come on, let's do it!" So we did, straining on our tip-toes to see him.

Glowing with happiness, I tried to work out if Elvis would be too old to marry me by the time I was grown, so that he could sing to me every day. Dreaming of being Mrs. Presley, I couldn't stop talking to Mom about Elvis for weeks as I floated around on a gold lamé cloud.

Cher

# 1

## *georgia on my mind*

Somewhere in the back of a drawer in my mother's house was hidden a small black-and-white photograph of me that I'd never laid eyes on. She couldn't bring herself to share it with me and broke down each time it was even mentioned. To the day she died, the pain of the moment that picture was taken in 1947 was as raw as ever, and the woman later known as Georgia Holt couldn't bear to be reminded of it.

From what little I'd learned, the tiny square of celluloid depicted me as a baby clinging unhappily to the rails of my crib in a Catholic children's home in Scranton, Pennsylvania. It was taken through a small viewing window by my tearful twenty-year-old mom, at that time still "Jackie Jean," her birth name, a singer from rural Arkansas working for tips as a waitress in an all-night diner.

She'd come to see me on one of her weekly visits to the home where my father had placed me before he took off on his latest moneymaking scam. I still can't believe he left her in Scranton with a baby, no money, and few skills, never to return. The nuns took in two types of waifs and strays: teenage girls who'd "strayed from the path of virtue," and infants "rescued from evil surroundings." I guess I fell into the latter category. The sisters charged my mother $4.50 a week, and with the tips she made at the diner, she was just able to make ends meet.

Often when I think of my family history it sounds like the opening of a Dickens novel, but it's true. Ours was a sad, strange story of Southern folk coming from nothing and carving out a life after the Great Depression. It wasn't pretty and it was never easy. Every day was a fight for survival for most of my family going back generations. Resilience is in my DNA.

In another photograph Mom kept for years, her maternal grandparents and their children were captured on the front porch of their funky-ass log cabin in the backwoods of Missouri, flanked by their hound dog. You can tell how hard their life was by the state of the cabin and the look on my grandfather's face. Not one person in the picture was smiling, least of all my great-grandfather Isaac Gulley, a railroad worker with a bushy beard. He once snapped the neck of my grandmother's beloved pet kitten after it got into their bucket of milk. They were so poor there wasn't anything that could be spared, not even for a kitten. She remembered that every day for the rest of her life because she loved that kitten so much and even taught it tricks, including how to push a doll's buggy.

I wish I knew more about my great-grandmother Margaret, who wore her hair in long braids and was the woman in her community who would go into the forest and gather herbs for medicine. With knowledge inherited from her own mother and the local Native Americans, or Original People as I now know they prefer to be called, she knew which herbs and roots to pick from the forest to make natural cures. She also knew some of the tribal dances, which she taught to her children. With the psychic abilities that also ran in my family, she sometimes had premonitions in her dreams and in 1923 had a vivid nightmare that her husband blew up and then fell to the ground in a million tiny pieces like confetti. It was so real to her that, the following day, she gathered her children around her to tell them. By nightfall her husband, Isaac, was dead. Isaac blew up stumps for the railroad for a living and that day he lit too close on the dynamite fuse. He was blown sky high in the explosion.

Widowed and penniless, Margaret struggled to feed her family, and when she lost their small farm, she could only afford to keep the two youngest boys, sending the rest to relatives they didn't know. Skinny, shy, and tiny for her ten years, my grandmother Lynda had to move in with relatives she hated. To pay for her keep, she was sent to work in a boarding house where one of her chores was to fetch the bread from the local bakery. That's where she met my grandfather Roy Crouch, a baker's assistant who'd fled an abusive childhood in Oklahoma to work in a café owned by his elder sister Zella—a tall, dignified, and colorful lady everybody adored. In those days in rural areas, history was passed down orally between generations. It wasn't written. It was the same in my family so no one seemed to know for sure how old Roy and Lynda were when they first met. I was told that Roy was sixteen and Lynda was twelve. Who knows?

The second youngest of nine children, Roy didn't get along with his mother, Laura Belle Greene. According to family folklore, Laura Belle was an imposing figure, almost six feet tall and part Cherokee. She had a fierce temper and beat her smart-mouthed son with a buggy whip. Despite that, I wish I'd known her, as she was, by all accounts, a remarkable woman who passed on her love of music to her children and, ultimately, to me. Once, when she beat him badly, Roy's sisters, my great aunts Zella and Clara who doted on their kid brother, carried him to the springhouse and dabbed his cuts with ointment. Desperate to escape, Roy dreamed of becoming an outlaw like Jesse James or Pretty Boy Floyd, but then he met Grandma Lynda and fell for the twelve-year-old farm girl with no life experience. After a moonlit swim together, she was pregnant and gave birth at the age of thirteen to my mother, Jackie Jean, in 1926. Lynda was too young to cope with a baby, and Roy, tired of her complaining, turned to other women and the illegal whiskey known as "moonshine" during the Prohibition years. When he was drunk, he sometimes beat her, continuing the cycle of violence that began when he was small.

Growing up I heard that he was arrested more than thirty times for violence and drunkenness, and having known him from childhood when he visited us in the summer, I could well believe it. After attacking the local sheriff, who tried to arrest him for bootlegging, Roy went on the run with Lynda and their baby, living the outlaw life he'd always dreamed of. They could only find menial labor, so he and Lynda picked cotton. My mother's earliest childhood memory is of being pulled over uneven ground on a burlap gunnysack while her mom picked cotton, my grandma Lynda stopping every couple of hours to nurse her. A thumb-sucker, Jackie Jean was given one of the fluffy white bolls as a pacifier. A full day's labor in the hot sun was worth a gallon of molasses that the little family ate with biscuits or stale bread—their sole diet apart from the occasional wild rabbit. The only time their bellies were full was when they sneaked back to Zella's bakery for a free meal.

They were saved from starvation by donated government "relief": beans, canned milk, flour, and lard. Lynda had to stand in line for hours to get them. It was the Great Depression, the worst financial collapse in the history of America, in which tens of thousands died of malnutrition and diseases. Jackie Jean was a sickly child who contracted rheumatic fever and strep throat that her grandmother Margaret treated with herbal remedies. When she became dangerously ill with German measles, her parents couldn't afford a doctor, so they handed her over to the Salvation Army until she was well enough to be returned.

Despite almost dying, my mother grew into a pretty child with a singing voice so powerful it could have been that of a grown woman. I guess this apple didn't fall far from that tree. People were astonished to hear her sing, and Roy would swell up with pride for the daughter he affectionately called "Jack." Lynda, still only a child, never took to motherhood, so Jackie Jean saved her love for her daddy, who was caring and fun—when sober. He took her everywhere, including to speakeasies, swinging her up on the counter to sing while he drank.

The first time he passed around his hat for her in the Shamrock Saloon in Saint Louis, with its spittoons and sawdust floor, he was astonished to collect sixteen cents. After buying some liquor, he gave the change to his daughter, who ran to the grocery store to buy a pack of tea, a block of ice, and a bag of sugar for her teenage mother, knowing how much she longed for the sweet tea that her own mother had made her. With her final penny, Jackie Jean treated herself to some candy.

The moment Roy saw that his five-year-old child with the voice of a blues singer could turn him a profit, he declared her the breadwinner. On a good night, people would throw so many nickels that when she stuffed them into her pockets the weight almost pulled down her pants. Although grateful for the money her daughter was earning, her mother was jealous of the attention she was getting and, tired of Roy's neglect and refusal to get married, ran away. She just disappeared and left my mom.

Roy looked everywhere for Lynda and listed her as a missing person. When he couldn't find her, he took Jackie Jean to stay with his sister Lodema and her husband, Wesley. Her uncle molested her. He swore her to secrecy, so she never told her father, and when she finally confessed to her aunt Lodema, she had her mouth washed out with carbolic soap. Helpless, she asked Jesus to save her, and maybe it worked, because she caught chicken pox and was moved to the kitchen, where she couldn't be abused. Jackie Jean's only escape was her singing, and she practiced every day with Roy coaching her. When they sang "Danny Boy" together, she felt safe. "I could fly away from the trouble and the pain when I sang," she said. Having found my own escape in music my whole life, I knew exactly what she meant.

After leaving Saint Louis, the pair headed to South Town in the poorest part of Oklahoma City, where Jackie Jean belted out numbers like "Minnie the Moocher" and "The Saint Louis Blues" on WKY radio. "One day, Jack, you're really gonna be somebody," her father kept promising. "Even Judy Garland don't sing as good as you do." She sang duets with bandleader Bob Wills's popular hillbilly swing band whenever they came into town. It was Bob Wills who told Roy: "That li'l girl is gonna make you rich." With his hopes raised and Prohibition lifted in 1933, my grandfather continued to drag her to every smoke-filled bar in town. No matter how tired or hungry she was, and barefoot on the counter because she didn't have shoes, she kept going until they'd collected enough for food and liquor. The stink of those bars remained with my mother forever. She always said the movie *Paper Moon* perfectly depicted her childhood, except that her father wasn't hawking bibles, he was selling her voice.

Roy never stopped searching for Lynda, and when he finally tracked her down, he got her pregnant again and persuaded her to come back. The couple had no money for rent and lived on day-old bread soaked in watery gravy. They were only saved from eviction because the landlady took pity on Lynda when she almost died from a kidney infection shortly before my uncle Mickey was born. Poorer than he'd ever been, Grampa needed a dream and Jackie Jean was it. Bob Wills had told him her talents were wasted in

Oklahoma, so Roy decided to take her to Hollywood, where, he was convinced, she'd become the new Shirley Temple, the child star who was making $1,000 per week.

It was in the winter of 1934 that my eight-year-old mother began hitchhiking the thirteen hundred miles west with her dad. Broke and hungry, they slept where they could, using Mom's voice to get into cheap hotels. No longer barefoot, she wore a beat-up pair of cowboy boots on the end of her matchstick legs, but the snow was so deep in places that it spilled over the top. A couple who gave them a ride bought my mom her first coat because they couldn't bear to see her shivering by the side of the highway, and a Greyhound bus driver ferried them across New Mexico for free before paying for their night in a motel.

Along the way, Roy put Mom to work selling Christmas cards on street corners and collecting empty soda bottles at movie theaters in return for free admission. Once inside, Jackie Jean stared up in wonder at the silver screen watching movies like *Little Women* with Katharine Hepburn or *Sons of the Desert* with Laurel and Hardy and vowed to be a star one day. Hollywood became her obsession, but when they finally made it to the slums of San Pedro in south Los Angeles, she was shocked to find that the fabled city looked nothing like it did in the movies. Even more distressing was the fact that everyone made fun of them, calling them "dumb Okies" because of their accents and shabby clothing. Life and genetics had already taught her that unless she was strong enough to keep putting one foot in front of the other, she wouldn't make it. She might have been dirt-poor, but she carried herself like a queen.

Roy was a farm boy who hadn't a clue how to get his daughter's talent noticed, so when the overnight success he'd hoped for never materialized, he took a job as a baker at a branch of Clifton's—the iconic cafeteria chain in LA. The moment his boss first set eyes on Jackie Jean, he gave her two dollars to buy some proper shoes, claiming to have found the cash lying under a table. And despite looking like a homeless person with lice in her hair, Mom still won every amateur singing contest she entered and appeared regularly on the radio singing with Jimmy Wakely and His Saddle Pals. She was even offered a scholarship with the Meglin Kiddies youth troupe, where Judy Garland had trained, but had to turn down this once-in-a-lifetime opportunity when she couldn't afford the required tap shoes.

While her father was at work, she hung out at the five-cent movies all day, dodging creeps in the dark. At night it was too dangerous for her to be left alone, so she slept on the bakery's dough tables. Once he'd saved up enough, he paid for Lynda and baby Mickey to join them from Oklahoma, but Lynda was horrified to discover that he'd fathered another child by a teenage girl. It was news to Jackie Jean, too, and she worried about her half sibling for a long time. Faced with the prospect of losing Lynda again, Roy slipped back to his old friend—bourbon. Addiction doesn't just run in my family, it gallops, and its unhappy consequences have been repeated with dreadful symmetry throughout my life. Forced to give up his Hollywood dream, my grandfather went back east with his wife and son. He tied a name tag around Jackie Jean's neck and put her on a train to his sister Zella in Arkansas. Although she missed her father and brother terribly, Mom spent the happiest six months of her childhood in her aunt's comfortable home.

Zella (who I loved) was a force of nature who loved Jackie Jean like a daughter. The kid who'd owned nothing was cleaned up, was put in pretty dresses, and had ribbons threaded in her hair. She won a statewide amateur talent contest in her category for singing the blues. Zella wanted to adopt her and one day send her to college, but when Jackie Jean found out that Lynda had walked out on Roy for good, leaving Mickey behind, she was so afraid for her little brother that she went back to keep him safe.

She found them living in the slums of Oklahoma City. Roy was still so desperate to get Lynda back that when he found out where she was working, he bullied her into visiting her kids. Too afraid to tell him that she'd married a Sicilian man, she agreed. Shocked by how her children were living, she returned a few days later with some money and clothes, but Roy forced her into bed. After the Sicilian found out what happened, he knocked several of Grampa's teeth out and told his wife that he'd adopt her children. Soon afterward my grandfather received a court order informing him that he'd lost custody, news that finally tipped him over the edge.

My mother's recollection of what must have been the worst night of her life was always patchy. It was only when I paid for her to go into therapy years later that the details were finally unlocked. Staying in that crummy place full of crawling things that bit them, Jackie Jean forced herself to lay awake for fear that men might break in and molest them. As she stared out the window, she told herself, "When I grow up, I will *not* live this way." She must have dozed off, because later she woke to the sound of hissing. Not quite awake, she imagined for a moment that the room was full of snakes but then saw a shadowy figure cross their room. Highly attuned to danger, she pretended to be asleep until he'd left. Choking, she suddenly realized that it wasn't snakes she could hear but gas. Jumping up, she grabbed Mickey and ran with him to a neighbor, who called the police. It was only later that my mom realized the shadowy figure she'd seen at 3 a.m. was her father. She recognized his gait and distinctive smell of fresh yeast. Roy had come back from his shift, turned on the gas, and left. She'd heard his steps disappearing down the stairs. The scariest part for her was that Roy was stone-cold sober, and for a long time she couldn't admit to herself that the only parent who ever seemed to love her and my uncle Mickey had tried to end their lives.

The children moved with their mother and Sicilian stepfather to a district of Los Angeles named Gardena. With identical houses and tiny lawns, that stretch of town went on for miles. Roy stayed in Oklahoma, and had no contact with the children he'd attempted to murder even though his daughter still missed him. That year was only made better for Jackie Jean by her stepfather, who gave her the affectionate nickname "String Bean." He was the only kind man she'd ever known. Once again, though, Lynda grew jealous of their closeness, and when my mom reached thirteen—the same age her mother had been when she'd given birth to her—she told her she'd have to go back to live with Roy. She was leaving the Sicilian for his nephew and taking Mickey with her.

I mean, jeez. My family. You couldn't make it up.

She couldn't face the chaos of life with her father, so Jackie Jean scanned the want ads and found work as a live-in maid in Hancock Park. Her employer's home was huge and her chores tough, but my mother never complained because it was the best place she'd ever lived. Vermin-free, it had clean sheets and there was a hot meal on the table every evening. As long as all her work was done, she was allowed to attend a local high school during the day and study late at night.

Mom became well-read, got good grades, and worked on improving her "Okie" accent by reading aloud to herself. Afraid that the rich girls at school might discover how she lived, she got them to like her by showing off her vocal "chops." She also played on her image as a nerdy bookworm, too busy editing the school yearbook to socialize or spend money she didn't have. With the encouragement of her teachers, she finally became the "somebody" her daddy always wanted her to be, although it broke her heart that nobody in her immediate family cared. Every night she curled up on the bathroom floor sobbing into a towel so that no one could hear her, and there were times when she even considered killing herself. Something stopped her, a determination to survive passed on through the female line. Studying hard for a scholarship to college, Jackie Jean was devastated when Roy wrote and begged her to come home. He'd fallen off a curb in Oklahoma City and broken several ribs, putting him in a full-body cast. At fifteen, she gave up her dreams of higher education, and out of a strange mix of pity, love, and duty, she went back to care for her father.

But she was determined to return to the city she thought of as home. She told me, "I knew I had to try to climb up and get back to Los Angeles."

Little did she know where that decision would lead both of us.

# 2

---

## *i'm so lonesome i could cry*

By the age of eighteen Jackie Jean was an accident waiting to happen. She looked like a movie star: built like a goddess with an incredible body, a mane of chestnut hair, and always dressed with perfect taste; you'd never know her clothes all came from the thrift store. But on the inside, she was still a country girl at heart and far too easy to manipulate.

She had been raised a Baptist, and it had been drilled into her by Roy that she should never have sex with a man until she was married. "Don't you ever, *ever* let a man touch you unless you're wed!" her father warned her repeatedly, no doubt reflecting on his own history. With his words ringing in her ears, Jackie Jean got it into her head that she'd get pregnant if she even French-kissed a boy. And after her childhood molestation, she was determined to avoid sex until she met "Mr. Right." My smooth-talking Armenian father, Johnnie Sarkisian, was Mr. Wrong from the outset, and when he asked my mother to jitterbug with him at a Harry James big band dance in Fresno, California, in 1944, her instincts warned her to be careful. The spoiled youngest son of a large Armenian family, Johnnie was a year older than Mom but wore the kind of flashy clothes and jewelry that gave him an air of greater maturity. He wasn't her type and was too short for her taste, but when they danced together her blouse got caught on his shirt button and she literally couldn't get away. By the time he'd unhooked her, she realized that he not only was a good dancer but possessed a certain charm.

They started dating at a time when life had a heightened reality and a sense of spontaneity because of the war raging across Europe. Even though Johnnie had been drafted into the US Coast Guard (before he was medically discharged), neither he nor my mother had any firsthand experience of World War II. When Mom's friend Ann started dating Johnnie's best friend Johnny Kevorkian, Mom was persuaded to go horseback riding with them but almost fell off when her saddle slipped. Johnnie saved her, his first grandstand play. His next was to teach her to drive and promise her his Buick convertible. After that, the couple started seeing each other regularly, but she wouldn't sleep with him because they weren't married.

One night in the club where Jackie Jean worked as a waitress and singer, a customer who knew Johnnie's weakness for gambling threw some money on the table and told him, "Stop mooning around her like a sick cow. Marry her." He challenged him to drive her to Reno, Nevada, where couples could marry with no waiting period. Cheered on by friends with a similar idea, four of them left that night. Beguiled by his charm and apparent stability, and impressed by his age and experience, Mom found him strong, quiet, and capable. Before she knew it, she was pronounced Mrs. Sarkisian in a hasty double wedding. Having just turned nineteen, and having not yet found her sass, it didn't occur to my mother to say no, even though she thought, *What am I doing?* and was so unhappy it was all she could do not to cry. Less than twenty-four hours after the ceremony and still a virgin, she walked out on Johnnie and fled back to Fresno, where a friend promised to help her apply for an annulment. My father followed and wouldn't hear of it. "How do you know you don't want to be married?" he protested. "You haven't even tried it yet. Give me three months."

Gullible and trapped, my mother was living at a time when women had little or no support from society, so, seeing no other way out, she went back to Johnnie even though she claimed she never loved or trusted him. "He could always outtalk me, outthink me, and outsmart me. I was no match for him, and he charmed me into it." And by *it*, I knew she meant sex.

The women in my family rarely chose their men well and Jackie Jean was no exception, but with Lynda her sole role model, she stood little chance. Beneath his polished veneer, my father would become a heroin addict with a penchant for larceny and a shaky relationship to employment. Not that she knew that to begin with. As newlyweds, my parents led a chaotic, nomadic existence, living on my mother's wages and staying with Armenian relatives until their patience—or funds—ran out. Johnnie's family was disappointed because no one had ever married a non-Armenian woman, but seeing as my dad was the "spoiled child" they forgave him. Except for my grandmother, who was very upset and said, "Hohvannes, she's too long for you!" The only relative who really welcomed my mom was Aunt Roxy, who wasn't at all traditional like the rest of them. She wanted to be an American girl and do everything my mom did. They got on like a house on fire. But it wasn't enough to keep her with my dad. So, miserable, she walked out after the three months were up and sought solace with her thirty-two-year-old mother. Instead of taking pity on her, however,

Grandma Lynda demanded to know if she was pregnant. When it turned out that she was, Lynda, a waitress who had no intention of being saddled with "a brat," took her to get an abortion.

With nowhere else to go, my mother reluctantly agreed and was taken to a sympathetic doctor in Long Beach, one of a handful of professionals who helped women illegally despite the risks of imprisonment (not unlike today). Mom was petrified. She told me years later, "I remember waiting in an old-fashioned chrome chair. The chrome was cold, yet the sweat was running off me, I was so scared. When they told me it was my turn, I got onto the table. But as I lay there, I somehow knew I couldn't go through with it, so I got off. Can you believe I came that close to not having you?" She was at a dreadful point in her young life with only two roads to choose from, neither of which were easy. Confused and afraid, she headed down one road but then turned back and took the other. I survived as a consequence, and I've never questioned how close she came to not having me. It was her body, her life, and her choice to make. Thank God she got off that table, though, or I wouldn't be here to write these pages.

Lynda was furious at Jackie Jean's change of heart and warned her: "If you don't go through with this, don't think you can come home to me." Distraught, Mom fled from the clinic where my heartbeat was almost stilled. Returning to Johnnie, she was so angry with her mother that they didn't speak for months. Once her pregnancy started to show and it was considered no longer decent for her to sing in public, Jackie Jean had to give up work. With no money coming in, my father moved them to the sleepy town of El Centro near the Mexican border, where he planned to run a trucking company that he'd persuaded his father to buy. Its drivers hauled fresh produce to the markets of Los Angeles, and, for a time, life was good. Johnnie found them a house and acted more responsibly at first, but then he started playing poker every night and often didn't return home.

Unhappy, stressed, and feeling trapped, my mother went into labor a month early and was taken to the only hospital in El Centro, with a small maternity unit. There was no pain relief, and the labor was long. She was exhausted by the time I arrived at around 7:30 a.m. on Monday, May 20, 1946. I was born under the sign of Taurus on the cusp of Gemini, so it's like there are three of us in here. Premature, I wanted to get the hell out of there, find me some wheels, and get going. But weighing only six pounds, I had to stick around the hospital a few weeks longer.

Grandma Lynda hadn't spoken to Mom since she'd fled from the abortion clinic, but the night before I was born, she had a psychic dream and woke my grandpa Charlie in the middle of the night. "Get up. We have to go," she told him. "Jackie Jean's having a baby girl." In a rare pang of maternal guilt, she made him drive all night to El Centro so that she could greet me.

While my mother was recovering in the hospital, a nurse came into her room and asked, "And what are you going to name your baby?" My mother had no idea, but the woman insisted so she replied, "Well, Lana Turner's my favorite actress and her little girl's called Cheryl. My mother's name is Lynda, so how about Cherilyn?" I believed Cherilyn was my name until the day years later when I decided to legally change my name to simply Cher. When I applied for my birth certificate, I was shocked to find that I was officially registered as Cheryl and asked my mother, "Do you even know my real name, Mom?"

"Let me look at that!" she cried, snatching the document. Presented with the evidence, she shrugged. "I was only a teenager, and I was in a lot of pain. Give me a break."

To celebrate my birth, Johnnie bought Mom a ruby and diamond watch in pink gold and furnished her with a cradle and buggy. Happy in her maternal cocoon, she became "the little woman" in the kitchen for the first time in her life, and even embroidered the tiny kimono the hospital sent me home in. I still have it because my mom had it framed for me as a birthday gift. Their home was modest, but they had enough, and she was happy. Then six months after my birth, Johnnie came home one night and told her that he'd lost his father's trucking business in a card game. Everything was gone. My mother couldn't believe what she was hearing.

Within days she had to vacate their home, hock her watch, and move into an ugly steel Quonset hut, an arched prefabricated building often used as barracks during the war. In temperatures of up to 120 degrees in the desert, it was like living inside an oven. When she threatened to leave again, Johnnie came up with some money and a plan. They'd go to New York, where he had a sister who he hoped would invest in his next venture. It sounded implausible, but Mom was so desperate to get out of that "metal coffin" that she had no choice but to pack our bags.

During an interminable fifty-hour ride on a Greyhound bus, they traveled twenty-five hundred miles across nine states, making multiple changes. On the way Johnnie confessed that he'd stolen a car and sold it in Mexico to pay the fare but almost got caught, and there was a warrant out for his arrest. Perhaps picking up on my mother's distress, I cried constantly, and she didn't know how to calm me. "I didn't do well as a mother," she admitted. "I was hysterical all the time because of the turmoil I was in."

Johnnie's sister Liz lived in a tiny New York apartment and had neither the funds to invest in any business nor the space to share her home. Walking the freezing streets wrapped in Johnnie's overcoat, Mom pressed me against her body to keep me warm. Her husband became increasingly paranoid every time he saw a cop and claimed it was too risky for him to apply for a job. With their money running out, Jackie Jean knew she needed to do something. She applied for a position as a hatcheck girl at the Copacabana nightclub on East Sixtieth Street, where the boss—a mobster—demanded to see her legs. After she nervously lifted her dress, he was so impressed that he upgraded her to cigarette girl so that his customers at the Brazilian-themed club and restaurant could admire them too. The club that would become famous in the fifties and sixties for hosting shows by Dean Martin, Jerry Lewis, and Sammy Davis Jr., and would later be immortalized in Barry Manilow's song of the same name, was bustling and Mom made good money. She was even able to pocket a few illicit tips, but after she received her first paycheck, Johnnie announced that they were leaving the city as the New York police were on to him.

Reassuring my mother that he'd get work in Scranton, Pennsylvania, a hundred miles northwest of New York, he promised to get us back to California. After another long bus journey, he checked us into a cheap hotel, but the jobs he'd bragged about never materialized. This was my mother's worst nightmare. When they were down to a few cents—enough to buy me two bottles of milk—she lost it completely. "You must do something, Johnnie!" she shrieked. "We have a child depending on us now." Years later, she was like a tigress when it came to protecting me and my sister, but back then she was unaware of how strong she was.

My father said he'd hitchhike back to New York to borrow money from his sister while my mother found work as a waitress. "But what about the baby?" she asked, horrified.

Raised a Catholic, my father had an answer for that too. "There's got to be a church organization around here that we can board her with until we've got enough money to get her back." Gifted in the art of persuasion, he then sold his sob story to a priest, who put him in touch with the nuns at a local home for children and unwed mothers. "It'll only be for two weeks," he promised Jackie Jean. "Then I'll be back for you and little Cherilyn and we'll all go home."

At first, Mom was calm. In her mind there was a plan in place. Everything would be fine, her husband and child would be back in two weeks. But once my dad left, the reality of the situation came crashing down on her. Mom didn't know a soul in the sprawling coal-mining town, she hardly had a cent to her name, and her baby was in a strange institution. When Johnnie took off, Mom moved into an eight-by-ten room that was little more than a cubicle and found a job in an all-night diner, where she was expected to work twelve-hour shifts from 7 p.m. to 7 a.m., seven days a week. As a mother, I can only imagine, and the thought chills my bones. The home where she left me was one of hundreds dotted all over the United States that took in poverty-stricken orphans and other kids until their families could afford to care for them. Jackie Jean was appalled by the idea of leaving me with these severe-looking sisters in black robes, even if it was only temporary. Her concerns were only magnified when she sensed the nuns' disapproval of her from the outset for being a Baptist. Powerless, she walked away in tears as my howls rang in her ears.

Returning to her cramped accommodation every dawn after her shift, she'd crawl into bed and cry herself to sleep. Alone in the world with no friends, no baby, and her husband gone, she didn't know how much longer she could go on and scanned the newspaper looking for a better-paying job. A lucky break came with a position in the Manila Bar & Grill, where she was hired as a waitress and singer. The owner was kind, the tips were good, and she was able to visit me twice a week. Everything began to feel more hopeful until to her horror Jackie Jean discovered that she was pregnant—by my father, the only man she'd ever had sex with.

Again, her life was spinning out of control. Aside from singing, the one thing Mom had learned was how to use her looks to get out of a bind. There was a regular at her restaurant, an older married man named Dave. He tipped generously, especially if she sang his favorite song, "My Man." My mother begged for his help.

"But where's your husband, kid?" he asked, and when she broke down, he agreed reluctantly, telling her: "You're asking an awful lot from a guy who's never even kissed you." He neverthe-less found a woman who'd perform an abortion for a hundred dollars and arranged for someone to drive my mother to and from the secret address. After the procedure, Jackie Jean was in so much pain that she had to be driven straight to the home of a nurse instead. She was in bed for three weeks to recover. When Dave visited Mom in her sickbed, she asked him what he'd have done if she hadn't survived. His reply shocked her.

"Kid, I won't lie to you. We'd have dumped your body in the river, or we could have all gone to jail." If that had happened, I'd have been adopted or remained with the nuns forever. Shocking as Dave's answer now sounds, prosecutions of those who carried out abortions were commonplace. Police kicking down the doors of clinics and private homes was as everyday as their raids on brothels and gambling dens. Those who were caught helping women faced prison sentences (once again, not unlike now) of an average of three to five years and lost their license to practice if they had medical qualifications. The women were generally regarded as victims and coerced into testifying, but the stigma of the trial could ruin them, so the risks were enormous for everyone.

As soon as she was healthy again after those three weeks, Mom hurried to the children's home to pay for my keep and collect me for a day out. She was shocked when the nuns forbade it. She wasn't even allowed to hold me. All they'd let her do was view me through a small window in a door. "As I looked in, you were standing in your crib holding on to the sides and crying. I was crying too. I felt so helpless."

Her protests fell on deaf ears and the mother superior was especially unkind to her because she worked in a place that sold liquor. She didn't even believe Mom was married and kept asking, "Why isn't your husband here? Isn't he concerned for his child?" Unsophisticated in the ways of the world, Jackie Jean was afraid that if she stood up for herself, the home might keep me forever. With no way to contact Johnnie and no one else to turn to, she decided that the minute my dad came back from New York she'd insist he get me out. My deadbeat father never returned or even sent word. He simply vanished. In time, she convinced herself that the only reason she was destined to meet him in the first place was so that I would exist. That was all he was good for.

"I cried so many nights in my tiny room wondering what I was going to do and where in the hell was Johnnie. I really hated him." All she could do was go to the children's home each week and demand to see me. The sight of my little face through the viewing window broke her heart, but it was on one of those visits that she borrowed a camera to take the photograph she held so dear. By early 1947, the mother superior declared that Jackie Jean Sarkisian was an unfit mother, and it would be better if she gave me up for adoption. Mom refused, but it was almost impossible to question authority as a penniless single mother.

She went to Dave again remembering that he was a City Council member. Reluctantly he agreed to help, saying, "I can't buck the entire Catholic Church, but I'll figure something out." After he took her to dinner on her next day off, she was fearful of where this might lead, but she would have made a pact with the devil to save me.

Dave offered to buy her train ticket. He then marched into the children's home and told the mother superior: "You have no legal right to keep Cherilyn Sarkisian here anymore." Frightened, she handed me straight over. To her dying day, my mother couldn't or wouldn't remember how long I was in that place, but it must have been several months, as I arrived as an infant barely able to crawl and when I came out, I was walking.

The behavior of those nuns haunted my mother her whole life. Mine is one of hundreds of similar stories of children kept by the Church or put up for adoption against the will of their frightened young mothers, who were condemned as being sinful or irresponsible. That kind of shit has been happening to women since the beginning of time. I have since come to know many wonderful and loving nuns in my life, but I still find it hard to forgive those who tried to take my mother's child and ruin both of our lives.

Almost fifty years later I finally expressed my feelings about that time in a song I wrote for my mom called "Sisters of Mercy." It was one of the few that I ever wrote, sang, and produced myself. I woke up one day in 1994 in a chateau in France, where I'd been invited to a songwriting symposium, and the words poured out of me in one sitting. They begin: *"Your faith is not faithful. Your grace has no grace. Your mercy shows no mercy. Is there no way out of this place?"* I didn't hold back, because it continues: *"There's a baby sobbing softly, in a crib that's now a cage. She's done nothing to deserve this, but it sanctifies their rage."* The chorus was *"Sisters of Mercy, daughters of hell."* When I first played it to Mom, she sobbed and sobbed, but I think it made her feel vindicated and took some of the pain away.

Furious, some elements of the Catholic Church damned my song as "extremely inflammatory." I understood their response; it was a tough song. But I did it for my mom, and it brought her some kind of relief. "Sisters of Mercy" wasn't a condemnation of the entire Catholic Church but a valid and heartfelt response to those who used their power to hurt my mom.

In all that time she was never able to share the only photograph of me in that forbidding institution, an image left lying in the back of a drawer. She couldn't get through five words about it without breaking down. And yet, of all the millions of pictures taken of me over the years, that was the one I most desperately wanted to see but never did.

# 3

## a dream is a wish your heart makes

One thing is for certain: my childhood was never normal, but it was only once I was older that I fully understood why I've always hated being left. Maybe that's why I always left first. Given my history, it's probably not surprising. My fear of abandonment undoubtedly stems from being separated from my mother as a baby, and my inner drama queen has become an integral part of the complicated human being that is me.

After Mom freed me from the nuns, she caught a train to Twin Falls, Idaho, where my grandpa Roy and uncle Mickey were living in squalor. Rescuing her twelve-year-old brother, she made her way to LA, where she settled him with Grandma Lynda temporarily while she eked out a living waiting tables. I was a little over a year old, so I have no memories from this time but had been told that I'd been babysat by my grandma's friends Edith and Mackie, while Mom worked her ass off. It wasn't until I was in my thirties and playing at Caesars Palace in Las Vegas that Grandma Lynda came backstage right before my show as I was putting on my makeup and introduced me to Mackie, who'd been her neighbor. I'd heard a lot about her and knew she was one of my babysitters when I was little. But then she produced an old wooden highchair with a worn decal of Bambi. "This was yours when you used to live with us," Mackie announced, eager for me to have it.

"Live with you?" I asked, so taken aback that I could barely speak. In my mind, I thought, *Fuck, the blows just keep on coming!* You know how sometimes if you start to talk, you'll end up crying? So instead I just sat in stunned silence and continued to put my makeup on. I knew I had a sold-out performance, and by that time in my life I was able to compartmentalize, which is a trick that served me well through the rest of my career. (This has happened to me more times than I care to remember, something upsetting right before I have to perform. It's strange, you kind of go into suspended animation.) It wasn't until much later that I was able to corner my grandmother, who told me that my stay in the children's home wasn't the only time I'd been left in the care of virtual strangers. When I was around two years old, Mackie took me in, as did Edith, who was a young mother at the time. I thought, *Damn, this abandonment is never-ending!*

"So how long was I with these women?" I asked, reeling.

"Oh, for quite a long time," Lynda replied. Having never had a normal childhood herself, this fact didn't faze her at all, and she revealed it to me casually, as if it weren't important that I'd been dumped again because my own family couldn't care for me. No wonder I felt so insecure and had separation anxiety throughout my life. The emotions that bubbled to the surface with this new information troubled me for a long time. I began to remember strange things, jigsaw pieces of the past that made me feel as if I had no connection to parts of my own story. I didn't know how to put the pieces together and needed someone to help me. "But I don't understand," I told my grandmother. "Where was Mom all this time?"

Lynda hesitated. "Well, she was young and busy and then she met this guy in Reno, and he was rich—"

I stopped her dead. I knew in that instant that Lynda, who was obsessed with finding my mom a wealthy husband, would have encouraged her to stay with a wealthy man, even if that meant giving me up. So, although Mom had fought for me in Scranton, pressured by my grandmother, she'd left me again. WTF?

The story of what happened after that unfolded gradually, and the timeline still isn't clear. After I'd been saved from the nuns, I was left with Mackie and Edith, and Mickey was placed somewhere else. Meanwhile, my mother and grandmother traveled to Nevada to seek divorces from their respective husbands. Taking advantage of what was dubbed "the Reno Cure," they had to establish residency for six weeks before their separations could become legal.

While in Reno, there was a local beauty pageant Lynda urged Mom to enter even though neither thought she would actually win. Mom was amazed when she was crowned the "Model Miss." She won a cash prize and her picture was in the paper for days. In one photograph, she was winking at someone in the audience, and when I asked who that was, she said it was my grandmother.

My grandmother was even more excited when she spotted Ernest Primm, a millionaire who was a regular in the Gardena Club in LA, where Lynda was his favorite waitress. Ernie was a middle-aged, balding Texan with a property empire that included Reno's Palace Club Casino and the Primadonna Club. It was a match made in heaven. My grandmother's greed and his money. Lynda was eager to introduce her single daughter to the man she called the "big boss." Grandma Lynda soon set her sights on making Ernest Primm her son-in-law. As she was fond of saying, "It's as easy to fall in love with a rich man as it is a poor man." And if you hear that often enough when you're young, you start to believe it, especially when your own mother sets you up.

To this day I feel sorry for my grandmother and the life she had, and I'm even more sorry that she instilled so much toxic stuff in my mom, who was so needy of her love and approval. She would tell me the same about marrying a rich man when I was growing up, and it's where she got her belief that if you were beautiful, you deserved a man who's loaded.

Lynda's scheming went better than she'd hoped, because Ernie fell for Mom after watching her sing "Can't Help Lovin' Dat Man" in a supper club. From then on, he was all over her like a cheap suit, buying her a mink coat and a diamond bracelet. This was a huge shift from her experience with my father, Johnnie, and she was dazzled. Ernie was also far better educated, and he drilled the hick out of her by teaching her how to dress, eat, walk, and even play craps. Using her natural poise and her fond memories of her statuesque aunt Zella, she threw her shoulders back and became such an elegant lady that few would have guessed she came from skid row (though she'd still talk like a sailor among friends, which is where I get it from). Still in her early twenties, Mom became fond of Ernie and knew they could have a wonderful life together once his own divorce was finalized. There was only one problem—he didn't want me around. Promising that I'd be educated in the finest schools on his dime, Ernie made it clear that I wasn't part of the deal. Mom chose to heed Lynda's advice to be patient: "He'll give you the moon with a string on it when you become his wife."

Once their divorces became official, the two women returned to LA. My mom entered and won another contest. This crown was for "Miss Holiday on Wings." She was photographed in a swimsuit sitting astride a model plane. The cash prize was a staggering

$750, much more than she'd have earned as a waitress in a month. This time she was spotted by a talent scout who offered her a scholarship to the Ben Bard School of Dramatic Arts, one of the most respected drama schools in Hollywood. This was all she'd hoped for when she swore on skid row that she'd have a better life. This would count as the first step in keeping the promise she had made to herself all those years ago sitting up through the night, watching over her little brother. But, still waiting for Ernie, she postponed her enrollment and I remained with Mackie and Edith.

One night she attended a gala event at the Hollywood Palladium. Mom was asked to dance by a devastatingly handsome young actor named Chris Alcaide. He towered over her at six feet four inches. Chris worked at Dolores' Drive-in on Wilshire Boulevard but was studying drama at Ben Bard's, which felt to my mom like fate. After a few more meetings, they started dating behind Ernie's back. The first time I met Chris, my mother watched as he folded at the waist. He threw open his arms and I ran into them. Ernie would never have done anything like that. *I'm going to marry that man*, Mom thought, knowing then that she could never be with a man who didn't love me. She walked away from Ernie and all he had to offer, telling him she wouldn't give me up. She and Chris were married a few days later, making him Husband No. 2. She then enrolled in the drama school where, coincidentally, Shirley Temple had first learned her craft. It was the closest Jackie Jean got to being like "Little Miss Miracle" as her father once dreamed.

Ben Bard, the founder of the drama school, was a former vaudeville and silent movie star who was a talent scout for Twentieth Century–Fox. My mother was in class with some heavy-hitters-to-be, including Rod Steiger, who went on to star in *On the Waterfront* and *In the Heat of the Night*; Stuart Whitman; David Janssen; and Robert "Bob" Mitchum. With all these colorful characters around me, it's no surprise that I ended up as a performer.

Life felt settled for Mom, Chris, and me. She had her classes at night, which she loved, and was booking commercials for Hotpoint washing machines, cars, watches, and even Beech-Nut peppermint gum on programs like *The Dinah Shore Show.* My babysitters would drop me at her drama class in the evenings and I'd watch rehearsals of productions like *Oklahoma!* and *A Christmas Carol.* Being the only kid there, I was made a big fuss of, and when I could no longer keep my eyes open, I'd curl up under my mother's coat at the back of the theater and fall asleep.

I memorized my first Shakespearean monologue at Ben Bard. At four, I didn't have a clue about ancient prose or iambic pentameter. I just liked the rhythm of the words and the sounds they made. Nor did I understand the play Mom was rehearsing, but I thought the spooky chicks were cool. I surprised everyone by coming out with the Song of the Witches from *Macbeth*, which begins, *"Double, double toil and trouble, fire burn and cauldron bubble . . ."* Nobody could believe that I could pick up something so complicated and repeat it. The skill was unique for a four-year-old and has served me well my whole life. Whenever the drama school put on a musical, my mom was given the lead because she was by far the best singer. I was accustomed to her singing at home, but it felt different watching her belt out the big numbers on a stage and I loved it. My mom and all the cast were so good at their performances that at four it felt real to me when she played Laurey in *Oklahoma!* and Michael Ansara, as the villain, Jud, attacked her. The moment Mom started screaming for help, I became so hysterical that I had to be taken outside. I only calmed down when Michael gently explained that it wasn't real. He was so sweet with me. He was devilishly handsome with dark features, and I felt a special affinity with the Syrian-born actor with the same look as me. He went on to play Cochise in the TV show *Broken Arrow.*

It was Michael who inadvertently caused Mom to leave her husband after months of fighting. Chris Alcaide was a jealous type who couldn't bear another man paying her any attention. This was especially true when he'd had too much to drink, which was often. At one cocktail party he spotted a tipsy Michael Ansara make a pass at her while she was getting their coats from the bedroom. Chris grabbed her and shook her until she thought her head would snap off. When they got home, their fight turned more violent. He pushed her up against a wall and closed his fingers around her throat. Her survival instincts kicked in and she cried, "What will happen to Cher if you kill me and go to jail?" In his drunken angry state, it was only his fondness for me that made him stop.

They divorced soon afterward, and at Lynda's suggestion Mom tried to win back Ernie Primm, but once he made it clear I'd never live with them, she walked away from him for good. I don't remember Ernie at all and only have a faint memory of Chris. I do know that he was very handsome, but then, all of my mom's friends looked like movie stars to me. They were all so talented and working across the arts: singers, dancers, painters, sculptors. I didn't know there were people who worked in offices. I knew there were cab drivers. From the age of four, this was my world, these were my role models.

Not long after she broke up with Chris she met the first true love of her life, a struggling actor named E. J. "John" Southall. She fell for him the minute she set eyes on him, something she had never felt before. My mom married John (Husband No. 3), but this time for love. He was and is the only man I think of as my father. Having declared that men are "things you love against your will," my mother was becoming a serial monogamist. The new man in her life was charming, handsome, and penniless. I suspect that one of the reasons the suntanned, sweet-talking Texan, who'd captained B-29 bombers during the Korean War, never made it as an actor was because he couldn't lose his accent. It wasn't so profound that people would start singing "The Yellow Rose of Texas," but it was enough to keep him typecast. If looking good were a marketable skill, though, he'd have been a millionaire. They made a spectacular couple.

My mom's best friend was Jacquie, known to all as "Jake." Her husband was Kenny. John and Kenny were in the same drama class. The four of them became very close.

An only child, John had no memories of his own dad, Eunice James Harmon Southall, known as "E. J.," who was gassed in the First World War and died in 1934 at the age of forty-one. My new stepfather was christened after him, but everyone outside his family called him John. Raised in Texas by his grandmother and two loving aunts, he was eager for a family of his own. Not long after he and Mom were wed, he told her to fetch me from my babysitters and bring me to live with them, which is how, at the age of four and a half, I found myself with a dad for the first time. In the back of my head I knew that he wasn't my real father, but I never gave it any thought. (I also knew there was another someone out there, a shadowy figure I sensed was a man that nobody talked about, a missing piece of the jigsaw puzzle.) Most important, the only man I ever called Daddy loved me and treated me as his own. That was good enough for me.

Like most budding actors, my stepfather was constantly on the grind and earned a living doing something else, in his case selling aluminum siding door-to-door with Kenny. They were both so handsome I'm amazed they weren't siding tycoons. Aside from Bob Mitchum and Rod Steiger, all my parents' actor friends had side hustles to pay the rent, doing anything from bartending to interior decorating. They didn't know how to have a nine-to-five, and none of them wanted that anyway. Lacking a formal education, my mom honed her acting skills and took any acting job she got. She even tried her hand at stunt driving and drove in a few commercials. She played a dance hall girl in the TV Western *Gunsmoke*, and had walk-on parts in shows like *The Adventures of Ozzie and Harriet* and *I Love Lucy*. In one hilarious episode with Lucille Ball that has been shown repeatedly over the years, my mom and two other actors played Paris models wearing gowns made of potato sacks and surrealist flowerpot hats. The woman Mom knew as "Lucy" liked her because she was young and pretty with dark red hair, so she hired her regularly. My mom admired and respected Lucy, so it made it even more difficult when she had to dodge advances from Desi Arnaz, Lucy's husband. She had a similar problem with Ozzie of *Ozzie and Harriet*, who once tried to show an actor—several times over—how to kiss Mom "properly" in a scene.

If she couldn't get walk-on parts, my mother picked up work as an "extra" for $25 a day and sought engagements as a lounge singer, but they meant late nights away from Daddy and me. When money was tight, we'd have to move in with John's mom, Betty, known as "Mamaw," and her husband, George, known as "Pa." I didn't mind it a bit because they treated me like a precious angel, which I loved. Meeting them was a huge shift in my life. The first time I met them I was taken to their house one night and Mamaw came out onto the front porch, took one look at me, and said, "So, this is my sweet baby?" They lived in a beautiful three-bedroom house with a big garden and fruit trees in Miracle Mile. With them in our lives, being a Texan became a badge of honor. Mamaw was Texan, Pa was Texan, Daddy was Texan, and I think he always thought we might go back there to live one day.

When my parents' work was steadier, we'd move instead to places like Crescent Heights Boulevard in the Hollywood Hills or to Laurel Canyon, where we had the first real family home that I can remember—a funky property off a steep, winding road called Lookout Mountain. North of Hollywood Boulevard, Laurel Canyon was a cheap district that attracted artists, musicians, and bohemians to its hillside bungalows and cottages nestled between faded mansions. I was five years old when we first lived there. My babysitter by then was a Mexican teenager named Maria whose job was to distract me from the distress of my parents' going out at night. Every time they left the house, I'd throw myself on the floor and pitch a fit, kicking, crying, and screaming. I was young, and I was terrified when they left at nighttime. I also knew that things had changed and I was overreacting a gargantuan amount. Sometimes, in the midst of these tantrums, I'd even ask myself, *Cher, what the fuck are you doing?* (I know it was early for that word, but I was only ever around grown-ups, so I'd heard it.) *They're just going to dinner!* But I didn't understand that feeling of abandonment, even if it was an emotion I came to honestly.

During the daylight hours I was unbothered by those fears, and instead had an adventurous streak. My favorite game to play with Maria was hide and seek.

One afternoon we decided to play it in the woods near our house. Excited, I skipped off—barefoot as usual—determined to find a good hiding place so that Maria wouldn't find me right away. It was only when I'd roamed farther than ever before and found myself in a small clearing surrounded by towering trees that I realized I was lost. I couldn't hear Maria calling anymore and the shadows were beginning to lengthen. Scared out of my little size 4 cotton underpants, I started calling her name in a scratchy voice as my imagination conjured coyotes and mountain lions lurking in the bushes to gobble up this knee-high snack. I was probably lost for less than twenty minutes before Maria found me, but it seemed like days.

My solution during the scariest or saddest moments of my childhood was to retreat inside my head. I think a part of me has been doing that ever since. Such was my imagination that I decided I was an angel sent from God whose mission was to cure polio, an infectious disease that caused paralysis and could kill children, who were the worst affected. News bulletins showed kids locked into breathing machines known as "iron lungs," or bent out of shape and walking stiffly in ugly leather and metal leg braces.

An early theory was that polio was carried by mosquitoes, so one day when Mom caught me jumping around in a dirty puddle, she went nuts and her Southern side came out. "Cher! Get out of there or I'm gonna snatch you bald-headed!" she screamed, convinced I'd be infected and die. I was so obsessed with the idea that I was an angel sent to cure the disease that when Jonas Salk invented a vaccine, I was so pissed off.

From angels my imagination leapt to Jesus, because not long afterward I thought I saw Christ's face in the folds of my organdy bedroom curtains. Half-asleep one morning, I looked up to see Jesus looking back down at me, and then he was gone. I should have said something, but I didn't, so I missed my chance to become Saint Cher.

Being on my own with babysitters so often, as both my parents were working, I invented invisible friends that only I could see. Being the peculiar kid I was, I came up with "Sam and Pete," two stubble-faced lumberjacks/truck drivers in jeans, plaid Pendleton shirts, and hats with flaps over their ears (though they didn't always wear their hats). They lived under the lemon tree in the backyard of Mamaw and Pa's house and dwarfed me with their presence. They were 100 percent real in my mind. I was just a kid, so where did I get that crazy idea?

Once I had those two giants in my life, I was happy as a clam talking to them about everything from why men drank to our dream places to live. We never ran out of conversation. In my head, they lived with Mamaw and Pa, who never questioned my need for fantasy friends.

Whenever I went to their house, I'd lay out a picnic under the lemon tree, near the trapeze my grandmother had made for me out of clotheslines and broom handles, and we'd have the nicest little tea parties, drinking homemade lemonade and eating cherry tomatoes that I'd pick fresh from the vine that grew on the side of my grandmother's fence. When my mother saw me chattering away to thin air and found out about them, she freaked out. It was Mamaw who calmed her down and told her not to be ridiculous. "She's just a child—an *only* child. It's just a phase." With Sam and Pete by my side, I was no longer quite so lonely.

Music was another refuge for my busy brain, and as a toddler I loved to join in with my mother, who always sang in the house. I'd run around in my underpants, singing into my hairbrush in tune with Mom.

For years whenever Grampa Roy came for his annual visit from Oklahoma (and before he had that one drink too many), my uncle Mickey would come over and we'd all sing together as a family. Roy, weak from years of alcoholism, could still play the hell out of a guitar, hee-hawing with glee all the while. That old man was a pistol and taught me many of my favorite tunes, like "Hey, Good Lookin'" and "Your Cheatin' Heart." I knew country music before any other kind, and the music of Hank Williams especially. Known as the "Hillbilly Shakespeare," Hank was immortal in our eyes.

Movies were another big thing in my childhood, an infatuation I inherited from my mom. It began for me when my parents took me to see *Dumbo* at Grauman's Chinese Theatre when I was five. That historic landmark, built on Hollywood Boulevard nearly twenty years before I was born, was a paradise for a kid like me. It was as big as a city and as amazing to me as the Great Wall of China. It was everything. If you couldn't have an out-of-body experience in that magical place, you were never gonna have one. Going there for the first time in my patent Mary Jane shoes, I was speechless with excitement, not least because it had the most colossal candy counter in the history of the universe, with candy I didn't even know existed. Staring up at it through the glass, I was so overwhelmed, I chose popcorn and a candy that I knew. We then followed a girl dressed in a beautiful Chinese costume into a red and gold theater so enormous that King Kong could have tap-danced on the stage. The walls were flanked with huge columns, and there were paintings, statues, and ornate moldings as well as an overhead light as big as a Buick. Having taken my seat next to Mom and Dad with my feet sticking straight out in front of me, I stared up in wonder when the lights were dimmed, the velvet curtains lifted as if by magic, and the music began. Then, miracle of miracles, images began flickering up on a giant screen. This was the first time I'd ever seen anything in color on a screen in my life. By the time the animals started singing and dancing, I was a goner.

I was so lost in that movie that I thought it was real, especially the baby elephant with the oversized ears who was made fun of until he was given a magic feather and learned how to fly. I felt so completely at one with his character that I was right there alongside him. I can remember deciding, *I need to be up there.* About halfway through the film and after drinking too much Coke, I was desperate to use the bathroom but couldn't bear to leave my seat. Refusing to miss anything, I made the conscious decision not to go to the bathroom even if that meant peeing my pants. Sitting in a wet patch for the rest of the show was a small price to pay to be in the presence of such greatness.

I floated out of Grauman's that day to declare that I wanted the black crows as friends and I was going to be Dumbo when I grew up, which seemed a perfectly logical next step to me. Seeing my mother laugh, I protested, "But, Mom, that's what I want to do!" In my brain I saw myself taking Dumbo's place, not being an elephant exactly but *playing* him. I was crushed when she told me, "You can't, sweetheart. There aren't any people in *Dumbo.* He's just an animated character, like Tom and Jerry. People can't be cartoons—or elephants. You'll have to go in a different direction."

The next picture they took me to see was *Cinderella* and I loved that even more. An equal-opportunity daydreamer, I announced afterward, "Okay, then I'll be Cinderella," thinking that since she's a human character, that would get around the elephant problem. Besides, Cinderella had the better deal. Dumbo wasn't given a single number to sing. In the back seat of Daddy's car, all the way home, I sang every word of "A Dream Is a Wish Your Heart Makes" as my mother jabbed his arm. "Listen, John! Cher's singing the whole darn song word for word and note for note!" she cried. "Do you hear this child? I told you she was special."

I guess I was who I was my whole life.

To save on babysitters, Mom and Dad started taking me almost everywhere they went. A favorite haunt was a faded adobe building called the Original Spanish Kitchen on Beverly Boulevard that had a painting on the outside at least a story high of a Spanish flamenco dancer. They also served the best enchiladas in the world. One night my dad and Kenny had a competition to see who could eat the hottest hot sauce. Daddy won, although he went purple with sweat popping out of his skin before throwing up. I was so in love with that place that, in my vivid imagination, I remember it having a beautiful flamenco dancer with a ruffled skirt I couldn't take my eyes off as she whirled and twirled around the floor. She was real to me, but with hindsight, I'm not really sure that there was one as I might have made her up. I was pretty loosely acquainted with reality. Either way, I longed for dance lessons even though I knew that wasn't something my parents could afford. My love of dancing is almost cellular and has never left me. On weekends we'd jump in the family's beat-up wreck of a jalopy and head north of Malibu near Trancas Beach to Cap's Place, owned by an old sailor who reminded me of Popeye but was known simply as Cap. It was a white house with green shutters down a steep slope. To reach the house you had to cross a rope bridge with wooden slats that swayed as you walked. I was the only kid taken along for the ride and there's a photo of me at Cap's Place finishing off an almost empty Brew 102 beer because I liked how it tasted and the grown-ups always laughed when I drank it.

The 1950s was the era of cocktail parties and martinis. Drinks flowed freely among the hopeful young actors who wandered in and out of our lives for card games, dancing, and potluck suppers. They were my crew. Before too long, our living room would be noisy with laughter and thick with cigarette smoke as they played canasta for hours and hours. Gossip, cocktails, and an overabundance of testosterone. I'd sit quietly in a corner, praying that if I was "as quiet as a church mouse," as my mother used to say, then nobody would notice me, and I wouldn't be sent to bed.

The women in the group became my tribe, especially Jake, who was like a second mother to me, but there was also Viv, Evelyn, Ginger, Jan, and an actress called Kathryn Reed who had the most fabulous red hair and went on to marry the director Robert Altman. Surrounded by so many funny, glamorous, kick-ass women, I soaked up everything about them, from their clothing to their makeup, their perfume to their mannerisms. These bewitching women were my life coaches. They were the ones who helped mold the Cher people see today.

Of course Mom was the most beautiful of all. I spotted her recently as an extra in a 1951 movie called *Grounds for Marriage* and she was so stunning that she took my breath away, although she was gone in the blink of an eye. That's how I remember her from when I was small. I have such clear memories, especially of her in one cocktail dress that made her look like a million dollars. It was pale blue chiffon with a little piece of matching lace across the front and a bunched-up pleat at the back that hung down longer than the dress. She paired it with some fabulous moonstone chandelier earrings that I used to play with when she was out, longing to be old enough to wear them someday, along with that periwinkle dress. When she gave them to me years later, I almost cried with happiness.

Daddy dressed stylishly too and was the most caring person in the world, good-natured, funny, and kind. He'd let me sit on his lap and steer the car while he laughingly worked the pedals. From then on, all I wanted was wheels, something he promised he'd buy me one day. He was adorable and everything you'd hope a father would be. When he drank too much, though, no more mister nice guy. That temper is a family curse and one I'm glad I didn't inherit.

Even though I hated all the arguments and the times when we were broke, as soon as I was able to express myself on the subject I begged my mother, "Please, let's never be like those other people. I'd kill myself if we had a normal life." God, I was so dramatic.

I needn't have worried, because my mother was far from conventional. She kept our lives from being dull even when that wasn't easy. She was the kind of mom who'd let me play hooky from kindergarten so that we could go to the beach on her day off. Still a kid at heart, she'd let us lie out beneath the stars on quilts spread across the front lawn while she whispered ghost stories to us and the neighborhood kids. In her car, we'd sing songs so loudly together that strangers would stop and stare. One of these songs, which Mom knew from her childhood (and which I've never been able to find again), went, *"I met a girl one time, I thought she was divine, say she had beauty galore. She took off her wooden leg when getting ready for bed. Took out her false teeth and the hair from her head. I slept on the chair 'cause there was more of her there. Oh, they can't fool me anymore."*

Every day was different, and the fun never stopped—until the days when it did. It was a case of feast or famine, just as it had been Mom's whole life. The daily grind reminded her of her childhood, where survival often depended on whether the crops failed or—in her case—how many nickels the drunks threw at her while she sang on the bar counter. When cash was scarce and we couldn't keep going to Mamaw and Pa's, we'd move to cheap apartments in the San Fernando Valley, a place I felt I didn't belong because none of our friends were there. I didn't hate the Valley per se, but I disliked it because I equated the Valley with harder times and I also missed being in Hollywood. I always knew the difference even when I was little. I just knew it wasn't the place I was supposed to be even though it had the greatest hamburger and hot dog stands. As soon as work was plentiful again, we'd leave the crummy apartments and hurry back to town to be closer to our friends and all the action.

It was unsettling to move as often as we did, and I'd sometimes wake up in the middle of the night after a nightmare and not know where I was. I'd have to lie still for a few minutes to get my bearings. Isn't it ironic I chose a career in which I'd be on the road my whole life and never know what town I'd wake up in? I still wake up sometimes not knowing where I am.

Wherever we were living and no matter how poor we were, she used to doll me up in my one good dress and my Mary Janes with little white socks that had lace trim. Then she'd drive me to Hollywood Boulevard to browse in the Broadway department store before buying us hot dogs. As we sat in her car eating them, my mom would tell me stories about the people walking by. It was fascinating because the people walking down Hollywood Boulevard were all really unique and interesting. "See that man in blue? I bet he's a magician," she'd say, or "Look at that lady's cheekbones. She could be the next Joan Crawford." My mom could have been the next Lana Turner, because, dressed in a tailor-made suit with a matching hat to complement her elegant posture (she used to poke me in the back and say, "Cher, stand up straight"), she was stopped on the boulevard one day by a stranger who rushed up and asked her, "Are you a movie star? Oh, you must be a movie star! You look just like one!" He was right; she did.

When times were especially hard, we'd leave California altogether to go to Texas. I was five or so when we relocated to Galveston, where Daddy got a job. I was enrolled in a new school and Gee stayed home with Mom. One of my teachers told me, "The way to remember the name of our town, Cher, is that it's *Gal* with a *Vest On*." After school, we went to the beach, where I played happily while Mom toasted herself in the sun, a habit I took to extremes as an adult. I'd been afraid of the ocean since I was flipped by a wave once when I was little, but I loved being near the water with my mom and remember Texas as a happy place that Daddy took us to many times.

I don't know why we left Galveston, but then, I never knew anything until the day it happened. I simply had to accept it. One day we packed up and moved three hundred miles northwest to live with my aunts Did and Ethel in Daddy's birthplace of Burleson. That town with a single dirt road had only one store and an icehouse where teenagers hung out for lack of anything better to do. People took their vegetables to a long cold-storage facility to be frozen for the winter. My aunts' home was built in the 1800s and was so small that I slept in a little alcove off the kitchen, where I was protected from mosquitoes by a net but warned to watch out for scorpions and rattlesnakes.

My aunts had very little, and with no bathroom in the house, we'd take turns to clean ourselves in the tin washtub filled with water boiled on the stove and placed in the kitchen, the only warm room. Having my hair washed once a week involved lying on the draining board next to the sink with my head tipped back into the basin while Mom shampooed it and then combed through the tangled knots as I cried out in pain. Every female in my family grew their hair long, even Grandma Lynda (whose long braids fell below her waist when they weren't wrapped into a crown on top of her head), so Mom wanted me to keep my hair long even though she threatened to cut it short if I didn't stop my whimpering. If she had, I think it would have hurt her more than me. We eventually bought them a bathroom and that was the end of the washtub and they were thrilled beyond belief.

I grew to love Burleson, and my mother loved my aunts but she didn't want to live in Texas. She and Daddy started arguing and from one day to the next were either madly in love or fighting almost to the death. After telling Dad for the millionth time that she didn't want to live in Texas, Mom packed our bags while he was at work and drove us back to LA. Not only was my dad not there, but there was some strange man in the car who I didn't know, and I was really pissed off. I didn't take to him at all, and I certainly didn't like the way they were together. I told Daddy about him when he showed up back in LA, which made my mom furious. The argument they had while I hid in my bedroom nearly ended their marriage.

I returned to Burleson decades later. I was pleased that the town was as I remembered it. I parked my car and stepped out as an old man walked by. Stopping in his tracks, he looked at me quizzically, grinned, and cried, "Cherilyn Southall? Is that you? Well, damn, girl, you all grown up!"

To this day, I have no idea who he was. He wasn't family, just someone who remembered me being in that tiny place as a kid. I was astonished and excited, even though I couldn't for the life of me place him. From the polite conversation that followed, I'd bet good money that he'd never even heard of a singer named Cher.

## unforgettable

One of my greatest childhood memories was going to get our first TV. My mom had a doctor's appointment and my dad said he would have a special surprise for us afterward. I was thinking, *Ice cream.* Instead, he brought us to an appliance store where he had bought this amazing giant TV. It was in a maple console. I'd never seen a TV in a piece of furniture before. It probably wasn't as big as it seemed then, but all I know is my mom was ecstatic. We brought it home and my dad and Kenny set it up. The console sat on the floor and everybody looked at it like it was a new baby. I wanted to be with the grown-ups oohing and ahhing, but my dad ruined it by saying I needed to take a nap before we could all sit down and watch a movie together. I thought, *What's the matter with him?* I tossed and I turned, but I couldn't fall asleep. I sat up looking out the window with my chin on my hands until my dad finally came in. Jake and Kenny were out in the living room with my mom all standing around the TV. Then *One Million B.C.* came on. It was unbelievable.

Victor Mature was my first movie star crush. I don't know why; I just loved him. I watched all his films, including *My Darling Clementine*, which I probably saw a million times. Mom finally said, "Well, of course you like him." I had no idea what she meant by that until much later.

In the time between my childhood and teen years, I dreamt of being an actress like those in the movies. Mom and I loved to curl up in bed together both munching on a bowl of popcorn. This was our special time. You didn't get to choose the movies back then, but it didn't make any difference what came on. I loved them all. Mom would tell me about the actors and actresses, all the Hollywood gossip she knew. Singing and the movies was what she loved and became what I loved. She seemed to enjoy every movie we watched, but I think she loved watching my reaction more than the movies. I could see it in her face. We watched great classic films, like *Gilda*, with Rita Hayworth, and *Gaslight*, with Ingrid Bergman. I adored Hedy Lamarr in *Samson and Delilah* and Bette Davis in everything. Lana Turner was my mother's favorite actress, her idol. She even dyed her hair blond to look like her. In *Homecoming*, Lana played a character called Snapshot and Clark Gable played a surgeon who falls for her after the war. That movie was one of my favorites. I didn't watch it again until thirty years later and immediately had an affinity for it that I couldn't understand. I'd completely forgotten seeing it the first time when I was little with my mom.

The movie I was craziest for, though, was *The Enchanted Cottage*, starring Dorothy McGuire and Robert Young, which had a huge impact on me. A film I plan to remake before I die, it tells the story of a badly disfigured veteran pilot who runs away to a remote cottage after his fiancée rejects him. There he befriends a very plain-looking woman. Once they fall in love, they only see each other as beautiful, thanks to the magic of the enchanted cottage. It offered such a great lesson about beauty being in the eye of the beholder—one that I carried into a film I acted in many years later.

With both my parents working, they needed a babysitter. Grandma Lynda wasn't an option, so Mamaw and Pa took on that role. They had an old-fashioned relationship and played by the rules of men. Mamaw would make Pa bacon and eggs, biscuits, and freshly squeezed orange juice every morning, even if she was dying of pneumonia. He just expected it. But they loved each other in their own way.

Mamaw was an amazing seamstress. She had worked at the Mildred Moore couture store in Beverly Hills, which made high fashion clothes for women. She worked with the finest fabrics and sewed them into the chicest styles, transforming the raw material into beautiful looks. I was blessed with the exposure to my grandmother. Mamaw also had a fabulous collection of hats and bags with matching shoes for her teeny tiny feet. When I was good, I could spend hours playing dress-up in her closet. Except I couldn't fit into her shoes. She had the smallest feet, like a child. My mom told me all actresses then had small feet like hers.

I loved being near Mamaw and oftentimes I'd sit under her Singer sewing machine swathed in velvets and silks or playing with buttons from her big round button box while she sat at the machine creating beautiful outfits for herself, for Mom, and for me. She'd tell me: "I'm trusting you with these now, Cher. Don't lose any." I swear that sorting those pretty buttons with rhinestones, sequins, and mother-of-pearl into little piles sparked my lifelong love of shiny things. Just ask Bob Mackie. I still love sifting through that button box. Even now it's one of my prized possessions. In case you are wondering, Sam and Pete were never allowed to go into the button box.

Mom was no longer Jackie Jean or even "Jack" by then. She'd changed her name to Georgia Pelham in 1949. Her best friend, Ann, from Fresno had died tragically young; she came from Pelham, Georgia. My mother thought a new name and a different hair color might make her seem more glamorous. As she put it, "I always set out to be a star. I just never arrived." My mom missed out on several major acting roles because she refused to sleep with men who promised her a break. Decades before the Me Too movement, the 1950s and '60s was the era of the "casting couch," and even though Mom was blessed with a *va-va-voom* face and body, inside she was still the naïve kid from the country. She even said no to a personal invitation from the infamous film producer, aerospace engineer, multimillionaire Howard Hughes. Afterward she'd complain bitterly, "I could have had my own show if only I'd lain on his couch."

As an actor you never forget those exciting moments when you get that call from your agents letting you know you booked an audition for a feature film at a major studio. The day that Mom was put up for an audition to play Angela, "the easy-living green-eyed blonde" in the 1950 MGM movie *The Asphalt Jungle*, she was over the moon. Her agent told her, "They want someone new and sexy, Georgia, so pad your bra." Nervous as hell, she met with the director and auditioned. At the end of the audition her agent told her, "Kid, you got the part!" It must have seemed like the greatest day of her life. What she'd always dreamed of was finally reality, but after five days she'd heard nothing and then she discovered she'd been replaced by an unknown actress named Marilyn Monroe. It proved to be her breakout role. As my mom would say, "Son of a gun."

Mom didn't have long to think about her disappointment at losing that role in *The Asphalt Jungle* because soon after, she found out she was pregnant. Not realizing the impact of her pregnancy on our family income, I was deliriously happy that a real baby would be left for us "under a leaf in the cabbage patch," which is where I'd been told they came from. I immediately forgot how miserable I'd been that my parents couldn't afford to buy me a $6 Tiny Tears doll that cried "real tears" and wet her diapers—although I did get one eventually, probably from Mamaw and Pa.

With Dad between jobs and with no income, we moved back in with Mamaw and Pa. Soon after the move I insisted that I wanted curly hair. Mom agreed to grant me my wish and took me to a salon where they used a crazy electric permanent wave machine that accidentally burned the silky black hair I'd been blessed with to a frizzle. It was so badly fried that I looked like an octopus, and she had to cut it all off. When I looked in the mirror at my horrible poodle cut, I burst into tears.

My distress was forgotten when the entire house was woken in the middle of the night by the start of my mother's labor. It was September 1951, and I was buzzing with excitement as Mom hurried into our car and was driven to the hospital. I was on the verge of hysterics when she returned a few days later with Georganne (named after Pa George), to be forever known as Gee. I couldn't wait to play with my little sister, but I should have been careful what I wished for, because from the day she arrived, I felt like yesterday's news. Everybody was so transfixed by my sister. Everyone in the house smoked and would stand around her crib oohing and ahhing and blowing smoke into her face. Nobody knew that cigarettes killed you in those days. No wonder she cried all the time.

Mom was always overly anxious, and the new baby took up all her time. I was told I was too little to hold her, so I didn't get to play with her as I'd hoped and could hardly get near her at all with all the grown-ups fussing. Disappointed and hurt, I retreated to the guest bedroom to draw, a new hobby.

Daddy must have seen me go to my room, because a few minutes later he came in and sat on the edge of my bed. He knew exactly what I was feeling because the first thing out of his mouth was "I don't see what's so great about that new baby? She's just a baby, right? She doesn't do anything but cry. That's no fun. But I guess we'd better keep her for a while and see how she turns out. Now, why don't you and I go get some ice cream?" It made me feel that my daddy understood what I was going through and how sad I was. I thought, *Okay, I have someone on my side.* And because he loved us equally, I don't ever remember thinking of Daddy as just "my sister's father." In fact, I felt I had priority because we'd been together longer. John Southall made me feel seen for the first time, and it was he who helped me grow to love Gee, even though I lost my treasured place as the only child.

That first Christmas with my new sister was one of the best I can recall. Gathered around a beautifully decorated tree at Mamaw and Pa's, all the gifts had been handed out when my mom pointed to a small box and asked, "What's that behind the tree?" When she pulled it out, I could see that the wrapping paper had an embossed velvet kitten and my name on it. "Did you buy this?" she asked Mamaw. "No, did you?" The question flew around the room, with everyone apparently nonplussed, until Dad said, "It must have come from Santa Claus." Breathless with excitement, I tore the paper and opened the box to find a beautiful stuffed cat with yellow fur and glass button eyes inside. I was instantly in love. I can't now recall what name I gave it, but I stroked that little toy until it lost its fur and fell apart completely.

We were all really happy in that first year of Georganne's life, but Daddy's drinking was still a problem. Sometimes it was controlled, but when he drank until he was drunk, he turned nasty. He would start what would become scary arguments with my mother, which sometimes turned violent. All his self-control was lost. I learned a few tricks to try to distract him if he was headed into that stage that ended in tears for everyone. For an alcoholic there's that one drink that turns everything to chaos. I would sit on his lap or ask him to come into the yard with me, but if that didn't stop him, I'd melt away and try to become invisible. Sitting quietly on my bed, I would become a nervous wreck listening to my parents screaming in the next room.

One night we were over at the home of the model Betty Martin, who'd been married to singer Dean Martin for eight years until he abandoned her along with their four children. The house was in Holmby Hills and Betty was famous for hosting Hawaiian-themed parties known as luaus, complete with flaming tiki torches and flowers flown in from Honolulu. I loved that gigantic house, the first I'd ever been in with two staircases, with the kids sent up one to spend the night upstairs. Later that evening Dad got it into his head that Mom was flirting with someone. My mom wasn't necessarily a flirtatious person, but men were always drawn to her. Livid, he grabbed her by her hair and started to pull her outside, but when she fell off her heels, he kept dragging her across the tiled floor in front of everybody. Not one of the men intervened.

I was playing with Betty's daughters, and we all came running downstairs to see what the commotion was, just in time to see five-foot-tall Betty march up to Daddy, poke him in the chest, and yell, "Hey! Nobody behaves like that in my house. Now get the hell out!" Mom was visibly mortified, all the other men stood still, and I felt my face redden with shame. It was one thing for Daddy to behave like that at home, but to show himself like that in public was quite different. Later that night, Betty made up a room for Mom and me. I was always grateful to her that we didn't have to go home.

The following morning, I hung out with her girls, Deana, Gail, and Claudia, who were roughly my age. They told me they were friends with another family living across the street and we decided to visit them. As we walked in their front door, I looked up and saw a small, pretty woman standing halfway up the stairs shouting at someone above her. She was wearing high heels and a pair of tight capri pants underneath a fabulous half-skirt in a beautiful, patterned fabric. The shirt she wore was in the same print with a little turned-up collar, and she carried in her hand what I assumed was a glass of orange juice.

When she saw us in the doorway, she immediately stopped shouting and said, "What are you doing inside, girls? It's a beautiful day. Go outside and play." She ushered her daughter, Liza, out with us. We did as we were told, and when we sat on the front steps Liza spontaneously burst into song with "Somewhere over the Rainbow." I remember thinking that was strange, as I'd never been around a kid who just burst into song like that, even though she was pretty darn good. It was only later that I realized she was Liza Minnelli and that the woman on the stairs was Judy Garland. Now I realize she probably wasn't drinking juice either.

Even though my mother loved my dad, there were times when she was so miserable that she'd leave him for a while, which was both a courageous and a foolish thing to do with two children to feed. "Anything is better than this!" she'd declare before bundling us into her car and driving away. The problem was that each time their relationship broke down she found it harder to make ends meet. She'd shift into survival mode and so, by default, would I. It didn't help that we'd usually have to move and I'd change schools, which meant I'd have to learn how to fit in again or try to stay hidden. This constant unpredictability made me hypervigilant about the moods around me and gave me what I call a faulty emotional thermostat as I, too, began to swing between extremes. There are photos of me taken when I was little where I'd be scowling in one frame and doing a Rita Hayworth pose seconds later. To this day I can jump right from happiness to drama, or from gleeful poses to Lady Macbeth, in a blink.

Finding work as an actress without an agent was hard at the best of times, so the minute Mom got home after a long day on set, she'd grab a Dr Pepper—her favorite soda, which became mine too—and then she'd hit the phone. It was horrible to watch and listen as she spent hours calling around to all the casting directors trying to pick up work as an extra. We had dial phones then and she'd be spinning it over and over again for hours. Mom would try all the casting directors that she knew, but everybody was calling at the same time for the same jobs so she wouldn't know how long she'd have to be on the phone before getting a job. These people loved her because she was so beautiful, but that could also be a disadvantage as she couldn't outshine the star, so they'd only put her in scenes that the star wasn't in. If she didn't keep trying for whatever parts she could get, she knew other actresses would, each of them hoping that a career-defining role was a phone call away. Mom's grit and determination impressed me, and I hung on her every word, knowing that the outcome would dictate the mood of the evening.

At the crack of dawn she'd get up and start doing her makeup for whatever job she'd gotten the day before. It was hard enough to make your mark as a woman anywhere in the 1950s, but to be in the sexist Hollywood system must have been rougher still. All the weight fell on my mother's shoulders. Unless we went to Mamaw and Pa, Mom had nothing to fall back on, least of all the men in her life, and she'd never received a dime from my biological father, Johnnie.

Mom could get painfully thin because sometimes she couldn't afford to buy lunch at work with the other actors. Often she pretended she wasn't hungry and would just sip on a Coke. At five feet seven inches, she couldn't have weighed more than a hundred and ten pounds soaking wet. She also made herself sick with worry and appeared to be in a constant state of stress. I couldn't help but pick up on the tension and feel it too. She'd vowed to be a better mom than Lynda, but she'd be the first to admit she often bungled it. And although Mom complained about Lynda almost every single day—such was the friction between them—every now and again they'd be thick as thieves, which was confusing. Lynda loved my mom but found it hard to show it in anything other than a passive-aggressive way, and when she did, it was fleeting, which only made Mom even more insecure. It was all too deep for me to understand.

Even though I was so young, my mother treated me like an adult confidante her whole life. I will never forget the time she broke down and asked me, "Cher, how on earth are we going to pay the rent?" Unable to think of an answer, a voice inside my head cried, *I'm a kid, Mom. How should I know?* I was always old beyond my years, maybe because I was treated like a grown-up from the earliest age.

Moving around so much took a lot of strength, and yet she somehow managed to do it, over and over, and to keep us fed and clothed, even though we lived like vagabonds. She put herself through high school by working as a maid and created a steady profession for herself. She did the best she could. I had never been prouder than when I came home from school one day to find her up on the roof with nails in her teeth and a hammer in her hand, replacing the shingles because she couldn't afford to pay someone else, a man, to do the job for her.

Although I knew my mother could take care of us, I still longed for the periods when she and Dad were reunited between arguments, because our lives would immediately improve. We felt safe and protected with our dad there. Everyone was happier when my parents were back together and our mother wouldn't have to work. It was just another instance of my childhood being great and then horrible. I learned early that most adults were unpredictable, so I couldn't count on them and had to be constantly vigilant. I never wanted a plain life, but a touch of normality was nice now and again.

Not many kids get to watch their mother in a public wrestling match with a neighbor on the front lawn, but I can say that I did. Mom was preparing to go to work as Queen Anne of Austria in a stage version of *The Three Musketeers* at the Coronet Theatre. While she was curling her hair into a million ringlets like Marie

Antionette before piling it up into a tiara, she asked me to let our dog out to pee. When I opened the door, the shaggy mutt we called Blackie immediately ran off, and I couldn't find him anywhere until I spotted the busybody who lived next door dragging him inside her house. A Swedish masseuse, she was built like Godzilla and always complaining about Blackie's barking. Not long after, I saw the truck from the pound pull up outside and began to panic. Running to Mom, I told her what I'd seen, and she abandoned her hair tongs and marched to the truck. The man from the pound already had Blackie in the back and refused to return him because he wasn't wearing a tag. Softening when he saw how upset I was, he said we could collect him that night and drove away.

After promising me that Blackie would be okay until she could retrieve him, my mother stomped to our neighbor's house, climbed the steps, and pounded on her door. The woman blew her off. I'd never seen my mom so angry as when she threatened to beat the shit out of her. Our neighbor was twice her size, so when she pushed open the screen door it knocked Mom backward down the steps. Furious and with perfect ringlets, my mother grabbed the woman by her hair and started swinging her around the front lawn. I hadn't seen anyone make a move like that since watching Mamaw's favorite wrestler, Gorgeous George, on TV. As I watched openmouthed, a man across the street yelled, "Go get her, blondie!" By the time she'd exacted her revenge, her hair and makeup had gone to shit, but she still drove to the theater in her old Studebaker and appeared in the play that night, rescuing Blackie on her way home. What a dame.

With such an unusual life, I often found it hard to relate to other kids with "normal" families. I had just started at a new school when a teacher announced that there would be "sharing day." The following morning, my classmates stood up one by one and shared corny details about their dolls, toys, pets, or what they did all summer with their perfect parents until I got so bored and thought to myself, *Oh fuck*. I didn't care about any of their silly lives. I was so over them already. When it was my turn to speak, I scowled and said, "I think this is dumb and I think you're all stupid. I hate being here. I'm not sharing. I'm going home." I marched right out of that building and no one tried to stop me. When I got home and told Mamaw what I'd done, she laughed until tears rolled down her cheeks.

When I was nine everything finally went south between my parents. My mother had left Daddy again, and the three of us were living on our own in a tiny little house on Corteen Place in the San Fernando Valley. The properties were laid out in a horseshoe-shaped cul-de-sac around a little court. One night, my mom's new boyfriend, Bill, was over and the four of us were watching TV. I hated Bill and couldn't understand what my mom saw in him. During a commercial, my mom asked me to take the garbage out, so I went in the kitchen, got the garbage, and took it out the back door, which slammed behind me. Unbeknownst to us, our dad was out front and heard the door slam. He thought Bill was trying to slip out the back, so jumping out of his car, he charged at the front door. The door flew open, covering Bill from my dad's view. Daddy ran into the kitchen and straight out the back door, thinking he was chasing Bill outside. Seeing my dad's rage, Bill jumped up and ran out the front door, past his car and into the dark. By the time Daddy had pulled himself together and charged back inside, he realized that he'd missed the idiot and hurled a glass of iced tea against the wall, splattering tea and broken glass everywhere. Then he ran into the kitchen and grabbed the butcher's knife, which looked bigger than it ever had before. My mom thought he was going to kill us. Daddy stormed out to Bill's Cadillac with the knife and started stabbing at the convertible, slicing the roof and the interior leatherwork. Seizing her chance, Mom grabbed Gee's blanket and pushed me out the back door toward the chain-link fence at the rear of our small yard. Barefoot, as Mom and I usually were, I climbed over it with my mother's help before she handed my baby sister over to me. Fortunately, Gee was too young to understand the danger, although she must have picked up on our panic. In her haste to get over the fence, Mom ripped her toenail clean off. We then ran as fast as we could to the first house we came to with a light on. Mom's toe was dripping blood as she banged frantically on the door. An old lady appeared through the glass and my mother begged, "Please let us in. My husband's trying to kill me!" We hid there until the police arrived. In the end, they let Dad off with a caution. They always gave Daddy the benefit of the doubt. The attitude at the time was to tell the man, "Hey, buddy, if you get rough with your wife, it'll scare the kids. Go walk it off." The cop even came inside and asked Mom, "Do you think you did anything to trigger this?" PS—I was thrilled Dad had trashed Bill's car.

That backyard got a lot of action. It was in the yard of that same property that I did a backflip off the swing set one afternoon and landed with my full weight onto the edge of a Yuban coffee can, which is where Gee kept her crayons. Without the lid, the rim of the can was very sharp. There was blood everywhere, my leg went all floppy, and my toes twisted into an unusual angle. Looking down, I saw my skin flayed to the bone. There was so much blood I started screaming for my mom. Mom stayed calm and wrapped my foot in white towels, which wasn't enough and they all turned red immediately. She called my doctor but he wasn't available, so she rushed me to the emergency room. She was fabulous in a crisis. I was gushing blood as we entered the hospital but we had to sit and just wait. I calmed down a little when I saw an older Asian man who was sitting in front of me and he was so calm even though he was covered in giant blue boils. It made me calm down seeing him sitting there so peacefully. I was so impressed with him and still remember exactly what he looked like. My mom only fell apart when I was brought into the operating room and the doctors started to use a long surgical tool with little pincers at the end to retrieve the tendons that had snapped like rubber bands up to my knees. As I was lying sedated on the operating table, the doctors told my mom that my tendons were cut. My mom watched as they inserted the metal pincer. Seeing the impression of the tool from beneath my skin, she passed out.

My left foot required surgery, and the doctors warned her that I might lose the full use of it, although she kept that bit from me. Fortunately, my natural athleticism and love of dancing were powerful enough to overcome any disability, although it gave me my distinctive loping gait. For weeks after the surgery, I had to wear a plaster cast that itched like hell. I lost count of how many pick-up sticks went missing down the side as I tried to scratch my peeling skin. For years afterward my toe would spasm and get stuck in one position, and I'd have to rub it to get it to move. The only nice thing about the whole accident was that I got to see Daddy, who visited and made a big fuss over me.

Because he and Mom split up so often, I thought their latest split was another of those times and fully expected Daddy to walk back into our lives any day. When that didn't happen and Mom seemed to hope that his absence would go unnoticed, I understood for the first time that love hurts. Even though I knew we were probably better off without him, I loved John Southall more than he could ever know. I was sad to my bones, but I couldn't even tell my mother how much I missed him because I knew that would only upset her more. It's true that in the four years that he'd been a mainstay of my life, from the age of four and a half to nine, I witnessed some horrible fights. I remember thinking, *Aren't they embarrassed to be acting this way?* I saw him pin her against a wall, drag her across a floor, bust down doors, and physically attack some of the men she dated, but his explosions were rare and always offset by his kindnesses. I was afraid when he whipped out his belt, but I never held it against him although I still can't stand the sound of a belt coming out of pant loops.

Despite all the violence and chaos that he brought into our lives, I forgave him. I still think of him as my dad. He really loved both me and Gee. I'm sorry my sister wasn't old enough to remember the good times. He was the first man I'd loved unconditionally even though sometimes I was afraid of him. Losing him was more than painful. One day he was there and the next he was gone. I hadn't read the signs well enough to be prepared for the loss.

# 5

## i'm movin' on

My parents gave me a tricycle as a gift and THAT was truly my first set of wheels. I got on the seat, looked around, looked up at my parents, and thought, *Okay, I think I've learned all I can from these people.* It was like, time to go. And then I pedaled around the apartment complex and didn't actually go anywhere, but I had my wheels and I felt free.

When I was four or five, I decided to run away for real. I don't know what happened that particular day, but I was through with everybody. We lived in Laurel Canyon and I was sitting on the curb by our picket fence, telling my mom, who was coming out to check on me, that I was pretty much going to leave. She was calm about it. I had my little doll-size suitcase packed with whatever a child of that age thinks is a necessity. Then I noticed that dusk was beginning to fall and I reasoned, *I'll wait till tomorrow.* My mom said, "Okay, good idea." As usual, she was supportive. Hitting the road was becoming a tradition for me.

A long way from friends, Mom, Gee, and I were living on our own in an apartment I hated deep in the Valley. I wasn't doing well at school and was missing Daddy less than a year after he'd left. One day when my friend Anita and I were walking home, we found a field and spent some time lying in the tall grass, where I tossed my lunchbox, having decided I wouldn't need it anymore. I was generally disappointed with the contents anyway, which usually comprised a Wonder Bread sandwich with an apple or an orange (never a banana because they went all weird. I didn't like them anyway). If I was lucky, there'd be a bag of Fritos and a small thermos of milk.

Looking up, I spotted an old dappled gray horse in a gigantic pasture. I was happy. I'd been on ponies before, and I loved going to Kiddieland (which inspired Walt Disney) with my mom and sister. I clambered over the fence and yelled for Anita to come with me. I led the sweet-natured animal to a concrete block. Tugging on its long mane, I climbed up onto its swayback. This horse was old. When Anita sat behind me we rode that poor girl around as far as we could until the pasture came to an end. The sense of freedom and adventure was crazy. It was only the barbed-wire fence at the edge of the field that stopped us. It marked the start of railway tracks on which sat a chain of stationary boxcars. Before I'd given it any thought and allowing Anita no time to argue, I yelled, "Come on!" and gave Anita a boost up with my cupped hands. I don't know how we managed it. I'd watched movies where outlaws and hobos "rode the rails" to escape their past and this looked just like that—dirty and musty with straw on the floor. Luckily, the space was unoccupied.

Settling into a corner giggling, I couldn't wait to tell our friends what we'd been up to. Our schoolgirl chatter was interrupted by a sudden jolt as the train started rolling forward. Jumping up, we looked out and the horse gazed up at us as we trundled slowly past. Anita gasped, but I cried, "Woo-hoo! This is way better than horseback riding!" Then the reality began to set in as our boxcar rolled right out of town. Within the hour the light began to fade, and my fellow runaway began to cry.

I tried to reassure her, but she couldn't be comforted. When we felt the wagons slow down before pulling to a halt at a loading station somewhere near Santa Ana, Anita ran to the door and I helped her down onto the tracks. I had no choice but to follow her because I wasn't brave enough to go on alone. Walking along the tracks, we spotted a railroad worker and asked for his help. Surprised to see two little girls in the middle of nowhere with night beginning to fall, he took us to a pay phone, where he gave us a handful of dimes. After Anita called her mother, sobbing, I realized that I'd better call my mom too. I could hear her initial sigh of relief that I wasn't dead. She hadn't been working that day and was waiting and worrying at home. But halfway through the conversation, I heard her tone change and knew that she was getting mad.

"Wait. Where are you exactly?" she asked. "Cherilyn, what did you do?" The use of my full name usually meant I was about to get my ass whipped.

I began to tell her what happened but didn't go into the details. "Well, we saw this horse and he looked really lonely, so we went for a ride . . . ," I said, knowing that no good was going to come of anything I said next. I then reminded myself that one of the strange things about my mother was that for minor infractions she'd get unbelievably angry, but for something big she'd be either stunned or so relieved I was still alive that it often passed unpunished. Or she'd be fascinated and say, "Well, I hope you've learned your lesson, young lady."

I couldn't tell whether she was going to go ballistic or quiet, but after a short pause, she said only, "I'll come get you." Miraculously, she was still calm enough by the time she'd driven the forty or so miles to reach us until taking one look at me, she yelled, "And what did you do with your lunchbox?"

I shrugged. "I threw it away."

Mom cursed a lot at home but not often in public, unless she was furious, so when she yelled, "Why the fuck did you do that?" I knew I was in trouble.

Sheepish, I replied, "It was just an adventure." And then, "I didn't get as far as I wanted." Me and my big mouth.

It was only later, when I was lying in bed, grounded, that the reality of what we'd done began to sink in. I had borrowed a horse and jumped on a train . . . and it was worth it.

By the time I was ten, I'd had so many scrapes that my mother and Mamaw had a bet that I'd never make it to twenty-one. I was in the ER so often my mom wondered if she should just swing by there first on her drives home from work.

Everybody in my family had a great sense of humor, even if it was a little outlandish. Most of the time I was well-behaved and quiet, but then a switch would flip. Once, as a joke on my uncle Mickey, I put a potato bug in an envelope and handed it to him. Mickey was terrified of bugs, so when he opened the mail I'd addressed to him, he completely lost it. He chased me out the back door. I ran away and tried to climb the fence. He grabbed me by the leg and pulled me down and smashed the bug in my face. I should have known he'd be that mad. When we were living in Laurel Canyon, on a really hot day we left the door open and a tarantula sauntered in, like they do. Mickey was the one to spot it. He jumped up on the couch and started yelling, "Get it, George! Get it, George!" My mom hit it with a broom hard but the legs kept going. My dad just sat there.

Just before I turned ten, we moved into what was my favorite house and the homiest place we ever lived. It was heaven to me. Even though our two-bed, one-bath redwood bungalow on

Beeman was still in the Valley, that matchbox property became a touchstone for all three of us after Daddy left. It had the look of a mountain cabin, with knotty pine paneling and a real fireplace inside, and apricot and peach trees in the yard. Mom, who'd never wallpapered anything in her life, learned how to do it in a day and decorated the bedroom I shared with Gee in a pretty print with powder-blue butterflies that matched the bedspreads, which I thought meant that we were rich. Best of all, Jake lived close by, and having her near was a blessing. It always made my mom calm to have Jake there. She had that effect on everyone around her but especially on my mom. The two were best friends.

Like a second mother to me, Jake was spontaneous and fun, a woman who'd throw potluck parties out of the blue, calling everyone up and telling them to bring something to eat and drink. She never got mad. You'd have to walk five thousand miles in any direction before you found anyone who didn't love Jake, and I adored her, but not just because she'd let me read her movie-star magazines when she'd finished with them. Once a successful singer who went by the name of Jacquie Reach, she'd been flown all over the Pacific to entertain troops during the war. When she came home, she made a living singing in clubs before marrying Kenny and having their son, Kevin, who was a handful. He would play with Gee often, which was surprising because while Gee always had her head in a book, Kevin was always getting into trouble. Somehow my mother got her hands on a used Cadillac. I don't know how. Soon, Kevin got into the car with a lighter and made burn circles all over the leather. My mother was so angry but Jake just said, "George, come on, it's done." Nothing fazed her. Sometimes Jake would sing for us, and I loved her voice, especially when she sang my favorite, "All the Things You Are." I have a lifetime of happy memories with Jake and Kevin. She was part of my family. My sister's voice was urgent when she called me decades later to tell me, "Jake's dying. Come quickly." I got there as fast as I could. I walked in, and she was asleep and so pale after a lifetime of being suntanned and rosy cheeked, so I grabbed her foot and shook it and said, "Hey, what the fuck do you think you're doing?" She opened her eyes and said, "Cher . . . ," to which I replied, "Don't Cher me. Wake up!" By the time I left, she was rosy cheeked again and singing all her old songs, including my favorite. That was the last time I ever saw her, but I'll love her forever.

The Beeman property was owned by a Southern couple who loved my mother like a daughter. Whenever it became available, they'd let her know and we three would move back in if Mom could afford the rent. We must have done that three times, and we sometimes lived there with Uncle Mickey, who'd share a single bed with his wife, Rita, while Gee and I shared the other and Mom had the only double. Mick was my favorite member of the family even though he'd smashed a bug in my face. He was the funniest person I'd ever met, and Mom was always in a great mood whenever he was around. Well over six feet tall, he was blond and handsome as hell. After a childhood that was almost as unstable as Mom's, he'd enlisted. When he left the army, he married my beautiful aunt Rita and they both taught at the Arthur Murray Dance School. Rita had had her legs crushed in an accident when she was buying ice. A man had backed into her and a doctor told her she would have to lose one of her legs. She told him, "Then I won't be able to teach you to dance." She kept the leg and became a great dancer. She and Mickey often brought their work home with them, and on any given day, I'd find them practicing the mambo and the cha-cha around our postage stamp of a living room as I tried to join in. They introduced me to the music of Tito Puente, who became my second musical hero after Hank Williams. Sometimes a little high on the pot they hid in a bird's nest in the backyard, they'd invite friends over and there'd suddenly be a party.

We had great Fourth of July barbecues at Beeman eating Southern fried chicken, corn on the cob, and coleslaw, before letting off firecrackers with the gang and our neighbors, including Mary and Hans, a sweet Dutch couple who babysat for us sometimes. The man had been part of the resistance and was taken to a concentration camp during the war. He somehow escaped. I remember he always changed his shoes to slippers when he got home. One year, running around, I burnt the sole of my foot on a hot sparkler. I never made that mistake again.

For Halloween, Mom let me wear her peasant skirt and flowy blouse and put a little lipstick and mascara on me, the first I'd ever been allowed. I was hopping from foot to foot with excitement as she applied it, desperate to go out looking like a grown-up. When I looked at my reflection in the mirror, the transformation was incredible.

It was when we were living at Beeman that I first began to dream up little plays to put on for my mom and Jake, marking out a makeshift stage on our living room floor. I loved to entertain them. I'd stretch a clothesline against a wall and drape a woven blanket over it as a curtain. My debut performances were short sketches that I wrote and acted out, and I was also the producer and director, agonizing over each production like a tormented Hollywood mogul. I'm sure seeing Mom at drama school sparked my love of performing, but like many people in show business, I was also really shy, which never made sense with my desire to get up on a stage. Maybe it was a need to express myself in a way that was more than just singing or dancing quietly alone, which was never enough. People often think of performers as outgoing, but that's not always true. I know of many big stars who are amazing onstage but can't do anything like that when they are offstage. It often feels like there are two Chers in me—the one who's anxious about going onstage and the other who feels completely at home in the spotlight. My mother and Jake were a willing audience, and my mom loved that I was like her in that way. Having been dragged halfway across America to perform at my age, she always clapped enthusiastically and praised me for each production.

Gee was my hired assistant and always played the girl, wearing braids I'd twisted out of yarn. She was too young to learn any lines, so I taught her a few basic actions and let her ad-lib. I was usually the man and became such a ham that I almost single-handedly put on an entire performance of *Oklahoma!* at one of the many schools I attended. That production was an obvious choice after watching Mom play Laurey, so I attempted a Cher version of the show that had made such an impression on me. I don't know how I had the balls, or why my music teacher let me go ahead, except that maybe she'd discovered I could at least hold a note. Casting was my biggest problem, as kids in the fourth grade aren't that interested in helping put on a full Broadway production, so I did it myself. I only persuaded four girls and one boy to take part and had such a ragtag cast that I had to do the rest, playing everyone from Laurey to the villain Jud, especially when the boy playing him quit midperformance. Complaining that I needed more time and more people, I ended up singing all the major numbers, from "Pore Jud Is Daid" to "I Cain't Say No." For my first-ever show, I think we did okay . . . It was a mess.

Attending that school gave me some of my happiest childhood days, and I made good friends there. Everything in the neighborhood was in walking distance, and as the unofficial head of our "Little Rascals" gang, I was the one who'd lead the others, run the fastest, and climb the tallest trees. It was a paradise for kids, and we raced around back and forth all day long, never running out of things to do. One whole fantastic summer we played log rollers by rolling barefoot around an empty lot on a four-foot-high cylindrical water drum. I talked all my friends into getting onto that old rusty water drum so we could get it to spin. A man would come out and yell at us for playing on it. Once he left, we'd get right back on. I wondered how easy it would be to join a circus.

If Mom had money in her purse, Gee and I could buy a ten-cent Popsicle from the Good Humor man, whose refrigerated truck played a melody as it drove slowly down our street. As soon as we heard that song, every kid would run to their mom and beg for money for a Chocolate Éclair or an ice cream sandwich. Better still was the Helms Bakeries man, who drove a large van and sounded a ship's whistle to let us know he'd arrived. Like the Good Humor man, he wore a uniform with a cap and tie, only his was khaki, not white. He came all year round, and as Mom had a sweet tooth too, we knew we'd stand a better chance of getting a treat if she came out to see him with us. His wagon had gigantic pull-out drawers in the back packed full of delicious treats such as frosted donuts, cookies, and my favorite, walnut squares with powdered sugar—sixty cents for an eight-by-ten-inch tin. When he rolled them out before our eyes, I decided I wanted to marry him when I grew up.

For my tenth birthday Mom threw me a party on the front lawn of our house. It had been a year since my parents separated, and even though the place was buzzing with people, it still felt like there was one person missing. Daddy was now living in Texas with his new wife, a nineteen-year-old he'd brought to meet us the last time he visited. Jane was pretty as a picture, with red hair, pale skin, and green eyes. I was crazy about her—and so was he. Even Mom liked her. She and my dad moved to Burleson, where they planned to start a new family, so I realized it was better not to think about him anymore. I might only have been a kid, but I'd already learned to compartmentalize sadness—something I became pretty good at later in life.

My parents' divorce didn't stop us from seeing Mamaw and Pa, though, who came to my party along with Jake, Kenny, and all of my mother's friends. Everyone did. My mother had done an amazing job to make my party special, decorating our front lawn with balloons and a lollipop tree. Mamaw and Pa bought me a $1.79 frosted Ralphs Bakery birthday cake, a longstanding tradition in our family. There was ice cream and a big pitcher of iced tea. We played silly games like Blind Man's Buff that Mom remembered from the happier days of her Arkansas childhood. Mamaw also bought me a daring white and pink seersucker two-piece, which was perfectly timed, as my old bathing suit was literally falling apart. I loved it. Mom knew that what I really wanted was an English racing bike for the freedom it would give me. I was the only kid in my group without one, so I'd have to borrow a friend's or ride on the handlebars of others. I never dared ask for a bike of my own, though, because I knew she didn't have that kind of money.

Halfway through my party, she drove off in her cranked-up wreck of a green Pontiac, so I assumed we must have run out of ice cream. Ten minutes later she pulled up to the curb and opened the trunk as my mouth dropped open. In the back was a beautiful maroon-painted English racing bicycle with gold pinstripes, three gears, and skinny tires. It looked nothing like any American bike I'd ever seen. Everyone gathered around as Mom, all smiles, presented me with the gift she'd bought wholesale from a friend who owned an appliance store. I hugged her. I was speechless. I grabbed hold of my handlebars as people clapped and laughed.

For the first time since my tricycle when I was four, I had my own wheels. So without a second thought, barefoot and wearing only my new two-piece, I jumped on my chariot and rode off. Leaving my own party, my friends, and the laughter far behind. I kept going and going and going and didn't come home for three hours. I can't recall where I went, but I just kept pedaling around and around our neighborhood, forgoing the safety of the sidewalk to go right down the middle of a busy street. When I eventually returned just after sunset, I found Mom waiting for me on the porch. She didn't yell. Instead, she said quietly, "Everyone's gone, Cher. Did you have a good time?"

"Yeah, Mom. I did."

Now that I was in double digits, I was in double trouble because I was becoming aware of boys. I didn't go from being a good child to being a bad child. I went from being a good child to a wild child. A cute boy in the fifth grade named Milton Broadlight brought me a corsage to what was basically a play date. We were ten. At the end of it he kissed me, and I thought, *Well, that was okay.* Yan Kovaleski was also in our class and he gave me a flower, a little bottle of perfume, and a decorative soap. I thought he was rich.

There wasn't much kissing going on at home as Mom was working all day and only going out on a few dates. Lou was our favorite because he made us all laugh and helped me get an A on a school project. At this point, if Mom didn't like a guy, she'd cut him off pretty quickly and was always so protective of us girls, constantly telling us, "Don't talk to strangers. Never get in someone's car, even if they tell you they have candy or a puppy." I was so shy anyway that, for a long time, I was too shy to even dial Information and talk to a stranger. "It's just a voice, Cher," Mom would say, chastising me. "No one can hurt you on the telephone." Hell, I didn't want to put the little fork in a drawer with a big fork because I was worried the big fork would be mean to the little fork, okay? That's how intense I was, and I'm sure I often pushed my mother to the brink.

For another birthday, my eleventh I think, she bought me a beautiful skirt and shirt set. The sleeveless top was pale blue with fluffy white clouds, and the skirt had clouds, too, but they morphed into flowers. It was so lovely that I decided to wear it to Sunday school. Mom was in one of her "let's check out every religion" phases, so that week she dropped us off at the Lutheran church, where I spent a happy hour or so coloring in the pages of a book of parables. Afterward, Gee and our friend Bobby ran a block and a half with me to the local convenience store run by Mr. and Mrs. Hornsby, who gave free treats to any kid celebrating a birthday. On the way, we chattered happily about whether we'd pick chocolate, ice cream, Coke, or the long black licorice that came in a big box separated by waxed paper. We were having such a good time that I completely forgot Mom was picking us up from church that day. When she got there, she found that we'd left and someone mistakenly told her that they thought a man had collected us, which is when she became hysterical and started driving around the neighborhood in a blind panic. By the time she found us back home in my room enjoying our treats, she was crying so hard that she couldn't even speak. She ran to her room, slammed the door, and sobbed so loudly we could hear her through the wall. I never meant to upset her; I just forgot. Whenever she ran out of emotional gas, she'd retreat to her bed, so I knew to let her be.

When she could no longer afford for us to stay on Beeman because work was scarce, we'd have to pack up and leave. This was always scary and unsettling, as we never knew where we'd end up. But the worst time was when Mom was so short of money that she couldn't even afford to keep us together. Gee and I went to live with Mamaw and Pa at their new house in La Puente, twenty miles east of downtown LA. I didn't mind it so much at first because it was there that Pa taught me how to drive his Ford, but the school in La Puente was much rougher than I was used to. There were fights and people could be mean. I went to the fair one day and a group of girls from my school came running up to us yelling "Run! Quickly run! Because there's some girls behind us. They have scissors and they're cutting people's hair off." I *absolutely* did not want my hair cut. Everyone in my family—my mom, my sister, my grandmother—all had long hair. And especially not by a bunch of bitches who weren't trained and probably would have clipped my ear too. I ran and we all scrambled to climb over a chain-link fence to get away. At school, there was at least one boy who was kind to me and would talk to me occasionally. One time, his girlfriend saw us talking for what must have been a few minutes. She found me later, opened her locker, and pushed my face inside, trying to slam the locker door on my head. She was tall and blond with short hair. She told me, "Meet me at the vacant lot." I thought, *Oh fuck, what's going to happen there?* I thought she was going to kill me. I saw a group of people gathering in the lot, and I really thought she was going to kick my ass. When I got to the lot, a miracle happened. I just remember a honking horn. I looked over and I saw my mom in the car. She opened her door and said, "Get in." When we pulled away, I could see the kids from my school gathered there. I know exactly what that girl would have done to me. Thank God for my mom.

Gee wasn't as affected by living in La Puente as I was. She was so comfortable with Mamaw and Pa. After all, she'd been born in their house. I just really wanted to be with my mom.

Mom stayed in town to be available for auditions and hoped that we'd be reunited soon, but the separation lasted for four months. She hocked our furniture and rented a tiny one-room garage apartment down a side alley with a teeny refrigerator, a borrowed hot plate, and the mattress on the floor. Every Sunday night we'd meet Mom for supper in a restaurant because she didn't have a kitchenette where she could cook us a proper meal. Alone, broke, thirty-one years old, and unable to care for her children, she came close to the breaking point and later confessed that she suffered from such severe panic attacks that she almost ran screaming into the alley in her nightgown—anything to get out of that room.

She wasn't the only one suffering during that horrible time. I broke down one Sunday night at dinner. Sobbing, I said, "I can't do this anymore, Mom. I want to live with you." She told me she only had a mattress on the floor. I said, "I don't care. I can sleep on the floor."

She told me, "You've seen how I'm living, Cher! I don't have a stick of furniture and I can't send you to school from there. Child welfare would take you away from me." I knew she was right, but I thought, *Come on, just fix it.*

I was still upset when I got back to my grandparents', but I didn't want to tell them in case I seemed ungrateful or hurt their feelings. Running inside, I took a hot bath and bawled my eyes out under the water. It took twenty-five years before a steaming bath didn't make me want to cry.

# 6

## because you loved me

School was never easy for me, though there were some good times. I loved drawing, sports, and history. I was really good at kickball, dodgeball, and handball so all the boys wanted me on their teams. Still, I was the poorest student in class and often felt embarrassed and isolated.

There was a time when we were so broke that my saddle shoes were literally falling apart and had to be padded with cardboard to stuff up a hole and wrapped with rubber bands to keep the soles from flapping. It was so Dickensian. I begged Mom to let me stay home until she could afford new shoes, but she refused. Knowing that I'd rather run away than face my classmates, Mom walked me right to the school gate within sight of my teacher so that I couldn't bolt. I still wanted to die, but she told me: "Did you hear about the man who cried because he had no shoes until he saw the man who had no feet?"

When Mom said things like that, I wanted to strangle her.

The year I was about to finish fourth grade after Daddy left was one of the worst for me. The only good part was my favorite teacher, Mr. Shippo, who was a history buff, and the way he taught sparked my love of history. He was a kind man and maybe thirty-five years old. He loved talking about history and would have discussions with us. He made our lessons come alive instead of just assigning us reading. He was the first person to try to explain to me about the Holocaust. One day I was looking something up in an encyclopedia and came upon a picture that was a bunch of naked bodies all piled on top of one another. The body on top had its head back, his mouth open, and dead eyes. I will never forget that picture. It was so horrible. I went up to Mr. Shippo and I asked what the picture meant. He brought me outside, took me under his arm, and told me what had happened. I didn't know that there were things in the world that could be that horrible. He could see how upset I was and he explained it in a very gentle way.

It was tradition that students dressed up for the last day of the school year, but at the end of fourth grade Mom couldn't afford to buy me anything special. She picked up some horrible brown sandals from a discount bin, and wearing them without socks, I looked like an old man from Palm Beach. I hated them so much I'd have rather worn the fucking shoebox. Then I pressed the ruffles on my old pink pinafore dress all wrong, and I didn't want to go to school, but Mom refused to let me stay home. Hoping to remain invisible, I almost lost it when the poorest girl in my class arrived in a white nylon net dress with little black flowers and matching Mary Janes. I tried to be brave about it, but a mean girl in my class looked me up and down and said, "Oh, Cher, you decided not to dress up?" I wanted to fall through the floor to China.

After that I took those hideous shoes off at every opportunity, running around barefoot, but that only had the effect of making them last longer. Although I have a million pairs of shoes now, I'm still happier barefoot and only ever wear shoes if I'm cold or going out.

As a kid who fantasized about owning beautiful clothes one day, I thought some of the outfits Mom bought me were embarrassing, especially those that were secondhand. She was a genius at finding things in thrift stores, and found me a silk shirt with French cuffs, which I liked, but to be honest it gave me the creeps to wear other people's castoffs. I was also mortified to think that someone might recognize it and guess where we got it from, complaining, "Everyone will know!"

"Nobody will, Cher," my mother scolded, adding, "I've bought some of my best outfits from here."

Money didn't grow on trees, as she was fond of telling me, and compared to her childhood mine was a day at the beach. If there had been a competition for who had the worst childhood in the history of the universe, my mom would have won it, because everything somehow reminded her of something terrible from her past. Those memories were precious to her in some way, and although dragging her awful childhood around with her her whole life was rough, she couldn't give it up.

No matter how bad I was feeling, my mother would always come up with examples from her childhood that were worse. In comparison, my complaints seemed like nothing. She'd win the misery Olympics with something like "Did you ever sing on the top of a bar for sixteen cents when you were five?" or "Did your mother ever nurse you on a gunnysack while she was picking cotton?" or "Did your dad ever try to gas you in your sleep?" Or one of the other million things. I mean, how could my life ever compete with hers?

Mom always reminded us that we should be grateful for what

we had. Even if our food wasn't fancy, she'd fill us up on corn bread, fried chicken, collard greens, and great salads and we'd make fudge and gingerbread as a treat. We certainly never starved, but there were times when we ate the beans until they went sour. Sometimes the milk would go bad or there'd be ants in the Rice Krispies. I hated those ants. I still do. Those are the times that being poor really got to me and I promised myself that one day I'd be rich and take care of us all.

Grandma Lynda was still working as a waitress and was married by then to my grandpa Charlie, her last and longest-suffering husband, who was the head baker at the huge Johnston's Pies company. I loved him because he was like a big kid and once let me eat an entire chocolate cream pie myself, telling Lynda—who was trying to take it from me—"Doll, just let her have a good time." They could have helped us out if they'd wanted, and Charlie would have brought food over for us had he known, but my grandmother never told him and would wait until we were destitute before she'd even offer.

Somehow I still found a way to have a relationship with her. I'd be enlisted to help with her two standard poodles, Samson and Chanson. I was convinced Lynda loved those dogs more than she loved any of us, because she was always polishing their nails and clipping their fur into ridiculous show cuts. She loved it if I made a fuss over them too. I was the only person in the family who got along with her because I didn't act like a child and knew how to give her the attention she needed. Maybe it was because she was sent to live with strangers after her dad died that she ended up the way that she was.

I loved it whenever Mom got a tax refund because we never had extra money. She'd take Gee and me to a mom 'n' pop department store with a great art section in the Valley, where I'd buy myself a drawing pad and all kinds of colored pencils. The first time I got my very own box of sixty-four Crayola crayons, I wouldn't even use them because I didn't want to blunt the points. I'd just open the box and stare at them in wonder. I'd never felt so rich. After our shopping spree, she'd take us to Du-par's restaurant at the Farmers Market on Fairfax, which is still there. I'd order fried shrimp or chicken pot pie and a Coke, while Gee always asked for French fries. Sometimes we'd head to the famous hot dog–shaped Pink's, or to our favorite Mexican food stand, Los Tres Burritos on Lankershim in the Valley, run by an adorable couple who served the best Mexican food I ever tasted—and for only nine cents. For a real treat we'd go to the Victory drive-in movie theater in Van Nuys, a place where we couldn't afford the food, so we'd hide popcorn, watermelon, and a bucket of my mother's Southern fried chicken under a blanket or in the trunk to save us having to buy any. It took forty minutes to get into the drive-in and we three would sit in that car singing old country songs together at the top of our lungs to pass the time.

One night at the drive-in, Mom told us we were in for a big surprise: "You're going to love this movie. It changed my life when I first saw it." When *The Wizard of Oz* started rolling in black-and-white, I was cranky. *We came all the way here to see a black-and-white movie?* I thought, *How the hell did this change her life?* But as soon as Dorothy opened that door to a world of color, my mouth popped open and didn't close for the rest of the movie. If there'd been a hook in it, I couldn't have been pulled in harder. With its perilous cyclone, scary witch, scarecrow, tin man, lion, and message about facing up to your fears, that film has never lost its magic for me.

Another night, we were in for an even bigger surprise, and this movie was about to change *my* life. I don't know why my mother thought it was appropriate to take my sister and me to see *Psycho* at the drive-in, but she did. Two days later I was taking a shower and suddenly the lights went out. My sister started growling and making noises from inside the laundry hamper, then she jumped out, screamed, and threw open the shower curtain. I was so scared I burst into tears. My mom was furious and gave Gee a spanking.

Rich or poor, Mom also always made Christmas special for us, trying to create what she'd missed out on as a kid. She'd save up for the most expensive silvertip tree, which we'd drag into the house and decorate together (I was in charge of the tinsel). Once it was finished, she'd bring out the gifts to place underneath, including the lovely handmade dresses sent each year by our Texan aunts Did and Ethel. Christmas 1954 was especially memorable because it fell immediately after Mom had left that horrid garage apartment and retrieved our furniture from hock. Money was still so tight that we'd moved to a poorer area on Bakman Avenue way out in the Valley. The apartment was really small, and we had no friends there like we had on Beeman, where we knew everyone in the neighborhood. It felt like we were going backward. Mom only had enough for a regular Christmas tree that year, which I draped with tinsel as always. Determined not to be defeated, she visited Grandma Lynda's friend "Nudie" Cohn. Nudie started off making pasties for strippers but went on to design fabulous country and Western clothes for TV stars like Roy Rogers and Dale Evans and became famous for Elvis Presley's gold lamé suit. (Later he would also make clothes for Sonny and me too.) Salvaging Christmas for us all, that kind Ukrainian sent Mom home with enough money for two new dolls as well as tiny cowboy boots, jeans, and a pair of white leather fringe jackets from his store. Someone took a photo of us sitting on a split-rail fence outside that apartment wearing them proudly. I still have that picture—I wish I still had the outfit too.

As soon as I turned eleven, Mom would leave me in charge whenever she was at auditions or on set all day. "You're a big girl now, Cher," she told me. "You have to help me look after your sister." She knew she could trust me as I'd been watching Gee since she was a baby and hadn't killed her yet, not even the time I gave her my little blue car to play with and she ate the wheels. My mom was hysterical and the doctor said, "Just go through her diaper for a couple of days and you'll find them." It wasn't always easy. If I cut her orange up wrong, she wouldn't eat it, but the upside is that Gee and I have a bond that's lasted our whole lives. All she had to do was give me a smile and look so adorable that my heart would melt all over again.

On the days when we weren't at school and Mom left me in charge, she'd make sure we had some food in the house before dashing out the door, leaving a trail of perfume and hairspray. "I'll try to be home before dark, and remember, never let anyone in the house," she'd say. Although she was a naturally tidy person, she often left behind a mess of powder, lipstick, and mascara in the bathroom. After the front door closed behind her, I'd play with her makeup and sneak to her closet and play dress-up with some of her clothes, posing in the mirror in shoes that were like boats on me and cocktail dresses that fell all the way down to the floor. As the person who pretty much ran our home by then, I'd spend the rest of the day wearing one of her sweaters like a dress as I straightened up the place, washed the dishes, did the ironing, and made the beds. No matter how many times I tried to teach Gee how to pitch in with the household chores, she'd always plead, "But, Cher, can you show me how to fold my shirt? And, Cher, can you show me how to put the pillow on my bed?" Until I ended up doing everything myself anyway. But she was funny and sweet, and quite content playing with her toys or—later—hiding behind the couch with her nose buried in a book, which she did from the day she learned to read. I'd then have some time to myself to draw or dance around the living room to my favorite songs.

At mealtimes, I could make us a BLT, a grilled cheese sandwich, or a peanut butter and jelly, but that was about it for my cooking skills. Not much has changed, although my pasta sauce is now so good that I've bottled it and given it to friends with the label "Diva Pasta Sauce." To be left in charge of the house felt important and helped me survive those early years psychologically. I couldn't do anything about paying the rent or buying groceries, but I could keep things straight for my mother. That was the only thing I could control, even though I wasn't perfect at it.

It was around this time that I first became sick. It was some sort of virus because none of the penicillin worked, and that was the only medicine we had. For two weeks I was ill with a fever of 103 degrees that gave me hallucinations. Mamaw came to take care of me, because Mom was working as an extra on the set of a movie called *Bundle of Joy* starring Debbie Reynolds and Eddie Fisher. The doctor didn't know what was wrong with me, so Mamaw bathed my head with cold water and gave me aspirin to bring down my fever.

When I was well enough to go back to school, Mom found out that I could get a free lunch if I helped out in the cafeteria between classes. I was embarrassed, so I'd try to hide in the kitchen, putting cookies in paper bags or doing some other chore in return for a hot lunch. When my job was done, I'd join my friends hanging out on the bleachers by the football field. I felt better knowing that being cool trumps being rich, and pretty much everything else.

My spelling was—and still is—appalling. And my grammar. Punctuation marks are like symbols to me that you throw in the air and they land where they land. I didn't understand it and still don't (as my Twitter followers well know). I never even read an entire book until I was seventeen because the words wouldn't arrange in my head. The teachers would repeatedly tell my mother that although I was smart, I didn't "apply" myself, when in truth I was applying the hell out of myself. What nobody knew back then was that I had an undiagnosed learning disability. There wasn't even a word for it. "Applying myself" became an expression that triggered anger in me for the rest of my life. In my heart, I didn't believe I was stupid, and I knew I wasn't lazy. I didn't understand why everyone else found it so easy and I just couldn't get it. I've now become an avid reader and know a lot about the most random topics, but it's all obscure and niche. I know details about particular subjects that catch my interest, like Napoleon, Lincoln, Lincoln's wife, Queen Elizabeth, interior design, directing . . . It changes but each time I'll go deep into whatever subject is interesting to me at the moment.

Math was a hundred times worse and might as well have been hieroglyphs. Numbers and I have never been friends. One day I brought home my report card and I had gotten a D in math. I was a little bit afraid of what my mom would say, but her response was so unexpected that I couldn't imagine where the idea came from. She said, "Don't worry, babe. When you grow up, you'll have someone to do numbers for you." My mom calling everyone "babe" was a habit that became a part of me, and Sonny used it too. The "babe" in "I've Got You, Babe" came from my mom.

I've had trouble with numbers throughout my life, and one day when I was older, my boyfriend Robert and I were driving up the street on the way to get lunch when I asked him what time it was because I couldn't read the clock in his car. He told me that it was in military time, but that didn't make a difference to me being able to understand it. He kept saying, "It's so easy, it's so easy." It was exasperating, and he said, "Just look. Doll, you're not applying yourself," and at that phrase I said, "Let me out." And I walked to the restaurant. To this day, woe betide the one who utters the words "You're not applying yourself."

# trouble

My mother never failed to surprise me, so I took it in stride when her fourth husband came along and swept us all off our feet. The real estate magnate Joseph Harper Collins fell in love with Mom when he met her at a party in the summer of 1957 and asked her to marry him immediately. She said yes two weeks later.

I was happy because I liked Joe, a barrel-chested, larger-than-life character who enjoyed having children around. Mom loved Joe. When they got married we all moved into his gigantic pink mansion in Beverly Hills. The wedding was in the Little Brown Church in the Valley, a wooden chapel dating from 1939 that Mom chose. Gee and I had new outfits for the occasion, and that was only the start. For a minute and a half we had a home on a hill with live-in housekeepers, headed by John Hames, a huge man with a wooden leg who made the most incredible pies.

We also had a heated swimming pool, which blew my mind because I loved swimming so much that I'd have sold Gee to know someone who knew someone who had a pool. But best of all, I loved that Mom could relax. All the stress left her life, as she didn't have to worry about money or work or putting food on the table. Once we moved into Joe's home, she became a different person entirely, happy and carefree. Joe loved company, so she'd invite friends and family over to the big house to show it off. Jake and the gang would drop by with their kids, and we'd play in the pool and have barbecues while Joe kept the cocktails flowing. We had so much fun in that house, and Mom, Gee, and I goofed around constantly. Even though Gee was still little, people always said we seemed like three sisters, laughing at the same things and finishing one another's sentences. We'd been happy before, but always with the stress of money just around the corner.

Living with Joe felt like another scene from the movie of my life. Thanks to him, I was sent to a fancy school and ate steak, and—for one glorious summer—lobster became my favorite food. Mom laughed a lot around him. He wore the most expensive of everything and his home was decorated with impeccable taste. But Joe swung too far the other way for my mother too, because beneath the panache, he was a party animal who liked to drink and was too wild in the bedroom. When he told her that he wanted to be more experimental sexually and involve other women, that was something naïve "Jackie Jean" from Arkansas simply couldn't face. Shocked, she told him, "You know I love you, Joe, but I can't do that." They tried for a long time to work it out, as neither Joe nor my mother wanted to face the end of their marriage, but the fantasy was over.

All four of us were brokenhearted when Mom finally said we'd be moving out. Packing up and leaving that time was hard for me because they'd seemed so happy and we all got along so well. My experience had taught me that when people broke up, everything went to hell, but Mom and Joe still seemed to love each other. We'd been having so much fun, I didn't understand why we were leaving. Gee and I lost yet another dad, and we missed everything about him, especially his good humor—and his pool. Joe rented a lovely house for us as part of the divorce settlement, a place with the coolest high-tech sound system and speakers throughout. This meant that when Mom was playing Elvis, Hank Williams, or Ritchie Valens, we could all hear it, and by "all," I mean my uncle Mickey, Rita, and their firstborn, Michael, who'd moved in with us again for a time. The house was ours for six months and then we'd be on our own, living on the money Joe had given Mom even though they'd only been married for less than a year. He even had John, who Gee and I loved, come help us at the new house for a while. Joe was a class act.

My mother admitted later that it was no coincidence that my biological father contacted her for the first time in many years in the weeks immediately after the announcement of her divorce from my millionaire stepfather appeared in the society pages. She'd last set eyes on Johnnie Sarkisian in Scranton more than a decade earlier. I have no idea what possessed her to agree to see him. Then came the question out of nowhere after she sauntered into my bedroom one night after school. "How'd you like to meet your real father?" She acted as if it were the most normal thing in the world for me to be introduced to the man who'd fathered and then just run away. Like asking if I wanted rye or wheat toast.

Amazed, I gazed up at her. All I knew about Johnnie Sarkisian was that he was that shadowy figure from the past that no one ever talked about. Besides, I already had a daddy I loved deeply and still missed.

Although I had no burning desire to see him, there was a tiny part of me that had always been curious. Within a day of my agreeing to meet my "real" father, Mom had me washed and dressed in my Sunday best, which meant that I couldn't secretly put on lipstick to hang with my friends at the roller rink, my new favorite thing to do. She even put curlers in my hair and sat me under the big domed metal hair dryer that nearly melted my ears. When the doorbell rang, she told me to go open it. Not feeling any particular way about it but still interested to meet the man, I did as she asked. I opened the door to see Johnnie standing there with his dark hair. He smiled at me, and I smiled back and thought, *Huh, so this is why my Mom looks at me funny sometimes.*

There was a sense of recognition at the genetic link between us because in him I saw my own olive skin and heart-shaped mouth. With thick dark eyebrows and almond-shaped brown eyes, he bore an uncanny resemblance to my favorite actor, Victor Mature, whom I'd always been a sucker for. No wonder Mom had commented years earlier, "Of course you like him."

"So, this is my baby?" Johnnie asked my mom happily. He was dressed beautifully and clearly had great style. A little shy, I stared at his fancy brown loafers and, intrigued, asked, "What are they made of?"

"Alligator."

"What?" I'd never even heard of alligator shoes, although I knew Mamaw had had some made from lizard. "And how much did they cost?" These were the first few words I ever spoke to my father, and he hadn't even stepped a well-heeled foot across the threshold.

"Eleven hundred dollars," he replied without flinching, a response that floored me. My most prized possession was the twenty-one-dollar white leather roller skates Mom bought me as a reward for finishing a color-by-numbers art project of Van Gogh's *Sunflowers* because I was never much of a finisher. Even at that tender age, I couldn't help but think that there was something unusual about his wearing alligator loafers.

Johnnie stayed for dinner, and I watched him with fascination. He seemed relaxed, easygoing, and even-tempered, like me. My sister and mother were a pair of volcanoes, whereas I was slow to anger (although if anyone pisses me off—and they have to go to unbelievable lengths to do so, believe me—they'd better leave the room, and then the state, and then the country, and then the planet). I also noticed that he ate very slowly, as I did. Mom had always been upset with me for what she called "dawdling" over my food, but when I saw him I thought, *Yes, I'm vindicated!*, because here Johnnie was. I had a new father and he played with his food too. Watching him, I understood that the reason Mom sometimes looked at me strangely was that he and I both had the same little half-smile.

I took all these connections in stride for the most part, but I watched him closely. I was different than my sister and my mom in some ways. My personality was more laid-back. I ate slower than they did. I smiled in a half-smile. My eyes were different. What I saw in him was the part of me that I could never explain before, because I'd never seen it in anyone else in my family. The thing you can't know unless you meet your other parent. This man walked in and it was like a missing puzzle piece for me. He did things intentionally and quietly like I did. He wasn't quick to anger.

Even though I knew that I was Johnnie's child, it was hard for me to think of him as my father. He was some other word that I couldn't quite put my finger on. My brain was full of complicated thoughts, some of which conflicted with the love I still felt for my daddy.

This surprise family reunion lasted longer than I'd expected, because my uncle Mickey liked Johnnie and kept inviting him to the house. Eventually, after he started coming over once in a while, and in a move I still find hard to fathom, Mom agreed to take Johnnie back. And then later, when we moved back to Beeman, she agreed to let him live with us. And then she married him again! I wasn't happy about it—it was happening too fast. I liked the guy well enough, but I didn't know him yet. I always had to dance around what to call him—"Johnnie" felt strange, but "Dad" definitely wasn't right. My dad was gone, so that was uncomfortable.

What was it about this man my mother claimed she never loved? He'd tricked her into a marriage she didn't want and talked her out of the annulment she wanted. He gambled, lost a house and a company, stole a car, and then abandoned both of us, only to return because he thought she had money. And still she went back for more. If he'd dumped my ass and put my child in an orphanage, I'd have stabbed him in the back with a knife. Well, maybe not a knife, because then I'd go to jail. A fork wouldn't do enough damage. A barbecue fork? Oh, fuck it, a fork.

It's hard to make sense of, but getting a husband was the go-to thing for women of that generation. It seems like Mom never quite lost the feeling that there was safety in marriage. Women were second-class citizens back then, that was the way the world worked (and frankly, we're still fighting for our rights). Whatever the reason, she kept seeking protection through marriage. Even now, it's hard to remember—was it seven or eight husbands in the end? Did she marry Johnnie two or three times? I could never figure out why she married him in the first place, so to remarry him when he hadn't changed and was no help whatsoever, financially or emotionally? To wed him three times seemed like an exercise in futility. But saying all that, he did have his good points. He was kind, he was a caretaker to some degree, and he had a magnetic charm.

What's strange to me now is that even though all these stepfathers and suitors passed through our lives, I barely remember a man in the house. There was usually only Mom, Gee, and me, the three of us creating our own universe, a club of like-minded females. And we were constantly surrounded by women.

Although my mother's life taught me how to be resilient, independent, and adaptable, it also showed me that marriage was rarely all it was cracked up to be. So when Johnnie moved in, I thought he was another man passing through. Only, unlike Joe, this one had no skills and was bringing nothing to the table. I understood that he was warm and charming, but to me he was so easy to see through. I thought, *Are you serious? You're so smart, yet you have the judgment of a fruit fly when it comes to him!*

Not long after he arrived back on the scene, Johnnie took me out to lunch to try to explain himself. He was soft-spoken. He could take the temperature of a room as soon as he walked in and then he wouldn't make a move immediately; he'd wait and wait and then make one. After ordering me my favorite malt, he said, "I want you to know that I haven't been to see you all this time because I've been in prison for four years." He was remorseful as he painstakingly described how he'd first started taking drugs because of the pain of emergency intestinal surgery and how that led him to heroin and, ultimately, a narcotics charge. He even showed me his surgical scar, which was huge and ran from front to back. Hard times then led him to a path of fraud and theft, he added. It seemed important to him that he tell me how horrible everything had been and how contrite he was, but at this age I wasn't interested in that part of his story. My mother might have bought his latest bill of goods, but I was more cautious and was waiting to see how I felt about this nice stranger who looked like me. I didn't dislike him, but I wasn't going to rush headlong into his arms until I knew I was firmly planted on the ground myself. I just didn't know if I could trust him—he was too smooth. Sucking my drink through a straw as he talked on, I tried to give him the benefit of the doubt, but I really just wanted to be finished so I could go to the roller rink in the Valley, put on the makeup that I'd hidden in my bag, and—as soon as I had on my magic wheels—show off to a boy I had a crush on named Foxy, whose job was to skate around the rink with a whistle, though mostly he was showing off his moves.

I don't recall anything about my parents' wedding in Vegas, but then I barely remember any of my mother's weddings, because most of them happened when I was really young. Or perhaps I didn't go. What I do remember is that not that long after we moved back to Beeman with him, my silver-tongued father talked Mom into relocating two hundred miles north to an area of Fresno known as Little Armenia. We were to live with his family—more strangers that I'd never met and didn't know existed until that moment. Mamaw put Gee and me on the train from LA to Fresno by ourselves.

I got my period for the first time that day. When I told Mamaw, she said they'd have supplies on the train, but all I could find there was a tampon, which I didn't know what to do with. Improvising, I stuffed a bunch of pieces of toilet paper in my underpants instead. I then carefully timed my reentry into the club car for when the train was going through a tunnel so it would be dark and I wouldn't feel self-conscious. Unfortunately, there were overhead lights in the car, and to my horror, when I got to the middle of the club car, all the pieces of toilet paper fell out of from under my skirt. Knowing I wouldn't survive picking them up myself, I whispered to my little sister to go grab them. She did—slowly, delicately, one by one, like she was a flower girl in reverse. She came to me and asked what they were. When I told her, she covered her mouth, giggling. I couldn't believe I didn't die of embarrassment by the time we got to Fresno.

Once there, I was introduced to my Armenian family members for the first time, astonished to discover how many of them looked like me. At my grandparents' house, dozens of relatives arrived to make a fuss of the prodigal son and his lost daughter. Only some of them spoke English, but they all seemed thrilled to meet me and constantly stroked my hair or patted my head.

Armenians are welcoming and I seemed to fit right in, so for the first time in my twelve years on this earth, it was my sister and my mom, not me, who were on the outside looking in. Johnnie's relatives were polite to my mother but didn't focus much on his "long" wife or her other kid.

Taking me to meet them was his slickest move yet, because as the adored baby of the family forgiven for his sins, he redeemed himself by presenting them with their missing grandchild. Although Johnnie had gambled away his father's refrigerated truck business, my grandfather had managed to keep hold of one vehicle and build the business back up again. Foolishly, he welcomed his son back with open arms. Watching Johnnie work the room, I understood how easy it would be to be sucked in by him. I was young, but I was not naïve when it came to him—I knew I was also a commodity, a big dose of extra firepower worth a few thousand dollars.

Still, I enjoyed meeting my grandfather Ghiragos, known as George; my grandmother Siranoush, known as Blanche; and my great-grandmother Noussapa, known as Lucy, plus aunts and uncles who couldn't have been nicer. They were mine and mine alone. Everyone seemed to have a lovely home and, better still, they introduced me to the most delicious Armenian food, including kufta and sarma (grape leaves stuffed with meat and rice, which my grandmother taught me to make). There was also shish kebab and a kind of sour pizza with spinach called lahmajoun that I still enjoy. Having never seen a man cook anything but barbecue food in my life, I watched in amazement as Johnnie and his sisters prepared what seemed to me like a banquet every night.

We must have been in Fresno for a while because we had our own house, and I went to a school that I don't remember hating for one full semester. I even made some friends who I'd play with near an aqueduct after class. We'd sneak into an orchard and help ourselves to plums, nectarines, and peaches, then stick them into the water of the aqueduct to get nice and cold. (I think the farmer pretended not to see us.) I missed my friends from Beeman and hated being away from Jake and my mother's girlfriends, so having other kids to play with helped. I don't know why we left Fresno, but on we went to Las Vegas to live with my aunt Roxy, my uncle Vincent, and my cousins Dickie and Geralyn. Aunt Roxy and Uncle Vincent owned a chain of successful dry-cleaning shops. Their big new client was the fourteen-hundred-room Tropicana, which had just opened as the largest and most expensive hotel in town, at the very end of the Strip. The shop was inside the Tropicana itself, and I used to go visit them in there. I loved Aunt Roxy instantly. She was a "balls to the wall" kind of woman who didn't care what anyone thought. She was hysterical and had a huge laugh. She'd met Mom before I was born, and they'd become fast friends back then. I also enjoyed living in Vegas in the mid-sixties and especially liked going to the all-you-can-eat buffet at El Rancho, with its Old West theme. I was just starting to settle into life there and being part of a large, loving family when the man who'd fathered me fucked everything up—like he always had.

Unbeknownst to any of us, he'd gone back to gambling and taking heroin, blowing any money he'd earn on craps and drugs. That was the thing about my dad. You couldn't trust him. He stole and then pawned my mother's last remaining diamond jewelry, all treasured gifts from Ernie and Joe. It all came to a head one night when Johnnie was preparing his latest fix in the bedroom of the house Aunt Roxy had rented for us and he nodded off, setting the bed on fire. Gee and I were in our room when smoke started curling under the door. Mom freaked out and grabbed us and then started yelling. She wasn't screaming that the house was on fire, she was shouting at Johnnie, calling him every name under the sun for almost killing us. He was so stoned he couldn't even respond. We left Vegas that night and within days were back living on Beeman.

I never questioned her decision or asked if I'd ever see my

Armenian family again. That would have been futile. I also knew that it was best to forget about the man with my smile who was half the reason I existed. He was a lot of things, but mostly, he was trouble. I think Mom always hoped that he'd become the man she wanted him to be, but he always disappointed her. I have no idea how he always got my mother to do what he wanted, regardless of whether it was right for her—or us. All she would say later was "Well, he could talk me into anything." No shit. Mom tried to act as if the whole Johnnie Sarkisian experience had never happened, only it had—and with consequences. Mom was pregnant again, and she found out not long after she'd left him. The last thing she wanted was another baby, least of all by him, so she had another illegal abortion and once again it almost killed her.

I was far too young to understand what was happening, but I knew it was something mysterious and scary. I wasn't allowed into the bedroom and had to keep my sister quiet, which is how I knew something was really wrong. Catching glimpses of Mom lying in her darkened room with her girlfriends going in and out in silence frightened me. I tried to read the faces of Jake and Colleen but couldn't. Everyone was whispering, and I was unable to be with my mother, again. Nobody took Mom to a doctor or explained anything to me, so I was convinced she was going to die.

Incredibly, she made a full recovery. Even more incredibly, she took Johnnie's ass back again.

During one of the respite periods when Mom wasn't with Johnnie, she moved us into a big Georgian-style house in Toluca Lake near the famous Bob's Big Boy. Her friend Colleen had been tipped off about a neighborhood that was about to be torn down to build a freeway and heard that its homes were available cheap on short-term leases. The one she found for us was two stories tall, with white painted brick, a high-ceilinged entryway, a gray slate roof, a big fireplace, and a brick chimney. It also had the biggest Christmas tree in the history of the world growing on the front lawn. To me that tree felt like it was a thousand feet high and twenty-five feet wide.

We lived in that big house in Toluca Lake with Colleen and her daughter Paulette for a year. I loved living with Colleen because she was so zen, a term she taught me. Gee loved it too because she was very close with Paulette. Colleen was a model with an ex-husband who supported her. She was a strange dresser in a fabulous kind of way, drifting around the house in beautiful Asian kaftans. While every other woman I knew plucked their eyebrows into fine pencil lines, she kept hers natural and thick. She had pale skin with dark hair like me, and I wanted to emulate her style. She and I would get up early and have our favorite Bigelow Constant Comment tea together in silence, because neither of us liked to talk in the morning. Then Mom would come down and start chattering away, breaking the stillness, as Colleen and I gave each other the side eye.

Our house was at least five miles from Hollywood and the places I loved, so my desire to escape took hold once more and I decided to sneak off—in my mother's red Pontiac convertible. I was thirteen and she was at work, so I skipped school, grabbed the keys, and told Gee to ride with me into town. I set off feeling strangely calm. Lord only knows how, but I made it all the way to our favorite hot dog stand on Hollywood Boulevard and back again. On the way home I ran a couple of red lights and bounced into a few trash cans but returned otherwise unscathed. Because I got away with it, I found the confidence to do it again and again, but the day I took my friend Della into town and back, I spotted my mother on the front lawn as we turned into our street and felt certain that the game was up.

Convinced I'd be grounded until I was an old lady, I faltered but kept the car rolling quietly forward. Mom was talking to Della's mother when I came to a stop behind that big old Christmas tree. Thinking I was so busted, I climbed out with a heavy heart, resigned to my fate, as I thought there was no way she hadn't spotted her red Pontiac. I expected to be murdered right there on the front lawn, but thanks to the tree, she never saw us pull up or even noticed that her car was missing. When she noticed us coming toward them, she smiled and said, "Oh, hi, girls. Have you been out for a walk?" That's when I knew that there was a God.

The Almighty became a daily feature of my life after I was sent to Villa Cabrini, an all-girls Catholic boarding school in Burbank. Johnnie Sarkisian, who'd been raised a Catholic, said his parents would want any child of his to have a religious education in the tradition of his family, even though I'd never been to Mass in my life. As was her pattern with him, my mother made some sort of deal where his family paid for my schooling. Despite her own horrible experience with nuns, she sent me to a place that was completely different from anything I'd experienced before. The nuns were tougher than any teacher I'd known, and among their many rules was a ban on patent shoes in case our panties could be seen in their reflection. There was also a prohibition on wearing makeup. Luckily, most of the nuns were so old and their eyesight so poor that they didn't notice when we did. I went home one day wearing so much eyeliner that my mother snapped, "Take that off, Cherilyn. You look like a hooker!" It wouldn't be the last time someone would tell me that.

All students had to wear uniforms for class, which I loved, as I couldn't be judged for my clothes. We could only wear nonuniform clothes on evenings and weekends, and I'd packed my favorite shorts, jeans, and crop tops, only to discover that none of those were allowed. The sole dress I brought was my pink pinafore, which I had to wear every single day, so I was given the nickname "Pinky Sarkisian," a name that matched my embarrassment. It was mortifying having only one spaghetti-stained outfit, and I still felt uncomfortable about my new last name. I guess because his family was paying for the school, my mom let me be enrolled as "Cherilyn Sarkisian."

The nuns were all very different from one another. My favorite was Italian and young with beautiful auburn hair and rosy cheeks. She was so sweet and looked like Sophia Loren, and I'm sure I loved her because she seemed so glamorous compared to the rest. For a minute and a half, I considered taking vows myself because I loved the drama of it. There's the costumes, the music, the lights streaming down, and the smoke from the incense that the priest swung. I just thought, and no disrespect to my many Catholic friends, *This is the original show business.* Every Friday a priest came to talk to us, but he got sick of my endless questions that were hard to answer, like "Father, why do little babies go to purgatory if they haven't had time to do anything wicked?" He didn't like that one bit.

One night in the dorm after lights-out, I started telling dumb jokes, things like "Sister Teresa waddles like a duck," "Mother Josephine's teeth are like stars; they come out at night," and "Mother Benedetta looks like the actor Joe E. Brown," while the girls giggled under their sheets. Unbeknownst to me, one of the girls sneaked out and woke Mother Josephine, our house mother, to rat me out. The following day the mother superior, Mother Benedetta, punished me. She started off by saying, "You know, Pinky, these robes we wear are sacred," and then—Bop! Wham! Shazam! After that she made me walk both ways across the lawn on my knees repeating the rosary before writing out "I will never say anything bad about the sisters again" two hundred times (fortunately, Mother Bernadette had all the girls help me so I could finish in time to play in the varsity volleyball game). She had this real New York attitude and sounded like the actor Sheldon Leonard, but at least she was nice. She told me, "Hey, Pinky, give me a break. Why don't you learn to keep your mouth shut?" Well, that was the end of my comedy career in that school.

Aside from mother superior, I loved all the nuns, the fun ones and the old ones. I also liked the new friends I made at Villa

Cabrini and became close to three girls in particular—Anita, Rose, and Donna, the wildest girls I'd ever met—and I began to enjoy school. I would have happily remained at Villa Cabrini but for that big mouth of mine. During the summer vacation I let slip to my mom that the mother superior had slapped me. Recalling her own encounters with a mother superior in Scranton, she was all set to drive over and give the nun a piece of her mind. I begged her to forget about it, but she never let me go back, so I sadly lost touch with Anita, Rose, and Donna. And, against Johnnie's wishes, it was back to public school.

Gee kept a list of all the schools she attended and claims it numbered more than twenty-five. The bright kid who was always reading, even at the table, was unlikely to be wrong. I never kept count. After Villa Cabrini, in January 1959, I started at Walter Reed. One night I went out with two of my friends and one of their boyfriends. We went for a ride in a '57 Chevy, which my friend's boyfriend double-parked at the now-iconic Kirkwood bowling alley on Ventura Boulevard. He ran inside for something, telling us, "If anyone comes, tell them I won't be long." We waited and waited, but other drivers started honking their horns for us to move out of the way. I slid into the driver's seat, slipped the Chevy into gear, and circled the parking lot to let them pass. Still the boyfriend didn't reemerge, so I did that a few more times and then I parked out on the street.

"Let's drive around the block, Cher," my girlfriends urged, so I did as they asked. Thrilled, they suggested, "Now drive us to Johnie's drive-in to get orange juice for our vodka," so I did that too. They'd stashed the vodka in one of their purses, but when we swung into the drive-up parking spot, a squad car suddenly appeared behind us, lights flashing.

It was humiliating to be pulled from the Chevy by armed police officers and given the third degree. Scared out of my wits, I tried to explain, but the boyfriend had reported his car stolen, so we were taken to the police station.

Everybody else's parents came to collect their children as soon as the police called, but Mom was out and they couldn't get ahold of her. There were no cell phones back in the day. By the time it was midnight, an officer moved me to an empty holding room with a window so that I could at least lie down. Exhausted and emotionally wrung out, I was finally falling asleep when I heard a noise coming from underneath the bunk. A hand suddenly shot out and grabbed my ankle. Crawling out, a wild old drunk started ranting, "Hey, you bitch!" I kicked him off, screamed for help, and remained glued to the wall until officers rescued me and closed the door on the bum they'd forgotten was sleeping it off in there.

My mother eventually came for me at 2 a.m. and, after taking one look at my tear-stained face, decided that I'd been punished enough. The worst part was that I never saw those girlfriends again, as their parents decided I was a bad influence and warned them to keep away from me; I was persona non grata. As a humorous postscript, years later someone pulled a photo of me from my junior high school yearbook in sixth grade and made it look like a police mugshot, although the cops never took one. After I became famous, that picture appeared in newspapers and magazines around the world as the real thing—an early case of "fake news" that made me laugh. I do kind of look like a criminal in it.

Although I sometimes acted like a grown-up, driving around the Valley, I wasn't at all the streetwise chick I appeared to be. So when my boobs arrived, boys weren't exactly running screaming into the street, but I found myself fending off advances from older boys and even some of my mother's friends. This was scary.

One of the first to cross that line was Colleen's boyfriend Huntz, an actor in a film series about a gang of New York teenagers. He was almost forty when he asked if I wanted to go visit Mom and Colleen on a film set. We were driving together on what seemed like an endless ride. I asked to make sure we were going the right direction because it seemed we were nowhere near the studios. Then, he put his hand on my thigh. I waited a few moments before I pushed him off and threatened to tell my mother, who'd have killed him. He told me I was being ridiculous. "Cher, come on, you're like a daughter to me, do you think I would touch you in an inappropriate way?" His words made me worry that I'd misinterpreted the situation, and I ended up apologizing to *him*.

Huntz had a friend and fellow actor named Gabe who was dating my mother at the time. We all had schoolgirl crushes on him. One night Gabe came over on his new motorcycle to show my mom, but she wasn't home, so he took me for a ride. It was the first time I'd ever been on a motorcycle and I was so happy, hugging his waist with the wind blowing my hair. *One day I'm going to have my own Harley-Davidson*, I told myself. (And I did. When I turned fifty, I got my own bike and went riding with my best friends Richard and Laurie Stark every Sunday.)

Gabe drove us to Wil Wright's ice cream parlor on Ventura, with its pink-and-white-striped tablecloths and wrought-iron heart-shaped chairs. He bought us two fudge sundaes with almonds on top. Then we rode around a while longer before heading back. After we got home, he went straight upstairs to see my mother and, out of nowhere, declared that he was in love with me. It was a shockingly inappropriate statement on any level, but especially since I was only fourteen. She immediately threw him out of the house. I heard the front door slam, and then she came stomping down to my room. Nothing could have prepared me for her reaction as she threw open the door and demanded, "What did you do with Gabe?"

"What do you mean, what did I do?" I asked, completely surprised. "We went for a sundae."

"No, what did you do with him?" Her eyes were ablaze.

"Mom, we drove around a bit and ate ice cream. That's all, I promise." Despite my protests, Mom was so upset. She was crazy about Gabe and she was broken-hearted. It really hurt me that she didn't believe me, and then she kicked me out of the house. I had no choice but to stay with my friend Della until she'd calmed down.

We never saw Gabe again. As I never thought of myself as pretty because of the bump in my nose, crooked teeth, and dark hair, it never occurred to me that he'd think of me in that way. Don't get me wrong, I wanted to be attractive—just not to guys who were twice my age.

So when Fred Smith, the cutest, coolest jock in school, asked me out on a date, I was beside myself. Fred was really handsome and on the football team; he was what we kids called a "sosh" (as in "social"), which meant a rich, popular kid, the kind who wore a certain type of clothes, like a Pendleton cotton shirt with cords. Mom was excited for me and bought me a beautiful mocha shirtdress from a store called Judy's that sold higher-end clothing. I felt fabulous when Fred picked me up and drove me to a friend's house for a party. He kissed me while I silently luxuriated in his football-toned chest and arms. We had a really nice time, and, for a hot minute, I thought I loved him. Then he drank so much beer that he threw up on my front lawn after driving me home. As I held his head while he puked by the big tree, my feelings remained. I was just so happy that he'd asked me out. The kicker was that he was so embarrassed that he never spoke to me again.

I'd had such a crush on him, but fortunately I had another crush to fall back on (it never hurts to have a contingency plan). An Italian family on our street had a cute son who was a senior in high school. He spent his weekends working on his hot rod as I handed him tools. Then he'd come to my room, we'd kiss, he'd want me to hold his other tool, and I'd say no. I liked his black roadster better than him.

Not that sex was far from my mind then, as the main conversations among girls at school were about how they spent their weekends fooling around with boys but never went to "fourth base." It all struck me as too casual, like they were checking things off a list. As someone who played sports, I'd had enough of their euphemisms and told them, "You're so childish. You're not playing baseball, you idiots. You're having sex!" I mean who did they think they were, Joe DiMaggio?

The neighbor was sweet enough when we were alone, but as soon as his friends came around, he'd treat me like an embarrassing kid. One day, when his buddies suggested a trip to Bob's Big Boy, he said, "Okay, let me get Cher." They laughed and said, "You're gonna take that kid?" and he ditched me. I was so hurt when he did that, I had revenge sex with him. I had never wanted to, otherwise I would have done it one of the five hundred other times he asked. But I was so angry at being dismissed, I decided to, if not lose, loan out my virginity to him.

When what turned out to be a massively overrated experience came to an end, I asked him, "Is that it? Are we finished?" Then I told him to go home and never come back. I wanted him to feel just as dismissed as he'd made me feel. Even though he kept trying to make it up to me, I never spoke to him again. Back in school, I reported to my friends that the "thing" they were constantly talking about was no big deal and that they should carry on kissing.

My mother warned me that the minute I lost my virginity she'd know because she'd see it in my eyes, so after the romp with the Italian, I ran to the mirror to check. I half expected to see the word *SEX* flashing in fluorescent letters across my forehead, but I couldn't spot anything different, and she didn't either.

There was another boy across the street who was very nice, but all he wanted to do . . . was my ironing. And that's really all I remember about him.

Soon, time was up for our white brick house and the big Christmas tree on the lawn, with both slated for demolition. We moved back to a duplex on Rosewood, two blocks south of Pink's, and I was so happy to be back in Hollywood.

The duplex needed some repairs—painting and plaster, and the big arched window in the front had been vandalized. The glass was completely smashed, so a friend of my mom's named Duffy and our next-door neighbor Coco, who was a fabulous model and another friend of Mom's, came over to help fit new glass into the window frame. A boy named Richard came to help them out as well. He was an actor and trumpet player who gave me my first real drink, with disastrous consequences. He took me to the Players Ring theater to see a play his friend was in. When it was over, he asked me if I'd ever had an alcoholic drink, so of course I said yes, although I hadn't unless you count the Brew 102 at Cap's Place when I was three years old. He gave me something called Country Club Stout Malt Liquor in a small can that I thought was regular beer. I wanted to look grown-up, so I drank it and ended up throwing up all over the stage, just like Fred Smith all over the big tree. Richard sweetly went across to the market to get me some Alka-Seltzer, and while I was still reeling, his friend started trying to kiss me. I pushed him off and yelled, "Are you out of your mind? I'm gonna throw up again!" And I did. I wish I could remember his name because he was really funny and had to be a bit desperate to try to kiss a girl who's throwing up.

One weekend, Mom went to New York to see a bunch of shows with the new man in her life, a banker named Gilbert LaPiere who she'd met at a party in LA. When she returned from Manhattan, she was raving about the musical *West Side Story* and brought back the record of the soundtrack. Man, I loved that show so much. Whenever I was left alone in the house, I'd play it full blast on the record player until it was something I felt I understood on a visceral level. Jumping around my living room really fast, I sang along to all the songs and made up the dance parts, moving my body to lift me off this planet. I hadn't seen the show, and the movie wouldn't be made until 1961, but I still identified with every character, "seeing" them in my head. They felt like they were mine alone. The love between Tony and Maria was what I wanted, not some dumb pawing from a teenage boy.

No sooner had we settled into the duplex on Rosewood when everything changed again. Gilbert had fallen hard for my mother, just as Joe Collins had, and he kept calling her from New York begging her to marry him. Tired of being alone and still trying to make it as an actress, once again she made a decision for the whole family and accepted Gilbert's proposal, making him Husband No. 5 (or 6, depending on how many times you count Johnnie Sarkisian). In an instant, Mom turned our lives upside down once more. After her announcement that we were moving to the East Coast soon after Thanksgiving, at eight and fourteen, Gee and I were again taken away from everything we knew and loved, which summed up our childhood. At the whim of what my mother thought best, I was learning that if I wanted control over my own life, then I'd have to find a way to escape.

While afraid I might lose the independence I had in LA, I was excited to go to New York. I was fourteen years old, and I was moving to a city I'd only ever seen in movies. The city of *West Side Story.*

# 8

## new york, new york

Once settled in Manhattan, we all relaxed, although the flight alone almost killed my mother. It was Gee's and my first time on an airplane, and we were having an absolute blast. Beautiful stewardesses in crisp navy uniforms escorted us to first class and served a multicourse meal, all prepared right in front of us—a salad with every ingredient you could want with a variety of dressings, a roast that they cut to our specifications, and ice cream sundaes with all the toppings. Gee and I were dressed in our finest, and we loved every second of being doted on. I didn't know to be afraid of flying yet, and being on a jet felt like the best ride we'd ever been on, better than anything at Disneyland. My sister and I fought over the window seat, desperate to look out the window to watch the world go by. Three rows behind us, my mother's anxiety kicked in big-time, and she had a full-blown panic attack. Gilbert's arm was black and blue from her squeezing, and a doctor on board had to administer oxygen. "What's the matter with Mom?" we asked each other. Gee and I kept looking at her wondering why she didn't see this as the great adventure we did. This was so exciting—but Mom clearly didn't feel that way.

Once back on solid ground, Mom perked up when she saw the apartment Gilbert had found for us. It was on East Fifty-Sixth Street, directly above a D'Agostino supermarket. My mother loved it, and so did Gee and I, because we each had our own bedroom, and the views were incredible. Our new stepfather was completely at home in the city, having been born in New Jersey, and was excited to show us Manhattan. There were too many fun and exciting distractions in New York, the best of which was that I discovered I could walk everywhere or take a cab, which meant I didn't need a car. In LA, you had to get into a car and you had to have a destination and you had to have someone to drive you. But in New York, you could just walk onto the street with everyone else, with all the hustle and bustle and energy. You weren't in the cocoon of a car. My mom didn't like that very much, but Gee and I thought it was amazing. You could just walk out of your house, and you were free.

I was due to start school in the new year, and until then, everything felt thrilling.

At first, Mom saw it as an adventure too. She and Gilbert went to plays, went out shopping, went to dinner at the city's fabulous restaurants where my mother was able to wear her amazing new clothes and jewels. They went to places like the Persian Room to see performers sing. Gilbert had friends in the city, so they would entertain in our apartment. This was all glamorous for my mom, and she enjoyed this new way of life, as the wife of a high-powered businessman.

I spent our first Christmas listening to 45s on the record player Mom had bought me. I knew Mom and Gilbert were going to be out that night, and I would be home with Gee, without plans. I probably was moping a little—my mom was adapting to Gilbert's way of being to fit in with his lifestyle, and that bothered me. Plus, I hadn't started school, so I didn't really have any friends yet. When our elevator operator Jesse sweetly offered to take me to a party on New Year's Eve, my mother immediately agreed I could go. Excited, I started to plan what to wear, talking to her about the options as I helped her bleach her hair. Distracted, I ran my fingers through my own hair, accidentally creating blond streaks on one side. Mom saw it and started laughing hysterically. Although I'd wished for blond hair when I was younger, I was over that by then. "Oh geez, Mom, what am I going to do?" I asked her. "All right, all right, sit down," Mom said calmly, and bleached the other side to even out the color. I was actually delighted with the finished product. Even better, she lent me her mink coat for the party as a treat—that was a shock and probably a little dangerous.

As I was getting changed, feeling terribly grown-up, sleet and then snow started to fall and the evening took on an almost magical feel. The first time I experienced a real winter was in New York. Looking out of the window of our high-rise apartment, I witnessed snow that was so heavy that I could barely see the building next door.

When I asked my mom what was happening, she laughed and told me, "That's a blizzard, babe." Weeks later, after a night at the movies, we walked out into Times Square to find the streets virtually empty as snow blanketed the ground. Gee and I ran around, slipping and sliding past the cabs parked on the curbs. The few brave cabbies who tried to drive found it nearly impossible to get anywhere. Sliding down the middle of a New York City street was the kind of fun we'd certainly never had before, and worlds away from Los Angeles. The only thing I'd ever experienced in Los

Angeles was a hailstorm, when I heard the crashing on the roof and ran outside to find frozen golf balls in the yard, then returned inside going, "Mom, Mom, what is this?!"

It was New Year's Eve on the brink of a new decade, and I was going to my first-ever Manhattan party. Jesse, who was in his twenties, took me in a cab three miles downtown to the East Village. The party was in an apartment block, and from the minute I stepped inside I felt as if I were walking into *West Side Story*. I'd never seen anything quite like the incredible guests there, all drinking and smoking and having fun. They looked and dressed nothing like any of the kids I knew. The guys wore colored shirts and black ties under black suits, with stovepipe pants. The girls were beautiful and fascinating, with hair teased a foot high and skintight dresses that pushed everything up. I was envious of their curves, not having any of my own. They had this style, this attitude.

I did my best to fit in and at least felt cool when the girls were impressed with Mom's mink. Jesse and I danced, and I lit a cigarette and talked with some people, just winging it. The fun ended abruptly when a fight broke out in the kitchen and a man staggered into the living room with blood on his shirt. He'd been stabbed and had to be taken to the hospital. Although I was shocked, I also found the episode strangely thrilling, as if the Sharks and the Jets were playing out their roles in front of my very eyes.

Jesse was a gentleman, but there was no spark, plus I don't think he knew how old I was, so when one of his friends asked me on a date, I said yes. We went out a few nights later, and it was great until he took me back to his place. He looked just like Bernardo. As soon as I walked in, I knew I was in trouble. I thought, *Oh God, Cher, what have you gotten yourself into? No good can come of this.* There was a tiny kitchen, a bathroom, and a bedroom with an unmade bed—and nowhere else to sit. A single lightbulb hung down from the ceiling on the end of a cord. It was creepy. The boy immediately started kissing me, and when he tried to get on top of me in what would now be classed as a sexual assault, I pushed him away and cried, "Whoa, dude! Stop. I'm not doing this, okay?" Even though he thought I was racier and a lot older than I was, I somehow managed to talk my way out of there, painfully aware that I could have been raped or worse. I never told a soul what happened and made a mental note never to put myself in such a dangerous situation again, although—of course—I did.

Gee and I settled into New York life, and Gilbert decided to adopt us, which made my mom happy. Gee would end up keeping our new last name, but I felt a little silly being known as "Cher LaPiere" because it rhymed. I think one of the reasons the man Mom called "Gil" liked us was because he had daughters the same age. The problem was that he was so square and traditional, with ideas about how to raise girls that were a million miles from mine. For years I'd been treated like a grown-up by my mother and was virtually the woman of the house. I was given a lot of responsibility and had earned her respect for caring for my sister and keeping our home clean while Mom worked. Within reason, I'd been allowed to dress how I liked, wear makeup, and smoke. But in New York, all of a sudden I was demoted. Mom and Gilbert treated me like a kid. One day I was a woman and the next they acted like I was five years old! I wasn't prepared to be subjected to rules and regulations. It was patronizing. When Gilbert pointed out that I was too young to be smoking, Mom feigned innocent surprise—"Oh my, smoking? I didn't know she was!" and quickly rescinded my cigarette privileges. Every time I saw her puffing away, I felt the injustice. (I once snapped a photo of her hanging out a window in our apartment, smoking while she looked over the busy city streets.)

Once the holidays ended, Mom and Gil enrolled me at a local high school. On my first day it was snowing hard again, so I arrived in a cab, which was my first mistake, because I almost got my ass kicked for being a "pussy." I was so different from all the other girls because I had no street smarts, so they didn't even give me a chance.

It was a tough environment that made me feel anxious—since I already hated school to begin with! Three weeks in, I quit. The decision came to me suddenly one day, and I begged Mom and Gilbert not to make me go back. I told them there was little point being there because I felt uncomfortable and wasn't learning anything, and that seemed to work. They weren't thrilled, but I'd bought myself a little time. I didn't have a plan, I just wanted to get out.

But without school, I had nothing to do and no way to make friends. I started to feel lonely, and it showed. Trying to help me out, Gilbert arranged for me to meet Joyce, the daughter of a colleague of his. Joyce was great—she wore dark eyeliner, pale makeup, her hair in a flip and was up for anything. She, in turn, introduced me to her friends, and suddenly I had places to go and people to hang out with. Wealthy girls who lived on the Upper West Side, who had all graduated already and had no clue how old I was but showed me how to live in the city—going dancing in nightclubs, shopping with friends, and being one of the gang, as attractive young men buzzed around us. It was half the girls, and half New York itself—I had found a new kind of freedom, and I didn't even need wheels.

No longer lonely, I hung out with these girls who were allowed to go everywhere and do anything, unless it was a Jewish holiday. On those weekends I was even invited to go to temple with their families, who were happy to have me along. Although my best friend Barbara's mother once said to me, "Cher, honey, we love you, but could you please stop singing for one minute?" I hadn't realized I was singing at all.

One day Barbara said she'd take me to Jones Beach. On the way there, Barbara jumped out of the subway car to ask directions, and to my horror, the doors closed behind her, leaving me alone as the train pulled away. She made indecipherable hand gestures at me through the train window, and ta-da! That, folks, is when the zipper on my skintight jeans decided to break. Thank God I had my bikini bottom on. Not that it would make that much difference to the onlookers. Mortified, and only in a short T-shirt, I had to cover myself with my purse. Sitting there, exposed and embarrassed, I felt like the eyes of all the men in the subway car were concentrated on my crotch. I went into some sort of fugue state so that by the time I got off the train, my hair was plastered to my face with sweat. I eventually found my way back to Barbara's apartment and collapsed into her mom's arms in a soggy mess. As my mother would have said in her Southern way, I looked like I'd been "ridden hard and put away wet."

For my fifteenth birthday, Gilbert took us to see the singer Eartha Kitt at the legendary Persian Room at the Plaza Hotel. Mom owned one of her albums, and we listened to it all the time. My favorite song was Cole Porter's "My Heart Belongs to Daddy," a number I performed years later. The only singers I'd ever seen were my mom and Jake. And though I loved their voices, this was a whole different level. Seeing Eartha at the Plaza was the first time I'd ever watched a female singer take over an entire room and hold it in her hands. She was tiny, but she was larger than life. I will never forget sitting in that opulent Art Deco room watching her onstage in a tight-fitting sequined dress with spaghetti straps and a fur stole. She held the attention of every man, woman, and child in the audience. At her peak in her mid-thirties, she was catlike in her movements. I wanted to be her, she was so mesmerizing, especially when she sang in French. When her set finished, she received a standing ovation with women cheering and men thumping the tables for more. Jumping to my feet too and clapping enthusiastically, I felt it again—that thing, a different kind of Elvis feeling. Looking back, I can see that she was one of those little signs, saying *Okay, Cher, go this way.*

In June, Gilbert and Mom took me, Gee, and Gil's daughters, Verna and Lisa, to Vermont for a vacation. Verna and I were over the moon to discover that the room we were sharing was clear across the hotel from Mom and Gilbert's. We did the Snoopy dance and called down to the front desk to order Cokes. I stripped off my travel clothes and was reading a magazine on the bed in only panties and a camisole when the Cokes arrived—delivered by a tall boy with beautiful blue eyes and blond hair. I was both embarrassed and intrigued. His name was Bodo and he was an Austrian ski instructor. Handsome as hell, he looked like a cuter Oskar Werner. Later that night at dinner, he was the maître d' and seated us. I was embarrassed, as he'd seen me in my underwear, but also DELIGHTED. After dinner, there were dances, and we'd hang out, and then he'd take me for a spin in his beautiful blue Thunderbird, in which we had our trysts. We had fun together, but by the time I'd returned to New York I'd lost interest. Like Bodo, none of the men I dated knew how young I was because I looked older and never confessed to my real age. And they never really wanted to know. When I look back at photos of myself from that time, I wonder why nobody said, "Hey, wait a minute. You're not eighteen!" With a new boyfriend almost every week, I was like a rough version of my movie heroine Holly Golightly, who had mesmerized me in the 1961 film *Breakfast at Tiffany's* with her independence, style, and guts.

Back in New York, Mom and Gilbert went to see Broadway plays and hosted cocktail parties for his banking colleagues, which we were expected to attend. One frequent cocktail guest was Noah Dietrich, a man who'd been hired by the magnate Howard Hughes to make him "the richest man in the world" and ended up running all of Hughes's businesses until they had a falling out. Noah was lovely, and I could tell his stories were fascinating because everyone really paid attention, but all I got from those stories was that Hughes was unhinged and made his life miserable. If only I'd known to listen.

To make sure we looked presentable for their grown-up soirées, Mom wanted us to buy dressier clothes better suited to our new lifestyle. She still tried to choose my outfits for me, and I stubbornly wasn't having it, so I'd ask Gilbert to take me shopping instead. With Gilbert, I learned the art of shopping with a man. I just made him think everything was his idea. He'd take a seat and let me pick the things that I liked, going in and out of the dressing room and showing him one outfit after the other. Gilbert would simply give his opinion, asking what I preferred, and agreeing to my choices. He never questioned the prices or the styles I picked. It was a wonderful feeling. I had a similar experience with Joe Collins when on a trip to Palm Springs. I chose several amazing dresses and he said, "You have a pair of high heels, don't you?" I fibbed a little and told him I left mine at home, so he bought me my first pair. When my mom saw us, she said, "You don't wear high heels. Why are you wearing high heels?" I wanted her to fall through the center of the earth . . . bless her cotton socks.

I set aside my jeans and crop tops in favor of more colorful outfits, and Gilbert bought me a black-and-white polka-dot dress with a black vest that had a matching polka-dot lining. It was thrilling to be able to choose clothes I loved, and not have to bargain or argue.

Shopping was just one example of Gilbert acting as a mediator between me and Mom. He was pretty genius at managing my mother when she was acting unreasonable, which seemed to be creeping in little by little these days. She was missing LA, her friends, and the life she knew. The more homesick she became, the more things became strained at home. I liked my life in New York, and I would miss my friends if we left, but nothing was worth seeing my mother so unhappy. And living with someone who is miserable is a miserable way to live. It didn't help that I was a messy teenager. (I still am.)

I tried to stay out of Mom's way, but things came to a head the day I disagreed with her over something at the dining room table. She was already on edge and telling Gil a story about something that had happened to us, but she got one part wrong, so I said, "No, Mom. It didn't happen like that. Remember?"

She stopped and looked to me. "I know what happened, Cher."

"No, Mom, you're forgetting the most important part."

Glaring at me, she said, "Are you disputing my words, Cherilyn?"

"No," I said, "but I was there, and—"

Without warning, she slapped me across the mouth. Unfortunately, the domed ruby and pearl ring in its prong setting Gilbert had bought her had twisted on her finger. It caught my lip and cut me. I remember that moment so vividly—where I was sitting, what was said, and exactly how it felt.

I was so surprised, and Gilbert was visibly shocked. Mom had often spanked me as a child, but she'd never hit me like that—she didn't believe in slapping. She said it was humiliating. It had happened so fast; I don't even think she realized what she was doing. Shocked, hurt, and then angry, I jumped up and glared at her. I really wanted to yell, "You should see yourself right now," but I held my tongue, marched to my room to grab my purse and jacket, and came back in. My mouth was bleeding. Gilbert looked at her disapprovingly, gave me some money, and I walked out.

The moment was proof of how much she was struggling, and I think Mom knew it. It was like, this isn't working, someone get this woman back to LA. I don't think we'd been in New York a full year before she declared that she couldn't face a second East Coast winter and had to return to the sun. In Manhattan she felt trapped in the high-rise and hated living for months in a frozen city. When she got irritable and took her unhappiness out on Gilbert, I felt sorry for him, especially as he went to bat for me on more than one occasion. What he didn't realize was that my mother believed that if a man wasn't as wealthy as she was beautiful, then he didn't deserve her. It was that same idea instilled in her by her mother when she was young: "It's as easy to fall in love with a rich man as it is a poor man."

*My grandparents on the porch in Arkansas, 1930s.*

*Mom and Grandpa Roy in Arkansas.*

*A signed photo of Mom for her daddy.*

*Mom, first place.*

*Mom at Ben Bard's in rehearsals for
Oklahoma! I was in the audience watching.*

*Mom and Colleen.*

*Mom on* I Love Lucy *in a flowerpot hat.*

*One of my favorite photos of my mom.*

*Mom and Ernie Primm.*

*Mom and me in Gardena, 1946.*

*In front of Jackie's house. Mom, Dad, Gee at six months, and me at five years.*

*Me being held aloft by Daddy Southall.*

*Mom, Uncle Mickey, and me.*

*Mom with Daddy Southall in Gallup, New Mexico.*

*Mom, Grandma Lynda, Grandpa Charlie and me. I was four.*

*The best tenth birthday gift ever.*

*Daddy, Mom, and Gee in Galveston.*

*Gee and me ready for church.*

*Gee and me on my tenth birthday.*

*At Beverly Park and Ponyland.*

*Sunbathing with Mom and Jake.*

*My first photo for modeling, at age fifteen.*

*My father and me.*

*Christmas in Encino with Mom, Gee, and Gilbert.*

*My sixteenth birthday.*

*Dancing with Gee. The blond streak in my hair is from an accident with Mom's dye.*

*First photo at Gold Star Studios. I'm watching the Wrecking Crew.*

*At Gold Star, circa 1962. From left to right: Phillip Spector, Darlene Love, and me.*

*In the Rudi Gernreich outfit the saleswoman told me I couldn't afford. I bought it in three colors.*

*Sonny and me on our Mustangs.*

*Sonny and me in London, 1965, after being turned away from the Hilton because of our appearance.*

The moment Gilbert capitulated to take my mother home, we boarded the plane. When we landed, she dropped to her knees and kissed the ground. I still have the photo. Gilbert relocated to the LA branch of his bank and bought her a shiny new Cadillac and a beautiful big house on Estrondo Drive in Encino, complete with manicured gardens, a swimming pool, and a view of the entire valley and the horses grazing on Clark Gable's estate. Happy to be home, she reconnected with her old friends and made new ones in our neighborhood, women she shopped, gossiped, and drank cocktails with to her heart's content.

In some ways I was happy to be back, but I'd loved living in New York and was bummed to lose the freedom I'd had there. My New York independence wasn't going to do me any good in a city where you needed a driver's license to do anything worthwhile.

Much to my chagrin, Mom and Gilbert insisted that I finish school and enrolled me at Montclair College Prep School in Tarzana. The only thing I enjoyed there was learning French with the principal's wife, Mrs. Simpson, who said I had a natural ear for languages. I also loved drama and singing with Mr. di Fiori, who told me the school was putting on a performance of *The Mikado* by Gilbert and Sullivan. I got up the courage to audition for the leading role of Yum-Yum and was devastated when Mr. di Fiori shoved me into the chorus instead. "You're a contralto, Cher," he informed me. "Your register is too low to sing with the girls but not low enough to sing with the boys." It was a quirk of my voice that would dog me for years. I thought, *Okay, so it's over.*

It was during my year at Montclair that I made my first young gay friend, Steve. It wasn't a strange thing to me. There had been gay people in my mother's circle of friends for years. There was Shirley, the fabulous one who looked like Brigitte Bardot. There was Scotti, who had a boyish face and who I loved because she treated me like a grown-up. Later there was Joan, Scotti's girlfriend who was young, blond, and extremely feminine. When

I was little, Mom had two hairdressers who were so bubbly and fun that I couldn't understand why all men weren't like them. Although I understood the concept of being homosexual, I didn't get why they had to hide it. I was shocked when I learned that during my childhood, it was illegal to be gay. In some states, if you were branded a "moral or sexual pervert," you could be sterilized or sent to jail.

Steve and I had the best times together and were both secretly relieved that sex didn't get in the way of our friendship. I only wished everyone I went out with could be as thoughtful and sweet. Not long after his parents gave him his first car for his birthday, he was invited to a gay party and begged me to go with him. "Sure," I replied, happy to go anyplace where I could dance. Steve wasn't coming out, but this was the first time he was prepared to be open about his sexuality in a public place, and where it was safe to do so because he had me in tow. When we got to the host's apartment, he was terribly nervous, but I talked him down. He was beginning to relax and had even started talking to another young man when there was a sudden commotion. We heard someone yell, "Police! Everybody stay where you are!"

We were in a back room when the officers burst in, so we fled to the adjacent bathroom. Steve locked the door, threw open the window, and climbed out, pulling me after him. We ran to his car and took off before the police could arrest him, although Steve almost couldn't drive for trembling. He was convinced that if his parents found out his secret, they'd lock him up, or worse. Shaken, we drove around for a while, but he was in such a state that it was really late when I got back to my grandmother's—where Gee and I were staying that night—which got me into a ton of trouble. She was uncharacteristically angry at me, so I told her the police had come to a party Steve and I were at because we were making too much noise. I couldn't have ever told her the real reason. She was from Texas, and that shit wouldn't play in Texas. I spent the next few days grounded but didn't much care. I was always happy to stay in and draw anyway.

At fifteen I was the subject of a few pieces of art myself, thanks to an artist named Tony Mafia. I don't know how my mom found him, but Tony had real talent and my mom commissioned him to sketch sepia-toned portraits of all three of us individually. When he delivered them, Tony went on and on and on about how I had an interesting quality with my dark hair and eyes compared to my blond mom and sister. I mean, my mom was beautiful, and my sister was adorable, but he said that like all children, Gee wasn't yet old enough to have character in her face. When Mom started oohing and ahhing over my picture, that made me stop and think, *Well, okay, she's a good judge of stuff, so I must be . . . something.* That was the first time I thought that I was anything at all, especially when she told me I should try modeling and sent me to a photographer for some portfolio shots. I was sitting in the studio between setups when the door opened and a man in his thirties came and sat across from me. It was the actor Telly Savalas, who later became famous in 1973 in the TV show *Kojak*. Staring at me as a smile tugged at his mouth, he said, "What would you do if I came over and kissed you right now?" When I rolled my fifteen-year-old eyes, he started to laugh. "Okay, okay," he said. "The look says it all." Good.

Months later, Tony asked me to sit for a mural of Italian-looking women that he'd been commissioned to paint for Martoni's restaurant on North Cahuenga Boulevard, south of Capitol Records. Martoni's was one of the places where the cool people of the film and music world hung out, although the likes of Frank Sinatra and the Rat Pack preferred Chasen's. For years anyone who went there to eat the best manicotti in the city was surrounded by various versions of me on the wall, although only one really bore any resemblance.

I was at Martoni's sitting for Tony one day when another

stranger started talking to me, only this time I didn't roll my eyes. His name was Antonino LoTempio, better known as Nino Tempo, a singer and musician with a beautiful voice who was thirteen years older than me. I liked him a lot and we were just starting to get close when his demanding friend flew into town from New York and took up all his time. His friend was a twenty-two-year-old music producer and record label owner named Phillip Spector, who was making music at Gold Star Recording Studios on Santa Monica Boulevard, which became one of the most successful studios in the world. Everyone from Brian Wilson to Jimi Hendrix to the Righteous Brothers to Ritchie Valens recorded in the place where Spector learned his craft. Once he became successful, he continued to use the same studio, and from the day he was flown in by a record company, Nino was expected to be on call. The pair had been roommates in New York. In Phillip's early records Nino played saxophone, piano, drums, and guitar, as well as singing backing vocals. Even when he wasn't needed, Phillip would call him up and say, "Come to the studio. I need an extra pair of ears."

Before Phillip arrived, Nino warned me, "Phillip needs me at the studio, so I'm sorry, but we won't be able to see each other as much." What I didn't realize was that this meant we wouldn't be seeing each other at all. Whenever I complained to Nino about it, he'd promise me he was working, but I became convinced Nino was lying and was seeing someone else. I didn't know anything about Phillip or have a clue how respected he was in the music business, and I didn't believe a boss would be that demanding.

At Gold Star, Phillip and his arranger Jack Nitzsche worked with artists like Jan and Dean, the Ronettes, Ike and Tina Turner, and Darlene Love, all of whom were backed by the session group that became known as the Wrecking Crew. Phillip had discovered a unique formula to create records with a dense, symphonic quality by multitracking one instrument upon multiple others and recording the finished result in an echo chamber. This became known as the "Wall of Sound," something that never previously existed.

None of this meant anything to this heartsick teenager sulking over Nino's lack of attention. He'd call and say, "Can we meet? I've got fifteen minutes before I have to be back in the studio." Without a car of my own, this was virtually impossible, and after a while I snapped and told him to lose my number.

He wanted to prove to me that he was working, so he took me to meet Phillip at his hotel off Sunset Boulevard, and I didn't much like what I saw. He might have been a demigod to many, but he acted weird, and I didn't like how he stared at me. Looking me up and down, he made a dumb-ass comment in French in front of his friend. "Voulez-vous coucher avec moi?" he said, smirking, asking me to sleep with him.

Without breaking a sweat, I gave him a look back and replied, "Oui, pour l'argent." You could have knocked him over with a feather. He didn't think I'd understand the question, let alone have an answer.

I split up with Nino soon afterward, and he called to tell me, "You broke my heart, Cher, and I never want to see you again." I didn't mean to hurt him, because he was a good guy, but I just didn't believe he was working as a full-time babysitter to a grown man. I was really happy for him when later that year he and his sister won a Grammy for the song "Deep Purple."

Living in LA without a license or car was taking a toll on my social life. My mom let me take my driving test in her Cadillac, but it was like a boat. Even though I had been driving since I was eleven, I failed. Next test, I aced it in Gilbert's more compact Buick Skylark. From that day on, whenever I borrowed that car, I had my Los Angeles version of freedom. Once I was behind the wheel, there was no stopping me, and I went out all the time because I could, having made the decision that there was no further use in my being at school. I'd had weeks off after another bout of mono and then I was suspended for a week for refusing to take my sunglasses off in class. The sunglasses and two ponytails in my hair were an homage to my heroine Holly Golightly. The principal of Montclair, Dr. Vernon Simpson, summoned me to his office and told me, "I could expel you, Cher, but I think there's something good in you. I want you to go home and think about that for a while."

My parents weren't happy, but my mom knew that school wasn't my path to my destiny. I promised them that I wouldn't just sit around at home and would go to acting school instead. Finally free of the confines of school, I could go in the direction I wanted as long as I followed Mom and Gilbert's rules. One night I borrowed Gilbert's Skylark and was driving down Sunset Boulevard when a white Lincoln convertible cut me off. I pulled into the parking lot of the famous Schwab's Pharmacy, shaken by how close he'd come to trashing Gilbert's car. I jumped out and yelled, "What the fuck's the matter with you? You almost hit me!" The man was wearing big, black-framed sunglasses, but I could still tell that he was unbelievably handsome, with one of the sexiest smiles I'd ever seen. When he took off his glasses, I realized that it was Warren Beatty. He'd been named the "New Star of the Year" for his Golden Globe—nominated role in the hit movie *Splendor in the Grass*, in which he costarred with the married actress Natalie Wood, who became his lover. My mother was nuts about Warren and so was my friend Penny, so I thought I'd better not let the moment pass for their sake. Buying time, I took a breath and asked, "Got a cigarette?"

"No," he replied, beaming. "But I can run into the store and get you some." He ran across the street to the gas station and did just that.

Ten years older than me, at twenty-five Warren was so drop-dead gorgeous I had to steady myself as he walked back toward me. "What's your name?" he asked.

"Cher."

"Well, Cher, do you wanna get something to eat?"

I hesitated. It was close to my curfew, and I was already worried I'd be late and end up grounded, but then I thought of how much of a fan my mother was, so I shrugged and said, "Sure."

"Do you want to come to my place for something?"

My knees almost buckled in the face of his charm and that smile—a devastating combination. "Okay." I followed his car to a big white modern house in the Trousdale Estates in Beverly Hills. It was a beautiful house with an amazing pool. He showed me inside, fixed us some cheese and crackers, then leaned in and kissed me. *Now, this is interesting*, I thought as I kissed him back. The two of us went swimming, with me in Natalie Wood's bathing suit, and we had a great time. Afterward I drove home in a happy daze at 4 a.m. and found Mom and Gilbert standing on the doorstep in their nightclothes, furious that I'd defied my curfew again.

"You will not go out again until you're twenty-one!" my mother yelled before sending me to my room, but nothing could burst my bubble.

The following morning the telephone rang. It was Warren. "Let's go to dinner," he said. I could hear his smile.

"No," I told him as my mother strained to eavesdrop.

"Then how about swimming?" Laughing at his random suggestion, I didn't want him to know how young I was or that I was grounded, so I told him, "My mother's pissed with me for getting home late, so I'm not going anyplace. We had a fight, and I can't go out."

Laughing, he said, "Let me talk to your mom." I wish I had a photograph of the look on her face when she realized who she was speaking to. She literally melted in front of my eyes. Ten minutes later, she was inviting him over. When she hung up, she cried, "Why didn't you tell me you were with Warren Beatty?"

"Well, you'd just told me I was grounded until I was twenty-one, so I wasn't in the mood for a chat." Any other mother might have been appalled by my teenage sarcasm, but my mom, who already loved Warren Beatty, was willing to forgive me. She begged me to introduce her to the star notorious for sleeping with almost every woman he encountered in Hollywood (and New York, and Paris, and London, and Kuala Lumpur). Later, when I was with David Geffen, Warren and I would become friends, and I loved hanging out with him, Jack, Robbie, Toots, Lou, Goldie, and his whole crew.

When I went to meet Warren, Mom was beside herself. "You have to tell me everything!" she whispered as I went out the door. He and I saw each other for two more dates and I enjoyed his company. But that was that. The last time he called, I was with Sonny. He said, "Do you want to go to dinner?" I said, "Well, I have a boyfriend." He said, "Okay, do you want to go to lunch?" It was so cute and so him.

I had agreed to go to acting class. Mom enrolled me in a twice-weekly, three-month drama workshop run by the actor turned coach Jeff Corey. He operated out of a small studio in a theater not far from his home in the Hollywood Hills. It was a smart move, because Jeff was someone who made a huge impression on me. Tall and lanky, the forty-seven-year-old had the corduroy style of a college professor and was equally intimidating. He had chiseled features, wild hair, and the bushiest eyebrows I'd ever seen. He was cranky sometimes, but mostly harmless. I loved him.

In the 1950s, he'd been blacklisted by the House Un-American Activities Committee for refusing to rat out suspected Communists in Hollywood during the witch hunts orchestrated by Senator Joseph McCarthy and J. Edgar Hoover. He was a brave and principled man. When I first went for an audition, however, he took one look at me and sneered, "I don't take children. How could you know anything about acting? You've no life experience."

Shocked that he thought of me as a child, I replied, "Bullshit!

I've got life experience, okay?" Staring him down, I thought of the million stories I could draw upon. Shrugging, he sent me away with Steinbeck's *Of Mice and Men*, telling me to come back when I'd finished it. He had no idea how difficult I found it to read or that I'd never completed an entire book in my life. I did my best, but the story of two starving migrant workers in the Great Depression was so gut-wrenching I couldn't get to the end. Worried that he'd grill me about it, I memorized a few passages in case. When I went back, he never even mentioned the darn book. He let me into his class. I was the youngest student that he'd ever accepted, and less than half the age of all the other students.

Jeff's reputation was legendary. He'd taught numerous Oscar-winning actors, including Anthony Perkins, James Dean, Anthony Quinn, Jane Fonda, and Rita Moreno, who won her Oscar in the film version of *West Side Story*. And a future me who also won an Oscar for *Moonstruck*. Jeff was hard on me from day one and I almost quit a hundred times. He had us doing all these quick-change exercises. One day we pretended to be on the telephone and then he yelled that the phone was now a detonator. When I placed it between my knees, picked up the imaginary receiver, and plunged it down as if setting off dynamite, he seemed pleased. But most of the time, I felt his judgment. More than once I wanted to cry in front of the class when he singled me out.

One day I asked him, "Why are you so hard on me?" Unexpectedly, he threw his arms around me and said, "Because you're the best in the class, Cher. You're an actor and I'm so proud of you. You're my favorite." Everything made sense, and I saw that this could be a possibility for me. I was excited. In the movies, the coach is always toughest on the best athlete. If Jeff was tough on me, it must have meant I was the best in that class and he loved me.

To begin with, nobody in the class took me seriously at all, but once I started to work, that changed. Jeff said that if I merely waited for a fellow actor to finish their line so that I could say mine, then

I wasn't acting. "Only when you've listened to what the person has said do you know how to say what you need to say." That not only made sense but came quite naturally. It was the best acting advice I have ever been given. My turning point came doing improv, which felt like a fun game. I found that I was finally good at something and had the ability to make people feel something. Jeff Corey still blew hot and cold with me, but I became eager to please him.

Unfortunately, my acting classes didn't alter the situation for me back home, where Mom was becoming unhappy again, and it felt like I had to walk around on eggshells. I'd be going through something that was bothering me and I'd tell her about it, but she always had worse stories. There was no question that my childhood was a million times better than hers, but I also felt anger because I didn't need to be reminded of that fact every single day. And my sister and I felt powerless to change what had happened to her. "At least your father didn't try to gas you!" she'd say, reciting the images always on her mind. Gee and I had no magic wand to take that pain away. Being unable to share my own pain, I just stopped talking at all. Gee became the only person I would confide in because she loved me unconditionally.

I couldn't fight Mom on equal footing, but I knew silence was the key. I'd answer her questions politely but then offer nothing more.

My sister, Gee, was the good one, who sat in a corner reading books about horses and collecting horse figurines. I now realize that she was merely absenting herself from the tension, because eventually she found her voice and clashed with Mom herself.

There was some tension building up in her marriage too. Gilbert was a sweet man who was crazy about Mom, and though she loved him, I don't know if she was ever in love with him. She was happier back in LA than she had been in New York, but the return wasn't what she hoped it would be either. At first, Mom and Gilbert picked right up where they left off—throwing parties, spending time with friends, living the suburban life that my mom seemed to have come to enjoy. But slowly, it started to feel like she was playing a part she didn't like, a part that I didn't like either. Mom went to therapy all the time. She cut her beautiful hair just like all the women in the neighborhood. Her designer clothes got more conservative; her life got more predictable. She may have told herself she was happy. But deep down, she wasn't. She knew it, and eventually Gilbert began to realize that all he was doing to make his wife happy didn't matter.

When my birthday finally arrived, I received my first-ever $100 bill—a generous gift from Gilbert. It felt like a big deal. I still have the photo of me holding it. That very week, I packed my bags and left home. Desperate to get out on my own, and tired of the ups and downs of my mother's moods, I persuaded my long-suffering stepfather to rent me a furnished apartment on Wilshire in Beverly Hills with Josita, our twenty-two-year-old German maid. It was heaven. Josita was a lovely girl but such a bad maid it was hysterical. She had no business being in anyone's house and, in the words of my mother, "couldn't find her own ass with both hands."

Josita and I had a blast in the Spanish-style place Gil found for us in a beautiful building with tall ceilings and turrets, on a beautiful tree-lined street. The first thing we did was light cigarettes in every room before jumping on the beds for the hell of it. Decorating on a budget, I went to the Akron home furnishing store and bought some madras cloth, the kind you'd use as an Indian bedspread. I made drapes and a go-go dress out of the same cloth and went dancing in it every night, although the things I made were so fragile that they made me feel as if I had to be home by midnight in case they disintegrated.

The deal with Gilbert was that Josita and I both had to get jobs so we could put money toward the rent, which was a hundred dollars. Gilbert got me a job as a clerk, punching time cards in Robinson's department store on Wilshire Boulevard. I had to wear a dress and keep office hours. It also involved math, which, as you can imagine by now, made it the worst possible job for me. I never understood the system, even when Gilbert kindly made me a chart to figure out which card went where. The work was boring and so were the staff, who all seemed ancient to me. Plus, they hated me because I was docking their pay. One day, I was about to punch my own time card when I said to myself, "Fuck this. I'm not gonna work here another minute." I went upstairs to say goodbye to the one lady I liked, and then I walked out not even bothering to collect my paycheck.

Jake helped me get my next and last-ever nine-to-five job, working at a See's Candies store in Beverly Hills. I loved working with the adorable blue-haired old ladies, but I didn't love serving the rich bitches who'd yell at me if the tip of my finger touched a candy or looked as if it might, even though we touched the candies all the time in the back of the store. That was intense enough, but then I'd have to operate the cash register, getting myself into a sweat and praying I didn't make some gigantic miscalculation. Plus, we had to wrap the boxes in paper with such military precision, no wrinkles, no creases, so you could bounce a quarter off the top. Who needs that stress? I was moved into the back room at See's instead to wrap candy and make up Easter and Christmas baskets in pretty tissue paper. I became like the Picasso of See's. Babe, rock and roll. I threw so much shit in there, the kids who received them must have lost their minds. I loved being back there because it was so peaceful, and I could sing to myself without anybody listening. The company rule was that I could eat as much candy as I liked in the store but couldn't take any home. Nevertheless, I'd secretly fill a bag with my favorite dark chocolate Scotchmallows, toffee, and chunks of Rocky Road and smuggle it out.

As has been the pattern of my life, I wore myself out working all day and burning the candle all night. I didn't drink anything other than Dr Pepper and I didn't take drugs; I went dancing in the smaller, cheaper clubs around Sunset Boulevard until I couldn't dance anymore and then I went home. I hardly ate anything either. I've never been very good at taking care of myself in that way. I ate reasonably healthily but sometimes forgot to. With my strange constitution, which crashes if I do too much, I became sick again— this time with hepatitis—and had to quit my job. I was so sad. I didn't get paid much, but I was having so much fun.

I'd met a guy named Red who worked as a jazz promo guy.

Josita's German boyfriend, Ulle, flew in from Europe, and she decided to go traveling with him, leaving me alone and sick in the Spanish apartment I couldn't afford to keep on my own. Taking pity on me, Red suggested I move into his place in Laurel Canyon until I got better. For the few weeks that I stayed with Red, I was sick with a fever and swollen glands, and my weight dropped to under a hundred pounds. Red took great care of me even though having me around must have been rough because I was really sick.

As I gradually recovered, I started worrying about what I'd do next and where I'd go. If I left Red's, I'd be homeless with no job. I couldn't face going home but I had no money, no prospects, and nothing to show for my sixteen years on the planet. Jeff Corey was teaching me a lot about acting but I'd seen my parents and their friends struggling to get work over the years, so I couldn't rely on a living from that. I'd thought my voice was a talent, but then I'd discovered that it was too unusual to fit in anywhere, which threw me. If I couldn't even get a place in a high school production, what hope did I have of being the acting, singing sensation I was destined to become?

I felt like a rudderless ship, bumping against one rock and then another before being knocked back by yet another wave. *Jeez, Cher. What the hell is to become of you?*

# 9

## tony meets maría

On a weekday night in November 1962, a Sicilian with an amazing smile joined our booth in Aldo's coffee shop. It was directly underneath KFWB, so all the radio promotion guys would come down after meeting with the disc jockeys to hang out and have coffee.

I was sitting with Red and my friend Melissa when there was a sudden buzz and I heard someone cry, "Hey, Sonny!" And then a bunch of people yelled, "Hey, Son, come to our table!" "Come sit with us!" Everyone was calling out to this guy. Based on all the commotion, I was expecting a tall, handsome man to walk up behind me. I turned around to look, and an intriguing stranger with a Caesar-style haircut walked toward us. He was wearing a black mohair suit, a mustard shirt with an oversized starched white collar, and a tie that matched his shirt. On his feet he wore Cuban boots with heels, the first I'd ever seen, though later the Beatles would be wearing boots just like them and calling them Beatle boots. I swear to God, it was like Maria and Tony in *West Side Story*: everyone else in the room faded.

To this day, I can see our Hollywood meet-cute in my mind. Grinning from ear to ear as people jumped up to say hello and shake his hand, Salvatore Phillip Bono was one of the most interesting men I'd ever seen. As he sat at our table, I noticed his beautiful hands with their long, tapered fingers and a gold chain-link ID bracelet with a watch face where the name would normally have been. Sonny definitely caught my attention. I was always interested in fascinating people because those were the kind of people I grew up around. He was the '60s version of my mom's friends. It wasn't love at first sight. I just thought this guy was special.

It was immediately clear to me that everyone loved Sonny, but at the moment he was fascinated by my friend Melissa, a knockout brunette Red suggested I invite to make up a double date. The two men knew each other from the promo business because they both schmoozed DJs into playing the latest releases. Easygoing with a ready smile, at twenty-seven, he was the youngest of three and the only boy in a Sicilian family. One of the first things he told me was that he was a descendant of Napoleon Bonaparte, but his father had shortened their name when he came to the United States. It didn't occur to me to question how a Sicilian could be related to a Corsican, and it didn't occur to me that he was lying. When Sonny was young, the family moved to Englewood, a working-class suburb of LA. After being kicked out of high school for hiring a Black band for the prom, he did every kind of job, including delivering meat and working as a masseur—until the day he spilled rubbing alcohol into the crack of a client's ass when the bottle slipped from his fingers.

A songwriter since his teens, his first hit was "Koko Joe,"

which had been inspired by having to unpack Koko Joe cookies while working in a grocery store. It did well enough for Sonny to continue writing, and he sang his own numbers as "Don Christy" (after his recently estranged wife, Donna, and his daughter Christy). That didn't prove successful, but a couple of his songs went on to be recorded by Sam Cooke, the Righteous Brothers, Jackie DeShannon, and the duo Don and Dewey.

Saying little, I watched him chatting up Melissa like a pro and admired the way he put everyone around him at ease. What he didn't know was that although he amused Melissa, he wasn't her type—she was gay. Then someone suggested we go to the Red Velvet Club on Sunset and Wilcox, and I was thrilled. As soon as we arrived, I went straight onto the dance floor to lose myself in music. Sonny only joined me because neither Red nor Melissa danced.

"I love your clothes," I told him. "Black on black. So cool."

"I love yours too," he said, sizing up my T-shirt and boy's jeans. (From the time I can remember, my grandma wore 501s, my mom wore 501s, my sister wore 501s. They were cheap and indestructible and are perpetually cool.) As Sonny told me years later, he couldn't figure me out that night. The truth is he wasn't trying to figure me out that night, he was trying to figure Melissa out. He may have wondered if I was gay or straight after learning that Melissa was the former, but she was just a friend who let me crash on her couch rent-free. Melissa lived in a complex with a pool at Franklin and Highland. The place was filled with the most beautiful women I had seen since I'd hung out with Mom and her girlfriends. These were strippers, hookers, actresses, and show-girls, all of them with knock-out bodies. Those chicks were the whole package—great asses, long legs, and fabulous clothes.

It wasn't long after that that Melissa told me I'd have to find someplace else to live. Her place was too small. Without any money, I had no idea where I'd go, as I couldn't go back to Red, and the last thing I wanted was to return to my mother's. That's when I spotted Sonny moving into the building next door. We'd only hung out that one night a few weeks before, but I was happy to see him. When he saw me waving through the window, he smiled and gestured for me to meet him. Running outside, I asked, "What are you doing here?" and he told me he'd taken a one-bedroom apartment in the building next door. I laughed at the coincidence. I didn't know until later that the whole building was owned by a wealthy family who'd bought it in order to get their daughter to come home from working as a stripper in Las Vegas.

Over the next ten days or so, Sonny and I hung out and became friends. He liked that I was quirky and nonjudgmental. I liked that he was funny and different. He was a grown-up without being too grown up, and I was a sixteen-year-old lying about my age. He took me to the park, or we'd talk in his apartment until his friends came over, at which point I'd see myself out. I neglected to tell him that I was about to get kicked out of the apartment until Melissa finally told me my time had officially run out.

Looking for a sympathetic ear, I walked over to Sonny's and sat on his couch to tell him I had no choice but to move home. Tears sprang to my eyes at the mere thought of it. I didn't mean to cry, but I think it made Sonny take pity on me.

"Well, Cher," he said. "If you cook and clean the place, you could always move in with me for a while."

In my mind I was thinking, *Yeah, OK, this old line,* but I must have had a look on my face because he shook his head and laughed. "Don't worry, I've got twin beds," he said. With a grin he added, "And honestly, I don't find you particularly attractive." I was both insulted and relieved. And that's how I became the potty-mouthed sidekick to a man eleven years older than me who was in the middle of a divorce.

I thought Sonny was the coolest person I'd ever met. If a girl called in those days and I answered the phone, she would invariably ask him, "Who was that?" and he would say, "Oh, that's just Cher."

One of the girls who came to the apartment told me that she knew Sonny was cheating on her. "That's just how he is, I suppose," she added with a tearful sigh. The news didn't surprise me at all. What surprised me is that she told me, a total stranger. Plus, I was just Cher. While waiting for his divorce, Sonny started seeing several women simultaneously, including one who claimed she was pregnant with his child, took his money for an abortion (along with that of two other men to whom she made the same claim), and flew to Hawaii to get her teeth fixed instead. That chick was so smart. She got a suntan and her teeth fixed all on their dime.

Almost all his relationships remained casual, because he certainly wasn't looking for love and most of the women were looking for a man who could support them. He was charming and funny, but he had no money, drove an old Chevy Monza, and lived in a one-bedroom apartment with a random teenager. He wasn't a catch.

Aside from keeping out of the way when his latest girlfriend was over, I became his housekeeper and general assistant, handing out beer and chips to his male friends who came to play liar's poker while I sat in the bedroom drawing or watching TV.

It was one of those friends who one day mentioned to him, "You know, I don't think Cher is eighteen." It could have been Melissa who tipped him off, but who knows? When Sonny asked me if it was true, I knew I couldn't come clean. Thinking on my feet, I came up with another lie: "Okay . . . I'm not eighteen now, I'm seventeen. But my birthday is in May, so I'll be eighteen in two months." He was a little cranky about it, but I guess I was so convincing that he believed me, even though I think a blind person would have seen the guilty look on my face. (I think whenever someone gives you an "Okay, but," everything that follows is probably bullshit.) With that, our friendship was back on track.

I learned so much from Sonny and enjoyed how he took care of me in his macho Sicilian way. When I got sick again, he took my temperature and tucked me into bed, got what I needed from the pharmacy, and kept an eye on me in case my fever got worse. I came to feel that he was the kind of guy who'd be there if something bad happened.

Before too long, I thought the sun rose and set on his Sicilian ass, even though I knew that I wasn't his type. My kind of body wasn't in style yet, and one day when I borrowed a bathing suit from Melissa to go to the beach, I watched Sonny's face drop when he saw me. "My God, you're skinny. You don't have any shape at all! Is that all there is to you?" He was looking right at me. He knew all the answers to those questions. With no curves, I looked like a matchstick.

As the weeks passed, Sonny and I became more like a brother and sister, or perhaps more accurately a father and daughter, because I was the insecure kid full of phobias, the teenager who didn't like silence and couldn't get to sleep unless the television was on, which is still sometimes true. In those days, TV programming ended at midnight and the station would play "The Star-Spangled Banner" before shutting off. For some reason, one night the waving flag followed by a black screen and absolute silence gave me a panic attack and I freaked out. "What's the matter?" Sonny asked, woken by my whimpering.

"I'm afraid, Son."

"Go to sleep, Cher."

"I can't."

"Then get over here, but just sleep, okay? Don't bother me." He pulled back his covers. I slid in beside him. He put the covers over me and then he rolled toward the wall. I tried to be quiet as a church mouse, just like when I was a kid at my parents' cocktail parties. That was our first night in bed together.

Like a guru, Sonny persuaded me to read my first book from

cover to cover, something I'd resisted for years because of my wonky (dyslexic) brain. It was *The Saracen Blade* by Frank Yerby and was set in Sicily at a time when the three religions coexisted there peacefully. Taking my time like he told me, I discovered that if I went at my own pace and a book held my interest, then I could finish it. I never knew that I could read for pleasure, and I'll always be grateful to Son for teaching me that. Six decades later, I still remember the story and the feeling of excitement is baked in the cake. Before too long, I began to hero-worship my roommate.

Although the feeling wasn't mutual, Sonny dug my weird sense of humor and was happy to do the things I liked because he was still a big kid inside. The women he dated wanted to be wined and dined at expensive restaurants, not taken shopping at Safeway for the promise of a pizza. Nor would they be happy to spend an afternoon painting together (he was terrible), modeling things out of clay, or heading to the park with a picnic. Having virtually raised my sister single-handedly, I was also glad to hang out with his four-year-old daughter, Christy, whenever she came to visit with his pet Yorkshire terrier, Scunci. Sonny loved that dog, and he loved Christy, who was cute as a button. She adored him too, and was always eager to please him. Sonny was a great dad.

I also found it strange that, practically from the day we met, Sonny didn't want to go dancing anymore, even though he knew how much I loved it. He realized I was a better dancer, and that made him feel uncomfortable, but he also didn't want me going dancing on my own either. I guess he was a little possessive, but the idea thrilled me because it meant he cared. Later I would find out that *possessive* and *caring* didn't exactly go hand in hand. Instead, once in a while he'd take me to Martoni's, where we'd eat and talk to his friends in the record business who hung out there. We'd also visit my uncle Mickey at his hip new club, the Purple Onion, on Sunset. The venue was small, with about 130 seats, but it was jumping. After he and Rita stopped teaching dancing,

Mickey's dream was to discover a new band and turn it into a supergroup. He bought the Purple Onion and, later, built another club called the Haunted House at Hollywood and Vine, billed as a kitschy Gothic go-go bar. Mickey made and lost several fortunes throughout his lifetime. We used to joke that at any point he could be traveling to work on a bus or in a Rolls-Royce. By the time he opened the Onion he was doing well again, thanks to a Beverly Hills headhunting business he ran, which later tanked when he invested in some singers who didn't make it.

He and Sonny got along great. He liked him so much he didn't rat me out to my mom, who would have killed me if she knew I was living with an older man.

While Sonny was out, I'd clean up the apartment and sing along to the radio. Listening to music was my life, and if I didn't have the radio blaring, I'd put on a record by Elvis, Ray Charles, Jimmy Clanton, the Platters, or the Everly Brothers, or the first single I ever bought—"Tequila" by the Champs. I also liked Ritchie Valens, Frankie Lymon, Jerry Lee Lewis, and Etta James—they all provided my daily soundtrack. I can't remember which song I was singing the day that Sonny walked in and heard me.

Sticking his head around the door of the bedroom, he asked, "Was that you singing?" He stared at me as if he'd never seen me before.

"Yeah," I replied, turning back to make my bed.

"You can sing," Sonny said.

"Yes."

"But I mean you can really sing!"

Bundling up dirty laundry, I replied, "Yes, I know!"

"Have you always been able to sing like that?" he asked, eyes wide.

"No, Son, I just started today."

"Huh," he said, before wandering off into the kitchen to make dinner, a role that he'd taken over since the day he'd first sampled my cooking. Not that I complained, because he could throw together anything and make an amazing meal. His mother had taught him well.

Sonny worked for Specialty Records, which made what were known then as "race records," featuring singers like Little Richard and Sam Cooke, who were friends that later became good friends. He liked the job, but the pay wasn't great, so he was still writing, pushing his own songs, and hustling for something new. He was tireless. One day I was reading a magazine on the sofa in the apartment when I heard someone honking their car horn. Looking out the window, I saw Sonny behind the wheel of a bronze-colored Cadillac convertible with the top down. I was stunned—it took me a minute to register—I mean, he'd left that day in a fucking Monza. He yelled, "Cher! Cher! Come on! Jump in. I'll take you for a ride!"

Laughing, I yelled, "Wait! What? Whose car is that?"

"It's ours!" he cried. "I got a new job." Screaming with delight, both at the car and his use of the word *ours*, I ran barefoot straight out of the house and into the leather passenger seat. I don't think I'd ever seen him so thrilled as he was that day. As much as the Monza had been a symbol of his lack of success, the Cadillac was a sign that life was about to change. The new job was with Jack Lewerke, president of California Record Distributors, a company that distributed music across the state, including almost everything produced by Phillip Spector on his label Philles Records. Lewerke liked Sonny and knew him well enough to bet that he could be the exact right person to work for the demanding Spector—and he was right. Not only was Sonny funny and engaging, but he was best friends with Jack Nitzsche, who was the music arranger for Phillip. And that sealed the deal. Sonny said he had eleven sides, and you had to know all of them, but Sonny could read him and they got on so well that Sonny was assigned as Phillip's "artist relations representative," working with him exclusively. This effectively meant becoming Spector's gofer at Gold

Star studios, where he was producing hit records. Remembering how hard Nino had to work there, I feared I'd see much less of Sonny, and I wasn't wrong. He was on call 24/7.

The job was a major step up, and he adapted to his new role with his usual enthusiasm and humor, talking to everyone like he'd known them his whole life, fetching coffee, and cracking jokes just like he'd done at Aldo's. He was excited to share the experience with me, but you couldn't just waltz a stranger into one of Phillip's sessions. Once he'd been working there long enough to get his footing, he got Phillip's permission to bring me to the famous Studio A to drop something off one afternoon. When I walked in, Phillip gave me the side eye and completely ignored me. Sonny had no idea that we'd already met or that I'd rejected his stupid pass. Neither of us let on. Phillip clearly didn't approve of my being there and told Sonny he didn't like girlfriends "hanging around" the studio, even though there were several cute ones there already.

I didn't care about any of that, as I was too busy soaking up the atmosphere of my first-ever recording studio. I was also incredibly shy in front of all the musicians, who were much older than me and clearly at the top of their game. As I wandered in, I was so nervous about stepping on something important and messing something up that I stood in a corner and peered at them through the glass. Sonny, who was an avid photographer, snapped a picture of me there that night, standing sheepishly up against a wall. It's a photo I still have.

The studio was small and dingy as hell, but I couldn't take my eyes off the musicians jam-packed into a tight rectangle. There were more people in that space than you could imagine, like sardines all one next to the other. I just thought *how is this physically possible?* Tommy Tedesco and Billy Pitman playing guitar right by Carol Kaye playing her bass, Leon Russell playing piano, and Hal Blaine playing drums, and these are only a few of the Wrecking Crew . . . all in this tiny space, I just thought, *How are they not hitting each other?* I was shocked. I had a romanticized vision of what a recording studio would look like from the movies. These players would become the most sought-after and famous studio musicians in America. Carol Kaye was the only woman in the room and one of the best bass guitar players in the world. She must have been a ball-breaker to go toe-to-toe with those guys. I guess they respected her, because I never saw anyone fuck with her.

Everyone smoked, so there were overflowing ashtrays and empty coffee cups lying around a stained carpet. There was also every kind of instrument from guitars to drums and at least two pianos. Off to the side was the small soundproof booth for lead singers to record their vocals in. All the walls needed painting, and there was a ratty old couch in front of a raised platform where Phillip stood in his sunglasses presiding over the entire operation like a film director. The sound equipment at Gold Star was anything but ordinary, and everyone was thrilled about the new four-track system, which allowed for the music, lead vocals, strings or horns, and backups to be recorded separately, overdubbed, then mixed and "bounced down" onto one complex, richly layered track. It opened up a new world for recording music and was perfect for Phillip's Wall of Sound.

On that first visit, I listened as the crew started laying down their sections for a Ronettes number. I adored those chicks with their hair piled a foot above their heads and was sorry that they weren't in the studio that day. Once the music started, though, I forgot I was in a shabby room off Santa Monica Boulevard. To hear these first-class artists play made the hairs on my arms stand up. Mom and I had always been tight singing together, but that day I knew that I was in the presence of some serious talent. Although I loved to sing, it was just for fun. Nino and Sonny had each drilled it into me that no one was better at making music than Phillip Spector. He was the king of the world, and that world wasn't mine.

Sonny took me to the studio a few more times in those early

days, and it was always a thrill. The only thing that made me sad was if Nino happened to be around, because he'd act as if I wasn't there. He would look through me. Sonny's new job involved anything from playing maracas and fetching coffee to picking up musicians and equipment. He was also enlisted to rattle the tambourine. On a bad day Phillip would put him on the "jawbone" (literally the jawbone of a mule), an instrument that must be beaten on the side with a clenched fist to make the teeth rattle and isn't very comfortable to play.

I didn't like the way Sonny was being treated, but I also knew he was there to watch and learn. He said, "You know what, I'm getting an education you couldn't pay for." Once he'd discovered all the angles in a situation, he could work them to his advantage, so if being treated like a lackey was the price to pay, then he was okay with that, even if I wasn't. Things were going great until the day my mother decided to pay an unannounced visit to the apartment. Although we'd spoken on the telephone, I hadn't seen her in quite some time, and she'd grown curious about my living situation. Knowing that I could never come clean about sharing an apartment with a grown man, I'd claimed my new roommate was an airline stewardess who was constantly away on flights. This meant that if Mom visited, I'd never have to introduce them.

The few times she did drop by, I insisted that she call first so I could quickly clear away any evidence of Sonny. Asking Melissa to open the window of her apartment, which was across from ours, I'd hurl his clothes, belongings, and underwear out of the window into hers, then run around and pick up anything that had dropped on the hedge between the apartments. Poor Son. I lost so much of his stuff, and one pair of pants ended up covered in the pasta sauce Melissa was eating when they landed on her plate.

The day my mother showed up unannounced, I was taking a shower. There was no warning, nothing. She buzzed me from the gate and asked to be let in. Half-naked, I ran around frantically hiding Sonny's clothes, throwing underwear into the kitchen cupboard where I kept the tea. I didn't have time to do anything else and, in my panic, calculated that Sonny's underwear would be the most incriminating. I let her in and ran to get dressed in the bedroom when I heard her say, "Cher, I think I'm going to make myself a cup of tea."

"Oh, fuck!" I cried, knowing that if she found the shorts it would blow a hole in my stewardess story. Running in, I threw myself against the cupboard and shrieked, "No, Mom! You're in my place now. Let me make the goddamn tea!"

"Calm down," she said, suspecting something. Pushing me to one side, she opened the cupboard. With an expression on her face that I knew only too well, she demanded to know who I was really living with.

My response sounded lame, even though it was true. "Well, his name is Sonny and he's separated from his wife, and he let me crash here for a while—but there's nothing going on, I swear!"

"And where exactly do you sleep?" she asked, marching into the bedroom to glare at the single beds.

"Well, um, this is my bed—and, um, he sleeps there."

"Bullshit!" she declared. "Cherilyn, you're coming home with me!" I was well and truly busted and there was no arguing with my mother when she was like this, so I grabbed a few things, left a note for Sonny, and went back to my old bedroom in Encino, where I curled up into a tight ball and became hysterical. Mom was furious and went straight to see the therapist Gilbert was already paying thousands to in the hope of making her easier to live with (not yet realizing that she was going through early menopause), and she asked him how she should handle the situation. He advised her to do nothing. "From what you've told me, your daughter goes through boyfriends in a heartbeat," he reminded her. "If you make a big thing out of it and forbid Cher from seeing Sonny, it could backfire, and you'll only push them closer." Instead he suggested that Mom take me on a trip to get me out of town and away from Sonny for a while. So off Mom, Gee, and I went to Arkansas for a miserable trip to visit family. I was thrilled to see my relatives, but I just didn't want to be there. I felt so far from home. Arkansas was not California. Racism had been something I'd been aware of since childhood and was confused by even then. On this visit to my aunt Zella in Arkansas, I was in the back of a car driven by a family friend and she said, "Wanna have some fun?" She then deliberately swerved her car toward a group of Black girls walking down the road just to kick dust in their faces. She barely missed one of them. I protested, but that was the end for me. She broke my heart. I kept talking about it back at the house, and as I did, I could feel my mother's tension rise until she took me into a bedroom and told me to keep quiet, which pissed me off. She wasn't racist either, but she was a realist.

"It isn't right, but you're not going to change any of their minds, babe," she told me quietly. "All you'll do is ruin dinner." Let me tell you, these people were my mom's friends, but I couldn't understand how we could be so far apart in our thinking. It wasn't the first time I'd been confronted with racism, though the first time I didn't understand what it meant. When I was a child, my mother's girlfriend Colleen dated a Black man named Paul. Mom had told eight-year-old me, "You must never speak about Paul to anybody else. You know we love him, and you know how happy he makes Colleen, but some people don't feel the same way about this, so no one can know because if her ex-husband finds out she's dating a Black man, she might lose Paulette." Back then I had no idea why this would make any difference. This was another time when as a kid I was treated like a grown-up, but this was the most critical time, when the consequences could have ruined peoples' lives.

I called Sonny a few times while I was gone, and he told me that his little Yorkie Scunci had passed away. We were both heartbroken. During my absence, Sonny was beginning to realize that I was the person he was closest to. "You know, it's funny, I miss you when you're not here," he told me, and my heart did a little dance because I could tell he really meant it.

Back home, I was certain that I'd be grounded until I was fifty and never see Sonny again. Fearing that the friendship I now cherished above all others was ruined, I longed for him, missing laughing at his corny jokes, soaking up his knowledge, painting with watercolors, and hanging out with my favorite person. Until we were separated, I didn't realize how deep my feelings for him truly were. This was far more than just friendship. He was my hero, and I could think of no one else.

I was eventually allowed out but under strict curfew, so the night Sonny dropped me home past the witching hour, Mom was standing on the doorstep. "You do know that my daughter is only seventeen?" she yelled. "I'm going to call the police and have you thrown in jail!" As far as she was concerned, my weird-looking boyfriend was no Warren Beatty, and he didn't get a free pass. He didn't even get a hall pass.

Her threat not only frightened Sonny but alerted him to the fact that I'd lied to him about my age yet again. "Sheesh, Cher!" he said, exasperated. Two words I would hear many times for the next eleven years. Suffice it to say, that put a bit of a damper on our relationship. Although I was certain Mom wouldn't carry out her threat to involve the police, the possibility was enough to scare Sonny away for a while.

No longer able to cope with my drama, she persuaded Gilbert to let me live in the Hollywood Studio Club, a chaperoned residence for girls who wanted to work in movies. Marilyn Monroe, Kim Novak, Rita Moreno, and several other famous names had stayed there. It was run by the YWCA, and its rules were strict—no men allowed and a curfew. I moved in as arranged but didn't much like it. My roommate, Alix Elias, was the only girl I got along with, and we stayed up late sharing stories about the men we were crazy about. Mostly, I was miserable away from Sonny. When my mother came to visit, she was shocked at how thin and unhappy I was. What she didn't realize was that, although I was only supposed to leave the club for acting classes, I was free to do as I liked as long as I was back before the doors were locked at ten o'clock, so I met up with Sonny before or after class if he was free. He was always happy to see me, and I could tell what he really missed was our special connection.

All of my drama was forgotten when Mom discovered that Gilbert had made secret arrangements to leave her. The most unkind cut of all was that he ran off with Beverly—one of her closest friends.

My mother fell apart and was inconsolable. She was so furious with Gilbert for leaving that she could barely function. Not only had yet another marriage failed, but when he left, her lifestyle went with him. Without a husband to support us, she would eventually have to go back to work. Although she looked great, auditioning for parts wouldn't be as easy as it had been a decade earlier. There had been times in my mother's life when she was still Jackie Jean that she contemplated suicide because the future seemed too bleak. This abandonment as her fortieth birthday loomed almost pushed her back to the brink. Even though she was never in love with Gilbert, she cared for him. I'd never seen her so depressed as she was after he left. She was alone again.

My sister, Gee, had recently turned twelve but seemed younger, although she finally came out of what I described as her "horse haze" to appreciate that some serious shit was going down. I was like a mother to Gee, having practically raised her. I had always given her the extra stability she needed. I couldn't possibly leave her to fend for herself in this situation. All I wanted to do was be with Sonny, but I had no choice but to go back home to act as a buffer. Nursing our mother through her depression was a lot to handle at seventeen, although this wasn't my first experience of taking care of her, and it threw me straight back to the time she almost died after an abortion, or the nights she was so worried about work and money or upset about Daddy that I had to comfort her.

She made a painfully slow recovery as I became the adult of the house again. Then a letter arrived from Gilbert telling her he'd moved to Oklahoma City with Beverly and was seeking a divorce. He'd continue to pay the bills, but when he warned her he might have to sell our house and cancel her credit cards, it was enough to get her up and take us out on a manic shopping spree to max them out. She drove us to Country Club Fashions at the Sherman Oaks Galleria and told me to buy whatever I liked. She bought a million things for herself and then, impatient with how slow I was being, started picking out things for me—skirts, shirts, slacks, and sweaters—all of which I hated. I refused to even try them on, which frustrated her. After wandering the aisles, I finally found a cut velvet jacket with white leather trim and a floral design, and a turquoise linen blouse with polished wooden buttons that matched one of the flowers. I loved my purchases so much, even though I just picked out two things. I hung them on the back of my bedroom door so I could look up at them, which is where they remained until Mom walked by my room a couple of days later and noticed them on the door.

Pulling the hanger down, she said, "I don't know why you got these. You never take care of your clothes, and you won't take care of these." She carried them back to her room, never to be seen again. It took me forever to forgive her for that.

After I went back to the Studio Club one afternoon to collect my things, Sonny picked me up to go see an art house film called *The Balcony*. I was stunned when I saw my acting teacher Jeff Corey up on the screen. It was a smaller part, but I was delighted. It was his first film role in twelve years after being blacklisted by the House Un-American Activities Committee, and I was so happy because I knew what it must have meant to him.

Laughing at my excitement, Sonny took me in his arms and kissed me, catching me completely off guard. I guess I'd finally grown on him. When I returned his kiss, we both stepped over a line. From that point on, there was no turning back.

# 10

## be my baby

Phillip Spector had a reputation for being moody, but he could be hysterically funny too. In those days, he wasn't unstable yet. He had quirks for sure, and his moods were mercurial. You had to read the room. You could joke with him until you couldn't. Everyone kept the atmosphere light and made sure that the studio was fun—that way, Phillip felt good about the work. Plus, he had great respect for the Wrecking Crew and singers in the room, so everyone was happy to be there. Mostly, it was about the music. That's where Phillip's head was. Always. One day the studio engineer, Larry, accidentally spilled his cup of coffee on a completed tape that had taken days to record. This meant that the whole crew would have to come back and record it again. I thought Phillip was going to kill him. Everyone held their breath as he erupted, but then—midstream—he made the choice not to lose it and just stopped. I think he realized yelling and screaming wasn't going to change the ruined tape, and it suddenly struck him as funny. After he found his way back to reason, everyone laughed, Phillip included.

It was a bit like my mom the day I jumped on a freight train as a kid. When the misdemeanor is so huge, shock almost takes away the anger. There was also a certain level of decorum to be maintained in the studio, where Phillip was in complete control. He could be your best friend or act like he didn't know you, but I didn't need to impress him. He'd needle me and I gave as good as I got, treating him as I would any other guy. Whenever he lobbed a comment my way, I'd lob a deadpan response right back. It got to the point where Sonny said, "Please, Cher, he's my boss. You can't smart-mouth him like that!"

The weird thing is that once I got around his bullshit, I grew to like Phillip. I think he grew to like and respect me too, because he let me hang out in the booth with him. He told Sonny I was funny and showed spirit. Returning home to my mother each night after a day surrounded by adults who showed me respect and gave me responsibility became increasingly hard. We barely spoke at all. Whenever Sonny picked me up or drove me home, he'd speed away as fast as he could. I was surprised when Mom suggested that we invite him in.

When he sauntered in with his buckskin pants and deerskin "Indian squaw" boots, similar to ones she owned, Mom tried not to like him but secretly did. She was always able to appreciate something that was different, and he had that ready smile that won her over too.

Grandma Lynda was a harder nut to crack. She was visiting that day, and when she spotted him, she turned around, came straight back into the kitchen, and asked Mom, "What the hell is *that* in the living room?" Sonny heard her too and thought it was funny, but Gee almost melted at the sight of him, sitting next to him and staring up at his face adoringly. I think he may have been her first real crush.

Even though Sonny was busting his ass at Gold Star, he was still hustling for his own career. In 1962 he and Jack Nitzsche had written a song called "Needles and Pins," which was recorded by Jackie DeShannon a year later. Phillip never considered Sonny much of a singer, but he went up in his estimation after that song became a success. Sonny took the opportunity to tell Phillip that I had a great voice too, hoping that Phillip would record me. Phillip had no interest, but Sonny didn't give up.

One day in the summer of 1963, Darlene Love didn't show up at the studio because her car had broken down. Phillip was already behind schedule in recording the Ronettes' next two singles, "Be My Baby" and "Baby, I Love You," and this delay frustrated him. Time cost money, so he told everyone, "Let's get something down anyway and I'll play with it and see how it sounds. Sonny, you join the backup girls." We all knew that if he asked for Sonny, he was desperate.

Undeterred, Sonny bounced up to the microphone like a puppy, and then I heard Phillip utter the words, "Okay, Cher, you too. Get up there. Sonny tells me you can sing."

I almost fainted. Was he fucking nuts? Darlene was one of the greatest singers of all time. I'd be too low for the girls and too high for Sonny. I tried to explain my vocal qualifications to Phillip, but he interrupted me, saying, "I don't care, I just need noise. Get out there and sing."

*But what if my noise is off-key?* I thought with a shiver. I stepped up to the microphone for the first time in my life and took my place next to Sonny, Fanita, and Gracia. I was shaking so much I had to lock my knees together and fix my focus on the little speaker that allowed us to hear the rest of the song. There were no headphones at Gold Star; we all just played and sang. It was so intimidating.

Phillip asked Gracia, "Okay, tell me what you'll be singing," and she went through her notes. When he did the same with Fanita, I thought I'd pass out on the floor if he asked me, as I wouldn't have had a clue what to say. I was planning on just listening to the girls and doubling up on Sonny's part, then hiding until it was over. Thank God Phillip never asked, but then I think he kind of knew not to.

We were counted in and started singing, and somehow a sound came out that seemed okay. I didn't know if it was luck or Larry's skills. I began to relax, but then Phillip made everyone stop. "Cher," he called. "Step back." I wasn't quite sure what he meant at first, but Sonny made a gesture for me to move away from the mic, so I took one step away and we started again.

Darlene was back in the studio the following day, and there was a collective sigh of relief. That woman was a force of nature, and still is, and the only one to stand up to Phillip if she didn't like something. The moment she walked back in, she took one look at me standing in her place and shook her head. Then she threw it back and let out that great big laugh of hers as everyone exhaled. Then she looked at Sonny and said, "What you doing here?" She joined us at the mic, and when we started singing, the same thing happened as the previous day. "Step back, Cher. Step back," Phillip instructed. "You're still cutting through." This went on and on until I must have been three feet from the others and virtually up against the wall. Eventually Darlene quipped, "She'll be in Studio B at this rate!"

When we finally got it right, I was blown away by our collective voices—Darlene's especially. If she was standing right next to me, I could hear nothing else. Being alongside them that day, I was just relieved I hadn't messed up the track. As a couch-surfing high school dropout, I was happy to have any job at all and shocked that it was this one. But I don't think I processed how amazing it truly was—it felt like it was too big for my brain.

Once we were finished and Phillip was happy with the song,

we were allowed to go home, but I was so hyped up that I couldn't stop talking. All the way back in the car and in bed that night, I drove Sonny crazy asking if he thought I did okay and whether Phillip might ask me to sing again. The good news was that Phillip not only invited me back, but for the next year, he hardly ever recorded a song without me singing backup for him. The bad news was that my nerves always got the better of me and I would pray that Phillip wouldn't ask me any questions about what I was singing. I could only join in with the others and latch on to their sound. I didn't have a clue what I was doing.

There were days when I locked myself in the bathroom crying because we had to do take after take, and I was convinced I was the problem. Ronnie, Phillip's girlfriend, who I'd become close to by this point, found me in there once and told me, "Come on out of there, Cher honey. You know you've got a great voice!"

Back at the mic, often half-frozen in fear, I'd stand between Sonny, Gracia, Fanita, and Darlene and there was something about our combined voices that Phillip grew to like. He called us his "funk" element, claiming that we changed the way a lot of his records sounded. Even so, every time Phillip came over the PA, I dreaded hearing my name. I sang backing for Darlene Love on her solo records, Bob B. Soxx & the Blue Jeans, the Crystals, and LaLa Brooks, who also had a hell of a voice.

I loved the work, I really did, and I also loved hanging out with everyone. The only thing that bugged me was my mom saying that I must be lying. She thought I wasn't working at all, but spending my time at the studio partying, not singing. "If you're really working, as you say, then why aren't you getting paid?" she'd ask. Sonny was on a salary from Phillip. Working for free was hard when the schedule left me little time for anything else. When I complained to Sonny, his reaction wasn't what I expected. "You should be paying Phillip for the education you're getting, Cher!" After I moaned that I'd missed another acting class with Jeff Corey, he went further. "Acting's horseshit, it's not going to get you anywhere. You don't want to be an actress, Cher, you're already getting somewhere in music. Gold Star's where it's at." I loved those classes, but I trusted Sonny. I shouldn't have. I probably could have done both. But he was already starting to take over my life, even if I didn't notice.

It made me think of a poem Sonny had written me a few months before. It came out of the blue, after a night we'd spent apart because he had to work late at the studio. I only remember the last line, where he wrote I was "a butterfly to be loved by all." I didn't know how prophetic it was at the time, but I knew that Sonny saw something in me. What I didn't realize was how much that scared him.

Jeff Corey became very emotional when I told him I was leaving his class. Smiling sadly, he said, "If you get serious about acting one day, then I think you could be great. Don't forget that." It took me almost twenty years to try acting again but I never forgot what Jeff said.

By the summer of 1963 Sonny had become everything to me, the all-seeing eye. I accepted that he hated my being involved in anything he wasn't a part of, but when he told me to give up the softball I enjoyed playing with my mom and our friends, I was devastated. As persuasive as ever, he convinced me that I didn't have time to "mess around with games" anymore and needed to focus entirely on my singing. That was rough because those once-a-week games were my last connection with my mom's tribe, and I never quite forgave him for making me step away from that important circle of friendship. My mother wasn't happy either and was even less pleased that she'd wasted money she didn't have on acting classes. Frustrated, she told me, "You're not going back to Gold Star until they pay you."

In Studio A the following day, everyone arrived to continue working on Phillip's all-important compilation album *A Christmas*

*Gift for You* (for which we never received proper credit, although Sonny got an honorable mention on percussion). It featured standards such as "White Christmas," "Frosty the Snowman," and "Here Comes Santa Claus," all sung by his famous stable of artists. Everything was ready when Phillip saw that I was missing and asked, "Where the hell's Cher?"

Sonny raised his hand. "Cher's mom doesn't believe she's working because she's not getting paid. She isn't going to let her come back anymore because she thinks she's partying." Phillip was so angry that he canceled the entire session and sent everyone home. He was superstitious about having the same people on every track. He told Sonny, "Cher's with you and I'm paying you, so what's the problem?" As far as he was concerned, we were two for the price of one. Sonny explained that this logic wouldn't sway my mom, so the next day he agreed to pay me something. I worked that day, and when we'd finished, Phillip wrote me a check for $25. I took it straight home and handed it to my mother in triumph, not knowing that it was the last check Phillip would ever write me. Mom was happy to see it, but she knew I was being taken advantage of. I was working enough to earn more than a measly $25. But Mom was depressed in bed, so I accepted her reaction.

She was becoming sadder and sadder, worried about the future because Gilbert was out of the picture. I did feel sorry for her, but given how mean she'd been to him, what did she think was going to happen? At the ripe age of seventeen, I decided that I'd finally had enough and told myself, *What can I do?* Grabbing my only coat and a handful of clothes, I threw them into a bag, opened the long window in my bedroom, kicked out the screen, and walked out. Mom was down the other end of the house, so I could have just walked out the front door, but I was making a statement. Half an hour later I walked into Sonny's apartment and told him what I'd done.

"What's your mom gonna do about this?" he asked, frowning.

"She won't do a thing."

The year after Gilbert left us was one of my mother's lowest points, and yet it was what drove me to Sonny and the start of the rest of my life. The day I moved back in with him was the beginning of the beginning. Something clicked when we got together then. As Sonny said later, he'd even missed my incessant singing. I was so happy to be with him, but I also felt guilty. Knowing that life would be lonely at home for Gee without me, I made sure to invite her over as often as I could and include her whenever possible. Even at such a young age, she understood my reasons for leaving and did well coping on her own when Mom went back to work.

With hardly any clothes of my own with me, I had to borrow some of Sonny's, including his Fruit of the Loom underwear. He put up with that for ages until, exasperated, he promised to take me shopping. He kept his word and, when he next got paid, took me to Wilson's House of Suede in Hollywood, where he picked out a black leather jacket for me that I loved so much I almost passed out. He also bought me a wine-colored mock-turtleneck sleeveless top that I thought was so cool. We picked out a great pair of stirrup pants, and a flat pair of boots with a wide shaft. When I zipped the boots around the pants, they bunched up at the bottom, which I thought was a design flaw. But I loved the look anyway.

For different reasons, Sonny and I were both on the periphery. High school dropouts with unconventional looks, we both came from rocky homes. We both grew up too quickly and couldn't settle in relationships, but once we came together, we enjoyed the same things, shared the same dreams, and thought the same things were cool. We fit together, and that suited me just fine. I was young and pliable and happy to be taken care of. And he made me laugh constantly.

In the music industry, Sonny could gently push the boundaries of what was acceptable in the workplace, and did so with his floppy Caesar hairstyle. I thought it would be fun to try something different too. My hair was so straight that I couldn't do much with it, so I cut my bangs to better frame the heavy black eyeliner I wore. I also started to trim my little side pieces like sideburns. This look became my signature for years, in fact until I had Chas.

Growing in confidence and happier now that my mother sort of accepted our relationship, I planned a surprise for her next birthday. Uncle Mickey had invited her to the Purple Onion for supper that night and I told him, "I wanna sing a song for Mom." This would be the first time I'd ever sung in a public place, and I don't know where I found the guts. Mickey thought it was a great idea and suggested I rehearse with the house band, Pat & Lolly Vegas. I didn't even know which key to sing in, so we played around until I hit the right notes. I rehearsed a few songs, especially "Danny Boy," one of my mother's favorites and a song she used to sing with Grampa Roy. I must have done something right during the rehearsal because the band happened to be auditioning for a new singer, which is why they were at the Onion. When we'd finished, they asked Mickey if they could just hire me. "She's a hell of a lot better than any of the girls we've auditioned." I was flattered and surprised. I said, "That'd be great, but I already have a job."

I don't know if someone tipped Mom off about my surprise, but she bought me a champagne beaded shirt at Corky Hale's boutique for me to wear that I lost my brains over. Feeling like a million dollars, I convinced my legs to carry me up to the front of the band and my mouth to open so I could sing the song. Mom said afterward that she was blown away by my performance—not so much the power of my voice, which she'd known my whole life, but what she called my "shining quality." Sonny was proud too.

Mickey was delighted and impressed by how many cool people Sonny introduced him to, including the DJ Sam Riddle and Little Richard, who was a piece of work and always joking around with Sonny, pretending to hit on him. Sonny loved Richard too, in a roll-your-eyes kind of way, and put up with his constant teasing. When I first met Richard, he was hysterical and asked Sonny, "Ooh, how did a fella like you get such a cute li'l girl, Sonny B-o-n-o?" I also met Brian Wilson, cofounder of the Beach Boys, who I found one day sitting on the couch at Gold Star. The Beach Boys were recording not far away at Columbia Studios, and Brian would come and sit quietly in a corner, watching and hoping to pick up a few tips from the master. Painfully shy, he offered to play piano, but Phillip passed, although he let Brian play the tambourine and sing backup on a few numbers. A tightwad, he'd enlist anyone if he didn't have to pay them.

Like Phillip, Brian was a troubled genius who wrote all those Beach Boys songs as if he'd been out surfing the waves his whole life, when he never had. He liked me because I was young and unintimidating, so we became friends. One day I was playing with the machine that punched letters into plastic tape for labeling equipment and decided to make Brian a bracelet. Because of my undiagnosed dyslexia, it came out as *I Love You, Brain*. It became our little thing, and, by the way, he *was* the brain, with an amazing mind for music.

We were still living in our Franklin apartment when Sonny's divorce from Donna came through in the fall of 1963. Under California law, there was a statutory waiting period of one year before he could remarry, but I didn't care about any of that because, as far as I was concerned, we were as good as married in my heart. Plus, without my mother's permission we couldn't legally wed until I was eighteen, the following May, anyway, so we settled into making a home for ourselves. When Sonny got a raise, he announced that it was time for us to trade up from our apartment. He found us a one-bedroom A-frame house up on Sycamore Trail in the hills behind the Hollywood Bowl. Our new home had a leaky shower and a dark backyard that was mostly dirt save for the fire pit. The rug was kind of hatchet too, but I loved it. With no furniture and not much money, we drove downtown to a secondhand store and bought an old iron bed, a lamp, a side table, and a funky chest of drawers to sit our TV on.

The bed frame was filthy, and while we were giving it a good clean, Sonny cried, "Cher, I think this is brass!" Excited, we ran out and bought about twenty boxes of steel wool Brillo pads, scrubbing it all night long until it was gleaming. That damn bed was brass, and it was beautiful. I was so happy and remember thinking that none of Sonny's former girlfriends would have done anything so hands-on, they just would have jumped on the mattress like idiots.

Sonny's sister Betty, who was my favorite, bought us some new sheets, and I was so excited that I kept saying how great they were because our old ones felt like sleeping on cardboard. To my surprise, Sonny got angry and hissed, "Stop going on about the sheets, Cher, okay? You don't have to act like we're paupers!" I didn't yet understand about his Sicilian pride and how important image was to him.

One day Sonny brought home a German shepherd puppy someone had given him, but we were honestly too busy to take care of a dog. There was only that small dirt backyard and no real place for him to run around, so the poor thing became needy. Sonny was cooking one night as I stood alongside him as his sous chef when the puppy got under his feet and yelped as Sonny shoved it to one side with his foot.

"Hey, Son, don't do that!" I said. Before I knew it Sonny had spun around and pushed me up against a wall. He didn't yell and he didn't hit me, but he had ahold of my shoulders and his face was clenched. I was so vehemently opposed to being manhandled, having seen Mom go through it, that I thought, *Fuck this*. I'd witnessed fear and I'd seen violence. I'd been beaten as a kid, and I wasn't going to be beaten as an adult.

Staring into his eyes, I said, "Let me tell you something. If you *ever* touch me like this again, I will leave your ass and it'll be the last time you ever see me." I wasn't kidding, and he could see that I meant it.

Aside from that incident, we loved being together in that house and made it as cozy as we could. We only had one table, and we worked on cleaning that up too before painting it blue and varnishing it until it had a kind of luminosity. Then he cut down the legs and surrounded it with scatter pillows. The house had awful old bamboo slat blinds that were falling apart and that I would have happily thrown in the dumpster. Sonny had other ideas and took me shopping, where we picked up three big rough-edged prints of cave paintings with antelopes and stick figures, stained to look old like parchment. When we got home, he took the blinds down and separated them one by one from the little strings that kept them in place. Then he wove three mats out of them with the prints in the middle, and hung them on the wall between the beams of the A-frame. They looked so cool.

One day not long after we'd moved in, Sonny called me all excited to tell me he was coming home with a big surprise. I thought he'd bought me something special, so my face fell when he rolled in a battered old upright piano that he'd found in a pawnshop for eighty-five dollars. "It has three broken keys, but they're all at the bass end where we never sing," he said. From the look on his face, you'd have thought he'd found a Steinway. I still have that ugly thing.

We were working constantly at the studio to finish the new Christmas album Phillip was putting together, and the fifteen-hour days felt like he was working us to death. The problem was that although Phillip knew what he wanted, we had to wait for him to work it out in his mind and let us know what that was. We all wanted to do a good job, but sometimes our mistakes became the hook that Phillip liked better than his original concept. Sonny sometimes stayed with him all night as he worked to get things right (Phillip didn't like to be alone), so I'd stay home watching TV.

Bored and a little fearful by myself, I spent a night with my friend and former roommate Josita, who lived in a two-bedroom apartment with her boyfriend, Ulle, and another girl. After an evening out together, we went back to her place, where they all went to bed, and I fell asleep on the couch. A few hours later I was aware of somebody lying next to me with their hand in my underpants. Half-asleep, I thought I was home and then suddenly remembered that I wasn't. It was dark and all I could see was the outline of a man. Frozen, I lay there, my heart racing, until he moved slightly away. Pretending to be drowsy, I got up and went into the bathroom, unsure what to do. When I heard a door close, I prayed he'd left, but the minute I realized he was still there, I ran past him into Josita's bedroom, screaming. Ulle jumped up and turned on the light and saw that their roommate's drunken boyfriend had returned home with his girlfriend, and seeing me lying on the couch, he thought he'd just lie down next to me and let his hands wander. It took me the rest of the night to calm down and I didn't dare breathe a word to Sonny for fear he'd murder the guy.

A few days later we went back to work on the Christmas album at Gold Star. It was all-consuming, but when we listened to what we'd created, we knew that it was worth it. I was totally wiped out after our marathon sessions of working every single night for a month straight, and I remember thinking, *How are all these old people still doing this?* I had no idea it was drugs—not everyone, but some were doing drugs just to stay awake. Then one day Leon Russell came in so drunk that he could hardly stand. It was out of character because he'd normally come in and sit down at the piano without saying a word. He and Glen Campbell used to go golfing, and the loudest things about Leon were his orange-and-blue-checkered pants and alpaca sweater. On this day, though, he was drunk as a skunk, and nobody knew what to do. He was staggering around the studio, and then he jumped up on the piano. Marveling, Phillip called out to him, "Hey, Leon. Have you never heard of something called decorum?'"

"No! Have you ever heard of something called 'Fuck you, Phil'?" Leon slurred before stumbling onto the piano stool to sit down and play.

We all died. I mean on the floor dying of laughter, Hal Blaine especially. Even Phillip was in hysterics, but we pulled it together when he finally said, "Okay, show's over. Back to work." Those were some of the craziest, happiest days of my life.

When the album was finished, Phillip booked a flight back to New York and everyone collapsed in a heap. Hours after he'd left for the airport, Sonny was passed out in bed when he received a call saying that Phillip had been thrown off his plane and urgently needed help.

"Go sort him out, bud," he asked me, yawning. "I'm too exhausted and couldn't trust myself to drive right now."

"Me?" I replied. "No, Son. Please. I'm tired too and I'm not even in Phillip's inner circle. Besides, what could I do?" He threw me his car keys. That was my answer. Exhausted, I navigated Sonny's big old Cadillac through traffic to a busy LAX. I eventually found Phillip passed out on a seat in the departure lounge, his suit carrier thrown over him. He was so scared to fly that he'd loaded up on drugs, and it was the first time I'd ever seen him under the influence. A member of the ground staff explained that once he was on the plane, he'd looked at his fellow passengers and freaked out: "You all look like losers. I can't fly with fucking losers, the plane's not gonna make it! I want to get off!" The stewardesses tried to calm him down, but he wouldn't stop saying it, so they had to taxi the plane back to the gate to throw him off.

When I shook him awake, he grimaced, squinted up at me, and said, "Cher. I need sunglasses." He didn't seem surprised that I was there.

"Well, okay. Can you walk?"

"Dunno. I really need sunglasses, Cher."

I managed to get him to his feet and then to a kiosk, where I helped him try several pairs on, telling him which looked the best. He eventually bought some Ray-Bans. I then made him drink gallons of black coffee before trying to book him another ticket, but American Airlines had banned him. I had to go to another airline and try to explain his drugged-out state. "Please, he was just so terrified of flying that he took something," I pleaded. After doing some verbal tap-dancing, I eventually got him onto another flight. Half-asleep and mumbling, he boarded without incident and flew home. I was too comatose even to be relieved.

A few weeks later we were asleep at home after another all-nighter in the studio when the telephone rang. It was November 22, 1963, the day Phillip's Christmas album was due to be released, and he was calling from New York. Sonny listened for a bit and then he collapsed into a chair and murmured, "Oh my God!" From the look on his face, my immediate thought was that someone we knew had died. When he came off the telephone, Sonny turned to me and said, "President Kennedy was shot in the head this morning. He was being driven through Dallas in an open-top car with the first lady."

Beside myself, I couldn't stop crying. Neither of us could move, we were so shattered by the news. JFK, who was in his forties, was the first president we'd ever known who seemed to understand our generation. I'd never connected with his predecessor "Ike" Eisenhower (who only ever seemed to play golf) or his wife, Mamie, with her bangs plastered to her forehead. JFK was young and handsome, a war hero with fresh ideas, and his wife, Jackie, was so beautiful and stylish. Losing him this way felt so surreal and so tragic.

That night Sonny and I curled up together weeping, and the following day we watched the news coverage on TV for hours. Phillip was upset too, of course, but what really killed him was that his prized Christmas album bombed because of the assassination. Nobody was in the mood to listen to "Here Comes Santa Claus" after losing JFK.

It could only have been a week or so later that I found out I was pregnant, which came as a huge shock, as we hadn't been trying at all. Having a baby wasn't part of our plan, not that we had a plan, and nor were we especially careful (the contraceptive pill was only available to married women). I'd also only just gained full independence from my mother, so this was the last thing I wanted. The weird thing was that once I found out I was going to have Sonny's baby, it was hard to be unhappy. Sonny was excited too, but worried that a baby would interfere with his work in the music industry. Plus, he already had a daughter.

In the end Fate intervened and I lost the baby. It happened spontaneously when I was sixteen weeks pregnant and home alone. I felt a burning pain and screamed because, having never been pregnant before, I didn't know what it meant. Sonny was at work and there was no easy way to contact him. By the time he pulled up to the house that afternoon I was sitting on the floor wailing and rocking myself in agony when he came running in. I didn't stop screaming even when we got to the doctor's office and into an elevator full of people. I was so scared because I was in so much pain and didn't know what was happening. They laid me on the table and made some bad faces and then started cutting. They kept on putting something in a metal tin that sounded like fish flopping or pieces of liver hitting a pan. It sounded worse than it was, because as he cut he was relieving the pressure and the pain. Then the doctor sent me straight to the hospital.

Sonny was right there for me, and we cried together at our loss. When it was over, Sonny took me home to rest, where I went quiet and withdrew into myself for a while. Within a week, though, we were right back at Gold Star to pick up where we'd left off.

To cement our future together, Sonny made a momentous decision. Sitting in a park one day listening to a guy playing sax, he turned to me and said, "Don't you think it's time you asked me to marry you?" Laughing, I replied, "Well, okay." We knew we couldn't have a conventional wedding, nor could we afford to drive to Mexico, where we could have applied for a license, so instead he had two silver rings made in a souvenir shop on Olvera Street with our names in raised letters. He'd wear the one that said *Cher* and I'd wear the ring that said *Sonny*.

The day he picked them up, he came home and it was time for our wedding. He insisted we do something to make it feel official, so I threw on a T-shirt and jeans and suggested we get married in our bathroom. I have no idea why, I just thought that was a good place to do it. We had a marriage ceremony of sorts, right then and there and with me presiding. It was all kinds of silly, but I meant every word as we stood barefoot facing each other between the shower and the window, the mirrored medicine cabinet behind us. I spoke my own made-up version of wedding vows, then he said a few words and we swapped our rings, kissed, and that was it. I guess we were kind of married and we told everyone we'd been legally wed. Our ad hoc ceremony was over in minutes, and then Sonny went into the kitchen to make spaghetti sauce while I hummed a happy song.

In my head, from the moment we put on those rings, I no longer carried the name Cherilyn LaPiere Sarkisian. I was Cher of Sonny and Cher, and proud to wear his name on my finger. A few weeks later, though, I lost my ring and was too scared to tell him. My God, what a nightmare that was. I even tried to hide my hand in case he noticed. The ring was missing for a couple of days, but I'd only been at the house and the studio, so I searched everywhere for it. One day I was washing up the spaghetti sauce pan and spotted something shiny at the bottom. I was so relieved to find my ring that I burst into tears.

I didn't tell Mom that we were unofficially wed, as I knew what her reaction would be. Things were better between us after she and Gee moved into a nicer rented house. My mother and Sonny even joined forces to buy me a six-year-old red convertible MGA for eight hundred bucks. I was so thrilled to have my own wheels again, but there was just one problem—I'd fibbed to Sonny that I knew how to drive stick shift. So, Gee and I had to figure it out one day, in the Hollywood Hills no less, which made it even more terrifying. After that, I took the long way on every journey just to make it last. I took such good care of that little car, filling it with gas and topping up the radiator like I'd been told. The only downside was that the MGA was tiny, and whenever the Ronettes flew into LA, all four of us had to squeeze inside. I don't know how we managed it with Ronnie and me up front and Estelle and Nedra smooshed into the little space in the back, but we always did—with a lot of laughing.

Unfortunately, the MG had an idiosyncratic habit of breaking down, which was a problem we couldn't afford to get fixed because the parts were too expensive. One day on Sunset and La Brea it happened again when I was out with the girls. The car died at a stoplight, right in front of a gas station. Without batting an eye, I jumped out, put up the hood, jiggled the two wires on the starter together, got back in the car, and started it. Hearing applause, I looked around to see the guys at the gas station hollering and clapping.

For much of 1964, Sonny and I worked with Phillip and witnessed the Ronettes become major stars. When they went on tour to England, their support band was a new British group called the Rolling Stones. Ronnie had a fling with guitarist Keith Richards even though her mother was on tour with her as chaperone. When Phillip came back to LA after London, he was wearing these incredible clothes. I remember a brown suede jacket with buttons, a bit like a peacoat but shorter, worn with a paisley shirt and flared pants. He also had a flat tweed cap, a double-breasted jacket, and a floral shirt he'd bought in a place called Carnaby Street. None of us had seen anything quite like this. His clothes were so exciting it made me start reading articles about the English look, which was clearly cool.

Meanwhile, Sonny's dreams for me were still being stalled by Phillip, who insisted my voice wasn't commercial enough and had the register of Paul McCartney. Sonny knew he had to try to find me the perfect song and create the right image to make it a hit. One night he took me to see the movie *Cleopatra* starring Elizabeth Taylor and Richard Burton. I wore a hairpiece Mom had given me—a kind of wide loose chignon—on top of my head above my thick black bangs, and made up my eyes Cleopatra-style with heavy black eyeliner and white eyelids, a look I kept for years. When we walked into the movie theater, the music was playing but the lights were still on. As we made our way to our seats, people started looking at us and someone asked if we'd come as Julius Caesar and Cleopatra. Sonny stashed that in his brain and decided to call us "Caesar and Cleo" in the hope of coattailing on the success of the movie.

Fooling around on the piano with the five chords he knew, he persuaded Jack Lewerke, who had recently founded the record company Vault, to record and release a song he wrote called "The Letter." To be honest, I didn't like it. Sonny thought it was worth a shot, however, and called in his old friend Harold Battiste, an arranger, composer, teacher, and jazz musician from New Orleans.

Sonny had learned from Phillip that the B-side of any record should be an instrumental with a ridiculous title so that it wouldn't detract from the A-side. He picked one of his own compositions, called "String Fever," written under the name S. Christy. The disc was released in February 1964 as by "Salvatore Bono and Cher La Piere also known as Caesar & Cleo." It bombed.

Our next release was "Love Is Strange," a 1956 hit written by Bo Diddley, in the middle of which Sonny included some corny dialogue. The B-side was "Do You Want to Dance," arranged by Jack Nitzsche. That record tanked. Undaunted, Sonny arranged for us to appear in multiact shows hosted by DJs like Wink Martindale on small-time circuits such as bowling alleys and roller rinks. Even though some of these places were a bit dorky, Sonny decided to change our look to mimic Dick and Dee Dee and April and Nino—the clean-cut acts, who were doing well in the charts. We were still trying to find our own image, and hoping to piggyback off their success. Sonny wore a suit, and I wore white silk crêpe pants with a shell beaded top and heels borrowed from my mother as we sang our new releases alongside songs like "Walking the Dog."

When I'd longed to be a singing cartoon character as a child, it never occurred to me that to achieve my dream I might have to perform in public night after night. Even though I had tons of energy and a resolve to be famous, I didn't know what famous was and might have been a bank robber if I hadn't met Sonny. It turns out, the thought of everyone looking at me was torture, and those nights, I was paralyzed by fear and, hyperventilating, told Sonny, "I . . . can't . . ." With a calm voice he told me it was okay, adding, "You'll be fine, Cher. You'll see."

Just as I was about to protest, he put his hand on the small of my back and shoved me onstage, and seconds later I grabbed his hand and pulled him on with me. Up at the mic, I remained glued to his side staring into his eyes and singing through him as I tried to make sound carry above the noise of tumbling pins and teens talking. The whole experience was a crapshoot, as no one knew our music, the house band was awful, and we had no one to sing backup.

Sonny wasn't a genius songwriter, but he was clever enough to be influenced by what he heard so that he could keep up with the trends. He learned from Phillip to listen to current hits and see which sounds were making it into the charts. The problem was that things were changing so fast. Beatlemania had hit America and the young British boys in sharp suits and clipped hairdos were all anyone could talk about. Their single "I Want to Hold Your Hand" sold over a million copies and was number one. More than seventy million people—including me—watched them on *The Ed Sullivan Show*, and the hysteria of the live audience reminded me of the Elvis concert my mother had taken me to seven years earlier.

Cashing in on their popularity, Phillip Spector wrote a song called "Ringo, I Love You," as if it were sung by a devoted fan to the drummer Ringo Starr. Having always ignored Sonny's pleas to let me cut my own disc, Phillip decided that I should be the one to record it. His only proviso was that I change my name to Bonnie Jo Mason to sound all-American. We recorded it in Studio B, a room about the size of my MG, and it was released in March 1964. Sonny used every trick in the book to get the demo played on local radio stations, but the feedback was terrible. My voice was so low that DJs thought it was one man singing a love song to another when homosexuality was still illegal. My single stiffed out of the gate. Bonnie Jo Mason was a flop.

When I listen to my early numbers, I cringe. I sounded so nasal because of teenage allergies. I'd also recorded an album of covers for Liberty Records in a separate deal, but they didn't like the way I sounded either, so nothing came of that. The failure of both convinced Phillip that he was right about me. Mine was only ever going to be the voice in the background. Sonny stopped hassling him to give me another chance and I stopped singing around the house.

Devastated, I was convinced that my career was over before it had even begun.

# 11

## baby don't go

Charlie Greene and Brian Stone were balls to the wall. They brought to mind the ruthless publicist played by Tony Curtis in the 1957 movie *Sweet Smell of Success*, although Charlie had a beard and Brian was so skinny we joked he had to run around in the shower to get wet. *Rolling Stone* magazine likened Charlie to a Chihuahua that spent its life trying to hump Great Danes. At eighteen years old, they had started a press agency in New York City. Too young and inexperienced— they spent more than they made—they folded after two years and set their sights on Hollywood. With only $8 between them, they hitchhiked to LA. Once in town, they snuck onto the Universal Studios lot. They took over a dressing room, called security, and ordered permanent passes for themselves and even took their lunches in the commissary. They started introducing themselves as press agents and continued this way for six months before being found out and getting kicked off the lot. They just lied but they were brilliant at it and totally committed to their lies.

They were fast-talking New Yorkers and really charming. Both of them. They were funny and they were completely different though both pretty cute. I don't remember exactly how Sonny first met them but it was through Gold Star. In those days, if you were in Gold Star and walking around, people just assumed you were meant to be there and were in the business. There was a sense of trust that if you were in the building, you were part of the brotherhood. Jack Nitzsche was producing a version of "Yes Sir, That's My Baby" for the two of them. Sonny and I were enlisted to contribute along with Brian Wilson, Darlene Love, Jackie DeShannon, and others, and the record was released under the name Hale and the Hushabyes. How did they just walk in and get all those people from the industry on a record together? Brian Wilson from the Beach Boys was gigantic at the time, and Darlene and Jackie. It doesn't make any sense in retrospect. That's how good they were. If they believed in something, they would just go to the mattresses and their exuberance was contagious.

Sonny met them at the perfect time. With Phillip frequently out of town, Sonny had kind of started to give up. We could get some small jobs as Caesar & Cleo at roller rinks or bowling alleys but nothing serious. We were really floundering. When we met Brian and Charlie, their enthusiasm brought back Sonny's drive. They were desperate to learn more about the music industry because they couldn't yet speak the "language," and when they realized that Sonny knew what he was talking about and was also well-liked and well-respected, they wanted to learn from him. Sonny agreed to teach them what he knew and in exchange Brian and Charlie let us use their office, telephones, and secretary. Their insane enthusiasm infected Sonny, and his excitement in turn made them even more excited. It was like we were the fuse and they were the match and all together we were a ball of fire. They signed us as Caesar & Cleo and we hoped things were about to turn in our favor.

Hot on the heels of the Beatles, the Rolling Stones arrived in Los Angeles to start their first American tour and came into Gold Star, where Jack and Phillip helped with a few of their numbers. Excited by the buzz surrounding these British kids, Sonny took me to their hotel to meet them. We arrived at the Hilton, but they weren't yet back from their interview, so he went off to make a call. A few minutes later, the band walked into the lobby and—spotting me alone—came over and sat down, talking fast and flirty in their English accents. When Sonny returned, he wagged his finger at them—"Hey, you guys, that's my wife!" He then introduced me to the nineteen-year-old lead singer Mick Jagger and the rest of the group. Although Brian Jones was supposed to be the leader of the band, Mick was clearly the star. Keith Richards, also nineteen, was sweet, funny, and shy. Bill Wyman and Charlie Watts, both older, were adorable, but it was Brian, at twenty, who caught my attention. He was so beautiful that I thought he looked like an angel, and uncannily like Mick's soon-to-be teenage girlfriend, Marianne Faithfull. He was the one I spoke to most. The rest had such thick accents that I could barely understand them. Not that I said much, and mostly I just smiled, because I was increasingly hesitant to open my mouth in the company of men if Sonny was around. I had learned to tell from a single glance when he disapproved.

I think the band liked us immediately. Their first taste of America had been uptight record executives in three-piece suits trying to make polite conversation. Record executives in London were more like the artists themselves in the way they dressed and talked. The band didn't like being around the American executives, who were so formal. They wanted to hang out with like-minded people who looked like them and just have fun. "Can't we stay with you?"

Brian asked. Sonny was flattered but didn't know what to say because he was reluctant to reveal that we didn't have any living room furniture and we only had two rooms. Embarrassed and a little out of his element, he whispered in my ear, "They want to stay with us. What should we do? Maybe they could sleep on cots." I shook my head and replied, "Son, c'mon, get real," so he told them the truth and they remained at their hotel.

"Come with us to our first gig," Mick suggested. The venue was the Swing Auditorium in San Bernardino, and when we arrived there on the old school bus the record company provided, the atmosphere was insane. It was the first big concert we'd seen. The thirty-five hundred mainly female fans who'd paid five dollars a ticket on that warm June night were manic. Standing at the side of the stage, we couldn't believe the noise. Those chicks went wild. When the gig was over, we all ran back to the bus but found ourselves surrounded by hundreds of frenzied girls. Because it was so hot, the windows were open, and they were trying to reach in. One, who was sobbing, with mascara dripping down her face, handed me a pen and a piece of paper for Mick to sign. Feeling sorry for her, I took it, and he signed it, but when I reached back to give it to her, a gazillion hands strained toward me to take Mick's autograph, grabbing me and almost dragging me out of the bus. Sonny had to jump up and pull me back inside as the slip of paper vanished into the mob. It was only when I got my hand back that I realized that someone had pulled the amethyst out of the ring Mom had recently given me for my birthday. I was shocked and burst into tears.

Even so, we loved being with the Stones. Some of the American newspapers said they were "Britain's bad boys" because Mick and Keith had been arrested in the UK with drugs on them earlier that year, but we never saw any drug use. They just made us laugh. Sonny hung with Mick mostly because he was old for his years and full of good advice. When he heard we weren't getting anywhere in the States, he suggested we try Britain: "Trust me, man, they won't be afraid of you there."

Fired up by watching the Stones perform, Sonny decided it was time to push me to the next level as a solo artist and wrote the song "Baby Don't Go" with this in mind. The lyrics were written just for me and told of a girl who barely knew her father and had only slept with one boy. Another verse spoke of having no money and shopping at a secondhand store. I loved the song from the start, and so did Charlie and Brian.

Charlie, Brian, Sonny, and I had become a real team, and their encouragement was amazing for Sonny. To save money and because we got along so well, we moved in with them, Charlie's girlfriend, Marcie, and Brian's girlfriend, who never washed her face but had the most beautiful skin. Marcie was a bit older than I was and had a great effect on me. She came from a rich family and one day told me, "Cher, there's more than just white broad panties." We lived in a funky old place they were renting somewhere in the hills near Laurel Canyon. The guys liked living together because they could meet and strategize at any time. With their encouragement, Sonny started pulling musician friends of his together so he could record the song.

Harold Battiste, who'd decided to stay in LA, did the arrangement and played the clavietta on the song for free. Then he talked his friends Leon Russell, Don Randi, and guitarist Barney Kessel into doing the same. There were other musicians as well but those three were a special favor. Studio time was booked at RCA and I was surrounded by people I knew. When I stepped up to the mic, however, my throat tightened. I froze. Panicking because I'd never sung lead, I begged Sonny to join me. "But, Cher, this is your song," he replied in frustration. "It's not written for two voices."

"Please, Son. Please. Just for the choruses. I can't do this without you." In my head, Sonny had become the magic feather given to the baby elephant in *Dumbo.* He eventually relented and our eyes locked while we sang together.

Wanting to test if he had a hit, Sonny went by himself to play the song for Phillip and offered half the royalties for $500. Phillip wrote the check right then and didn't say anything. Probably the most expensive test anyone's ever taken.

We were so excited about the song that we went right from the studio to Mo Ostin, the senior executive at Reprise. Charlie and Brian's enthusiasm boosted Sonny's confidence and spurred him on to be bold. Nobody had any time to prepare Mo Ostin. The four of us just walked into Mo's office and said, "We're Sonny and Cher and we're ready to play this for Mo." Mo had already signed Sonny and me as Caesar & Cleo, which of course we knew, that's why we went to him with our song, trying to impress the boss. We didn't know that Mo had no idea who we were when we walked in. We went through the entire meeting thinking he knew who we were. Charlie and Brian were talking so fast you'd think they were on coke. The moment we played Mo the song, he freaked out. We were all excited, thinking we had finally brought him something he liked, and the whole time he thought we were two independent musicians pitching ourselves as something new. It ended up working in our favor, because he loved the song so much he offered us an amazing deal that was a hundred times better than the one he didn't know we already had. Sonny just said thank you. We raced to sign the contract before he could find out his mistake. Mo was teased mercilessly for years after for having accidentally signed his own artists.

"Baby Don't Go" was released on Frank Sinatra's Reprise label in September 1964, and Sonny & Cher was born. Even though the song was originally meant to be just for me, Sonny put his name first. It sounded better.

Once we had the demo, Sonny persuaded his friend the DJ Sam Riddle to play it on his popular radio show, where its success or failure depended on audience reaction. In those days listeners picked which songs were played, so we enlisted everyone we knew to call in and ask for ours. There were two telephones in the house we were sharing with our managers, and Marcie and I manned these while Sonny, Brian, and Charlie called in from elsewhere. Mom and Gee called in from home, and other friends were recruited too. We didn't stop dialing until our single became the most requested song on the Southern California airwaves. We were so excited when it became a regional hit, and in Texas too, even if it didn't dent the national charts.

We followed that up with our first album. It was also called *Baby Don't Go* and featured mostly covers and a few of Sonny's songs. Sales were modest but encouraging. Convinced that this was the break we'd been waiting for, Sonny made a momentous decision. "We can't be singing background forever, and I think we have a shot at this," he told me, his eyes bright. "It's time to leave Phillip and try to make it on our own."

In November 1964, he and I stood at the microphone in Studio A along with the Blossoms and a few new guys I'd never worked with before to record our last-ever backing vocal for Phillip Spector. It was for "You've Lost That Lovin' Feelin'" by the Righteous Brothers, a song still considered to be the ultimate example of his Wall of Sound. Phillip had signed the talented duo of Bill Medley and Bobby Hatfield earlier that year, referring to their sound as "blue-eyed soul." He flew in two favorite writers from New York and set them to work creating the perfect song. Despite his having all that he needed to produce what would become a number one hit around the world, earn a Grammy, and be listed as one of the best songs of the century, recording it was far from easy.

Phillip was possessed. He was working so hard because he knew the song was brilliant, and when Bill Medley put the vocals on it, no one could breathe. Everybody was standing completely still. Everybody just knew that this was genius, that this was a once-in-a-lifetime song. When Phillip played the final version back, there were only a few of us in the room: Brian, Sonny and me, Bobby Hatfield, Jack and Cynthia Weil, and Barry Mann, who'd written the song with Phillip. When we heard it, we knew that we were hearing something totally unique. Seeing our reaction and exploding with joy, Phillip jumped in the air and screamed. "It's a fucking giant!" I never had that experience again, even on my own songs.

Happy to be leaving on such a high note, we were released from our punishing schedule but broke without Sonny's wages. As I only ever got paid that one time, I had nothing to fall back on either. Free but scared, we discovered that making money outside of Gold Star was going to be tough. The world was starting to shift musically, politically, and culturally. Kennedy was dead, the Vietnam War was only halfway through, and there were race riots across the Southern states as the civil rights movement was gaining momentum with Martin Luther King Jr. and Malcolm X leading the way.

Young people were finally speaking up and protesting about what was wrong. We had decided that we wanted a different kind of world than our parents and grandparents had lived in. A more inclusive world because what we'd inherited, in our eyes, was a mess and we weren't going to have it anymore. As a byproduct, there was an explosion of color and vitality in the art, fashion, culture, and music scenes, especially in California. When it came to my personal fashion, everything started with meeting Colleen and Bridget.

One day I was walking down Sunset when I spotted a beautiful blonde with her hair in long braids wearing the most amazing bell-bottom pants that made me chase her down the street. I'd never seen "bells" at the bottom of pants that huge. She told me they were called "elephant bells." Hers had big flowers all over them and were laced with rawhide. I asked her where she got them and she told me,

"My friend made them," introducing herself as Colleen. She took me to her tiny cubbyhole at the back of a dry cleaner on Sunset, where she and a flame-haired Irish girl named Bridget were creating pants in every color. A little older than me, they became my closest friends and went on to make many of my all-time favorite outfits. Those girls were the first to teach me to dress how I feel. Inspired, I started to take them some of my own designs and we spurred one another on with bigger and bolder ideas. Some of the pants they made had embroidered butterflies or were embellished with leather. We'd go to the Home Silk chain store and buy thick drapery cotton in every color with stripes and paisley prints. They also made pants from something called "rough-out," a thick double-sided suede that took a year to break in. I only ever had one pair. They had belt loops in the shape of the symbol for spades, but the legs were so stiff that they felt as if I were walking in a cardboard box. They eventually softened, and I made myself a pair of matching moccasins that laced up the back. I thought I'd died and gone to heaven.

Sonny had always dressed on the edge even when he was a promo man, but I began to style him, living vicariously as I pulled random clothes out of his closet and pushed him to dress even more out-there. I wasn't yet brave enough to wear some of the looks I persuaded him to try—nor did I have the money—but I was on the brink of being as fearless as he was. I also cut his hair, trimming it into the distinctive mop top that ended up making him look like a cross between a Roman emperor and Napolcon.

While my personal style was really taking shape, we were still dressing in what felt like ridiculous costumes when we performed. It wasn't until a travel mishap that we began dressing as ourselves onstage. We can thank luggage handlers for our success because they lost all of our bags. We were booked to appear at the bottom of the bill at a gig near San Francisco. I think the headliners were the Beach Boys and the Dave Clark Five. It took Sonny forever to persuade me to fly, insisting that we'd never make it in time otherwise. I reluctantly agreed. As we boarded the plane, I was panicked, but when the crew shut the door I almost blacked out. From then on, Sonny referred to flying with me as "white-knuckling." I was relieved when we landed, but then furious to discover that our luggage wasn't on board. We had nothing but our regular clothes to wear onstage. Stepping into the spotlight in our floral bellbottoms, funky tops, jewelry, and striped pants, we sang "Baby Don't Go" and were surprised at the reaction.

The Northern California kids flipped out when they saw us. I mean, they really lost it. Because of how we dressed, they assumed we were British, and the gig was a big success, which had a knock-on effect on our record sales. From then on, we did away with the cheesy suit and my breakaway skirt and decided to wear our everyday clothes instead.

One day we were driving down La Cienega Boulevard when I spotted an amazing bobcat-fur vest blowing in the breeze outside a sandal store owned by an Armenian leather worker named Andrew Makhokian. "Whoa, Son!" I shrieked. "Stop! Back up!"

"What?" he cried, wondering what was wrong.

"Look at that! Oh, Sonny, I just have to have it."

He parked the car, we ran in, and I tried on the vest. It was too big for me, so I made Sonny try it on. He bought it and wore it for years until he made the mistake of loaning it to Jerry Wexler for a costume party. The two already had bad blood, and after the party Jerry said it was stolen. That vest helped create Sonny's signature look, and I had one made to match, although I never liked mine as much. We also bought a rough-out suede leather bag that was shaped kind of like a banjo, and two hand-tooled leather belts. Son's looked a bit like a Viking belt and mine had a lyre on the buckle with studs across the leather. Nobody was wearing studs then.

After "Baby Don't Go" became a regional hit, Charlie and Brian called the president of Atlantic Records, Ahmet Ertegun, telling him Sonny and I weren't happy at Warner Brothers/Reprise. He then signed us to Atlantic Records, which was a surprise, as it predominantly produced R&B, jazz, and soul records.

Determined to make me a solo star, Sonny signed another deal, this time with Imperial, to release my cover of Bob Dylan's "All I Really Want to Do," the first of many of his songs that I recorded. I was a huge Dylan fan and loved his writing, as did Sonny, although he never thought much of his voice, which was a bit rich coming from him. Our friends the Byrds released their version first, produced by Doris Day's son Terry Melcher, who ran into Sonny one day and told him, only half-jokingly, "I'm gonna bury you." None of us could have foreseen that our corny cover, sung by a "married" couple, would fare better in the charts.

A year or so later we were in a New York recording studio, where Sonny was doing some mixing. Bored, I started playing with a typewriter. There was a warehouse-style elevator in the building, and as I was tapping away, the wooden doors slid open. Out stepped Bob Dylan. I almost fell off my chair. The minute he spotted me, he gave me a big smile and came straight over to tell me, "Cher, I loved your version of 'All I Really Want to Do.'" He was so friendly—but I was so shy I could hardly respond. Of course, when Sonny came out of the studio the two of them talked as if they'd known each other for years. Sonny handed someone his camera (he always had his 35mm with different lenses) and had a photograph taken of us all.

Sonny and I set off on a West Coast tour, and I insisted that he drive us everywhere. I'd inherited my mother's fear of flying. We did many shows in thirty-eight days, and for several of them, I almost didn't make it to the stage because I was so sick with nerves. We sang at venues in Anaheim and Long Beach, then from California we headed to Washington, then Texas, almost always at the bottom of the bill and in some very strange venues.

When sales of our records finally brought in some dough, Sonny found us a beautiful Japanese-style property off Barham Boulevard that was really interesting looking, black and red with shoji greens, and not far from Universal Studios. It was an extravagant gesture on his part, but I loved it there and was so relieved to be on our own again.

Tireless in his pursuit of our dream, he was always moving us on to the next thing, and he never stopped writing songs, even if that meant staying up all night—the time when he was at his most creative. So hyped up that he couldn't sleep, he'd sit at the piano or the kitchen table scribbling away. Sonny wasn't the best piano player in the world, so it was funny to see his technique during one of his marathon songwriting sessions. He would chord with his right hand and just use the index finger of his left. He didn't know that many chords so he wrote all of our songs with the same three or four.

Regardless of his ability and our sad piano, he kept going, and once he was happy with a song he'd rush into the bedroom and shake me. "Hey, Cher, wake up! Come sing this for me." I'd shuffle into the living room rubbing the sleep out of my eyes because I'd just been dead to the world, and he would play me his new song, but without any preparation, I felt shy and embarrassed. "Come on, bud," he'd say, trying to encourage me. "It's okay. It's only you and me." During one session when I was especially reluctant, he got exasperated. "You're being ridiculous, Cher. There's only us here. Now just sing the song!" I did as he asked but barely even registered how it sounded.

One night in early 1965 he woke me up to play another new number he'd written. He had a habit of scrawling lyrics on old shirt cardboard, filling in both the white and brown sides before handing it to me. He had the worst handwriting in the world, so as I squinted at it through sleepy eyes, I tried to make sense of what he'd written. Then I listened to him singing it and, can I tell you, Sonny's voice wasn't amazing in the daytime, so imagine having to listen to it at 2 a.m. *"I got you babe,"* he sang, a little off-key. On first hearing, I wasn't impressed. "I don't like it," I declared, yawning. "I don't think it's a hit." I'd already asked him to add some modulation when he wrote me a song, which made it more exciting and was something Phillip did in some of his tracks. "I don't care what it is, I just want a modulation," I'd insisted.

Two hours later, he shook me awake again. "Cher, Cher, I think I've got it! Come and listen." With one eye open, I listened to the new version and nodded. "That's better." I loved the modulation, and I liked that he used "babe," the term of endearment my mom had passed on to me, but overall I still didn't think much of the song. It wouldn't be the first time I was wrong. When he wanted me to sing it back to him, I told him, "Okay, okay, but then I'm going back to bed."

Within weeks, we recorded "I Got You Babe" at Gold Star and Ahmet stopped by to listen. My mom knew Ahmet from years before and had been telling him every time she saw him, "I have a daughter who sings." Each time Ahmet would dismiss her, saying, "Yes, Georgia, yes, Georgia." Then as I was recording in the studio my mother walked in and Ahmet looked at her and asked her, "What are you doing here?" She told him, "I've been trying to tell you I've got a daughter who sings."

We released "Babe" as a single, and Sonny's friend Sam Riddle promoted it heavily. It was the summer of '65, and our lives were about to change forever. The Beach Boys invited us on tour, and we did gigs with them in Birmingham, San Diego, the Hollywood Bowl, San Jose, and the Cow Palace in Daly City—where we reconnected with the Ronettes (minus Ronnie, whom Phillip had kept with him). Everywhere we went, the teenage audience went wild for our look, rather than our music, which pleased me more than it did Sonny.

Back in LA, we traded up to a house on Hemet Place, one block above Hollywood Boulevard, which had a cathedral ceiling in the living room. I'd never been in the house before, but when I first walked in, I heard myself say, "I used to live here." I had such a strong sense of déjà vu that it was spooky, because I knew the layout of the rooms and felt completely at home. I guess my great-grandmother's psychic powers, passed on to Grandma Lynda, occasionally manifested themselves in me.

We set up the brass bed and the few pieces of furniture we'd acquired, and Sonny hung a large painting of us that a fan had done over the fireplace. He moved his piano into the garage beneath the house to make more room and so as not to disturb me at night. Knowing what a great team we made, we invited Bridget and Colleen to come live in our garage apartment and set up their workshop. Sonny bought them an industrial sewing machine so that they could more easily work the skins and rougher fabrics. I was in my element there. Bridget, Colleen, and I would all design together and Bridget would sew everything. We'd all work down there at once. Colleen would be designing a shirt while Bridget was sewing a pair of pants, and I'd be there with leather strips to lace up handmade moccasins. I started designing paisley and striped outfits for Sonny. For ages, I bought nothing at all off the rack.

We were happy together and we were starting to really make progress, but I was still cutting our hair and making our clothes. If Sonny didn't cook, we'd go to a funky little Italian place right off Hollywood Boulevard that was so small it was like a walk-in hot dog stand, with just a few tables and a counter. It shared a drive-way with a gas station. Sitting in the restaurant, you could see the pumps. Run by two friendly Italians, the joint served pasta, garlic bread, and a glass of wine, all for one dollar and fifty cents.

Almost as good as the food was the entertainment, because the restaurant attracted the weirdest diners, including a magician with a monocle and a painted mustache and a Fortune Teller who'd eat half her meal and leave the rest for her daughter, who came in after her. We left her our wine, as Sonny hardly drank, and I was still underage with no taste for it. Nor did we use drugs, even though marijuana was popular; neither of us was interested.

My experience with narcotics had put me off for life. I'd seen what happened when my biological father set fire to the bed in Vegas on heroin. I never saw anybody who did drugs having a better life. Luckily, the addiction to alcohol and drugs that ran in our family for generations jumped right over my sister and me.

With some money in our pockets and both of us feeling more hopeful than we had in a while, Sonny decided that we needed to ramp up our profile even more. He agreed to a cameo role for us in a low-budget comedy called *Wild on the Beach*. It was a lame project trying to cash in on the success of the beach party films with singers like Frankie Avalon and Annette Funicello. Sonny was convinced his song "It's Gonna Rain," in which he did most of the singing—or rather talking—would cash in too. It didn't.

The film took only a week or so to make, and we were in it for about two minutes. As this was Sonny's first time on a film set, he studied the director, Maury Dexter. With the success of the recent Oscar-nominated Beatles film *A Hard Day's Night*, Sonny wondered if making a movie was something we should think about too.

He also thought back to Mick Jagger's advice that people in Britain would really "dig" us. This was echoed by Jack Good, a British friend of ours who was the producer and creator of *Shindig!*, one of the most popular music shows in the United States at that time. Jack invited us on but took us to the side afterward and told us that he could never get us on as regulars, as the sponsors wouldn't allow it because the older audience couldn't understand what we were. He told us, "You need to sell everything you have and go to England. You're too far ahead for folks here. The Brits will get it. They'll appreciate you and think you're amazing."

Sonny took his words to heart and came home one night to announce, "We're going to London."

"What? How?"

"Charlie and Brian are going to hock the rest of their office equipment to help raise the money for the fare. We'll give up the house, the TV, and sell the cars." I wasn't sure it would be enough. Sonny had returned the Cadillac when he left Gold Star and had since bought a black convertible Mercedes 190SL with a red leather interior, which was beautiful but not worth much. And my beloved MGA was basically worthless after the engine burned out. I put water in the radiator, but nobody ever told me it needed oil too.

To plan our trip, we met Charlie and Brian over lunch and then went back to their office on Sunset and Highland. When we walked in, we found a large man with a big mustache waiting for us in a chair directly facing the door. Charlie and Brian's body language betrayed them because, pale-faced and shaking, they hurried into the office and slammed the door.

The visitor introduced himself as Joe DeCarlo, an associate of Frank Sinatra, Jilly Rizzo, and other prominent Italian Americans. He was also the Las Vegas manager of Louis Prima and Keely Smith, a successful husband and wife who'd toured together as a bandleader and a singer throughout the fifties. When we walked in, the man was scowling with his arms folded, and within minutes he and Sonny were laughing, bonding over their shared Sicilian heritage. Sonny then took "Joe D" into an office and shut the door so that they could talk some more.

Later that night when I asked him about Joe, he told me that Charlie and Brian had borrowed some money from "the wrong people" and Joe had been sent to collect or maybe to break legs. Typical of Sonny's negotiating skills, he'd smoothed things over and persuaded Joe to let them pay back the loan in installments. Sonny also asked for tips from Joe's experience with Louis and Keely, suggesting that if our careers became more successful like theirs, Charlie and Brian could pay him back quicker.

Son was the youngest child of a family of Sicilian immigrants, so he was tough and clever in a difficult situation. He and his family had experienced a lot of racism, as no one in America respected Italians after Mussolini joined forces with Nazi Germany in World War II. He was picked on at school by bigger boys, and he learned to fight back. When I asked him why, he said, "Because I knew that eventually I'd wear them down." That ethos summed up Sonny perfectly because he was successful at everything he tried—eventually. He had his nose broken so many times in fights that his septum was badly deviated and required surgery about five years after I met him. He'd never much liked his nose anyway, so when the doctor said, "Why don't you let me fix that for you while I'm fixing your septum?" he agreed. He loved his new nose. I loved his new nose too.

I liked Joe from the outset. One of his best friends was Jilly Rizzo, Sinatra's right-hand man. Jilly and Joe D also introduced me to Vincent Alo, known as "Jimmy Blue Eyes"—the inspiration for many a movie mobster—in an Italian restaurant in the Valley. Though I sensed these guys had a history, they were always perfect gentlemen, so old-fashioned and polite to the ladies. One night I was in a club with Jilly and Joe D when Jilly leaned over and offered me some advice. "If ever you get involved in a fight, Cher, make sure that there's an ashtray on the table."

"Why?"

"Because if you bash someone hard enough over the head with it then they're pretty much done." I had to laugh. "Good to know, Jilly." Joe DeCarlo may have been a gangster, but I never knew it for sure. Years later when we were on the road together, I'd lie on his bed, and he'd tell me what he called "bedtime stories" about how he'd once been shot in the back by his partner who co-owned a club with him, and later he was acquitted on a charge of trying to murder that partner and dump his body in the Everglades. I never knew how much to believe. All I knew was that I loved him to the day he died. What impressed me more than his wild stories was that Joe had served on a special reconnaissance mission on Iwo Jima in Japan during the Second World War. The others pulled out and left him alone on the island and he had to survive on raw fish because he couldn't risk a fire. He could never stand the smell of fish again, even in a restaurant. Joe was also on board the USS *Missouri* to witness the official Japanese surrender. No matter if he'd been lying or telling the truth, he was a father figure to me.

With a couple of suitcases and wearing clothes we thought were fabulous, Sonny and I, accompanied by my sister, Gee; Charlie; and Brian, flew to London in August 1965. We gave ourselves two weeks to try to make it there. If it didn't work out, we'd fly home, broke and done. For the journey, Sonny dressed like Tom Jones in a shirt with ruffled sleeves and his trademark fur vest. I wore my personally designed salute to the American flag, a pair of red, white, and blue horizontal-striped bell-bottoms in a loose knit material with an industrial zipper and a huge pull ring. Paired with a matching bell-sleeved blouse and red leather Capezio shoes with little heels, that outfit was my pride and joy and is one I still have to this day. My mom secretly kept it and she presented it to me out of the blue a few years back. I could hardly believe it.

Charlie gave me a sleeping pill for the flight so that I wouldn't hyperventilate, but my body has such a low tolerance for drugs that I was still half-asleep by the time we landed. After our fourteen-hour "red-eye," I was a wreck in desperate need of a hot bath and a cooked breakfast.

"Mr. and Mrs. Bono checking in," Sonny told the dapper receptionist at the Hilton hotel, who stared at us over the rim of his spectacles. The man behind the desk looked us up and down as if he had an unpleasant smell under his nose, saving his most withering gaze for Sonny's caveman vest. Giving the register a cursory glance, he replied, "I'm sorry, sir, but we don't have any reservations in that name."

Sonny smiled. "Oh, but I think you're mistaken. I have the confirmation telex."

He shook his head. "No, I'm sorry, sir, our hotel is completely full." And then he walked away.

My partner in crime then leaned over to look at the leather-bound register and found our names entered in ink. With his camera around his neck, he turned the book around and fired off a few frames as proof. "Excuse me!" he called. "Excuse me, sir. There it is, Bono! B-O-N-O. Booked in for two weeks."

The man returned to repeat, "As I explained, Mr. Bono, the hotel is full." He was so dismissive and arrogant, I could have cried. He wasn't even rude to us in a nice way.

By the time we reached the revolving doors, escorted in person by the manager, there were two members of the press standing outside. I couldn't imagine they had anything to do with us because we'd only just arrived. No one in England even knew what Sonny & Cher was. But as we pushed through onto the street, the reporters accosted us.

"Sonny, Cher, did the Hilton just kick you out? Was it because of how you look? What did they say?"

Too exhausted to speak, I let Sonny handle everything. All I wanted to do was get into a tub, then lie down. I kept my sunglasses on to hide my bleary eyes, until Sonny told me to take them off and smile for the photos.

When the journalists had what they wanted, he made a few calls and hailed a couple of taxis to take us to another hotel. I can't remember where now, but it was prewar and not very nice. Our bed was lumpy, there was no TV, and water trickled out of the shower. We slept for twelve hours straight.

Cranky and fearing that we'd wasted our money by coming, we had no gigs lined up and no clue how to begin, but by the time we'd bathed and dressed, we were famous. Photos of us being kicked out of the Hilton were on the cover of the evening newspapers, and the telephone started ringing off the hook. It was crazy-ass crazy. Everyone wanted first crack at us for interviews and for us to appear on their TV and radio shows. It was madness. I guess nobody else looked quite like us and people were fascinated. People said later that Charlie and Brian had arranged the whole Hilton fiasco to get publicity for our arrival, but I don't think that's true. The man at the desk looked at us as if we were dirt under his fingernails, and I doubt he was that good an actor. Whether it was genuine or not, boy, did it work. The hotel even invited us back to apologize and hosted a press conference and photo-call for us there a week later. Our managers then spread a separate rumor that a Saudi prince had asked Sonny if I was for sale at the Playboy Club, and that one did the rounds for years.

The odd little song that Sonny had scribbled onto shirt cardboard soared to the top of the British charts and remained there for two weeks. Our previous songs quickly followed suit. Within days we were singing "I Got You Babe" on the TV shows *Top of the Pops* and *Ready Steady Go!* and posing for what felt like hundreds of photos in the clothes we wore every day, all of which seemed to blow people's minds. The difference in London was that not one person called us freaks and everyone seemed to accept us as merely quirky. Soon, we'd have people running up and wanting to touch us. There was one lovely moment when we went to buy Sonny some cigarettes in a tobacco shop and a sweet old lady pulled out a notebook and asked me to sign it. That was so touching, and I happily signed the first British autograph of my career, with the same *Love, Cher* that I'd been practicing since I was eleven.

Some of my happiest days ever with Sonny were on that first trip to London. We never stopped laughing as we shopped and went to clubs, met the most incredible people, and found ourselves the center of attention everywhere we went. This was how I'd imagined fame to be, only better. Sonny and I had both always wanted to be singers. We had been moving one foot in front of the other doing what we had to do to get here. We were grateful for each other and everything that had happened to bring us here. I could have ended up as a struggling actress or a waitress in a diner like my mom and grandmother before me, and Sonny could have ended up hauling beef or as a song promoter. Sonny told journalists, "Up until I met Cher there was a piece missing and she was the missing piece."

We never stopped working. I kind of didn't know where I was sometimes. The food was not great, but the trip was more than we ever hoped for. So much happened in such a short span of time that much of our British experience became a blur. I was totally exhausted as we went from talk show to talk show, then to music shows, then to press interviews. We did everything, and everyone was so friendly, but the farther north we got, the stronger the accents became and the less I understood what people were saying. Finally, I just smiled and said yes. It was intense and fun. It felt a bit like being on a giant Ferris wheel, seeing only snatches of things as we sailed by. I saw fleeting glimpses of some famous sights, such as Piccadilly Circus and Buckingham Palace, though we were so busy we never had time to linger. Gee was having the time of her life, too, but later, the crowds became hard to deal with. Maybe I could have handled them if I'd been able to have a rest, but everything was absolutely nonstop. The most chaotic appearances were at record stores because the kids who had lined up for hours went wild when we arrived and there was never enough security to keep them back. We'd never had fans like that before. We were pushing through screaming throngs of teenagers who all wanted to be close to us. I wasn't used to that kind of adulation. I'd only seen it with people like the Stones or people who were "famous," and I didn't see myself that way. We'd only been there for two weeks.

At night, the kids melted away and we were taken to some of the hottest London venues, like the newly opened Scotch of St. James and the Ad Lib Club. Just a few weeks earlier, we wouldn't have been allowed within a mile of these exclusive venues, but now we found ourselves in with the in crowd. The Rolling Stones introduced us to the Small Faces, four crazy kids we met on *Ready Steady Go!*, and to Rod Stewart, who was in a band supporting the Stones. I was mad for Sandie Shaw, whose love of being barefoot matched mine, and Dusty Springfield, who was stunning. We also met John Lennon and Paul McCartney. Looking around at all those famous people, I joked that if someone set off a bomb it would have been the end of music.

The highlight of London for me was the shopping. Ever since Phillip Spector had returned from England with such unusual clothes, I'd wanted to go. With appearance after appearance—we achieved a record for being on the most TV shows in one week—we constantly needed new things to wear. Sonny must have received an advance from the record company because he gave me some cash and told me to go have fun. I never had my own checking account or wrote a check myself in all the years we were together. I didn't even know the name of our bank. It wasn't that he forbade me to do these things, but I never thought to ask as I'd never bought big-ticket items before. I was also nervous to write anything in front of anybody because of my word blindness.

Together, we went to the famous Anello & Davide dance and footwear store on Drury Lane, where John, Paul, George, and Ringo had their bespoke "Beatle boots" made. I bought a pair in black and a pair in white and sometimes wore one in each color. Then we headed to Carnaby Street and some psychedelic boutiques on the King's Road in Chelsea, where Phillip had bought some of his best outfits. Gee bought some amazing purple paisley bell-bottoms with white laces, and I picked up a green corduroy jacket and some cool stovepipes, along with a double-breasted rabbit-fur coat that cost me thirty-five pounds and made me so happy that I skipped out of the store wearing it.

Thanks to an Indian model Brian hooked up with, I also discovered a newly opened boutique called Biba on Abingdon Road, Kensington. When I first walked into it, I stepped over the sign that hadn't been hung yet; they were still setting up and there were clothes lying on the floor, but I didn't care and wanted to buy everything. The clothes spoke to me: they were chic and unusual with mixed bohemian and modern styles, industrial zippers, and pants that were between bell-bottoms and straight with a tiny flare. Casting aside my hippie persona, I chose a plastic pantsuit in taxicab yellow and some zipped linen suits with tunic tops. By the time we left England, we spotted many of our young fans walking around in their own versions of our clothes, which we loved.

We'd have gladly stayed—despite the food—but news of our success had hit the United States and we found ourselves number one in both countries. Incredibly, we even knocked the Beatles' single "Help!" off the top UK slot as "I Got You Babe" sold a million copies within two weeks and was certified gold. That sentimental little tune Sonny had played to me in the dead of night and that I'd told him I didn't think was a hit was loved the world over by people with whom it resonated somehow and found its lyrics tender and sweet. Unbeknownst to me, I'd be singing it to audiences for the next fifty years.

A week of media appearances was arranged for us in New York and our flights were booked. Hilariously, when the British producers found out that they couldn't get us onto *Ready Steady Go!* for the second time, they came up with the idea of having the Rolling Stones and the singer Cathy McGowan do a spoof of us, lip-syncing "Babe." I wish we could have hung around to see that. Cleverly, the record companies quickly rereleased our earlier singles and they became instant hits too. We had five songs in the top twenty, which only Elvis Presley and the Beatles had done before. It was like a dream. Cher and Sonny went into this trip with nobody knowing who we were and we came out with everybody in the world knowing "Sonny & Cher."

Hearing "Babe" today still reminds me of that time. It felt like my song because my mom and I called everybody babe, which is why Sonny wrote what became our anthem. As Sonny always said, something came together, and that song about our love for each other represents the realization of a dream, thanks to our British fans. Waving goodbye, we climbed into a Boeing to fly back to America. After reassuring a nervous Gee that the airplane was perfectly safe and wouldn't crash, I secretly accepted another pill for my nerves and told Sonny to wake me when we landed—and take me straight out for a burger.

# 12

## i got you babe

A rriving at the recently renamed John F. Kennedy Airport in New York was surreal. We stepped off the plane to five thousand screaming teenagers holding up banners and rushing toward us as we entered the arrivals hall. I nearly turned tail and ran.

The police and fire crew helped us to our waiting limousine, but the fans still almost ripped off the door. Some thought we were one of the so-called British Invasion bands that had started with the Beatles and now included acts like the Kinks, Herman's Hermits, Gerry and the Pacemakers, and Peter and Gordon. Everything British was suddenly the hippest thing going on in America, so it was funny that we were American and had to go to Britain to get famous first. Having escaped from the crowds, we were driven to the Hampshire House Hotel south of Central Park, which became our Manhattan base. It was good to be back in New York and it felt so different from when I'd lived there with Mom, Gee, and Gilbert. No longer a crazy teenager who didn't have a clue what I was going to do with my life, I was now the "someone" I'd always wanted to be.

Sonny and I went into Atlantic Records to record some new tracks. Ahmet Ertegun welcomed us home and then invited us to one of his legendary parties, this time at his beautiful brownstone on the Upper East Side. We were introduced to all kinds of cool people who we didn't know. Everybody was excited to meet us now that we were so famous. We met the rich, famous, and titled. I even met Andy Warhol, who seemed nice but didn't say a thing. And I came face-to-face with Baby Jane Holzer, the socialite and model who spoke in such a baby voice it made me laugh.

Ahmet's wife, Mica, was one of the loveliest people I ever met. Romanian with skin like porcelain, she had a fabulously posh accent. I adored her. She had fled her homeland after the Russian occupation and made her name in America as an interior designer. In her thirties, Mica was a tad naïve, so when she accidentally walked in on Otis Redding and a few musicians smoking a joint, she told her husband, "Ahmet, you're not paying these people enough. They're so poor they have to share the same cigarette!"

At the last of the Ertegun parties we attended in some palatial venue before we flew home, Mica wore a stunning *Dr. Zhivago*-style coat in brown fur with leather toggles, and I gasped. "Oh, Mica, that's the most beautiful coat I have ever seen!" I declared. From the party we went straight to the airport to catch our flight back west, and when we opened the trunk of our limo, her coat was there, a gift for me. These days, I'd rather die than wear fur, but in the sixties I didn't know better, and I loved her for it.

When Sonny and I had flown out of LAX a few weeks earlier, we'd been so broke that we'd had to hock or sell pretty much all we owned. By the time we flew back, we were rich—at least on paper. We were talking the whole flight back about what we were going to do. Charlie and Brian were saying they were going to walk into a Cadillac dealership with a bag full of money and wait for a dealer to come up to them thinking they were bums so then they could dump out the bag of money right there and buy the new car all in cash.

Of course, nobody handed us wads of cash and we were put straight back to work finishing the final tracks for *Look at Us*. With our sudden rise in popularity, we needed to pull together the rest of the album because people were clamoring for it. Sonny hired many of the musicians we knew from Gold Star and recorded covers like "Unchained Melody" and "Then He Kissed Me." The rest were existing recordings. There was also an old Ma Rainey number called "See See Rider" with one line adapted about going to the Hilton and not getting in. The new album sailed into the charts, as did *All I Really Want to Do*, my first solo album of covers for Imperial. Our star was burning bright, but everything was happening so fast that we were dazzled by it and couldn't even see our own reflection.

Such was the public interest in us that Freddy Apollo, from the venerable William Morris Agency, agreed to represent us, even though he had serious misgivings about our look. Freddy was a pistol and the brother-in-law of Jerry Ridgeway, who was appointed our new tour manager. The "suit people," as we called them, told us that being married was a big part of our appeal. They were horrified when they found out that we weren't and soon afterward issued a press release that claimed we'd tied the knot in Tijuana, Mexico, in October 1964, almost a year to the day after Sonny's divorce. We didn't create the lie, but that one also stuck for years. They also advised us to change our wacky look, warning that it would soon become dated, but—knowing that taking this kind of advice hadn't helped us in the past—we ignored them. Ironically,

Freddy Apollo would much later get into drugs, especially acid. He'd grow his hair out long and start wearing the wildest clothes with beads and fringe, becoming crazier than we ever were. That happened to a lot of those guys.

We were invited onto NBC's *Hullabaloo* music show, hosted by Sammy Davis Jr., appearing along with the Supremes and the Lovin' Spoonful. We sang "Babe" and the Stones' "(I Can't Get No) Satisfaction," and as a closing number we joined forces with Sammy, bizarrely, to sing the Herman's Hermits hit "I'm Henry VIII, I Am." Sammy was a great, fun guy and an exceptional talent. He and Sonny became friends and shared a passion for photography, chatting about cameras for hours. A couple of weeks later we had what still ranks as one of the most exciting invitations of our lives when we were asked to appear on CBS's *The Ed Sullivan Show*, the biggest show in America watched by as many as seventy million people and, more importantly, where I'd first seen Elvis. Also the Beatles, but Elvis was the man. To be following in those footsteps wasn't something we had ever thought possible. It was proof not only that we'd "arrived," but that we were popular enough that the show's all-important viewing figures would soar. That didn't stop me—and even Sonny—from shaking in our boots.

When we arrived for rehearsals and spotted Ed Sullivan, I was so excited to meet him but also anxious because I knew how powerful he was. We'd been warned that one acerbic comment from him on national television could bury us because everyone trusted him and he was so famous, he was like George Washington. Unexpectedly, he didn't even come near us. He just stood to one side with his arms crossed and watched us rehearse. All he knew was that our being on his show would bring in younger viewers. I wore my new kelly-green corduroy peacoat and pants with my Beatle boots. Sonny wore taupe pants with a red-and-blue-striped T-shirt and his bobcat vest. Once the cameras started rolling, I went into a sort of altered state, but our host sprang to life and gave us a glowing introduction, calling us "two fine youngsters" and "the current sensations of the recording field." Having (incorrectly) claimed that we'd both graduated from California high schools, Mr. Sullivan added, "Within the past three months they have amazed everyone in show business by getting five hit records in the top fifty in addition to two albums, which is just incredible." And then he spoiled it all by saying, "Give a big hand to Sonny and *Chur!*"

Despite being thrown by Ed Sullivan's mangling of my name on national television, we opened with "I Got You Babe," then I sang Sonny's song "Where Do You Go" as he leaned against my shoulder. Our last number was another of his compositions, this one called "But You're Mine," with lyrics that stated he wasn't pretty but belonged to me. I never questioned why we sang unknown songs on a prime-time show, as it might have made more sense to sing "Baby Don't Go" and "All I Really Want to Do," but with hindsight I realized Sonny was showcasing himself as a songwriter and trying to promote our new material. It would have helped our songs so much more to do the ones that were hits, and we could have sold so many more albums and records. I mean we were playing to seventy million people. It was dumb to do that. Almost as quickly as our time in Sullivan's spotlight began, it was over. We were wheeled in, wheeled off with another parting reference to Sonny and "Chur," and sent home.

Back in LA we'd given up our house, so we moved back in with my mother for a time while we looked for a place to live. Someone smart advised us to buy, not rent, which would be a first for us both. When we heard that a show home was being sold on the estate where Mom and Gilbert had lived in Encino, we decided to go look. The estate was built by Marvin Wilson, whose brother Ronnie was an interior designer Gilbert had hired once to decorate the family room for my mom's birthday.

When we viewed the $75,000 single-story property at Academia Drive, we bought it on sight. It had what felt to us then like a huge living room, a massive bathroom, the most gigantic closets, and a swimming pool with a view over the Valley. We liked what Ronnie had done inside and purchased all the furniture, too. It wasn't quite the house of my childhood dreams. I would have rather been in Los Angeles—I never lost that. Still, I was pretty excited about it, and since it was our first proper home together, I wasn't going to look a gift horse in the mouth. I adored Ronnie, who was in his twenties, and he and I turned out to have a meeting of minds. I had no idea he was gay; all I knew was that he was fabulous and drove the most amazing metallic-blue Corvette. I wanted one just like it. It is not surprising that he went on to become the interior designer to the stars and decorate nineteen homes for me over six decades.

My mother and Gee were moving too, as Gilbert's alimony was dwindling. Sonny assured me that we were helping them financially, and they found a rental on Balboa Boulevard, a few blocks from us. I know we went to the house at least a few times, but I don't remember what it looked like, I was working so much then. I was either working too much or resting up, but it seemed like a nice enough house. Later I started wondering if we actually were taking care of them right. I never knew how much Sonny gave them.

Our lives were so insane during this period. Still a teenager, I had Sonny, a beautiful new house, and money to spend. I was so insecure about becoming poor again that I started buying two of a few key household items in case we needed to replace things that had worn out. There was no logic to owning two electric frying pans or two hair dryers—I'd have been a broke housewife with great hair—but it made me feel better because since childhood I'd been accustomed to losing what I had or being forced to trade down to a worse situation. I think it went back to the incident when my shoe had to be held together with rubber bands. Sonny didn't ever seem to fear being poor again and treated himself to a dirt bike because the many paths cut into the hillside around our neighborhood were perfect for riding.

Despite having everything we wanted, Sonny and I never seemed to enjoy the fruits of our labors in the same way that our peers did. We could only do what he wanted to do. We didn't go out to dinner or to movies anymore, and he didn't want me to see my old friends or go anywhere without him except shopping. Nor did we go on vacation unless it was a day or two tagged on to the end of a gig. If I complained, he'd look at me like a disapproving father and tell me, "This is our time, Cher," which I understood. We'd both been poor before, and Sonny knew better than I did that fame can be fleeting. I'd just never expected the pace to be so relentless.

Trying to capitalize on our popularity while we had it, Sonny continued to add more to our already overloaded schedule. He worked us constantly with hardly a moment between gigs, recording sessions, and interviews. We also made appearances on TV shows, like the one hosted by Danny Thomas, *Shindig!*, and *Hollywood Palace*, hosted by Milton Berle, the comic I'd enjoyed watching on Mamaw and Pa's first television. I liked being on these shows—and especially working with "Uncle Miltie," who was hilariously dressed up in a bobcat vest and wig pretending to be our child, "Sonny Junior"—but I couldn't help but feel that the television industry thought of us as just a novelty act. And it was tough that Sonny gave us more to do in a day than could comfortably be done. He loved doing live shows, which I liked but made me nervous beforehand, and he was so driven that he didn't appreciate how easily I tired or how my virus came back with a vengeance whenever I was overworked. When I visited my doctor one day, he was surprised that I didn't have the scar everyone had on their arm from their childhood vaccinations, but I probably was moving from one school to the next at the time that they were administered. He gave me my missing shot and it got infected, making me dangerously ill.

Weak, I'd beg Sonny for some time off so that I could rest. "It's too much," I'd tell him, but there was always another item to be checked off the list.

Being famous was rough but it was fun. I loved not having to worry so much about money and spending so much time with the man I loved.

The icing on the cake for me came when I was asked to design a fashion line of Sonny & Cher clothing for Gordon & Marx of California. I was ecstatic. This was beyond any childhood dream. Everything in the collection I put together was a copy of the things Sonny and I wore, including unisex faux-fur vests, sleeveless tops, and elephant bells. Our line sold out so quickly that the company couldn't keep up with demand. There were no dresses and none of the new miniskirts that were all the rage, because Sonny wouldn't let me wear them. I guess he thought they'd sexualize me too much and compromise our image or attract the attentions of other men. In a strange way, his jealousy flattered me. It sounds crazy now— jealousy doesn't mean love—but it didn't feel that crazy at the time. I remember when I finally got to wear a miniskirt. Twiggy was coming over and I really wanted to wear a dress to meet her. I got this little golden colored minidress, cotton brocade, very short with shoes to match. To appease Sonny, I wore something underneath that was almost like a pair of bloomers but not quite. They were my own thing, just something slightly longer to put on under the dress so that I could pass the outfit by him but also still look cool.

Having discovered our address from a magazine article Sonny arranged, teenagers would turn up at the gates to our Encino house eager for a glimpse of us. We also had an "S" and a "C" on the gate. Before the article it didn't seem like a big deal, just something fun, but then after, we'd see kids coming up to our gate that was so clearly labeled. Loving the attention, Sonny would invite random fans in to talk and tell us what was troubling them, so I never knew who was going to turn up next. He also signed me up to pen a

"Dear Cher" column for *Teen Beat* magazine. I started by reading the letters and responding myself, but I got so busy that the magazine had one of their staff do it, which is a shame because I'm sure the responses about acne or boyfriend trouble would have been much more authentic if I'd written them from my own nineteen-year-old perspective. Regardless, every young girl I met seemed to want to tell me her problems, something I hadn't counted on at all. I'd wanted to be famous, I really had, but when it happened, it was a lot more of a responsibility than I imagined.

One girl named Joey, who was seventeen and still in high school, became a regular visitor with our English friend Ray. I would later learn that she was the younger sister of the woman who'd owned our apartment building on Franklin (and I had once asked her what kind of mascara she wore that didn't run in the pool). She also looked a lot like me. One day she came alone and seemed surprised that I was there, telling me she was expecting to meet Sonny and Ray there. It never occurred to me that there might be something strange about that. Instead, I told her, "Well, I'm going shopping if you want to come." She jumped at the chance, so I took her in my beautiful new Excalibur to Paraphernalia on Rodeo Drive, where we had a blast trying on wacky vinyl outfits in primary colors that were cleaned by spraying them with Windex. After that first shopping trip, she started hanging out with us all the time, which I loved. She and I got along so well and called each other Betty. We still do today.

The only time Sonny allowed me out of the house on my own was to go shopping. I guess he thought retail therapy made the hard work feel worthwhile. I loved being out on my own and would go whenever I got the chance. During one of these outings, I was walking near Rodeo Drive when I spotted in a shop window an amazing pantsuit with a psychedelic check pattern and a big red stripe down the front. Walking in, I said to the sales assistant, "Oh my God, I love that! Where does it come from?"

She took one look at me, said, "It's very expensive, miss," and turned and walked away.

I followed her and asked politely, "But who's the designer?"

With a sigh she replied, "Rudi Gernreich."

"Could I try it on?"

The sales assistant gave me a thin smile. "Miss, as I have already explained to you, that item is *very* expensive." She was so dismissive of me in my little crop top and bell-bottom pants that I lost patience.

"How many colors does it come in?" I asked.

Looking at me askance, she replied, "Three."

"Great. I'll take one in every shade."

"Oh . . . I see." I watched her expression shift. "Well, do you want to try them on?"

"No. I'll just take them," I replied, pulling out my credit card and slapping it on the counter. The bill was more than I ever thought anyone could pay for anything, but it was worth it to see the look on that bitch's face. As soon as I left the store I broke into tears. I called Sonny. "I did something terrible," I sobbed. "I spent so much money!"

When I told him the whole story, he said, "It doesn't matter. It won't make any difference. Come home." Relieved, I made my way back.

Sonny was a homebody, but he'd occasionally take me to nightclubs, never to dance, but to meet people in the industry and catch up on the latest trends in recording studios. I was often too tired to stay out late, and I didn't see the point if I wasn't allowed to dance or talk to anyone without him. He told me that anything a couple couldn't do together wasn't worth doing. I wasn't even allowed to wear perfume because he didn't like the smell. That was disappointing because I loved perfume, but I still didn't realize that I was slowly having to give up a lot of myself. He wouldn't even let me listen to music. Meanwhile, Sonny gave up nothing. Truthfully, I don't think I ever met a person before or since who was as private as Sonny. He hid so much of himself, and after the beginning of our relationship, he never asked much about me either. At the start of our time together, he asked me lots of questions, shared a lot about himself, and seemed to relish getting to know me as a person, but that tapered off. The changes in how he treated me came very slowly, so I didn't even notice. It was very Machiavellian (an author Sonny loved).

I'm not even sure there was a lot to ask about me, to be honest, because I was becoming more and more a shadow. Only when we worked was I the person in front. I was becoming less and less of an interesting person to Sonny, even though I was interesting and funny to everybody else. The thing he liked about me in the beginning was me being this salty waif, which wasn't what he wanted in a wife.

At the end of 1965 we went back to the East Coast. We stopped in New York for some time in the studio and it was there that we received the strangest invitation of our careers. There was to be a swanky New York society soirée where Jacqueline Kennedy would be the guest of honor. Her hosts were the millionaire Charles Engelhard and his wife, Jane, and when they asked who the former first lady might like to invite, she shocked them by replying, "I'd really like it if Sonny and Cher would come and perform." The invitation was passed to us through our agent, who accepted on our behalf. That's how the most unlikely couple in the history of the world was allowed into the hallowed sanctum of one of the largest private apartments in the exclusive Waldorf Astoria Towers. We were permitted one rehearsal with our four-member band in the afternoon. Then we worked out which songs to sing and how to set the volume for the space. We'd never played a house before and were accustomed to arenas, not long living rooms with low ceilings. I'd never seen so many silver plaques, coffee sets, and ornaments. *Why do they have so much silver stuff lying around?* I wondered, although I later discovered that our host was the heir to a platinum fortune and the items I was ogling were platinum and worth a fortune. Not that this meant anything to me, as I didn't much like them.

When we returned later that evening, the twenty or so invited guests were milling around sipping champagne in black tie and satin gowns. They were the crème de la crème of Manhattan society. We arrived up the back elevator and went into the living room to set up. Everyone else was far away in the dining room. We weren't invited to the dinner. I was far too nervous about meeting the widow of JFK to eat, so I couldn't have cared less. Sonny dressed in his trademark vest, but I'd gone to Bendel's and bought myself a beautiful French green velvet military-style jacket and matching pants, which I wore with my black Anello & Davide Beatle boots. I looked like a little soldier. I'd cut my fingernails into squares rather than ovals, which nobody else was doing back then, and my hair was shaped into a point at the back like I'd seen in a magazine. There was a time when I'd cut my bangs to a point too.

Once the dinner plates were cleared, we made our way to the far end of that silvery salon to sing a few of our bestselling numbers before the guests were served dessert. I'm sure it was a surprise to everyone, but they clapped politely. When our set was over, the staff started to hustle us out the door, but Jackie asked, "But, wait, where are Sonny and Cher? I wanted to talk to them over dessert." So, the staff raced after us and brought us back in.

Shortly afterward, all the men adjourned to smoke cigars, and the women in the room stood up as one and walked out. Nothing was said, and with herd instinct, I followed. The ladies gathered in a mammoth bedroom with an en suite bathroom, where everyone settled down to gossip while they tended to their hair or makeup before dessert. A strange-looking woman with dyed black hair and an enormous string of pearls marched up to me, lifted my chin in her bony hand, and said, in a masculine voice that seemed accustomed to giving orders, "My dear, you have a pointed head. You are beautiful." I couldn't think how to respond, although in my mind I was thinking, *My head isn't pointed. It's just not flat.* Fascinated by the grand woman with massive earrings standing in front of me, I looked around and saw that no one else seemed to notice how odd this wild old broad was, and I wondered why.

"And you're so skinny!" she added, sucking in lips coated in lipstick under an enormous nose. "Why aren't you a model? Richard must see you! You'll love him—he's divine." I had no idea who Richard was and assumed he was at the party, but this odd woman remained where she was, running her eyes up and down my 102-pound frame. I felt like a butterfly pinned to a board. Once she'd seen enough, she flipped open a beautiful compact that looked like something Catherine the Great might have owned and held it up high, her head thrown back, to apply more red lipstick on a face that was heavily powdered in white. I was mesmerized.

At nineteen I was the youngest by far. I settled on the edge of the bed with my hands clamped between my knees, unsure of what to say or do. Jackie Kennedy, who was thirty-six, sat down next to me with such an elegant bearing that she reminded me of my mom. Tongue-tied, all I could think to ask was, "How are Caroline and John Junior?" recalling how brave her children had been at their father's funeral just two years earlier.

"They are very well, thank you," she replied in that breathy, almost transatlantic accent. "'I Got You Babe' is one of our favorite songs, and the children love to sing along." She was so sweet and kind. When we went back into the dining room, Jackie sat us immediately to her left and was great at putting us at ease. Sonny gave her something for the children, two little Catholic saint medals, which as a woman of faith she appreciated. She told him that he looked "almost Shakespearean" with his pageboy haircut, and from that moment on he was like putty in her hands. Well, I think he was putty before, but that only helped.

As if the week weren't memorable enough, I received an invitation to be photographed for *Vogue* the next day, and I almost fell off my chair. The supermodels of the day were women like Anne St. Marie, Linda Morand, Benedetta Barzini, and Jean Shrimpton. But the androgenous teenage British model Twiggy had also come to the fore, making pencil-thin girls like me fashionable. I later discovered that the invitation to appear in *Vogue* came from Diana Vreeland, the editor of the magazine and one of the most powerful women in fashion. This industry legend was the lady who'd admired my pointed head at the party. With a striking appearance herself, she was an innovator and a champion of those who were unusual looking or showed character—women like Penelope Tree, Veruschka, and Anjelica Huston. Diana had the nerve and foresight to see that we were the new women, even though we weren't beautiful in the traditional sense at all. I'd been waiting for Diana my whole life.

The mysterious "Richard" to whom she'd referred at the party turned out to be Richard Avedon, the forty-two-year-old superstar photographer. He was adorable. I had an immediate crush on him. Richard was not very tall and was quite thin, with sunken cheeks in a beautiful face. His clothes were plain but super chic and he always shot in his slippers. He had lots of beautiful hair and wore his glasses on top of his head until he was ready to shoot; then, with the slightest nod, he'd drop them to the bridge of his nose without them ever falling off. He'd wait patiently until I was zipped or sewn into the newest outfit while Ara Gallant, an eccentric makeup man and hair designer, supervised. Once the hairdresser Suga had done something amazing with my hair, I'd be brought forward into the lights, where I'd wait stiffly for instructions.

My childhood fantasies were coming true, but I was skittish and so utterly clueless that at first, I remained like a statue. I was accustomed to Sonny having his camera in my face, but Richard was a stranger. After a while, though, I forgot about everyone in the room except the man behind the lens, who was so great at making me relax. During my first photoshoot he shot only two setups of me, one of my naked back with my face shadowed in profile and one closeup of my squared-off painted fingernails. I didn't want that first session to end. Diana wandered into the studio with a cigarette and declared, "Oh, Richard, I told you she was divine. Isn't she the most beautiful creature you've ever seen? *J'aaadoore!*" The experience was mine and mine alone. I felt completely free.

I would go on to shoot with Richard numerous times, contributing countless pages for *Vogue*. He would get me posing and dancing, even jumping for him. He loved to capture his models in midair. "Yes, Cher!" he'd cry enthusiastically. "This is so amazing! Beautiful. Jump higher!" A few years later, Richard would be assigned to shoot a two-photo spread of me and it should have taken a day. But our one-day shoot ended up lasting several days, and the magazine published twenty photos of me over ten pages. The headline was "SHE DARED: Fashion to Enjoy. The Price Is Right. The Girl Is Cher." They put me in outfits costing less than a hundred dollars, which they scrunched up and accessorized with expensive jewelry and shoes to make them look far better than they should have, although Richard assured me that I looked good in everything.

Richard and his stylists made me feel truly beautiful for the first time in my life. Nobody else could have persuaded me to pose virtually naked in a backless dress, despite fearing what Sonny might say. I knew he was coming back to pick me up and would want to look at the Polaroids. I was nervous because I was certain he'd flip out when he saw my backless pictures. Although I was seated in the shots, it was clear that I was naked beneath the fabric I was holding to cover my breasts. "I don't know how I got talked into this," I told Diana and Richard. "Sonny's going to kill me when he sees these."

That's when Diana Vreeland showed me what she was really

made of, because when Sonny arrived, she moved in on him like a pro and with the kind of charm I'd only previously seen in Warren Beatty. Cornering him and gushing about me, she told him how amazing the photographs were—"like a piece of art"—with my hair going to a point, and said that no one had a back like mine, and reminded him that *Vogue* was the most prestigious magazine in the world. She completely won him over before he'd seen a single shot.

When the shoot wrapped, I shyly asked Richard if he thought I might ever appear on a *Vogue* cover, and he smiled and shook his head. "You can have blonde hair and brown eyes or dark hair and blue eyes but you can't have dark hair and dark eyes. You'll never be on the cover." When I did make it onto the cover for the first time six years later, he was one of the first to congratulate me.

Meanwhile back in Los Angeles, Princess Margaret, the queen of England's sister, had flown in for a series of charitable events with her husband, the photographer Lord Snowdon. Having read all about us in the English press, the princess invited us to perform at the Hollywood Palladium. This came as a surprise because the old guard either had no idea who we were or thought we were freaks. It boggled the imagination how much that wasn't our audience. The best that could happen is we'd live through it. We did not want to accept, but we couldn't say no to Princess Margaret. I think we were wearing white outfits but we should have been wearing camouflage. The whole event was a fiasco. It started late, the princess had laryngitis, and Frank Sinatra dropped out at the last minute so Bob Hope introduced us instead. There was no stage, so we stood on the dance floor. The acoustics were so bad that, coupled with sound problems, we performed terribly. Peter Bogdanovich, a man I would later truly dislike for a myriad of reasons, was then a critic for the *Saturday Evening Post* and claimed that we howled like a pair of coyotes. The audience must have agreed because very few people applauded, and halfway through our set Princess Margaret asked for the sound to be turned down because she had a headache. The engineer then accidentally cut the mic and interfered with what we could hear, which threw Sonny completely. He got angry, I was mortified, and we couldn't wait to get off. It was like a bad dream that we couldn't get out of; we just had to stand there and wait for it to be over.

Peter Bogdanovich did more than just attend the concert; he moved in with us for three days to write a six-page profile to be published in April. The title of the article was "They're What's Happening, Baby." I never liked doing interviews because I didn't know what to say, so I let Sonny do all the talking and usually only spoke when I was spoken to. Hoping to get me on my own, Peter asked to go shopping with me for extra color, a trip that got me into so much trouble. Wandering through Century City, we came across someone who was physically debilitated, and I got really quiet. When he asked what was wrong, I said something about how sad that made me. He misunderstood my reaction and made it sound like I was grossed out by what I'd seen, which was the exact opposite of what I'd said. That's not who I was; it was more who he was. He also quoted me as saying that I sometimes felt like punching my mother (I thought every daughter secretly did) and he also printed our full address so that even more fans could come calling. The whole thing felt like a betrayal.

After Sonny read the finished article, he lost his mind. Mad as hell, he declared, "No more interviews for you!" It was meant to be a threat but felt to me like a promise, and I thought, *Thank God!* I was more than happy to step back and become Sonny's shadow.

In January 1966 we were invited to headline at the legendary Hollywood Bowl, a venue we'd only played at the bottom of the bill. To be at the top this time, with the Righteous Brothers, Jan and Dean, and the Mamas & the Papas supporting us, was a thrill; it was even more thrilling when tickets sold out in twenty-four hours. For the gig I wore my yellow plastic trouser suit with my white Beatle boots and felt like a million dollars.

Of course we would end our set with "I Got You Babe." I was loving playing concerts, but this closing number made me nervous because our fans would almost always rush the stage. Sure enough, the moment the first few chords were struck at the Hollywood Bowl, the kids pressed forward, with several of them making it up onto the stage even though they had to wade through a pool of water to get to us. I grabbed the mic and told them: "Hey, hey! Stay cool, okay? If you all come up here, then we can't sing any more songs." To my astonishment, it worked.

Grampa Roy was visiting my mother from Oklahoma at the time of our headline gig, so I arranged complimentary tickets for him, Mom, and Gee. My mother was so excited and so proud. That was a very happy night for her and poignant for my grandfather, the man my mom and I got our voices from. That night, watching me onstage as the crowd went wild, Grampa Roy almost choked on his tears. He leaned into my beaming mother and told her, "That's you up on that stage, Jackie Jean. It's you!"

At another concert in San Francisco, the crowd got so whipped up with excitement as we were onstage that they broke free and stormed us. One girl started grabbing at Sonny's moccasins and he had to hop backward to keep her away from it. He had all his money in that moccasin because he said nobody would think to rob you there. This girl was pulling on it and he kept hopping backward. I was thinking, *Oh shit.* The people all around us from our group were laughing their assess off at how he was dancing backward to avoid her. She got one of the shoes but not the one with the money.

Almost knocked over in the rush, I looked up to see girls in bell-bottoms with their hair dyed black to look like mine bearing down on me, hands outstretched. I kicked free and ran like hell backstage, where a security guard mistook me for a fan and put me in a headlock that almost choked me to death. He was gripping me so hard that I couldn't even cry out for help, then slammed me against a wall, knocking the air clean out of me. Finally, our managers spotted what was happening and jumped on the guard to get him to let me go.

Afterward, my mascara streaking down my face, I told Sonny, "That's it. I'm not doing this anymore!" It took all his powers of persuasion to convince me that it wouldn't happen again, that we just had to give it one more year.

As a way of making me feel better, Sonny took me to the seaside town of Sausalito for the day. I'd always wanted to go to that pretty town right on the water, and we had one of the best days of our lives there. It was foggy and atmospheric with little artisan stores. We ate pizza in a pizza parlor and literally skipped up and down the street together, making waves in the fog like a couple of kids. It was one of those perfect, carefree days, and it was so nice to take a break.

It was shocking to see the impact our music and style were starting to have. Girls were buying our clothes and wearing Cleopatra-style eyeliner. Some even started ironing their hair flat to look like mine, and boys began to dress like Sonny in furry vests. I never imagined we'd wield that sort of influence. It was surprising but cool.

I had only ever witnessed that kind of adulation we seemed to be getting on one occasion, sometime before we were famous, when we were standing in the hallway backstage at the Cow Palace in the San Francisco Bay area. We were hanging out with the other musicians all waiting to go on, including the Beach Boys and my friend "Brain." Farther along the corridor there was a sudden shift in the dynamic. Whoever or whatever was coming seemed to be creating their own weather system, and people pressed back against the wall as if physically affected by what was passing. As it did, I caught a glimpse of someone in sequins swooshing past in a tornado of perfume and hairspray. It was Tina Turner, following behind her husband, Ike, but the energy was all hers. It was so powerful. Tina and I were friends longer than most of our fans have been alive, and well into her eighties, she never lost that incredible presence. I miss her mightily.

Sonny was determined to make me a star as bright as Tina was back then—and continued to be—but he sensed that world events were already changing the dynamic of our industry beyond his control. The midsixties brought in the counterculture, with ideas advocated by people like beat poet Allen Ginsberg and Timothy Leary, the Harvard psychologist who recommended the use of psychedelic drugs for mind expansion.

Leary became famous for his "Turn on, tune in, drop out" message, which I thought was dumb. I never took drugs, and the idea of taking acid didn't turn me on. I was already pretty tuned in, and I had no intention of dropping out. So, while everyone else was tripping, playing acid rock, or marching in the streets to protest the Vietnam War, Sonny and I were the straight, square couple who sang middle-of-the-road songs, didn't engage in drug culture, and now in the era of free love we became uncool for being married. Sonny was never a march-in-the-streets kind of guy, but for some reason he felt compelled to abandon his antipolitical stance and he released a statement condemning the use of marijuana, which made us look like part of the Establishment and alienated our younger fans. I didn't want to smoke pot myself, but I didn't care if other people did. My uncle smoked pot and even my mother sometimes did. Him speaking out against it struck me and our audience as so uncool. Drugs might not have been our thing, but I was far more liberal in my views and didn't agree with telling people what they should or shouldn't do, especially as Sonny previously insisted that we avoid radical causes. Knowing it would fall on deaf ears, I didn't tell him how ridiculous I thought it was to do the PSA. His antidrug stance seriously backfired, because our record sales dropped almost immediately and offers began to dwindle. William Morris even switched us from the musical concerts department to the personal appearance department, which we knew was the first nail in our coffin.

Keeping us relevant and in the public eye required a great deal more time and energy after that, and the more Sonny took on, the moodier he became. Looking back, I think some of his mood swings at this time could have been because he was starting to abuse prescription meds.

That Christmas, I bought him twelve beautiful leather-bound journals with his name and the year tooled in gold leaf. There was one for each month so that he could keep a record of our time together. I secretly hoped that writing down his feelings might help lift him out of his darker moods. And write he did, so much so that he'd wake me up in the middle of the night to read me what he'd written, just as he had with his songs, urging me to listen to something he thought was profound. When I'd nod off, he'd shake me again. "Wake up, Cher! You have to hear this."

He continued to write his thoughts in those journals and would leave them lying around for me to find. Every so often I'd add my own comments as a way of communicating with him indirectly, and he'd write something back. It's strange that the notebooks became the way we expressed ourselves to each other. For some reason, he was more open to my opinions when I wrote them than when I said them out loud.

It wasn't until years later that I was shown an entry from the late sixties, as it appeared in a book Sonny published. It moved me deeply. Sonny wrote: *Today is my 33rd birthday. I am never sans Cher. She lives inside my body. Cher is truly a star from the top of her head to the bottom of her feet. Thank God I have Cher. She is my stabilizer. She is my generator too. She's my reason.*

I wish I'd known how he really felt because I never would have guessed that in a million years.

# 13

## good times

S onny being Sonny, always thinking about what's next, he decided he was going to make a film and we would be the stars. Sonny promised, "Ours will be like the Beatles films only better." He would talk about it constantly over cards, beers, and clam-eating contests with his pals every week. Sick of hearing him go on about it, his friends eventually turned on him and said, "Then make it yourself!" which was the push he needed. One of those friends was Francis Ford Coppola, a UCLA student and budding filmmaker who'd made a couple of low-budget movies. The other was Billy Friedkin, a young documentary maker who also wanted to make films. This pair of poker buddies was years away from making their iconic movies *The Godfather, Apocalypse Now, The Exorcist,* and *The French Connection,* but they were

Sonny's good friends and in the film business so he trusted their advice.

Although I'd loved my acting classes and had hated giving them up, I was a little wary of Sonny's movie dreams because I knew they'd be novelty films and not the serious dramas I'd wanted to pursue. But Sonny was brimming with self-confidence, and even though he'd never written a screenplay in his life or appeared in anything other than cameo roles, he decided overnight that he was a filmmaker now. He hired his poker buddy Billy Friedkin to be his director, even though Billy was in his twenties and had never directed a movie before. He hired a screenwriter as well but eventually took over the writing himself, firing the other guy due to creative differences—one of them being that Sonny would call up everyone in the early hours demanding a writers' conference, just as he had woken me in the middle of the night to hear his songs and read his journals.

Their discussions about the film were endless. One night I got fed up with how long they went on, so I marched into the living room to tell them that their script was dumb and embarrassing, and I wanted nothing more to do with it. Sonny immediately jumped up and cried, "That's great, bud! We can make a movie about you not wanting to make a movie!"

Calling in favors from friends, he persuaded Harold Battiste to arrange the score featuring six of Sonny's songs. Harold had never written music for a movie before and had to read a book on scoring before starting, but he arranged a cool slow jazz version of "I Got You Babe" for the opening that I loved.

Sonny eventually got backing from Paramount to make the movie, which he decided to call *Good Times*. The movie is really funny. It's kind of stupid and corny, but it's funny. Sonny called it a "romantic comedy with songs." The script is full of musical numbers, skits, and silly jokes. We played ourselves with a version of Sonny as a naïve singer desperate to make the two of us movie stars. He gets tricked by a scheming producer into accepting an awful script, and he and I are then seen fantasizing about the kinds of roles we'd love to play instead, from Tarzan and Jane, to a sheriff and a showgirl, to a "gumshoe" private eye with his moll. The whole time my character isn't having any of it. The film spoofs so many other movies that Sonny had seen: *The Maltese Falcon*, Tarzan films, *High Noon*, and every other Western Sonny had ever watched.

We filmed much of it at our home to make it "even more authentic." We even used our own cars—a pair of 1964 Mustangs gifted to us by the Ford Motor Company and customized by George Barris, the famous "King of Kar Kustomization," who also crafted the Batmobile and the Monkeemobile. I was given a candy-pink Mustang with pink fur carpets and ermine trim, while Sonny's was painted in forty layers of Murano gold paint with black-and-white fur seats. Those cars come up for auction every so often. I still get a kick out of seeing them.

The first day on set Sonny was busy running around playing his new role as a budding filmmaker. I swear if they would have given him one of those little glass director's viewfinders, he would have walked around set with it up to his eye just to look the part. While he and Billy Friedkin were busy running around, I didn't have much to do. I was wondering how I was going to fit in. The truth was I never thought he was going to get it made, so once he got funding I was thinking, *Oh shit, this is real. I'm going to have to do something.* I remember I'd just started birth control and had gained fifteen pounds. I felt huge. Great timing to be on camera. While I was standing waiting for my parts, I met the actor George Sanders, who'd been in many classic films, like *The Picture of Dorian Gray*, *All About Eve*, and *Forever Amber*. He'd even been nominated for an Oscar. I remember I kept thinking, *I feel so bad for him to be in this film after he's done films of such stature.* Later he'd go on to play the voice of Shere Khan in *The Jungle Book*. He started talking to me and immediately he was so wonderful. I said to him that I felt like we'd met before, and he replied, "That's called déjà vu," and that's what got us talking. It was the first time I'd heard that term. He was so cosmopolitan, like a gentleman from back in the day. I think it surprised him that I knew so much about his period of filmmaking, but I loved his work and had so much respect for him.

When shooting would wrap each day, Sonny and Billy would sit in our living room and discuss what cuts to make. They'd have long discussions, then rewrite portions of the script and talk about what needed to be re-shot, their conversations lasting late into the night.

One of the best parts about shooting the movie was all the time we spent at the Africa USA wildlife park. The first day at Africa USA, a guy walked straight toward us from a distance with a tiger next to him that was off leash. I was freaking out as they got closer and Sonny kept telling me, "Cher, just stay calm." I was wearing shorts, and when they came right up to us, as the trainer was talking to Sonny, the tiger named Sarang licked the inside of my leg and it was like rough sandpaper. He was huge, a fully grown tiger. I almost passed out. My favorite animal at the park was a beautiful elephant named Margie. Sometimes I'd just lie out in the grass and Margie would hang out beside me or I'd hop up on her and ride her around the park. The hair on her back was sharp, so they had to take a blowtorch and burn it off before fitting her with a padded seat. I don't think she was fully grown but she knew how to lift me up with her trunk and place me on her back. She was so kind and I was never afraid—after all, she was a fellow actress. Some of the people who worked at Africa USA told me they also had alligators but they were in hibernation. Nobody told me where they were in hibernation, but I didn't think much of it until I was wading across a lake in the park. I was halfway through and I thought, *Oh my God, where would an alligator hibernate but in a lake?!* I almost drowned myself rushing back to the shore. It turns out that the alligators were actually hibernating in a metal bin, but every step out of that lake I imagined sleeping crocodiles inches from my feet.

Two times, things got a bit out of hand on set. The first was a scene where Sonny played Sam Spade and I was Brigid O'Shaughnessy. The villain of the scene was meant to shoot me in the back, but the blanks in his gun were too heavy and really hurt when they hit me. I was just wearing a thin blouse or dress, so they hit me hard. Billy just kept telling me that I had to man up. It hurt so bad that I started to cry, and then I fell back against the armoire, which started to rock. Luckily, one of the prop men caught it just in time. I said, "Screw you, Billy," and walked off.

The second time was when Sonny was being Jungle Maury and there was a lion cub in the scene with him. The cub was little, but even a young lion is still very strong. At the end of the scene, Billy yelled "cut" and Sonny was walking off. I guess the lion really liked him because he jumped onto Sonny's back, knocking him flat on his face.

The movie was starting to win me over. There's one scene where a group of chimpanzees are playing poker together. It was hysterical. All the chimps sat around the table arranging their cards in their hand and picking which to play next. It looked like a real poker game. One of the chimps was smoking, which he loved doing. It was one of my favorite scenes in the movie.

I think the person who was happiest about Sonny's film was my mother, who dropped by every so often. She would tell everyone proudly, "I always knew my daughter would be a movie star." I had to laugh. Being able to meet George Sanders was just a huge bonus.

Our lives were so crazy at that time that I didn't think anything could surprise me anymore, but then we met someone who was in a different league of crazy. It was on a trip to New York accompanied by our friend Joey. We were staying at the fabled St. Regis hotel on East 55th Street when we met up with Francis Ford Coppola, who was in town working on a new movie. In the lobby, we bumped into the artist Salvador Dalí. Turns out he spent every winter in the St. Regis. The famous surrealist looked us up and down and invited us to a party that his wife and muse, Gala, was having in her suite, number 1610. We went as requested and Dalí received us graciously, wearing a velvet blazer and looking as weird as he always did. His pet ocelot, Babou, lounged on a couch nearby.

Everyone was either beautiful or bizarre and all of them looked as if they were high. Several wore frilly black lace and carried silver-topped canes. The rest were staggering around speaking French so quickly that I wouldn't have understood them even if I'd paid more attention in Mrs. Simpson's class. It was like stepping into a bad Fellini movie and, for once, Sonny and I weren't the strangest people in the room. Feeling terribly square, I didn't know what to do or say. I guess I did a good enough job pretending to be cool, because as we were leaving, Dalí declared, "You must come to dinner tomorrow night." It was a command, not a request.

The next night before dinner, Dalí greeted us in his studio, which was small and dimly lit. Within moments of arriving, it was immediately apparent that an orgy had recently taken place. An open door led to a large room where people were naked or in various states of undress. One bra-less chick came out wearing a see-through blouse that might as well have been Saran Wrap. Not knowing where to sit or what to say, I settled into a big plush armchair and tried my best to look unfazed. Joey sat in another chair, but Sonny and Francis were such sissies that they huddled together on a little one-seater sofa on the other side of the room. They just sat there like schoolboys until reaching forward to help themselves to a box of chocolate candies fashioned as facsimiles of the famous Dalí melting clock. Everyone in the room gasped. The candies were an art installation, not to be eaten. I'm surprised we didn't get thrown out right there.

Shifting in my seat, I felt something digging into my side, so I twisted around and saw a strange object sticking out of the crack between the cushion and the chair. Curious, I pulled it out to discover a gorgeous painted rubber fish. I was even more entranced when I switched on the little remote-control gizmo attached to it and the fish's tail swished rhythmically to and fro. I assumed that it was a toy for the bathtub.

Dalí was watching me, so I said, "Oh my God, Salvador, this is beautiful!"

"Yes," he said, his smile crooked. "It's lovely when you place it on your clitoris."

I couldn't drop that fish fast enough as Sonny and Francis immediately lost all control, turning into fourteen-year-old boys. Wheezing with laughter almost to the point of hysteria, they grabbed a large coffee table book and brought it up to conceal their faces. It happened to be Dalí's own book of paintings, so all I could see was the photograph of Dalí's mustached face on the cover, shaking up and down, as Dalí's real mustached face gazed at us quizzically. With no help from them, I somehow managed to never lose my composure. Inside, however, I was—how can I put this?—screaming. And with that, Dalí announced, "Shall we go to dinner?"

Accompanied by an entourage of the bizarre orgy people, we walked a couple of blocks to the restaurant, where we were joined by the Franco-American artist Ultra Violet, who was wearing a man's shirt and tie with a velvet skirt. She sat next to me and, saying nothing, repeatedly tapped my leg with her cane. *If she does that again*, I thought, *I'm going to smack her.*

Less than ten minutes after we'd sat down, Dalí rose to announce, "I forgot, we have a previous engagement." With that, they all got up and moved to the next table a mere five feet away. Apparently, they were over us. We were so relieved that we could no longer hold it in. The boys started pounding the table and we all screamed with laughter. I'm sure Dalí thought we were all cretins, but by then we were beyond caring.

Back in LA, we accepted an invitation to appear on the first season of *The Carol Burnett Show* on CBS, hosted by one of the funniest women in show business. It was groundbreaking in its style of comic variety and especially in being hosted by a woman, and we were thrilled to be introduced by Carol as "leaders of the new wild, way-out movement," though in my ears that sounded like an old-fashioned way of explaining who we were. The way people described us always made me laugh. To prepare for the show, I was sent to Berman's costume house on Highland to be fitted for an outfit. Waiting in the fitting room, I became increasingly nervous as—at twenty—I'd never been professionally fitted for a dress before. Staring at my own reflection in the three-way mirror, I saw the door open behind me and in walked the most incredibly handsome man. He was in his late twenties with tousled blond hair and the most amazing blue eyes and looked like he'd just spent the summer in Greece. I took one look at him and said, "You're so much younger than I thought you'd be!" Quick as a flash, he replied, "And you're so much smaller than I thought you'd be." Because I was taller than Sonny, everyone always thought I'd be a giant. That was the first time I met Bob Mackie.

We both laughed and that was the beginning of a friendship and collaboration that lasted from that day in 1967 to now—and counting. Even though I only met Bob Mackie once or twice in those early years, I knew in my heart that we'd work together. What I didn't know was that he would become, hands down, one of the most important men in my life. Feeling fabulous in a cute scarlet minidress with billowing lace sleeves that he adapted just for me, I stepped into the limelight on Carol Burnett's show to sing my latest solo single, "You Better Sit Down Kids," a number Sonny wrote. I smiled as Sonny sauntered on in a green paisley Nehru-collar jacket and black pants, and we sang a couple of numbers together and messed around a bit, nudging each other and laughing. He always knew how to relax me onstage. By the time we joined Carol for a lavish finale, it was so much fun that it didn't feel like work at all.

Sonny was still working hard on our film despite Paramount pulling out and had plans to make another movie that would star just me. He also had plans to produce a Sonny & Cher musical called *The Beat Goes On* and an animated film. The more projects, the more excited and nervous he became, and I just went along for the ride trying to smooth things over as I always did.

When *Good Times* was finally released, it got good reviews. The *New York Times* described it as "sprightly" and "a bit of good-humored silliness," and the *Los Angeles Times* said it had charm. Sonny was described as a natural and my performance was said to be "effortless." I didn't know if that was an insult or a compliment. Despite positive reviews, it wasn't a success in the box office and Sonny became depressed and frustrated. He'd overextended us financially for the film, and now he was on his own because he'd already fired Charlie and Brian for focusing too much on their new acts, like Buffalo Springfield and Iron Butterfly. Those two were gone before I was even told, and when I asked him why, he claimed they'd stolen from us. I read later somewhere that we had to pay them $250,000 to buy ourselves out of their contracts.

Refusing to give up on us, Sonny arranged a meeting with the William Morris Agency, who were supposed to be advising us. We walked in and sat at the end of a long table with a bunch of somber-faced suits. When Sonny asked them to do more to promote *Good Times*, help get our next movie filmed, and push our musical career to the next level, no one said a word. Then chairman of the board Abe Lastfogel, a strange little man in his sixties, stood up and said, "The future looks bleak," before walking out. Everyone else then got up and followed him.

Sonny was furious, but it was Joe DeCarlo who stepped in to save us, along with Harvey Kresky, who worked at WMA but quit his job to help manage us, even though we remained on the agency's books. We'd always loved Harvey because he was the only one at WMA who really understood us. Young and hip, he didn't wear a suit and was tall and handsome.

I became pregnant again in the summer of 1967. Sonny and I were pleased, if anxious, but I soon had another miscarriage. It began while I was out shopping with Joey in Hollywood buying something to wear to see Muhammad Ali in a fight later that night. Doubled over in a store bathroom in pain, I knew I was losing the baby but managed to make it home before the bleeding started. The next day it was back to the hospital again. I had naïvely thought that getting pregnant and giving birth was going to be easy.

We were going from city to city to try to keep our careers alive, but our sales dropped from millions of copies to tens of thousands. With more time on our hands and entering an election year for the first time as public figures, Sonny decided that we should get involved in politics. There had been a hike in organized crime, more civil rights protests, and increasing political fallout from the never-ending Vietnam War. People all over the country were protesting. Sonny offered our services to the presidential campaign of US attorney general Robert Kennedy—whom he'd briefly met—because he was convinced that the younger brother of JFK was what our country needed. Times had changed and so had the music. We had become passé compared to twentysomething artists like Jimi Hendrix, who was playing his guitar with his teeth; Cream and Eric Clapton; and Led Zeppelin, whose music I was crazy about. I'd have been more than happy to change with the times and go more rock and roll, but my thirty-three-year-old husband would veto any such suggestion, so that was that. I knew the rules.

By this time, I was pregnant again and soon suffered my third miscarriage. Each time I lost a baby, it was worse than the last and yet another knock to my confidence. I was only twenty-one but began to wonder if I'd ever be able to have a child, something I very much wanted, even with the difficulties in our marriage. The thing I hated most was that following the loss of each baby, I'd almost inevitably run into someone who'd ask about the baby or how I was feeling. Then I'd have to go over and over what had happened, which only prolonged the whole experience and made it ten times worse.

I didn't understand what was happening and told Sonny tearfully, "I don't want to do this anymore. It's too painful." In a bid to find out what was wrong, I went to see my gynecologist. "You have an angry uterus, Cher," he told me. "Putting it in layman's terms, this means your uterus goes into contractions too early for no reason."

Whenever he was at a low point, Sonny would turn to his writing, and after figuring we'd exhausted every other possible means of revenue, he began to work feverishly on our next movie, which he planned to call *Chastity*. His story of a young homeless woman hitchhiking and wandering in search of something would, he was convinced, reconnect us to our younger fans and the youth culture. He became even more passionate about it after Billy Friedkin called one day and said, "I'm coming to pick you both up in ten minutes because you must come and see this new movie. It's unbelievable!" The film was *The Graduate*, starring Dustin Hoffman and Anne Bancroft, and we both loved it because it was something so different and new. I think Sonny secretly aspired to make something equally as good.

To help him finish off *Chastity*, he hired a "secretary" to take dictation, a woman who happened to be young and blond. That old chestnut. One night I woke up thirsty. Barefoot and sleepy, I wandered through our open-plan house down the strip of marble path to get a glass of water. I padded past our living room and then our den, which was sectioned off by a wrought-iron gate with a little palm tree on each side. I couldn't see much through the gate but could make out what looked like two figures. Still groggy and not thinking much of it, I kept walking into the kitchen. As I got my water, I could hear noises, like rustling and whispering. At that point I knew something was wrong, but kept walking back toward our bedroom, when I saw the shadowy figures of Sonny helping his new assistant out the front door. It was such a fucking cliché. It broke my heart, but you've got to give him an A for effort.

I just continued walking to the bedroom and lay down on the very edge of my side of the bed. I heard him come in behind me and start to say, "Cher, I—" but I held up my hand and said, "Don't say a word." I must have just shut my brain off because somehow I was able to fall asleep. In the middle of the night, I got up, packed some clothes in a bag, and went to Mom's. Whenever I'm in a tight spot, then and now, I always get the feeling that I want to talk to my mom.

My mother was furious when she found out what had happened and then told me, "Cher, honey, I have to tell you that I've been hearing stories about him for some time now." I couldn't bear to hear any more; I was still grappling with what had happened. Just waking up was too much. I was overloaded with sadness. My mother had seen every trick in the book when it came to men, and she never forgave Sonny for hurting me, especially after he called early the next morning and told me it was my fault.

When Sonny came around to further plead his case, Mom held her tongue. She wasn't going to start yelling at Sonny when my sister and I where there. She knew how bad I felt, and she wasn't going to add insult to injury. As always, Sonny used his charm and persuasiveness to win me over. He told me he was sorry but insisted I was to blame for not having enough sex with him. "I wouldn't have had to look outside our marriage if I was sexually satisfied," he insisted. That was such bullshit, but by the time he'd finished I found myself apologizing.

The incident drove a wedge between my mother and Sonny for quite some time. Not long after, she wrote me a letter with a list of her grievances and then just stopped talking to me.

I tried to forget what had happened and was relieved when Sonny and I moved into a new house. We had been invited to a party by the actor Tony Curtis. The star of *Some Like It Hot* and *Spartacus* (and a man who would marry almost as many times as my mother) was throwing himself a birthday party at his Italian Renaissance mansion at 141 South Carolwood Drive in Holmby Hills. We had no idea why we were invited because we'd never met Tony before, but we soon discovered that he liked to surround himself with "hip" people, and I suppose we fit the bill.

When the gates to the house clanged opened and Sonny drove us up the long driveway to Tony's house, I gasped because I'd only ever seen a property like that in the movies. With so many rooms, and set in acres of manicured lawn, it was stunning. There must have been a hundred famous faces at his party, but walking into the oak-paneled foyer with its elegant staircase, Venetian mirrors, and crystal chandeliers, I only had eyes for the house.

The 12,200-square-foot property was built in the 1930s and boasted nine bedrooms and ten bathrooms. Many of the ceilings were painted with frescoes to look like the sky, and every room featured ornate marble fireplaces. There were stables and an Olympic-size swimming pool. One previous owner was Joseph Schenck, the founder of Twentieth Century–Fox, who designed a screening room with a secret door said to have been created for his lover Marilyn Monroe to make a discreet entry and exit whenever she visited him.

Walking around the amazing property with my mouth open, I told Sonny, "We're going to live here one day."

He looked at me and laughed. "Okay, bud. If you say so."

When Tony Curtis greeted us, he threw open his arms in welcome. "Oh, you're here, my daahlings! Welcome." In a black velvet suit with a silk shirt and long black scarf, he was everything I hoped he'd be and more, a fabulous cliché of a movie star and utterly amazing. He reminded me a bit of Diana Vreeland with his grandness, and we both adored him instantly. I told him how much I loved his home and he beamed at me. "Well then, you must come and see my other house, my dear," he said, interlocking our arms and taking me on a tour. "I moved out six months ago. It's a smaller version of this one—and it's for sale." I couldn't wait.

We drove to 364 St. Cloud Road in Bel-Air a few days later, and Tony was right, it was a mini version of his Carolwood mansion but just as beautiful. We both fell in love with it on sight. When Sonny saw how happy I was wandering around the rooms imagining us there, he told Tony he wished he could buy it for me. As smooth as silk, Tony replied, "As it's you, daahling, I'll let you have it for two hundred fifty thousand dollars." Sonny said nothing and let Tony carry on with his sweeping arms as he gave us the full tour of the billiards room, paneled library, dining room, six bedrooms, bathrooms, and huge swimming pool. When we eventually got back in the car, I stared at the man I loved and said simply, "Son . . ."

"I know," he replied with a sigh. He looked back at me and nodded. "All right. We'll swing it."

I don't think I could have loved him more than I did in that moment. I finally had my dream house. Tony let us move in within weeks even though Sonny hadn't raised the money to pay him yet. Denis Pregnolato, who worked for Sonny and me but was also someone I considered a good friend, moved into the smaller wing, and we invited friends and family over for a barbecue on the patio right away. Most of them were tongue-tied because, like us, they couldn't believe we lived in such a grand place.

Once we were in the new house, Sonny confessed that he'd spent all our spare cash and couldn't afford any furniture. We'd sold the Encino house fully furnished, so for a long time all we had was a beautiful four-poster canopy bed with wooden posts, and a huge mahogany dining table with fourteen velvet-covered chairs for when Sonny's family came to visit. We also had a little table and chairs in the sunroom where we ate breakfast, which Ronnie Wilson kindly decorated for us as a housewarming gift. He put up lively floral wallpaper printed with different colored poppies, as well as beautiful drapes and seat cushions to match. I didn't care about the lack of furniture in the rest of the house. I was in heaven. Nouveau riche we may have been, but as I used to say, better nouveau than never.

I loved that house, but it also marked a distinct change in my relationship with Sonny. One of the moments that most clearly marks the shift came when I asked Sonny if we could go out and do something fun since we were always either working or cooped up inside. Finally, he took me out one night to see the war movie *The Dirty Dozen* starring Charles Bronson. I was content when on the way home afterward he turned to me and said, "You really liked that movie, didn't you, Cher?"

"Yeah," I replied with a smile. "I thought it was great."

There was a pause and then he looked at me strangely. "Do you know why you liked it so much?" What came out of his mouth next completely blindsided me: "Because you're sexually frustrated." It was the first time I ever thought that something wasn't right, that maybe Sonny wasn't my friend. Then suddenly, Sonny said, "Let me out of this car right now!"

"What?" I asked, thinking he was joking.

"Pull over. I want to get out of this car—now!"

Without warning, Sonny was out of control, shouting at me to let him out of the car. I was frightened, so I pulled over and did as he asked. Once he climbed out and slammed the door, I drove home as quickly as I could and went running in to find Denis.

"Den, you have to help me! The craziest thing just happened on our way back from the movies. Sonny lost his mind. He made me stop the car and let him out on Dead Man's Curve. Please go get him because he's walking home and there's no sidewalk there and I'm afraid."

Denis raced out and found him. When Sonny came back into the house, he was furious. "How dare you leave me there?!" he yelled, before storming out. I stared at the angry space he'd left and asked myself, *What the hell just happened?* I thought that I must have done something without realizing because I couldn't make sense of his reaction. It was mind-boggling in the true sense of the word. (Years later, I figured that he probably caused a fight to have a reason to leave the house for a date.) As was often the case with Sonny, his outburst was quickly forgotten, and he carried on as if he hadn't done anything at all. It was something that I would look back on and realize was a pattern. Sonny knocking me off balance and then a moment later acting like it never happened.

His outbursts often came when I didn't expect them. While living on St. Cloud I had taken up tennis lessons. I was desperate for a distraction and some physical activity that would keep me from going insane, so I'd asked Joe if he could help me, as he was the one person I felt I could confide in. He was also the only one who could sit down with Sonny like a father and have a heart-to-heart. I told him, "Joe, I have to do something, or I'll go out of my mind. I've got to get out of this house, and I can't just be shopping all the time. I need to do something physical. I really want to learn how to play tennis. Can you please speak to Son?" Joe was the one person who knew what my life was really like, and he agreed to help.

After talking to him persuasively on my behalf, Joe took me shopping and I bought some full whites and tennis shoes. Then he drove me to the Hollywood Hills for my first lesson with a coach, who had to be a woman. I loved every minute, and the experience took me straight back to my days playing softball with Mom's friends. I only had one-on-one sessions with the coach at her home, and I never saw anybody else but her.

One day she happened to be hosting a party right after my lesson. Some of her guests started to drift in as I was leaving. I said hello to a couple of them in passing, and then Denis Pregnolato, picked me up and brought me home. When we got back, he reported to Sonny that he'd seen me talking to some men.

I had no idea that they'd spoken, but later that night I looked out of my bedroom window and spotted flames. Peering closer, I saw that Sonny was stoking the incinerator in the back yard. When I realized he was burning my tennis clothes, I felt such a rush of anger and then complete hopelessness. I'd so enjoyed my lessons. I couldn't believe he was being so controlling. I felt utterly betrayed. By Denis. By Sonny. Something inside me clicked that night.

Nothing would get in the way of Sonny's dream to make me a star while winning the respect he craved, so when he couldn't persuade any studio to invest in his project after *Good Times* had gone down the toilet, he had to take out loans. It was, he said, a gamble worth taking and one that would show the motion picture industry what young people wanted to watch. When he'd finally raised enough, he hired a fifteen-member crew and a director (who'd only ever worked on commercials and knew nothing). The man looked like a cliché of a Hollywood director and was kind of a hack. He charmed his way into being Sonny's friend, and we all flew to Arizona to try to salvage our careers once again, but things went south from there. To keep down costs, I wore my own clothes—a wine-colored T-shirt, suede pants, and moccasins—and carried the same cowhide purse I'd swung at attackers on Sunset years earlier.

Sonny always said that *Chastity* was inspired by me, and I guess I could've been offended, but I wasn't. The plot featured a smart-mouthed teenage hippie who had no focus and was wandering through life with no talent other than raw energy. The storyline was thin to begin with and Sonny's fiddling did nothing to improve it. My character, Chastity, *was* kind of interesting. She hated to be touched but secretly yearned for a normal life. She bummed rides across the Southwest, stole a car, and drove to Mexico, where she was seduced by a lesbian in a bordello before falling for Eddie, a clean-living law student she was too unstable to stay with. The bisexual part was inspired by Sonny thinking I was Melissa's girlfriend when we first met.

A British actor named Stephen Whittaker was cast as the law student, and he and I hit it off immediately. He'd recently played a bad boy in *To Sir, with Love* and this was his second movie. We started to chat between scenes, and I enjoyed his company because we really talked, and he was genuinely interested in what I had to say. It was great to find someone I could relate to, and not in a sexual way. He was just a boy my own age with stars in his eyes who understood my love of acting.

In the early hours of June 6, 1968, Sonny took a telephone call that stopped production for a few days even though the budget and the timings were so tight. Robert Kennedy had been assassinated by a lone gunman at the Ambassador Hotel in Los Angeles. At the age of forty-two, he'd just won the nomination in the Democratic presidential primary and had been celebrating with his campaign team and journalists when he was shot. We'd only met him once or twice, but that had been enough to impress us, and if we hadn't been working on the film, we could have been with him that night to celebrate, as we were due to go campaign for him when the shoot was over. Kennedy's murder came almost two months to the day after the assassination of Martin Luther King Jr., another great loss to the world. Within a few weeks, Sonny and I were invited as one of the few white acts on the bill to perform at the Soul Together concert, a benefit concert for a fund in Martin Luther King's name, at Madison Square Garden. This was our first time playing at that holy temple of music and we were grateful to be part of an ensemble cast.

The headline acts were Aretha Franklin, Jimi Hendrix, the

Young Rascals, and Sam & Dave. We were at the bottom of the bill with King Curtis & The Kingpins. Sonny wore a raven-black checked pantsuit, and I wore a pale pink satin full-length Egyptian-style dress. I'd designed it, and my seamstress Sadie had made it for me. The last time I wore it the dress fit me perfectly, but when I put it on this time it felt a little tight. While Sonny went off with Aretha Franklin to find a drink, I went to observe the crowd from an archway where I'd stay out of sight. Suddenly aware of someone standing next to me, I turned to face Jimi Hendrix. He was wearing a velvet jacket, a voluminous silk shirt, and some amazing rings. Smiling, he introduced himself and asked, "Have you got anything?" At first, I didn't know what he was talking about but soon understood it was drugs, because he added, "Everyone's looking for stuff backstage."

When I told Jimi that I didn't take drugs, we made small talk. All I knew was that Jimi was cool and I liked him; he was so nice and polite. I didn't know what I had expected but it wasn't that. Really handsome, he was such a gentleman. He had an interesting personality too, and I loved his style and the way he moved. He was only a few years older than me, so when he died two years later of alcoholism and hard living, I was very sad. His name was added to a long roll call of talented musicians, singers, and industry experts who had died so-called rock-and-roll deaths in the late sixties. Among them were the angelic Brian Jones, Janis Joplin, and Brian Epstein.

After the gig, we returned to Arizona to finish shooting *Chastity*, where Sonny was busy supervising the crew and trying to keep costs from spiraling out of control. He wasn't too busy to notice how well I was getting along with my costar Stephen. Jealous and worried that Stephen and I might have an affair, Sonny moved my scenes to a different time of day so that my costar and I were rarely together anymore. The atmosphere on set was horrible then, and what Sonny did was so unfair, as I didn't even know Stephen that well and there would never have been the opportunity for us to meet secretly since we were shooting constantly. I didn't even have a crush on Stephen. I just liked having someone younger and freer to talk to, with beliefs more like my own. Sonny's possessiveness ruined everything, and I was so mad at him for that. The script was already disjointed, but Sonny made it worse by cutting all scenes of intimacy between Stephen and me, not even allowing us to kiss. That was dumb because I was supposed to be falling in love with the guy. From then on, the whole film no longer made sense.

When the shoot was finally over, we returned home at last, where I discovered I was pregnant again, which explained why my dress had been tight at the concert. My doctor told me, "Cher, I want you to rest for a month. I want you to lie down, I don't even want you to go in cars or do anything that could jostle you." The idea sounded quite appealing after the previous few years, although in retrospect I'm sure Sonny freaked out at the thought that I might not be able to work, as we didn't have any money. While I was resting, Sonny kept his fast pace of life. He'd be out all day working on edits and often up late into the night. The cutting room became his second home. In September he attended the Democratic National Convention in Chicago, where there were riots in the streets. He'd come up with an idea for a bill suggesting a way to place young people in the legislature as "junior senators" to give them a voice and help bridge the generation gap in politics. He'd met with all the senators' wives to pitch it. Senator George McGovern showed interest in his bill, and when he came back, all Sonny could talk about was McGovern and how he should be our next president. Sonny had had to cut his trip short because he got caught up in the rioting when students accused him of being rich and part of the Establishment. He didn't help himself at all with that image when later that year he agreed to shoot a thirty-minute government film called *Marijuana* for distribution in American schools. In it, he warned teenagers that if they became "potheads" they could ruin the most important years of their lives. As a man in his midthirties, dressed in gold silk pajamas sitting in our opulent home, he came across as someone completely out of touch with the audience. Year after year, students in ninth to twelfth grade were forced to watch that film, so his message made us both look like fools, especially when they weren't listening to us anyway.

Sonny's behavior could be erratic and moody, but it never occurred to me at the time that he might secretly be taking drugs himself. He was so staunchly antidrug I never dreamed this could be true. But one day, I saw something I wasn't supposed to see. I was resting on our bed when our bodyguard Big Jim wandered through our bedroom with something that he placed in the cabinet in Sonny's bathroom. I didn't think anything of it, but after Jim left, I went looking for a razor to borrow from Sonny to shave my legs, and what I found instead was something I didn't expect. Inside the cabinet was a square white-plastic bottle about seven inches tall with hundreds of blue Valium pills in it, the kind of container a pharmacist stores bulk pills in before divvying them into individual prescription bottles.

Sonny's bathroom was private, and I knew intuitively that I shouldn't go in there, but I'd had no idea it was because he'd secretly been taking the Valium and prescription painkillers he kept for pain from his kidney stones. Had I known back then, it would certainly have explained the mood swings that made him so hard to read, or the nights he'd shake me awake to talk about something. That's why I'd bought him his diaries. I don't suppose for one minute he thought of those pills as the "drugs" he publicly condemned like pot or LSD. As I was soon to find out, this wasn't his only secret.

In the middle of all this turmoil Sonny called me from his office one day to say, "I'm coming home and we're getting married."

Taking a breath, I simply answered, "Good." In my head,

we'd been married since we swapped rings in the bathroom, so this was merely a formality. The ceremony had to be done quickly and privately so nobody would find out we had been faking our marriage from the beginning. It was different then, and living together before marriage was really frowned upon. We wouldn't have been able to be accepted as role models. In that day the truth getting out would have been a career ender, but it wasn't as if I'd always planned a dream wedding anyway. That wasn't my style.

I pulled on some bell-bottoms and a cool top and was ready when Sonny came home shortly before Joe D and his girlfriend, Margie (who later became Margie Perenchio), turned up to our house to act as our witnesses. When our attorney arrived, we went into the library, where a justice of the peace performed the brief ceremony. Then we signed the documents to make our relationship legally binding. It was over in minutes. There was no white dress, no cake, no guests, and no flowers. My ceremony had been better and longer. But I didn't feel cheated. Far from it. I was happy that it was done at last. Sonny went straight back to his office with the all-important piece of paper, and I went back to my room to rest. What happened didn't make what we already had feel any more special. We were still together, I was carrying his child, and now we were husband and wife with a certificate to prove it. That was all.

I was so happy when our baby survived the first few months without my uterus kicking it out. Sonny was convinced it was a boy, as that's what he wanted because he already had Christy. I didn't care. I just wanted our child to be born alive and healthy. As my due date got closer, the anticipation of becoming parents did wonders for our relationship. Although Sonny was as busy as ever, he was tender with me and calmed me every time I started to panic about the birth. Rarely without his camera, he took dozens of photographs of me as my little belly swelled to not-so-little.

In early 1969 my friend Judy Allison threw me a baby shower at an LA hotel. Standing behind a long table, heavily pregnant in a voluminous Indian paisley blouse, I opened the gifts of toys and baby clothes as Cass Elliot, Liza Minnelli, Joey Maalouf (now Steiner), and others cheered me on. Holding up the tiny rompers, bonnets, and booties for everyone to see really brought it home to me that this time, it looked like I was going to hang on to this baby.

On Sonny's thirty-fourth birthday, February 16, 1969, I started to have contractions and he drove me to the hospital, only to be told after a few hours that it was a false alarm, so he took me home. The same thing happened again a few weeks later. Then on March 3 at around 6 p.m., I called him at his office to tell him, "This is it!" to which he replied, "Okay, bud. I'll talk to you later," and hung up. Thinking it would be another wasted journey, he carried on working.

"No, Son!" I cried into a dead receiver. I was so scared that I could hardly speak because my teeth were chattering so much.

Joe D was with him that day, and he looked at Sonny like he was crazy and said, "Don't you think you ought to go to the hospital in case you miss the birth of your child?" Sonny suddenly appreciated what I had said on the phone and ran for his car.

It was a huge full moon that night—I remember looking at it on the way to the hospital. Just gigantic. When I arrived at Cedars-Sinai in the back of our ridiculous Rolls-Royce limousine, Sonny was waiting to take photographs of me from every angle, trying to make me laugh even as I shielded my puffy face, side-eyeing him the entire time. After sitting me in a wheelchair, he gave his camera to Denis Pregnolato and instructed him to take photos of him wheeling me along the corridor.

"Remember, Cher, I want a boy!" he told me, laughing all the way.

"I'll kill you if you don't stop taking pictures!" I was half-laughing, but I didn't want photos of me thirty pounds heavier, sweaty, and in pain. He assured me that I'd thank him in years to come, and he wasn't wrong about that.

Every part of my body was trembling as I was wheeled into the labor ward. I was petrified of what was to come and felt completely unprepared as my labor progressed, especially when Sonny had to leave me and go to the waiting room—as was the custom back then. He instructed Denis to take even more photos of him looking pensive out of a window, smoking a cigarette, and in medical scrubs. The entire event was captured in celluloid.

Still panicking, I only calmed down when my wonderful gynecologist, Dr. Alfred Heldfond, arrived. He was accompanied by his Swedish nurse, Elizabeth, a woman who'd become my closest friend during my pregnancy and was so wonderfully kind to me. I loved Elizabeth so much—even more when I found out later that her mom had died that day, but she still insisted on attending.

In those days, there were no epidurals, so you were either totally conscious and in pain or completely out of it. After I was given the drugs, I couldn't see anything. Everything was just blurry. In the early hours I was told to push, then I heard a baby's cry and I asked a dozen times, "Does my baby have all its fingers and toes?" before falling asleep.

Sonny came the next morning and told me we had a seven-pound-eight-ounce baby girl, and she was beautiful. He didn't seem to mind at all that she wasn't a boy. I named her Chastity Sun, "Chastity" because it was my name in the film we'd just made and "Sun" after her dad.

I couldn't believe how tiny she was. Unbelievably cute, she had great big eyes and so much black hair that she looked like a little Eskimo. I was very happy, but after they took her back to the nursery, I got myself into such a state of anxiety about having to care for her that I asked for a pill to help me sleep. It didn't work and I had a terrible night sweating, scared stiff that I didn't have a clue how to be a mother. It didn't help when the next morning, the intercom chirped, "Mothers, get ready to see your babies," and no one wheeled mine in. When I asked a nurse, she said firmly, "I can't talk to you about that. You'll have to wait for the doctor." I collapsed in a panic, calling Sonny, and managing to get out only "Son, the baby!" in between my sobs. When Sonny rushed to the hospital and found out Chas was fine, they were simply trying to bring her temperature up in an incubator, he absolutely lost it on the entire staff. I could hear him yelling from my hospital bed.

When Sonny came in again the next day, he went to check on Chas in the nursery, and when he came back, he was quietly furious, trying to keep his temper under control for my sake but unable to hide his anger. "What's wrong?" I asked, afraid that something bad had happened for real this time.

Sonny frowned. "Your mother was here."

"What? When?"

"Just now. She told the staff she wanted to see her grandchild."

"Is she coming to see me?" I asked, pulling myself up on my pillows in preparation.

"No, I'm so sorry, bud. She left already." He was so angry with my mom that day that I didn't think he'd ever speak to her again. I had almost forgotten why she and I weren't talking this time, but her decision not to see me broke my heart.

Once I was allowed home from the hospital, Chas went into her pastel nursery surrounded by everything she could possibly need and more. I went straight back to our four-poster bed, but in the middle of that first night I woke to find myself alone. Sonny had gone out.

Looking up, I thought, *I can see the ceiling.* You couldn't see the ceiling from our bed because of the canopy. Realizing I was lying on the floor and feeling feverish, I got up to go to the bathroom but was barely able to keep myself upright. Then I felt a kind of rushing sensation and terrible cramping and made it to the bathroom, where I had a hemorrhage. There was blood everywhere and I passed out on the floor. I came to and tried to pull myself together, but by then I'd passed out again.

I don't know how long it was before Sonny came home, but when he found me, he fell to his knees and rocked me in his arms. He immediately called the doctor, who arrived to give me shots to stem the excess bleeding. The doctor remained with me all night to make sure I was all right. Looking back, I wonder where the hell Sonny went the first night I came home with our baby, but at the time I was too tired and weak to even think. Despite his not being there, I have to say that Sonny was supportive and concerned, maybe out of guilt for wherever the hell he'd been at a time when I so needed him. Either way, I don't know what I'd have done without him.

I slept for the next three days. I was so weak that I couldn't even hold Chas, and Sonny fed me steak to try to build my strength up. He stayed by my side and promised me that the baby and I would be just fine. He was such a great dad and took good care of us both. Soon he was stirring pasta sauce with one hand and cradling the baby against his chest with the other. When Chas was about three months old, my mother dropped by—her first visit in almost a year. She walked into our bedroom just as I was getting dressed, Chas was lying on the bed, bawling because she was hungry. I was about to feed her.

Mom took one look at me and her new grandchild, and the first thing out of her mouth after months of silence and my almost bleeding to death was: "This baby is insecure." Sonny was furious. My mother always had one foot in the past, one in the future, and could be kick-ass and fabulous one minute, but then, with the flick of a switch, she'd change. It's hard to explain complicated people, and everyone in my life seemed to be so complicated and fragile, always acting out—me included. In fact, I might be the queen of that.

When I eventually recovered, I dried my eyes; picked up my child, praying that my mother wasn't right about her being insecure; and cuddled her. I was a mother now and determined to do it to the best of my ability.

# 14

## *the harder they come*

Three weeks after giving birth, I flew to Page, Arizona, for my second *Vogue* photoshoot with Richard Avedon. I panicked at first because I couldn't take Chastity with me, but Sonny insisted I do it because the exposure would be good and keep us in the public eye. The German nurse he'd hired to take care of Chas was good with the baby but too strict with me. She was so tall and built like a wrestler and acted as if I would drop Chas or somehow hurt her. I didn't know much about taking care of a baby, but I wasn't a complete idiot. She hardly allowed me to touch my child, and it got to the point where I'd sneak in early in the morning, grab Chas, bring her back to my room, and lock the door. The German woman would follow, clomping down the hall after me because she'd had one of the first spinal infusions

235

and it made her footsteps really heavy and uneven. She'd call to me outside my bedroom, "Mrs. Bono. Please open ze door!" I couldn't wait to get rid of her once I got home from the shoot.

Gee flew with me to Arizona, while Sonny stayed home to organize a new tour and work out the final recording schedule for my next album. Thank God. It was the first fun thing I'd done in months and was really wonderful because I was on my own with Gee, Richard, and Ara Gallant, and I met a man named Maurice Hogenboom, who was a photographer and model that the casting director had selected to be shot with me. He was beautiful, very sweet, and about a thousand feet tall. This shoot was to be the third installment in a series Diana Vreeland had organized: Veruschka had already been shot in Japan, Toots (Anjelica Huston) was shot in Ireland, and now I was to be the third spread to finish out the series. I had my figure back already, so they didn't have to hide a bump, and they dressed me in Giorgio's modern takes on Native American dress. They gave me some outrageous makeup that looked like I was wearing feathers for eyelashes or had a cow's skull inked on my forehead. And they draped me with turquoise Navajo jewelry— sparking a lifelong love. There were also some fabulous embellished belts with fringe, bone necklaces, and amazing arm cuffs.

I felt free and relaxed on set. Everyone was treating me like an adult and nobody was trying to control me. Arizona in April was freezing, and one day I had to get into a lake and stand about waist-deep in the water for a while holding a piebald pony by a rope halter. Richard set up his cameras on the shores of Lake Powell and had us posing up against red rocks or mountain backdrops. I was shivering so badly. Richard kept giving me shots of brandy and I got so drunk. When we got back to the hotel, my sister put me right in a bath. While I was still tipsy, Sonny called and my sister kept pushing my head underwater so I couldn't say anything. She made up some believable excuse for Sonny and then told me I shouldn't be talking to him because I was drunk.

While we were in Arizona shooting, Diana Vreeland got fired from *Vogue*. Grace Mirabella took over and cut down my spread from what was supposed to be twenty pages to maybe six and didn't publish them until more than a year later, in August 1970, in a spread entitled "Cher-Okee in Indian Country."

I came home feeling really good about the shoot when Sonny sat me down and confessed something that pushed me over the edge. "We're broke, Cher. We owe the IRS two hundred seventy thousand dollars in back taxes and we don't have the money. We're going to have to go back on the road, bud."

I didn't cry. I didn't yell. I didn't even think, *Thank God I bought two hair dryers*, because when you've lost everything, trust me, having two of everything means absolutely nothing. Most of all I felt scared. Holding our baby, close to bankruptcy in a mansion that suddenly felt too big, I sat very still, trying to take in what Sonny was telling me. As if talking to a child, he explained that he'd had to sink several hundred thousand dollars of our own money into making both movies and that we also owed another unspecified amount in loans. I thought of all his fancy cars and then I thought of the moment I'd begged him to buy me the house. "We'll swing it," he'd told me, and I realized that the house of my dreams cost almost exactly what we owed. That's how people in the movie industry or music business get into such trouble. You come from nothing and suddenly you've got all this money and you're doing *Ed Sullivan* and people are screaming for you all over the world and you think it's gonna last forever. Then one day it dries up and you realize you never had any backup.

As someone who didn't know my ass from first base when it came to money, I'd always felt lucky to have Sonny, believing he was both savvy and shrewd. It never occurred to me that he didn't know enough about finances and might not be the best man for the job. Neither of us had ever stayed long enough in any job to pay income tax, so I guess he hadn't factored that in, or maybe he'd simply ignored it. Everything had happened so fast that paying taxes was probably the last thing on his mind. We didn't have a business manager, only Charlie and Brian, who knew nothing about the music business, and we'd never have let them take care of our money. Joe D knew more but he was a gangster. I'm pretty sure he stole jewels, and I doubt that he ever paid taxes.

Sonny had been keeping the bad news from me until the baby was born and assured me that he'd tried everything he could to save us from ruin. I could tell how much it hurt him to admit screwing up. We were so broke that he'd been borrowing money from our chauffeur, Joseph. How do you like that? You've got to give him an A for effort. He'd not even paid Tony Curtis in full for our house yet, so we couldn't sell it, and the property market had dipped, so there'd have been little return anyway. Sonny also told me he knew it would break my heart to leave that house. Our only hope was to sell our latest movie to a studio and go back to doing gigs, even though we'd no longer be playing the big venues and the money would be far less.

"So that's how things are, Cher," Sonny told me finally, his voice flat. "There's nothing else to do but start again." Then my hearing went out and I was completely inside myself. I could see in Sonny's face that he was afraid and trying to hide it. Having just had a baby, my hormones were totally out of whack. The worse a situation is, the quieter I am. I was silent. The worst part was this was just a beginning and I didn't know if it was the beginning of the end, really the end. I started to have a horrendous panic attack and was shaking with fear. Sonny took me by the shoulders and said, "Look at me. Just give me two years and I promise we'll be bigger than ever." He seemed so determined and had so much energy. Most of all, though, he had a great belief in us as stars. Something about the way he looked at me made me believe him.

"Okay, Son," I told him as bravely as I could, wiping my eyes. "Two years."

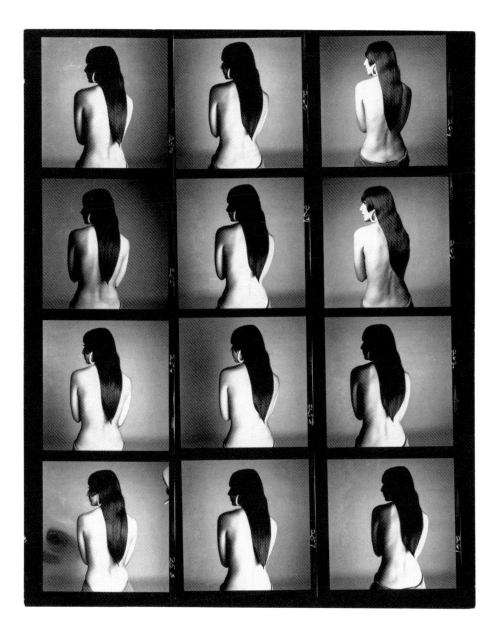

*First photograph with Richard. Mrs. Vreeland was there.*

*Our first managers, Charlie and Brian.*

*Sonny and I join hundreds in Hollywood to protest police brutality, 1966.*

*Needlepointing my life away.*

*With my beloved Scunci, 1970s.*

In the pool with Sonny at the Encino house.

Break time on the road.

Joey and me.

Ready for an awards show.

*Just arrived at the venue, preparing to go onstage.*

*Serang and me. He licked my leg, and his tongue was like sandpaper.*

*Son, me, and Margie.*

Chastity *movie shot with Sonny in the director's chair, my friend Joanna, and me.*

*Shaking hands with the audience at the Martin Luther King Benefit at*
*Madison Square Garden, June 28, 1968.*

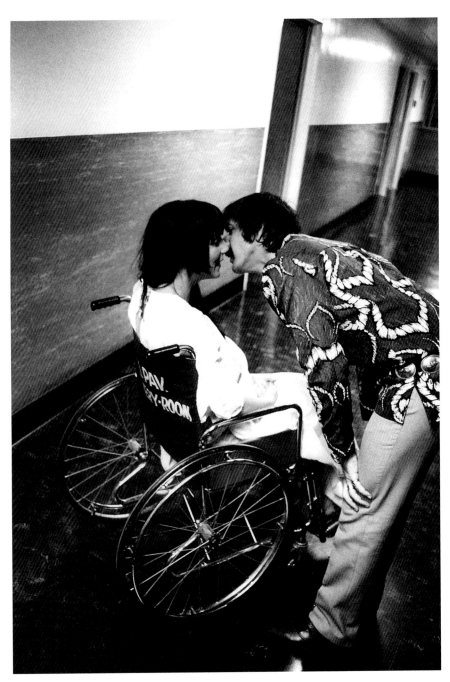

*Son kissing me as I went in to have Chas.*

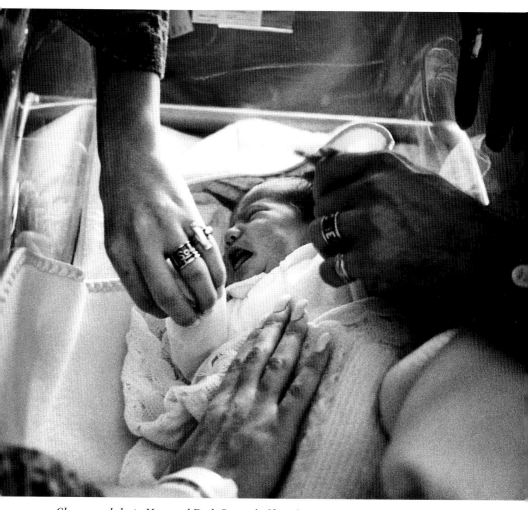

*Chas snuggled up. Mom and Dad. Sonny & Cher rings.*

*Mama plays with Chas. Working the Blue Room, Fairmont Hotel.*

To start the next phase of our career, we all went to London to appear on a British television show called *This Is Tom Jones*, hosted by the singer. That May night in Elstree Studios also featured a teenage Stevie Wonder singing a medley of his songs. I had been a fan since I saw him on *American Bandstand* in 1963 as Little Stevie Wonder singing "Fingertips." Then, the host and I sang "The Beat Goes On." Tom was in a tux, and I wore a Native squaw dress. It was Sonny's idea to storm onto the stage and forcibly drag me off as if he were angry with me for singing with another man, leaving Tom shrugging and perplexed. It was all pre-rehearsed, but the irony was that Sonny's act wasn't that far from the truth.

We flew from London to New York, where I learned that Grampa Roy had passed away at the age of sixty-three. I couldn't attend his funeral, but Gee did, and told me that Mom was very upset to lose the man she still adored.

From New York, Sonny came with me to Alabama to finish recording my sixth solo album and my first for Atlantic. Entitled *3614 Jackson Highway*, it was named after the address of the Muscle Shoals studio in the town of Sheffield, where it was recorded. Some of the greatest artists had recorded there: Aretha Franklin, the Rolling Stones, Joe Cocker, and Stevie Wonder to name a few. It was made clear to Sonny even before we arrived that Jerry Wexler, a producer and partner at Atlantic Records who was said to have coined the term "rhythm and blues," was going to be the producer, but that didn't stop Sonny from giving his opinion. When I arrived with Chas and Sonny in tow, I could immediately tell that Jerry wasn't happy. Sonny claimed he was there to support me and take photos, and it was he who took the picture of me in a beaded outfit standing outside the studio with the band that was used on the record sleeve. But he couldn't stop interfering, and he and Jerry didn't get along at all. Sonny and Jerry argued so much that Jerry ended up in the hospital and I ended up lying in the cemetery across the street where I'd talk to the dead guys.

The record was released on June 20, 1969, less than three months after I became a new mother and not long before the release of our movie *Chastity*. Sonny wrote in his diary, *It's a great album. I think it's the best she's ever done.* A few critics said nice things about my voice, but it failed to change our fortunes. Atco canceled my next album and dropped me.

Our film *Chastity* came out the same month, distributed by American International Pictures, but it was given an R rating, even though there was nothing in it that should have gotten it labeled as "risqué," so the younger audience we were trying to target couldn't see it without being accompanied by an adult.

The movie was panned by the critics. Deflated, we both came down with the flu and were too sick to attend the premiere, which was probably just as well.

Without a hit record or movie, the plan to go on a concert tour was dead in the water. There wasn't enough work for us to support our agent Harvey Kresky from William Morris, so he left to be with more successful clients, while Joe D gamely stuck with us. Sonny put our house on the market, and aside from the upcoming gigs we had at the Flamingo in Vegas, he booked us into the only other dates we could get, doing the supper club circuit and performing in hotel and casino dinner theaters.

Sonny and I didn't know what to expect but were relieved to be working, so, in September 1969, we put Chastity in a travel crib and hired a nanny named Heidi, who turned out to be the sweetest woman in the world. Sonny put a band together. They traveled separately in a van, and we had our car with Chas in a wicker cradle as we set out on a schedule of back-to-back shows starting with three weeks at the Elmwood Casino in Windsor, Ontario, Canada. I'm sure the venue was perfectly fine, but coming from where we'd come from, it felt horrible. We stayed in a motel across the street and there was a railway station nearby that kept us awake all night with the whistles of passing trains. The plumbing in our room didn't work properly and there was mildew on the paper-thin walls. We un-packed, and Sonny asked for a hot plate and started cooking pasta sauce in our room for us and the band because we couldn't afford to pay restaurant prices. I wanted to curl up and die.

For our stage appearances, Sonny dressed in his tuxedo with a fancy shirt and bow tie. He decided I needed a more grown-up look, so he asked Sadie to make me a Grecian-style dress, to which they added a beautiful bronze-colored chain that went from the shoulder and looped down to the hips and back up. I looked like some sort of goddess. On my feet I wore Roman sandals Sonny had the movie outfitters Western Costume make for me. Dressed and ready, we'd leave Chas with Gee or Heidi and take the service elevator to the ground floor, where we negotiated our way through the busy kitchen while trying not to slip on any grease or walk into a waiter flying past us carrying five plates. Standing by the swing doors and trying to keep out of the way, we'd listen for our cue from the previous act and then walk on waving and smiling as if we were playing to a sold-out Hollywood Bowl. As always, I'd get past my nerves by staring at Sonny rather than making eye contact with the "audience" as we sang our sad set.

Having played to thirty thousand screaming fans, now we were lucky if we had an audience of more than a hundred. At one of our first midnight shows at the Elmwood, we had to play for four people. Four. A lot of the places were real dives. One night I had a panic attack at the thought of having to stand on that stage for an hour. I didn't think I could go on. Freaking out, I told Sonny, "I can't do it. Not tonight. I just can't!" He was gentle with me and said, "That's okay. Just come on with me for the opening and then you can walk off anytime you want. I'll just do a song until you can come back." When it got too much for me, I did as he suggested and walked off to watch him singing from the wings. We had gone from performing for huge crowds of kids who loved us and knew every word of our songs to small groups of people who didn't know us, didn't necessarily like us, and might be best described as ambivalent or even mildly annoyed. These audiences weren't here to see us perform; they were coming to have dinner or for drinks at the midnight show. I wasn't used to begging an audience to like us. This was my worst nightmare. It's a thousand times harder to come back than to become. Becoming famous is hard, but making a comeback is almost impossible. I have done it so many times, but this was my first time. Sonny knew me well and the right thing to say because knowing I could walk off whenever I wanted made it easier for me to go up onstage each night and sing with him.

Wanting to keep us in the public eye, Sonny arranged for us to appear as guests on any TV show that he could get us on. We flew to Philadelphia to cohost with Mike Douglas on his TV show, inviting him to come onstage and sing "Baby Don't Go" with us. Later, Mike asked Sonny why we were performing in supper clubs, and my chameleon of a husband didn't even flinch. "I think it solidifies you as a performer," he replied, sounding as if he meant it. "I think you must get in touch with the general public, not just a certain age group. And you must entertain when you get up there." He added that our audiences were very engaged with us as a couple, but that his dream was to push me forward as a solo artist and be the force behind the music.

Later in the show, we brought Chastity on for her first-ever television appearance.

For the first two years of her life, we were working constantly playing small gigs around the United States. Chas reached so many milestones, like sitting up or crawling for the first time, in hotels and motels. Chas was our only entertainment and such a gift. Being with her was like having Christmas every day. She was so happy and adorable that her little feet never touched the ground because everyone from the band to the hotel staff wanted to cuddle her. Once her blond hair started coming through, it grew out with black tips, so she looked like a little punk rocker decades before we even knew what that was. After watching many rehearsals, she started pretending to conduct the band. One time I put my T-shirt on her and my headband around her belly so it looked like a little evening gown. She jumped around "conducting" and got so excited. An unbelievably good baby, she was the sole focus of our long road back to who we once were. We had no money, no big house, and no fancy meals, so the three of us just hung out together. No matter how difficult our circumstances, Sonny could always make me laugh. And in a weird way, struggling again helped revitalize our relationship. Being poor narrowed the focus of what we could do, what was important, and how to best spend our time. It made us feel like it was the three of us against the world.

Trying to engage the audience and using me as part of an experiment, Sonny came up with one of his crazier ideas. He thought I should sing the "Un bel dì" (One Fine Day) aria from Puccini's *Madame Butterfly* that I'd memorized as a kid. "Doing that as a solo halfway through the act would be different and interesting," he insisted.

I said, "Please, I really don't want to do it. Isn't this already enough torture?" He said, "Cher, c'mon." Nobody liked it and most people looked at me with their mouths open, but of course the night we stopped doing "Un bel dì" someone came in and requested it. OMG.

Everything was hard at that time: the accommodations, the hours, the people in the audience. Each night was like a war, and we lost almost every battle. Finally, at a second show at the Elmwood in Windsor, Ontario, I got tired of people wishing they were somewhere else. It was a midnight show so a lot of the people in the audience were drunk and didn't care, so I just turned my back to them and started talking to the band and making them laugh. (Thank God bands laugh at anything.) A heckler in the audience yelled out something and it made me think, *Okay, man, fuck you.* I don't remember what he said, who could know, but I said something back that must have been funny enough because even some people in the audience started laughing. Son just kind of took a step back, looking at me like *Okay let's see where you're going.* Usually, he'd be giving me side eye, but he just kind of waited. It felt good because I finally got to say how I was feeling. Then Sonny joined in and we started to have fun between ourselves so it didn't really matter what the audience thought because we were just enjoying ourselves together.

We started moving toward this new kind of act and got braver with what we said onstage, but it was always hit or miss. We'd say something one night and the audience would roar, then we'd say it another night and they'd be silent. It was starting to work, but it wasn't working enough. It was a glimmer of hope, but we were still in these hotels every day stuck performing two shows every night. I wanted it to be like it used to be.

One evening while I was in our hotel room, someone from our group brought up a man who analyzed handwriting. He'd done it for some other people in our band and we'd had a lot of fun listening to what hc deduced. This stranger didn't know me or my story. I was in another room when I wrote something down. When I returned, he looked at what I'd scrawled and put his hand on my shoulder.

"You're unhappy," he told me quietly. "Don't worry. You won't be with your husband forever."

I was so shocked I could barely speak. I was also terrified because I worried that what he'd said might get back to Sonny. After he left I couldn't stop thinking about it. I felt anxious and afraid. It was like the Bermuda Triangle of my life. It was awful. I didn't say anything for a few days, but finally I went to Sonny and told him, "Son, I'm unhappy. I don't know why, but I'm so sad." He took a beat, then exploded. He yelled, "You're so ungrateful. Do you want me to divorce you?" I was stunned. The first thing in my mind was *I'm never going to tell you how I feel again.*

# 15

## ladies and gentlemen, sonny & cher

I guess it's true what they say about necessity being the mother of invention, because slowly, we developed an act that eventually people would line up to see. They didn't come for our singing; they wanted to hear our jokes. We weren't experienced as writers and it took a long time to figure out what audiences liked. Son and I started to just talk to each other onstage, and if it was funny we kept it. Sonny began to see that this was a thing. I'd always been a bit of a wiseass, and when I first met Sonny, it had amused him. Now in front of these audiences, I was getting to speak more loosely again. I just was who I am, kind of like my mom, which is where I got my sense of humor, as well as from my uncle (the funniest man to ever draw breath), my grandpa, Jake, and, after she got a little bit older, my sister. Growing up, having a sense of humor was prized—but never in a gazillion years did I imagine that I'd become a stand-up comedian. It didn't happen overnight, but after months and months of refining our act, our shows started selling out. I'm talking *months*.

Mostly I'd poke fun at Sonny and he'd fire back with retorts. I'd make jokes about his mom's overeating, while he teased me about my nose or being too thin. His height and his singing were easy targets, as were his hopes of becoming a sex symbol. "You'd have to come out naked and on fire to attract the attention of this audience," I'd tell him, adding, after a beat, "Well, maybe just on fire . . ."

Our dynamic started to change because I'd taken us into a new area just by accident. All of a sudden we got excited again like when we started Sonny & Cher. Our stage personas were the opposite of our real relationship. He wasn't being himself when he played the aggrieved husband allowing the occasional comeback—the hapless victim of a glamorous bitch. He was just being smart and enjoying himself, which made it fun for the audience—and for me. Being onstage suddenly felt like acting or playing a game, and it was one I began to enjoy. The more fun Sonny and I had, the more the band laughed and, finally, the audience too.

The jokes were so good that they made the audience listen to the songs, which rounded out the show. Instead of playing to a couple of drunks with their backs to us, we found ourselves wisecracking to couples who identified with our marital gags and bought tickets to watch us joke around. As 1970 rolled in, we developed more of a following. Each performance, we would go onstage with a rough idea of what had happened the night before and then try to polish it and make it better, refining in real time to get a solid twenty minutes. The band became our accomplices. They'd belly laugh at our jokes and people in the audience would crack up along with them.

As time went on, we got better and better. It helped that people would clap for us now, which made being up there more fun and made our performance more relaxed. Sonny would say something about himself, like making fun of how he dressed in the sixties: "I did look a little weird and stupid."

"Yeah," I'd reply. "What's your excuse now?"

Or "Hey, Cher, do you remember when kids used to try to rip my clothes off and scream?"

"Now they'd scream after you ripped your clothes off," I'd snap. Timing was everything.

He'd tell the audience, "Christmas this year was really nice. My mother cooked, and she really knows hows to stuff a turkey, doesn't she?"

Expressionless, I'd arch an eyebrow and say, "Yeah, straight into her mouth."

Sonny was the perfect foil, and for a straight man he could be hysterical onstage. He'd often make himself laugh so much that he couldn't even sputter out his lines, which made me crack up until neither of us could continue.

In a far better frame of mind, we celebrated Chas's first birthday in early March 1970. Sonny was a big kid in her company, and I could happily watch them both for hours. He was so creative and so nutty about her that he'd make up absurd fairy tales with an Italian twist, like the tale of Good Princess Garbage who loved garlic or cleaned up pizza boxes. Those were the kinds of stories he'd tell throughout her childhood.

We were so busy traveling and working that our world consisted only of the three of us, Denis, and Joe D. When I heard from Gee that Mom was getting married again, I was happy for her. At forty-four, she was still beautiful, and Hamilton Holt, a silver-haired Southern gentleman whose name she took—and kept—was lucky to have her. I couldn't attend their Florida wedding, and when they moved there for the three years that their marriage lasted, we could only get down there to visit twice, as we were working constantly.

We continued touring our act as Sonny added more and more dates with the help of the William Morris Agency. We'd spend a week in one venue, then do a series of one-night stands in adjacent cities. We marked my twenty-fourth birthday and Sonny's thirty-fifth on the road. On my second Mother's Day as a new mom, we found ourselves in a crummy hotel room, where Sonny tried to cheer me up by writing *Happy Mother's Day I Love You, Mom* on the bathroom mirror in soap. I picked up his camera and took a photograph as proof.

Our new agent, Freddy Apollo from WMA, came to see our new act and liked it so much that he arranged for us to appear before an audience of comedians at the Century Plaza Hotel in Los Angeles. Bill Cosby was at the height of his career, and we were on right before him. It was a nightmare rivaling our performance for Princess Margaret. For reasons I can't now imagine, we were offered a television script not long after for a new television special called *The Sonny & Cher Nitty Gritty Hour.* The show went okay, but it felt too formulaic and less spontaneous than what we did on tour. Nothing came of it and we were soon back on the road with our twice-nightly shows. I felt permanently tired. The good news was that responses to our performances were better, so we were making money and starting to gain a following. Sonny kept saying, "Cher, we're heading someplace. We're gonna get someplace. You'll see." I figured we'd at least be able to pay off the government, which I was still nervous about, but Sonny kept saying, "I promise, I promise." In this case he gets a real A for effort because Sonny kept pushing for us to get bigger and better bookings, and before I knew it we had an eight-minute role in a popular TV show called *Love, American Style* that aired in January 1971. I played a girl who was excited because her boyfriend was about to drop by and propose, and Sonny played a kooky friend of his who was in love with me and had himself mailed to my address to persuade me out of the marriage. His ploy worked, of course, and we skipped off into the sunset to eat Italian.

It wasn't until one night in June that year, almost exactly two years after Sonny told me, "Just give me two years, Cher, and I promise you we'll be back on top," that everything changed. Fred Silverman, the thirty-three-year-old executive who'd taken over as head of programming and development at CBS Television, came to see a performance we gave in New York after he'd spotted us somewhere. We were appearing for three nights at the Royal Box supper club in the fifty-one-story convention hotel the Americana, where a few years earlier Lennon and McCartney had announced the formation of Apple Corps. Fred liked us and talked to William Morris about booking us as substitute hosts for a late-night episode of the hugely popular *Merv Griffin Show* in mid-April.

Being invited to host a prime-time television talk show was a huge deal for us. Merv had started out as a singer with big bands and ended up on Broadway and in films before being invited to host his own TV show in 1962. Every family in America watched it, including ours, and when he went on to create the game shows *Wheel of Fortune* and *Jeopardy!* he became one of our country's first billionaire media moguls.

The format of Merv's talk show was different from anything we'd done before, and we were completely out of our comfort zone. Previous guests had included people like the author Gore Vidal, singer Judy Garland, actress Janet Leigh, director John Huston, and boxer Muhammad Ali. Our schedule had us interviewing the editor of *Cosmopolitan*, Helen Gurley Brown, who'd written the bestselling book *Sex and the Single Girl*, and the actor Michael Blodgett, who'd starred in the movie *Beyond the Valley of the Dolls*. We also chatted with actress Jackie Joseph, a regular on *The Doris Day Show*, and I was filmed away from the studio with football player Fred "the Hammer" Williamson, which I loved because I was such a football fan. Our turn in the spotlight seemed to go well and the reviews were enthusiastic.

Unbeknownst to us, Fred Silverman had spotted some potential in our act and was looking for a more contemporary variety show to attract younger viewers weary of longstanding hosts such as Merv Griffin, Dean Martin, and Dinah Shore. Wanting more feedback, Fred sent two of his best producers and writers, who'd recently worked together on *The Andy Williams Show*, to watch us and help him decide if we were good enough to have our own gig. When Allan Blye and Chris Bearde wandered into the Fairmont Hotel's Venetian Room with its crimson carpets, elaborate lights, and giant F's on the walls, they joked that it reminded them of the dining room of the *Titanic* "just before it hit the iceberg, but with fewer people."

Incredibly, though, the pair enjoyed our odd little act, saying later, "God bless them, they came out and did their funny exchange and sang their hits and there was something there. As singers they were just okay, but as comics they were hysterical." After the show, they came backstage, and we all hit it off immediately. They decided we didn't have experience but had raw talent. By the time they landed back in LA, they'd already written the formula of a new show for us, based on what Sonny and I had developed on our own, and within days Fred Silverman offered us a chance to record a summer pilot, *The Sonny & Cher Comedy Hour.* We got six episodes because CBS was releasing a miniseries about the six wives of Henry VIII and we were the lead in. Thanks, Henry.

It felt surreal to be embarking on this exciting new adventure together after all we'd been through. Sonny was especially pleased, strutting around telling everyone who'd listen that he always knew we'd make it. Knowing that we'd need good legal representation to negotiate the new contracts, Sonny remembered the lawyer Irwin Spiegel, whom he'd always hoped to hire. When Sonny was young he was in court watching a trial for some reason. The man who was in the right should have won, but instead the guy who was clearly in the wrong won the suit. Irwin had represented the guy in the wrong, and from that day on Sonny decided if he ever needed a lawyer that's who he would hire. He was just another suit as far as I was concerned, but he went with Son to their first meetings with CBS. There was one detail I cared about most, and I told the executives, "I'd really like Bob Mackie to design my costumes." When I said that, everybody looked at me like I was crazy. I might as well have said, "I'm leaving Sonny to run away with Dumbo." We had no money, and there was no way we were getting someone of Bob Mackie's stature to design for me. They told me the designer Ret Turner had already been assigned. Then they started talking business and I got up and left. I called Bob and asked for his help. He agreed to collaborate with his friend Ret, who was the head of wardrobe for NBC. He too was a legendary figure.

We were given two months to tie up our touring commitments and prepare for our first show. We felt ready for it and were thrilled and delighted at the opportunity. We got our first live audience for *The Sonny & Cher Comedy Hour* by telling nearby shoppers there would be free food and drinks from the Farmers Market. Thankfully, it was the only time we needed to bribe anyone to watch our show. Not that we knew that the day our pilot was filmed at Studio 31 in CBS's Television City at Fairfax Avenue and Beverly Boulevard. We were both just praying it went well. Sonny was more nervous than me for a change, which secretly amused me. I watched him jumping about the stage like a grasshopper and thought, *Son, come on! Get it together. We've been doing this shit for years.*

Once in a while if my stage fright was really bad on the road, I'd take a quarter of one of Sonny's Valiums to take the edge off, but that day, I wasn't afraid. I had our routine down, having memorized my script on first sight. The show was almost identical to what we'd been doing for the previous two years, only without the constant traveling and the bad nightclubs. With our experiences on the *Nitty Gritty Hour* and *Merv Griffin* under our belts, I felt better equipped to perform to a camera and a small crowd. We also had a great crew helping us with everything from costume changes to planting cue cards in case we forgot our lines (as Sonny often did), so it was no longer us against the world.

Ret Turner did a great job as head of costuming and quickly became one of my dearest friends. He'd often pick up Chas after her dance classes and bring her to set, where she would show us her new tap dance routines she'd learned that day, then he'd let her twist his red hair into many little ponytails all over his head. It was a family dynamic as well as a work dynamic. Our budget was so small to begin with that we only had a few outfits each. Ret made a full-length white dress that I wore to open the show, and we adapted it repeatedly and in all kinds of clever ways: it started as a Grecian-style halter-neck and ended up as a cutaway. Ret and Bob put cherries on it, a heart for Valentine's Day, fringe, necklaces, or whatever they had on hand. There was no money for the beads or bows I longed for. Carol Burnett's soundstage was just across from ours, and Bob Mackie designed for her show, so we'd often borrow or steal pieces from her wardrobe to dress things up. Luckily, she and I were the same size. They even raided our rivals at NBC, working miracles with whatever they could find, especially when it came to the crazier character costumes.

As the magic hour approached, we took our places on the specially designed set and I squeezed Sonny's hand. His chief concern was the presence of Fred Silverman, who'd flown in from New York and was watching from the wings with Chastity in his arms. He'd come to visit Carol Burnett and check up on his new show *All in the Family*, which was filmed on a soundstage near ours. Fred was all smiles, but even with that teddy bear look of his we knew he was one of the suits and the man to impress. A reporter and photographer from *Life* magazine were also waiting, camera and notebook poised. The stakes were high.

An animation of us created by graphic artist John Wilson rolled and an announcer called out, "From Television City in Hollywood . . . ladies and gentlemen, Sonny and Cher!" I stood there, taking it all in, thinking, *Ah, THIS is what I'm supposed to do.* Ever since I'd sat open-mouthed at Grauman's Chinese Theatre as a five-year-old I'd wanted to be up on a screen in my own show. I'd had the same feeling watching Elvis. Twenty years after *Dumbo,* it was finally happening. There was a dramatic drum roll, then the stage wall lifted for our arrival. It was covered in dozens of gigantic round lightbulbs like those on a vanity mirror, each bulb printed with cartoon versions of Sonny's and my faces. We walked up the stairs from the back and onto the stage, our fingers interlocked. Dressed in coordinated white outfits, we opened by singing alternate lines of "The Beat Goes On" until it was my cue to step forward and pretend to get carried away by myself, just as I'd done in our nightclub act. Sonny faked indignation and tried to cut in, but I kept cutting across him or blocking him from view until he stopped the music altogether, hands on his hips, as I carried on singing a cappella. "What am I, chopped liver?" he asked. "This song was written for both of us, sweetheart."

I nodded, (beat) then replied, "*Was.*" The audience burst into laughter, and I carried on singing. Eventually I stopped and let him have his turn, staring him down.

"Are you upset because I wanted to do my spot?" he asked.

"Goodness to Betsy, no," I replied, using an old-fashioned phrase while flashing the audience a knowing smile.

Giving up, Sonny allowed me the spotlight, but I swayed my hips so provocatively that he interrupted again, stepping in front of me saying, "No, no, no. She's the mother of my child!" To me he cried, "Can you stop that? Use your feet, that's what I do, and snap your fingers." He got his first round of applause with his aside, "Cher only moves that way onstage. After the show, *nothing* goes on."

The seventy-eight-year-old veteran comedian and vaudevillian Jimmy Durante was hilarious as one of our first guests. (He was an old-timey guy—it would take us a while to get younger people to come on.) Jimmy was in the first of our "vamp" skits, featuring me dressed as notorious women of history, such as Cleopatra, Pocahontas, and Mata Hari. After the skit, I would sit on top of an upright honky-tonk piano with my legs crossed or lying along the top in a gorgeous red gown singing the best song about being a "scamp, a vamp, and a bit of a tramp," before spelling out V-A-M-P. I loved that part because I was not just singing but acting, and the whole act was so much fun. The audience seemed to love it too, and the studio made it one of my signature sketches because of the great feedback. The whole experience reminded me of our movie *Good Times*, which Sonny had virtually written by himself and suddenly seemed way ahead of its time.

I'd be lying if I told you I could remember every detail of those first few shows, but I do know that it took us a while to find our footing. Fred Silverman was like a protective father figure to us and kept assuring the executives at CBS that we'd be a hit if they gave us a chance. Looking back at that first season, it was hard work but it taught us new skills. It's one thing to be funny off the cuff but an entirely different challenge to be reading lines and make them funny. Was it perfect? Absolutely not, but it was a great change to be off the road and on our own stage. Because Sonny didn't memorize his lines, he'd squint to read the cue cards stuck to the back of props. I'd let him flounder around for a while, riffing, going along with him wherever he went and following up with a one-liner. The show was written for Sonny to be the straight man with me landing the zingers, but we developed our own thing. I told him, "Son, don't read the damn cue cards like you're reading the damn cue cards, just blow it out and be silly like you always are." Sonny respected me as an artist and he also knew I had his back, so when I was abrupt with criticism about our act like this, we were talking as two equals, and he listened. I didn't have time to explain at length, and he knew I was speaking up to be helpful to him. He soon leaned into his own style of comedy and was hilarious. He'd go freewheeling, running around the stage like a large child. He often had me in stitches, and people loved him. Our techniques and personalities were completely different, but we came together to make something perfectly whole. As we figured out what worked, we were able to play off each other and Sonny began to feel more free experimenting and going off script. It was like the show had a life of its own, and eventually we could just be. It was something entirely new, which is always difficult, but once it took shape it was magic. I don't remember a single show when we were angry with each other. We could be having a bad day, but the moment we got to work: we were Sonny & Cher. What you saw was really what was true. We had so much fun and we were equal. Performing in that show was a perfect playground—we both understood what it was to be two kids playing. If Sonny came walking through the door right now, we'd be Sonny & Cher. That's all we were meant to be and that's what we were.

Knowing that our lifestyle was going to change, we hired a British nanny named Linda Koot for Chastity. She was in her twenties and fit enough to chase around after our very active daughter. Linda brought her on set almost every day to eat lunch with us and hang out with our crew of people. Chas had no idea we were working and thought the whole show was one big game in which everyone played dress-up and had fun. Knowing she was in safe hands with Linda, we could focus on our weekly routine, which began early every Monday morning with a read-through of the script. Everyone sat around the table making suggestions and asking questions. The monologue in our pilot was pretty much the same structure as what we performed on the road but everything else developed as the show evolved. There was all kinds of different material: the recurring "vamp" segment based on famous women throughout history; a sketch called "the launderette" with me playing Laverne and Teri Garr playing Olivia; "the fortune teller" with my head inside a vending machine telling Sonny his future; "Mr. and Ms.," a gender-bending sketch with me as the man of the household, along with so many others. During the first six shows we were just trying things to figure out what would stick, guided by our director, Art Fisher, whose voice would yell "Cut!" from beyond the bright stage lights like the voice of God. When his voice would come over the speaker, Chas would look up in the ceiling and ask, "Is that Art Fissue?" We were working hard but having such a blast. Our producers Chris Bearde and Allan Blye did a great job, and our reviews improved week after week.

The only problem everyone had was with my hair, which hung well past my waist. Stylists would be sent to my dressing room to prepare me for each new sequence, only to take one look at my thick black mane, freak out, and say, "What the hell are we supposed to do with *this*?" Frightened by the challenge, they'd try to squash it under wigs, which was a disaster until we finally found Renata, who'd worked in German opera and used their style of fixing hair for wraps so that finally the wigs slipped easily on and off. I did my own makeup for years because I never liked the way the professionals made me look. I didn't have a makeup person until Tommy Cole did my makeup for *Mask* in 1984, and I didn't get someone consistent until *Witches of Eastwick* in 1986, which brought me one of my closest friends, Leonard Eagleman, who would continue to do my makeup for every film afterward. Within weeks of shooting our show, my skin broke out in tiny bumps due to the coating of foundation I had to wear for hours at a time under hot stage lights. My face began to resemble that of a hormonal teenager. I can't have looked too bad, though, because our reviews continued to be positive. Critics described Sonny and me as "endearingly mismatched" and applauded the producers for leaving in the bits where he screwed up and had to ad-lib. Our show wasn't what people expected to see on TV, but that's why it worked. It was just a married couple poking at each other, and people seemed to tap into that, especially when the cameras focused on how we looked into each other's eyes or how Sonny would brush a stray hair back from my face. Fred Silverman said of us later, "When we started, they were very in love and very close and it was my hope that they would be on the air for twenty-five years." I'm sure that's what Sonny hoped too.

We were working on the show every weekday: Mondays were a read-through, Tuesdays were for rehearsals, Wednesdays were camera blocking and dance rehearsal if they were needed, plus costume fittings afterward and recording opera tracks if there were any, Thursdays and Fridays were taping days when we'd block and shoot everything including the "chroma key" sequences that used blue screen, a technology that Art Fisher had pioneered. Friday was the day the live audience filed in to watch us open and close the show. By the weekend we were exhausted, so we took off to recover and spend time with Chastity, who'd learned to swim at six months and loved splashing around in the pool with us. It was a lot, but we did our best to make it work. Some weekends we'd go to Oxnard Beach, where Sonny had bought us a funky little house. It was there that I had one of my happiest days. I was sitting out on the back steps watching Sonny walk to the beach with Chas when suddenly she stopped, came running back to me, gave me a big kiss, and said, "Mommy, I love you so much," before heading back to join her dad. It was such a healing moment.

By the time our summer pilot season ended on September 6, 1971, CBS was delighted with the ratings and immediately offered to renew, giving us thirteen more episodes of *The Sonny & Cher Comedy Hour*, set to air from December 27 to March 20, 1972, taking us to just before Chas's third birthday. They brought in some exciting new actors and writers, including Teddy Ziegler (who I loved), Freeman King, Peter Cullen, Murray Langston, and a young writer/comic named Steve Martin who'd had success with *The Smothers Brothers Comedy Hour* (a show canceled by CBS after only one season due to an offensive sketch involving a spoof sermon). Steve would go on to tour with us after the show and then become a huge star doing comedy and film. They also hired comedian Teri Garr, who was funny enough to have her own show and was teased mercilessly by the boys. They all fucked with her constantly: if she had pigtails they would pull them or stick them in inkwells or black paint, step on the heels of her shoes, or draw on her face while she slept or whatever. It wasn't mean-spirited, they were just childish idiots. I was always getting after them, telling them to behave or there would be trouble to pay. She and I became fast friends.

Things felt different now that the show was picked up. We had more confidence in everything we were doing. It was like a dream. Sonny and I now had much bigger dressing rooms with couches and a bathroom. I loved it. On Thursdays and Fridays things got especially lively because Ret would go to the Farmers Market and get tons of fun things to eat, then set them up in my room. People would just casually pass by on some pretense, then come in and sit down and eat our food. Everyone from the studio would hang out in my room then, even Allan or Chris might drop by because I had such an unreal spread from Ret.

As someone who'd always loved fashion, I felt like a kid set loose in the dress-up box at CBS now that we had the budget for a parade of costumes. Being fitted for them as they were pinned and cut to hug my body took me back to the days of watching Mamaw make beautiful clothes or trying on Mom's dresses while she was at work. From the start, the "suits" at CBS complained about how much my gowns cost, but they stopped bothering us when they realized people weren't only tuning in for the comedy but also to see my costumes. The money spent on the gowns was bringing in extra viewers.

Each week I'd have a solo. Alone onstage in one of Bob's breathtaking gowns, I would sing an old song that I loved, often from a classic movie or one my mother would sing. Before I started to sing, I'd ask the stage manager to go find Son. (It was something I did even after we were divorced.) He would then come over to the set and stand behind the camera to watch me. The stage lights were bright, so I could only see his shadow, but knowing he was there was a comfort. Afterward, he'd come up to me and tell me what he thought. If there was something he thought I could do better, he'd tell me and I'd do it over again, but I could tell by the look on his face when I'd aced it. I couldn't have done those solos without him. When it came to my singing, I trusted him.

Working on television was so completely different from what I knew. Each week we had new guests, new songs to perform, new scripts to learn. When it was the two of us onstage, we could make up our own jokes as they came to us. "Do you believe in reincarnation?" I asked him one night. When he nodded, I paused for a couple of seconds and then hit him with "Then come back taller." Jokes about his height always got the best laughs.

When we'd started with the summer show, it was hard for Chris and Allan (our producers) to get guests, but the moment we went into prime time, and our ratings went sky high, people started begging to get on. We couldn't beat them away with a stick. Our show ultimately brought on huge names like Truman Capote, Muhammad Ali, Elton John, Tina Turner, Twiggy, Redd Foxx, Kris Kristofferson, Hugh Hefner, Bob Hope, Jean Stapleton, the Jackson 5, and Billie Jean King, among many others. A number of our guests were serious actors and musicians who wanted a chance to goof around, put on tights, and wear kooky costumes. It felt amazing to invite Tony Curtis and our old friend Glen Campbell to goof around with us, as well as the comedian Phyllis Diller, who played the harpsichord and was funny and serious all at once as she tried to get me to crack up as "the princess who couldn't smile." We also had *Charlie's Angels* actress Farrah Fawcett, who became a friend. Years later, when Farrah was sick, she would ask if she could spend her last days in my home because she wanted to see the ocean. Ryan denied her, saying, "If she wants to see the ocean, she could stay at my house."

Carol Burnett came on the show several times and was always a pistol. We were destined to be friends from the beginning. We're two Tauruses, c'mon. That dame could make me laugh with just a look, which of course is no surprise given her comic genius. Chastity worshipped her and had seen her so often on TV that she thought of her as famous, which wasn't how she thought of me at all.

Once we wrapped each night, my life was very routine. I would come home, go upstairs to look at the baby, take off my eyelashes, brush my hair, put it in a ponytail, wash my face, brush my teeth, then watch TV and go to sleep. That was it. I didn't go anywhere and the work was hard on me. I had an especially demanding schedule because we had more male guests than female guests, and they often wanted to do a segment with me instead of Sonny, especially if it was a male singer who wanted a duet.

I got even busier when Sonny decided that in addition to preparing and filming a show each week we should also get back into recording new music and out on the road. "We have to make the most of this second chance, Cher," he insisted, stopping just short of repeating what was becoming his mantra: "This is our time." I knew from the look on his face that it wasn't a suggestion, but a statement of what we were doing. And who was I to argue with the man who'd kept his promise?

To capitalize on our success, he sent me to work on a new album for Kapp Records with producer Thomas "Snuff" Garrett. Because of our pressing television schedule, I was given one week to finish the record. The good news was that I immediately loved "Snuffy," who was a natural comic and great at his job. Never musically trained, he'd started as a disc jockey in Texas but had such an ear for a hit record that he was a millionaire by the time he was thirty. It was the first time Sonny didn't get involved because he was so busy putting together our new live show for our concert tour. I wanted to take more time but there was none, and Snuffy was a "get it done" kind of guy anyway. So I'd go into the studio and put the vocal down a couple of times, maybe listen to it and do it a couple more times, but that was it. I'd always know the songs perfectly before showing up because I knew I wasn't going to get any real time to sing, and back then you couldn't clean up a vocal like you can today.

Entitled *Chér* (with the accent I'd adopted when I was eleven and practicing my autograph to make me seem chic), my seventh album's cover photo was a black-and-white close-up by Richard Avedon depicting me pensive, with wet hair combed down over my face. I fought with everybody for that album cover. I was the only one who seemed to like it. The single the record company released was "Gypsys, Tramps and Thieves," and it became my first-ever top ten hit as a solo artist and even earned my first Grammy nomination. The sad truth is that although it was the first time I felt I'd been recognized by my peers, and without Sonny's name appearing anywhere, we were working so hard, I honestly don't even remember how it felt. When you're doing an album and a TV show and costume fittings and photo shoots and concerts and being a mom, it all becomes a big blur. That song has never been one of my favorites because I don't really like story songs much, tunes like "Ode to Billie Joe" by Bobbie Gentry, even though that was also a huge hit. "Gypsys" has the same kind of vibe, as did the other contenders that year—Janis Joplin's "Me and Bobby McGee" (released after her tragic death at the age of twenty-seven from a heroin overdose), Joan Baez's "The Night They Drove Old Dixie Down" (I loved that one, it's an amazing song), and Carly Simon's "That's the Way I've Always Heard It Should Be." In the end Carole King won the award for her brilliant song "Tapestry."

As Snuff Garrett liked to remind me, though, we weren't making music just for me. I never got the opportunity to pick my own songs back then. They were always chosen for me by Snuffy, Sonny, or whoever was producing—always a man. "Gypsys" became so successful that the album was reissued with a new cover, renamed to match the single, and went gold. I had to hand it to Sonny—he pushed me, but he sure knew what he was doing when he sent me back to the studio. I couldn't argue with a hit.

With something like fifty concerts under our belts by the end of that year, it took an enormous amount of time and effort to juggle performing, our TV show, and our private life. One of them had to take a hit. Sonny would always remind me. "We thought we were solid money-wise last time, but we weren't." Sonny packed our schedules so tight, not giving me enough time to catch my breath. Some weeks he arranged with production to shoot two episodes in three days so we could go straight on the road and get in nine days of touring. This was a bargain for the producers because it saved them money, but it meant double the number of costumes, fittings, dance routines, and last-minute script changes for everybody who worked on the show. That hectic schedule could only happen about once a month. Our dear friend George Schlatter (a creator of *Laugh-In*) once said, "If Sonny and Cher were driving into Hollywood from the Valley, Son would take a gig on Mulholland to break up the trip." George was making a joke but it was kidding on the square.

# 16

## i will always love you

One day we arrived for the read-through, and the script was so all over the place it had to be rewritten. Realizing we had a moment of freedom, Ret and I turned to each other like *let's get out while we can* and made a beeline for the door. I was still in my fishnet tights and leotard but rammed on my cowboy hat, made by Bob, as we jumped into my turquoise Ferrari. (I'm in love with Ferraris. My favorite was my Dino—if it was a guy I would have married it and we'd still be together.) Ret and I drove to Saks Fifth Avenue in Beverly Hills, where I saw a pair of beautiful black leather Charles Jourdan boots and bought them on the spot. As we wandered through the store, we suddenly found ourselves in this amazing round room that was all mirrored and filled with thousands of perfume bottles. I picked one up, sprayed it in the air, and told Ret, "Oh God, I love this. Sonny doesn't want me to wear perfume, but maybe I could just wear it for the show?" Ret nodded his head. Then I became aware that something was going on in that room besides me finding a perfume. I looked up to see a crowd of women had started to gather around us, pointing and whispering. When they didn't look away, I asked Ret, "What are they looking at?"

He laughed and said, "Well, you, of course. You're on television now, honey. Everyone knows who you are." I was so busy working I hadn't been out in the real world to see that I was famous again, but this time in 4k.*

Sonny and I had never been wealthier or more in demand. The IRS had been paid off and we now had fame, money, and respect. This was the fantasy we'd always imagined, although we never did walk into that Cadillac dealership with a brown paper bag full of cash. I was realizing that television fame was different than what we'd had from our records and concerts. Neither of us could believe it.

I was finally able to wear the kind of beautiful, beaded gowns I'd always dreamed of. Bob made one covered in shimmering red beads with an open stomach that just killed me. He and Ret still sometimes went on costume raids for dancers, but for me and the guest stars, they were able to create whatever they wanted with a budget that grew to five thousand dollars per dress. Bob always said my size 6 body was like a coat hanger he could hang anything on and it would look good. Bless him. At twenty-five years old and 108 pounds, I was finally getting some definition, especially once we started to do dance routines for our production numbers. Also, my body type had finally come into vogue.

Astonishingly, I was named one of the ten best-dressed women in America, along with the fashion designer Carolina Herrera and

---

* "4k" provided by Slash Electric Alexander Edwards.

Liza Minnelli. That felt surreal. Nobody would have believed it if they'd seen me in the sixties. Sonny, of course, made fun of my nomination in our next show and teased me mercilessly, claiming that my ass-kicking new outfits only accentuated my "size 38" nose.

Bob Mackie and his team knew exactly how to show off my figure, although they had to turn around each new costume within a couple of days every single week. Not one of his costumes allowed for underwear, so I lost count of the hours I stood naked in front of him and his staff at his studio on Melrose Avenue as they studied me from every angle and worked out how best to style me. Elizabeth Courtney, the celebrated dressmaker who'd fitted dresses for Marlene Dietrich and Marilyn Monroe, among others, oversaw everything. People would close in on me to tug at this and pull on that, or I'd have to whip the dress off and flip it around. Thank God, we were all friends, and most were gay men, so I never felt embarrassed.

Because Sonny and I were married, we were almost free of censorship on the show and could get away with *much* more innuendo than if we'd been single, which I found out later when I had my own show and always had two censors on my set. But Sonny and I were supposed to adhere to a law that had been passed twenty years prior, the Code of Practices for Television Broadcasters, which outlined how to dress "within the bounds of decency." Bob and I found the whole idea insane in an age when women were wearing their tits up to their shoulders. I mean, you had Raquel Welch, Marilyn Monroe, Barbara Eden, and Jayne Mansfield. Bob cut everything just on the edge of getting canceled. I don't know how we got away with it. He'd make cutaway backs and open sides, showing off my long torso but often with little strips of fabric to cover up the offending part. It was a pain in the—well, midriff. Of course, those strips would flap to one side as I moved, or Bob would abandon them altogether on occasion to see if anyone died of shock, and when they didn't, he exposed more and more of me, which I didn't mind at all. It was fun. I'd always dressed in pants, and this was the first time people saw me as feminine or sexy.

Our scripts also pushed the envelope and were on the razor's edge of risqué. People loved it. To remind our audience of the wholesomeness of Sonny & Cher, we started bringing on "the president of our fan club" for our closing song, "I Got You Babe." Dressed in a mini version of our outfits, Chastity would wander onstage, and I'd pick her up and hold her in my arms as she waved shyly at the audience. She just seemed to get it.

Our "easy viewing" show became a Monday-night institution as the families of America tapped into our vibe and turned us into a top ten hit, pulling in millions of viewers at a time. Someone described us as "television's favorite odd couple" and "the unlikely darlings of prime time." The television network carried out endless market research, and the verdict was that most people thought I was talented and beautiful with fucking amazing clothes, but Sonny was the lovable one, the silly one, the giggling fool. Fair comment.

Now that we were bigger than ever, Sonny was on a mission to keep us there. It wasn't enough to have cash to burn. He wanted to make us so much money that he knew he'd never have to cook meals in a motel room again. I don't blame him. Ditto. When we were down, we might as well have had "loser" stamped on our foreheads. Then the moment we were back everyone wanted to be our new best friend. Sonny was doing everything he could to keep up the momentum and spent all this time talking about the show and the latest deals he'd made. He seemed to be turning into one of the "suits" we'd always made fun of, as if being an entertainer wasn't enough for him anymore. He wanted to be a mogul. I was starting to miss the smiling Sicilian who'd rest Chas on one hip as he stood at the stove stirring pasta sauce.

When Sonny started smoking cigarillos, I felt compelled to challenge him. "Really, Son?" I cried the first time I saw one jammed between his lips. "You're smoking fucking cigars now?"

He looked up at me that day as if I were a sixteen-year-old and said, "Why don't you go buy yourself something?" I told myself he was tired like me, and just as overworked, but I was starting to feel that something was wrong. I reasoned that we still performed so well together, even if our time at work had become more fulfilling than our home life. Where had all the fun gone? Instead of spending as much time as possible with me and Chas, who missed him terribly, Sonny and our lawyer Irwin lost hours in meetings puffing on their cigarillos while booking more gigs, discussing new contracts, and negotiating bigger record deals. Sonny loved playing the big boss man, the wheeler-dealer. He didn't want to be just an entertainer anymore. That felt beneath him now. Gone was the happy-go-lucky Salvatore Bono that I first fell for at Aldo's coffee shop, and it bothered me, who he was becoming.

He even set up something he called "the Benevolent Army of El Primo," in which everyone—including me—was issued a nylon jacket embroidered with their name and rank. He was the self-styled El Primo, of course, and I was Prima Donna, while his "Primaderes" or "Primadettes" had stripes on their epaulettes to signify their status, from private to sergeant. I had the most for my "years of service." Our growing staff received a letter telling them that they'd been accepted to "serve under his Supreme Dictatorship" and could rise through the ranks to win a bronze, silver, or gold Sonny-style mustache, with the proviso: "Your conduct is expected to be no less than excellent and will be judged by your performance under His Supremeness." The idea was funny and the message tongue-in-cheek, but I was the one living with El Primo. I never wore that jacket, but I do still have it.

Work was a safe zone—we never ever fought on that set, but at home Sonny seemed to be disconnecting from me. One night I was watching something on television about abortion and casually commented that I thought women should be allowed a choice. He snapped at me almost as much as he did the time I told him I was unhappy or after *The Dirty Dozen* when he told me I liked it because I was sexually frustrated and yelled, "Let me out of the car." Whenever he got mad like that, it just made me shut down, even though he'd never laid a hand on me. I never understood why I didn't talk back or fight with him, but I just knew I couldn't win. You learn after a long enough period of time that it's not worth it.

Spending time with Chas, my love of fashion, and being in the CBS family kept me going, but I was still only in my twenties. I longed to have my own opinions and make some friends. I was starting to feel so closed in. We didn't go to dinners, concerts, or movies (except *The Dirty Dozen* and *The Graduate*). All I did was work, go shopping, and spend time with Chas.

Then something came along that I wanted more than anything. Tony Curtis's Holmby Hills mansion had just gone on the market. It reminded me of all the fun we'd had with Tony, going to dinners and dancing at the Factory, which was packed with every star imaginable. Tony was so social and he loved both Sonny and me. And, thank God, Sonny loved him and spending time with him enough to go out. That house represented happy memories for me. I broke down in tears asking Sonny if we could buy it.

"We're going to live in this house one day," I'd told Sonny that night five years earlier when we sped through the open gates and climbed the hill to the first mansion we'd ever seen. "Okay, bud. If you say so," he'd replied, laughing.

He wasn't laughing the day I drove him crazy, begging him to purchase the real deal. In the ten years we'd been together, I'd rarely cried or asked for anything. I didn't have to ask more than the one time—Sonny wanted the house too. It was a gargantuan symbol of how we'd come back and triumphed. It felt like my "I'll never go hungry again" Scarlett O'Hara moment. I hoped this shiny castle on the hill would change things. Like many women, I was so blind.

As opposed to the house on St. Cloud, which was completely

empty when we moved in, we had "the big house" redecorated by our friend Ronnie Wilson, so it was decked out. He went on buying trips to Europe, filling it with antiques and damask, oil paintings, and cut crystal for a fraction of the price it would have cost in America. God, it was stunning. There was a large guardhouse, a tack room that had once been part of the stables, riding trails, and a staff wing as big as a house. I'd had Chastity's bedroom decorated in the way I imagined to be every little girl's dream—pink and white with beautiful wooden carvings in the ceiling corners, a dusky pink carpet, a painted wrought-iron canopy bed with white netting, and fabric-ed walls decorated with little men dressed in pink, playing instruments. In the corner sat a life-sized lion that Hef gave her when she was born. There was no accounting for taste, because very early on she claimed that the tack room was her favorite space. She called it "Dracula's Hideout." Go figure.

The kitchen was my least favorite room because it was so dark and industrial. It was a working kitchen so there was nothing pretty about it, and it was so far away that a previous owner claimed you could starve to death just trying to get there. The upstairs was as lovely as I remembered it, though, and I had my own walk-in closets for my clothes and shoes. Our bedroom had a yellow theme with a mahogany four-poster bed and walls covered in fabric. The paneled library was my favorite space and one of the smallest. It had two leather sofas and beautiful mahogany bookshelves that we filled with books we had no time to read.

I couldn't wait to show the house to my sister and my mother. Jackie Jean Crouch, now Georgia Holt, could never have imagined back in Arkansas that she'd ever cross the threshold of a place like that. Neither could I. Walking around, admiring everything, my beautiful mom with her fabulous hair, chic clothes, and elegant posture fit right in. That was quite a moment for us both.

From the moment we bought it, we called the house on Carolwood Drive "the big house." I will never forget the day we moved in. When those wrought-iron gates opened and I looked up at this 12,200-square-foot, nine-bedroom, ten-bath mansion, my first thought was *Oh God, I'm going to have to live with him for the rest of my life to pay for this.*

Despite having the most gorgeous home, Sonny never wanted to throw parties or invite friends and family over unless it was for Thanksgiving, Christmas, or Chastity's birthday, when he pulled out all the stops. Not that I had any friends of my own to invite. Sonny had stopped Joey from coming around but never gave me an explanation other than that hanging with girlfriends was "dumb." Joe D was long gone and suing us for hundreds of thousands of dollars, and I wasn't allowed to fraternize with the band. That left my sister, Georganne, who was busy making her own way as an actress.

Bored and lonely, there were a couple of times when I was so mad at Sonny that I almost defied him—the night he burned my tennis gear and the day Brian Wilson's wife, Marilyn, invited me over for a Tupperware party. Sonny and I had kept in touch with "Brain" since our Gold Star days and were delighted when he married his childhood sweetheart Marilyn. Thinking that an all-female event at her house to sell kitchenware couldn't possibly be considered subversive, I accepted her invitation, only to be told that I couldn't go. "What? Why not, Sonny?" I asked, tears pricking at my eyes. "They're my friends. They're just girls. There won't be any men there!" Why the hell couldn't I go to a party in the afternoon, for goodness' sakes? There was no threat.

He looked at me and said, "There's no reason for you to go to a Tupperware party, it's dumb." It was like he thought such an event was beneath me, beneath "Cher." But it was not something he should have been able to tell me I could or couldn't go to.

It was a breath of fresh air when a twenty-one-year-old named Paulette walked into my life one fine day in June 1972, at an event twenty miles north of Washington, DC. The moment we met, she spoke to me in Armenian—"*Inchpes es?*" (How are you?). And I replied, "*Lav yem*" (I'm fine). Those are two of the only three phrases I know in Armenian, the last being "I love you." When Paulette explained that her surname was Eghiazarian and her parents were of Armenian descent, we felt instantly connected.

She was four years younger than me, and her life seemed like something out of a movie. The daughter of a former intelligence officer in World War II who became a founding member of the CIA, she'd lived all over the world—from Africa to the Middle East. After leaving high school, she did some modeling before traveling with a surf team based in Hawaii. She'd been to Woodstock in a camper and visited exotic places like Puerto Rico and Corfu. Eventually, tired of spending her days being stoned on a beach, she'd gone home to visit her family in Washington with no idea what she was going to do next.

As part of a deal Sonny made for us, that month we were playing in the round at the Shady Grove Music Fair in Gaithersburg, Maryland. The wacky but enormously funny Steve Martin was our opening act. It was a venue we'd played before, but now that we were television-famous, we were expected to attend a meet and greet before the show with congressmen and other dignitaries. When I walked in with Chastity and wandered over to a table of food to find some of her favorite cheesy Goldfish, I spotted Paulette immediately because she stood out from the crowd. Striking, with a deep tan and long brown hair, she was wearing a black tank top and bell-bottoms with gold chains. Intrigued, I went over and asked, "Who are you? You don't look like anybody here."

Looking around at the suits, she laughed and replied, "Well, no." Bubbly and open, she explained that she was only at the gig because she knew the owner of the venue.

The next night Paulette was back, this time on the arm of our road manager, Jerry Ridgeway. They made a beautiful couple. Sonny had a rule that our male crew couldn't bring random women on the tour, only steady girlfriends, so Ridgeway said she was and asked if she could accompany us to our next gig. When Sonny agreed, I was delighted because I was so starved for female companionship. Neither of us could have imagined that from that chance encounter we'd end up becoming best friends for over fifty years, our lives intertwining in all kinds of strange and complicated ways.

When we went to New York, my new girlfriend was there too with Ridgeway, all of us staying at the St. Regis hotel. We hung out, went shopping, and hit it off immediately. We liked the same things and had a similar sense of humor. Paulette taught me so much, and I couldn't hear enough about her amazing adventures. As with many of my friends, she adopted a pet name for me, because it was impossible to use my name in public without turning heads. To Paulette, I will always be "Cheralina" and to me she is "Pauli." Whatever we did, it was fun, and she knew how to carry herself. She never got overwhelmed when people would come up to mc on the street or take my picture when we were out. Maybe it's because she'd been in Washington, but she handled it all perfectly.

Sonny didn't seem to mind that I had a friend, probably because he thought Pauli was too young and not as smart as he was, so he never considered her a threat. In our world she was naïve (and in her world I was naïve). Sonny knew he'd be able to control her too. What he didn't bargain for was that hearing about her adventures threw my own situation into sharper focus. I didn't want her life, I just was starting to wonder if I wanted mine. Pauli has always been a warm, fun person who still acts like a teenager. I couldn't help but admire her. She reminded me of my mom's best friend Jake, who was open and always joking.

Having Pauli for company changed everything for me, and I was happier still when she flew back to LA with us and moved in with Ridgeway, who was living in Malibu. Paulette openly admired my life, believing that Sonny and I had the perfect marriage with the perfect child, that I had a perfect wardrobe and was living in a perfect world. She had no idea of the tension building up inside me. In truth, I was finding it hard to eat and to sleep. Weight was falling off me. For Paulette's birthday she had chicken cordon bleu, which I love. I remember trying to get myself to eat it and I couldn't take a bite. That scared me.

The confusing thing was that, although I was deeply unhappy, I still loved Sonny, but I was no longer in love with him. We were an amazing team on TV but at home things were falling apart. He didn't notice me anymore, so he didn't see it. We were madly in love for the first few years and entertained each other endlessly, but *The Sonny & Cher Show* changed him beyond recognition. I was able to live with him because I compartmentalized my feelings and was used to censoring what I said and did around him. Since we'd been together since I was so young, I knew the rules and how I should behave not to cause any problems. We had been like a sister and brother, father and daughter. We'd been partners. Family. And we had the same dream. That kept us together. But he didn't seem to care how I felt anymore, or that I even had emotions. He was indifferent toward me, too busy trying to make an empire and be a mogul.

With my anxieties mounting, I had never felt more stressed but didn't have any idea what I could do. I was starting to feel trapped. I didn't know how I could go against him or stand up for myself. I honestly didn't know how. It was a bitch, okay? And to top it all off, I couldn't tell anyone. I didn't trust anyone because I was afraid that something I said would get back to Sonny. So I just needlepointed myself to death—it was how I kept my mind occupied. I knew that the consequences of breaking away from Sonny would be enormous, not only for me but for Chas, who adored her father. And I had no desire to have more children with him. Although I did my best as her mother, they'd always had a special, secret kind of relationship that didn't include me. He would joke with her the way he used to with me. When he and I had first gotten together, Sonny had made up some of his own words. One he used a lot was "No sampian," which meant "No thank you." He didn't really use his made-up words with me anymore, but he did with Chas. He treated our daughter like the son he'd always wanted and called her El Primo Jr.

Toward the end of October 1972, we'd had an especially busy time taping two shows back-to-back so that we could perform in Reno. I was ready to drop, but instead we had to fly to Las Vegas to play two gigs a night in the Sahara hotel's Congo Room, something we'd done on and off since spring.

Paulette flew out to join us in Vegas, and I'd never felt more in need of a friend. She loved being with us and helped me in all sorts of ways, from getting magazines and my favorite candy to helping me into my gowns. After our shows she'd walk me to my room, where I'd peel off my eyelashes and ask her what she was going to do that night. She'd tell me some variation of "I don't know, go to the bedroom of one of the guys in the band to drink beer, smoke pot, and pass around guitars. It's not that exciting, Cher."

Soon after she arrived, she and I went looking for Sonny to ask him if I could go to a fair that the rest of the band were going to. Even though he never listened to any new music and wouldn't let me play it at home, I thought he might come along and was excited. I found him in our apartment suite talking business with Denis and Irwin, discussing how much money we'd made, so I said, "Oh great, let's go to Europe." Sonny looked at me with a frown and said, "Why? You can't make any money in Europe."

"No," I said, "I thought we could go on vacation."

He rolled his eyes and said, "Cher, c'mon." It didn't occur to him that I might need a break.

Then he called me over to sign something, saying, "We got a

contract with Caesars." I just sighed to myself and thought, *There is no "we" here.* I had no say in the decision and the thought filled me with absolute dread. In that moment, I couldn't articulate my feelings, so I just said, "Okay," and signed a new contract for us to perform in Vegas every summer for God knows how many years, tying us into something I didn't want to do because touring so much felt like it was killing me, and I knew Chastity was suffering too. The realization that my husband would always put business first over me and my feelings winded me. All of a sudden, I was pissed off, frightened, and felt completely trapped.

Remembering why we'd come, I forced a smile and said, "Hey, all the guys in the band are taking their girlfriends to this fair. It sounds like fun, wanna go?"

He barely looked up at me and said, "No, just go with Ridgeway and Paulette." From then on I started to feel hopeless and, soon, desperate. Between the signing at Caesars, shutting down the idea of a vacation, and telling me to just go with Ridgeway and Paulette to the fair, I felt pretty much defeated. After our shows, I could hear music rising from the busy hotel below through my open French doors. There I was, twenty-six years old and in what had become a loveless marriage. Sonny had given me the vehicle and the confidence to become the somebody my mother always told me I would be, and then he just lost interest. Mom had called me selfish and so had he. Perhaps they were right, or maybe I wasn't the selfish one. Maybe it was them? I stepped barefoot onto the balcony of our suite and stared down. I was dizzy with loneliness. I saw how easy it would be to step over the edge and simply disappear. For a few crazy minutes I couldn't imagine any other option. I did this five or six times, and each time I'd think about Chas, about my mother, about my sister, about everybody and how things like this could make people who look up to me feel that it's a viable solution, and I would step back inside. Then one morning everything changed. That night between shows I went out on the balcony again and this time I thought, *I don't have to jump off, I can just leave him.*

Paulette was oblivious to what was going on beneath the surface, and the next day she chatted on about what she'd been up to in LA, but I was tuned out. Then she casually mentioned that Bill, a young guitar player who'd joined our band, had asked for an eight-by-ten photo of me from the office. I thought nothing of this because people asked for photos of me all the time, it wasn't unusual. She added that she'd also spotted Bill trying to draw my likeness on an Etch A Sketch the band had, which I thought was sweet. Laughing, she said, "I do believe that Bill may have a crush on you, Cheralina!"

Bill was the total opposite of Sonny (even though they were both Aquarians). Bill was tall with a Texas drawl and twenty-one years old. I knew he was good at electric guitar because I'd noticed him playing my riffs back to me one night when we performed the Carpenters' "Superstar." I thought, *God, he's really good, and he's really listening to me.* I'd shut down the romantic side of myself and thought nothing of this except that he was talented.

I still didn't think anything of it when I heard from Paulette that Bill and his girlfriend hadn't slept together in months and I found myself asking his girlfriend to join us at the Caesars Palace spa that afternoon to find out if it was true, which it was. I didn't have any plan, I was just acting in each moment as it came. I still hadn't been able to really eat or sleep and I weighed ninety-eight pounds on the first day of my period. A little later, Pauli casually mentioned that between our two shows that night she and the rest of the band were going to see the Righteous Brothers play at the nearby Hilton hotel.

After our first show ended, without thinking, I ran offstage and changed my clothes, slipping on jeans and a T-shirt. Son came in, and as he was taking off his tuxedo, I was rounding the corner out the door and called out, "I'm going to see the Righteous

Brothers with Pauli and Ridgeway," and then I was off down the hallway. I didn't wait around for his reply. He called after me, "Are you crazy?!" But I was already gone. I hurried toward Paulette's room, running into all the guys in the band on the way as they were coming offstage, and we all went together to the Hilton's Casino Lounge. My heart was pounding the whole night. The lounge had tables with horseshoe booths. Bill's girlfriend slid in first and one of the guys sat down on the end next to her, then Bill slid in on her other side and then me. As I was scooting over to sit alongside him, Bill grabbed my arm and pulled it so hard that I smashed right into him and his leg was pressed close to mine. When he put his hand on my knee, I thought, *Well, that's unexpected.* To this day I don't know how he was so bold.

There was just enough time for me to run from the lounge act in the Hilton to our second show at the Sahara, which was in my favor because Sonny didn't have time to start a fight. There he was waiting in a fury. "You are in so much trouble, Cher!" he yelled. "Are you out of your mind?"

"No, Sonny. I'm not," I replied, far more calmly than I felt, dressing quickly as he carried on giving me a tongue-lashing. Ignoring him, I ran straight out onto the stage ahead of him, still buttoning up my pants. I felt somewhat out-of-body as I kept acting without any kind of plan (and I still hadn't eaten much of anything). It was as if I were knocking over dominoes one after the other. I just kept going even though I had no idea where I got the nerve. Once the show was over, I barely took my bows, and Sonny and I exited in different directions without a word. Running to the dressing room, I dropped my clothes, and by the time he had joined me and was trying to talk to me, I was dressed and out of there. He was so shocked; he was totally unprepared. He didn't know where I was going or what I was going to do.

I found Paulette and told her, "I wanna do what you do after the show."

She looked at me like I was crazy and said, "Sonny would *never* allow you in that room."

"No, no. It's okay," I lied. "I've got permission."

Paulette eyed me with suspicion but sighed. "If you say so."

She took me to the drummer Jeff Porcaro's room. Everyone was happy to see me, but they were nervous as hell. They couldn't figure out how I'd escaped and worried that they were going to pay for it with Sonny. Just as she'd described, our guys were sitting around smoking, drinking, and hanging out in a way I hadn't enjoyed in years. I was sitting there with everyone when Bill showed up. He sat for a while, talking with the guys, then stood up slowly and said, "I'm going to the lobby to get some smokes."

Making a split-second decision, I jumped up and said, "Okay, I'll go with you . . . I need a magazine."

Paulette did a double take, and fearful of the fallout, she protested, "But I just bought you every magazine they have!"

To which I replied, "Baby, there's a *Popular Mechanics* you missed," and left.

As Bill and I wandered down to the lobby and outside toward the casino entrance, I asked him, "Are you really going to get cigarettes?" He nodded. I said, "Well, I'm not going to get magazines."

He stopped with a "Huh?" so I spelled it out for him: "I'm only coming along because I wanted to be with you."

Shocked, he started walking around me in a big circle, and did that a couple of times. I think his mind had been blown in the literal sense of the words. I could see him thinking a million conflicting thoughts, like *What does this mean? What is she saying? What's gonna happen? Will I lose my job? Or more?* We walked on into the casino and past the slot machines to a stand selling cigarettes, where we ran straight into David Brenner, the stand-up comedian who was our opening act. He almost passed out at the sight of me on my own in public with Bill. Me with a guy by myself? He might as well have seen Frankenstein with Dumbo. David came up to us, kind of shaky, saying, "Hi, guys, what are you doing?" David and Sonny were really close, and I figured he wouldn't want to be the one to break this to him. I replied coolly, "Oh, we're just buying cigarettes." David looked so nervous, but I'd already done it, I'd kicked over the can, milk was spilled.

Bill bought his smokes and then said, "I don't want to go straight back to the room."

He didn't say it in a sexy way, it was more that he was confused, like, "I don't want to go back to a room full of people right now." I didn't say anything. He showed me outside to a big brick wall behind the hotel. "This is where we all come to get high before the show," he told me. I nodded. We leaned against the wall quietly side by side, then Bill suddenly blurted, "We all wonder how you can live this way." It was the first time anyone ever said this to me and I didn't know how to react. I never thought other people would notice, and the idea of everyone in the group talking about it made me embarrassed. Then Bill pulled me toward him and kissed me. It felt like my head almost exploded off my shoulders. Bill was a great kisser, but more than that, Sonny didn't like to kiss. This was what I'd imagined in sixth grade when I knew that kissing was in my future.

We went back up to Jeff Porcaro's room, probably twenty minutes after having left, and sat down with everyone. Soon after, the phone rang and it was Sonny. "What do you think you're doing, Cher?" Sonny asked. "What the fuck do you think you're doing?"

"Oh, I dunno. Just hanging with the guys."

You could have heard a pin drop in the room.

"Have you lost your mind? Come back to the room."

I had no idea who I even was at that moment, because I told him, "Well, you know, Bill wants to understand more about his publishing rights, so I thought I'd bring him up to our suite." I got up and Bill got up with me. I don't know what I was expecting. I said it like it was a thing, but I had no idea how Bill would react. If I were him I would have been thinking, *This is a bad idea, that's my boss upstairs, I'm not going to go up to your room.* He had to have balls the size of SOMETHING HUGE. When we walked into our suite, Sonny was waiting in a chair, staring at us in complete silence. Bill had never seemed taller to me than when he stood beside me as we faced my husband.

"Could you go into the bedroom so we can talk?" he asked Bill quietly, and Bill left the room.

Still staring me down, Sonny looked different somehow. Pinched. Shaken. "What are you doing?" he asked, but I didn't answer. Then he asked, genuinely curious, "What do you want to do?"

I couldn't believe what came out of my mouth next. I remembered that Sonny had ruined the entire script of *Chastity* just because I was talking to my co-star and I said, "I want to sleep with Bill." It all seems crazy now. I didn't mean it, but I thought saying those words was the only way that he would let me go. I'd already tried telling him I was unhappy using those words, and I'd learned my lesson. I thought maybe this would work instead. I just wanted it to be over.

The silence was deafening. Then he said, "How long do you think you'll need?"

And looking back I have no idea what made me say what I did next: "Two hours." The whole conversation was insane. I went from not arguing with him to saying that. And meanwhile Bill's in the other room by himself with no clue what's going on and I'm sure if he guessed for a million years he wouldn't have thought that.

"Okay," Sonny said, and, without another word, he got up and left the room. I walked into the bedroom where Bill was sitting up against the headboard with his legs outstretched, his ankles crossed, just sitting there smoking a cigarette. I knew I'd just put him in jeopardy, and I knew that wasn't good. I sat down next to him. He was wearing a new leather jacket, and the smell of a leather jacket will remind me of him forever.

Then we just started to talk, which I never did before because I didn't trust people not to go to Sonny. I don't know what made me drop my guard and open up to Bill that night, but I told him everything. He asked me, "How did it get this way, what happened that you're living like this?"

I responded honestly, trying to figure out the answer as I gave it. "We've been together since I was sixteen. Somehow it just happened. It just progressed. We were happy, then at some point he stopped caring."

Bill asked, "How can you work with him every week?"

I tried to find words that would make it make sense. "I'm so happy on the show," I told him. "Sonny cracks me up and we're like two kids up there. There's no boss and there are no rules. It's just fun and he acts like he used to when we were first together and in love. It's like it's all good again."

He couldn't understand it. I didn't understand it myself, but he listened. To this day, I can't believe I told a complete stranger everything about our private life. I acted purely on feeling because I felt that I might have an ally and I needed one. Bill was a twenty-one-year-old guitar player and Sonny was Sonny of Sonny & Cher, not to mention thirty-seven and his boss. Still, Bill came up to the suite with me, and then went into the other room when Sonny told him to and waited. He could have left at any time. We didn't know each other at all, he didn't owe me anything, but he stayed and I poured my heart out to someone I hadn't ever spoken to before. I didn't know his morals or his character. He could've gone straight to Sonny. But he didn't. "We all feel so bad for you," he told me. That's all that happened—we sat and we talked and I cried. Nothing else. Both of us were so exhausted. Besides, I wouldn't have done that in my own bedroom, I don't care what I was going through.

The next thing I knew it was the middle of the night and Sonny was back. It was about 5 a.m., and he treated me very coldly. Devastated, I lay there and told myself, *That's the last time. You are never going to do this to me again.* I was so fucking angry. I knew then for sure that he didn't love me anymore. A little later, I was still half-asleep when he came around my side of the bed, picked up my hand, and pulled my wedding ring off my finger. It took me a second to realize what he was doing, but I was too exhausted to care.

I woke up in the late afternoon, still in a daze. There was no sign of Sonny, and I had no idea what I was going to do next. He and I were supposed to be onstage twice that night, but there was no way I could do that. When I went to see Chastity, I found her room empty and discovered that Sonny had sent her back to LA with the nanny. I was so angry that he'd done that—another of his unilateral decisions, exerting his control.

I told Paulette to tell Bill I wanted to talk to him and she told me he was leaving for Texas. I said, "When? I want to talk to him before he goes." By that time it was getting dark. I jumped up and pulled on a long thick sweater and a pair of boots. I was so out of it I didn't put anything else on underneath. Bill met me in the dressing room and asked if anything was going to happen with us. I said, "I don't know what's going to happen. Period." Then I walked outside. For the next hour I walked up and down the Strip trying to figure out where to go, but people recognized me and kept coming up and asking for my autograph, saying, "Hey, Cher! What are you doing on the street?" Others told me how excited they were to see our show later. It was all so surreal; it was like being in a cheap Fellini set in Vegas. Keeping my head down and trying not to cry, I sought refuge in an empty, overgrown lot just to get away. Eventually I went back to the hotel to find Sonny. As I wandered the upper corridors of the Sahara looking for my husband, I repeatedly told myself, *I'm going to do this. I really am.* I eventually found him sulking in his dressing room, where I walked in and blurted, "Sonny, I need five hundred dollars in cash. Now." I only had charge cards and had no other way of getting hold of any actual cash. He just gave me the money. He didn't say anything.

Ever since we'd first started living together, he'd been secretly convinced I'd leave him one day, something he didn't properly tell me until years later, although he'd written it in a poem he gave me back when we were still working for Phillip Spector. There was a line "a butterfly to be loved by all but not by one." But it was just poetry and I was seventeen. When you're seventeen, what do you know about anything? On the day he knew that moment had finally come, he also realized there was nothing he could do to stop me.

As I was leaving, he murmured something, but I just kept on walking, so he lobbed a final comment my way: "America will hate you for breaking us up!"

Twisting back, I recoiled at what was such an obnoxious thing to say, but then it hit me: *Oh God, that's probably true.* He had rarely been wrong, and he knew that would sting because I'd always worried about what people would think. I loved the show, I loved the audience, but I just couldn't care anymore. He'd backed me into a corner and I didn't know what else to do. Staring at him coldly, I told him, "Last night I didn't care if I was alive or dead."

I went to my room and packed a bag before hurrying to Ridgeway's room, where I figured I'd be safe and Paulette might hide me. That's where I found Bill sitting on the couch. Ridgeway and Paulette were going to drive him to the airport. "Come with me, Cher," he begged. He was brave to ask, but I couldn't even think straight enough to give him an answer.

I can't recall what happened next or in exactly what sequence, but something clicked inside me when I found out that Sonny had slept with Bill's girlfriend the previous night out of revenge. My mind was going a mile a minute, and I suddenly blurted, "Don't go to Texas, Bill. Come to San Francisco with me. Sonny gave me money for tickets." For some reason, the only place I could think of to escape to was Sausalito, the sleepy seaside town where Son and I once had a perfect foggy day together. I thought of it as a safe place, and at that point, I just wanted to feel safe. I deliberately didn't specify Sausalito in front of Pauli and Ridgeway, because I didn't know what they would tell Sonny if he pressed. I was instinctively protecting myself by giving them plausible deniability.

When Bill agreed, I borrowed a pair of sunglasses from Paulette, and Ridgeway reluctantly pulled their rental car around to the back of the hotel, where Bill and I jumped in. Sitting in the front seat, Paulette kept turning to see me cradled in his arms and said, "I'm so happy for you!"

"Shut up, Paulette!" Ridgeway snapped, his eyes full of fear in the rearview mirror. "I'll probably lose my job for this. Do you not understand the ramifications here?" And of course, he was right. I was one half of the most successful couple on television and the headline act at the Sahara, leaving it all a few hours before a sold-out performance. The gossip was flying everywhere. I don't recall the flight that evening or what Bill and I talked about—if anything. We arrived in San Francisco in the early hours and took separate cabs in case anyone spotted us, but then our drivers both got lost in the notorious Bay Area fog. Later I discovered that Sonny sent private detectives to follow us, and they got lost too. There was no way he was going to let me go off on my own. Unable to find our way to the coast, Bill and I ended up back at the airport before eventually checking into some bullshit hotel at around 4 a.m. When we walked into the lobby, the guy behind the desk jumped up and cried, "Hey! Cher! Wow! Welcome . . . where's Sonny?"

"Oh, um . . . he's coming in on the next plane with the rest of the band and the dancers."

Bill stepped in and said, "Two rooms, please."

After Bill let me into my room, I fell onto the bed and he lay down beside me and kissed me tenderly like before, although I could tell he was nervous this time. A little later, we made love, and it was unbelievable. I knew then that I would never have sex with Sonny again. The next few hours were an odd mix of joy, relief, and exhaustion that ended abruptly when the telephone rang. The private detectives must have tracked us down. I picked up the receiver to hear Denis Pregnolato say, "Cher, it'll be really bad for Bill if you don't come home right now."

"Okay," I replied, almost in a whisper, "I'll be on the next flight." I got up immediately and flew to LAX on my own. It was the first time I'd been on an airplane or even in an airport alone, but I hardly realized. Meanwhile, Bill flew to Texas to avoid reporters.

Bill was a quiet guy, but my God, he had some balls to go against Sonny Bono. He was dead set against my going back, but I knew I had to for his sake. I was still putting one foot in front of the other hoping what I did was okay. The Sahara hotel had put out a press release saying our show had been canceled because I was suffering from exhaustion and that the TV host Johnny Carson would fill in for us. The press immediately picked up on the news, and gossip columnists started a rumor that Sonny and I had had a fight in Vegas and that I couldn't go onstage because I had a black eye. I don't know what Sonny told CBS, but that week we would be back filming the show and somehow we were hysterical.

It's difficult for me to describe what it was like to leave Sonny because I was so sleep deprived, hadn't eaten, was so confused, so upset, so in turmoil, not knowing what was going to happen next, not knowing what Sonny's reaction was going to be to anything. I'd taken each step based on instinct without any real thoughts in kind of a fog, but the truth is, once I started there was no turning back.

Almost delirious by the time I got back to the big house, all I wanted was to go to bed, but Sonny was there sitting on the top landing of the steps and looking really bad. I could see in his face he was also exhausted. I was too tired to care. Sonny told me, "You should apologize to Irwin." Irwin came to the house about an hour later and I did apologize to him. It didn't occur to me how ridiculous that was. Irwin sat me down to discuss the legal implications of my walking out, with Sonny in the room the entire time. I barely knew Irwin and also didn't like him since, besides being generally an unpleasant man, he'd been responsible for both losing Joe D and the contract at Caesars. He explained very matter-of-factly that if I persisted with my disastrous course of action, I'd be in breach of all my contracts, potentially costing me millions. I told him I didn't care. I was too tired to deal with him. Then he asked me, "What do you want, Cher?"

Nothing had prepared me for his question, and I hesitated for a moment, both Irwin and Sonny watching me think. Finally finding my voice, I said, "I want a place in Malibu where I can go on weekends, and five thousand dollars a month in my own checking account. If Sonny agrees, then I'll do the next show. If he doesn't, I won't." Sonny didn't bat an eyelash. I didn't know it then, but I could have asked for so much more and gotten it: I had no idea how afraid they were of me and what I might do. It really stuck in their minds that I said I didn't care. All those men in suits had had me at their mercy for so long. Now I was telling them what I wasn't going to do.

Irwin stared at me for a moment and then said, "Okay." Just like that. I couldn't believe it. Everything had changed in forty-eight hours. Feeling a flood of relief, I went to bed, where I passed out into a deeper sleep than I'd ever had before.

The next thing I was aware of was a few hours later when Sonny came and sat on the edge of the bed. He didn't say much and had the demeanor of someone who was beaten. He didn't even seem angry and looked so gaunt it occurred to me that he'd probably not eaten for days either. He sat down on the floor, and I was crying. He said, "What's the matter, bud?"

I said, "I want to talk to Bill." Then I fell back asleep, still exhausted, and Sonny left.

An hour or so later his assistant Sharon shook me awake.

"Bill's on the phone." She took me into the staff wing to take the call so Sonny wouldn't hear it.

"I don't know what to do," I cried when I heard his voice.

"Let me come to you. I don't want you to be alone." I told him I was getting a place at the beach and he could come be with me there. A week later he took a cab to Sharon's. I picked him up there wearing a light turquoise suede outfit I'd just bought and drove him to my new condo in Malibu down the street from the restaurant Moonshadows. Pauli had said to me, "You know, when you're in love you wear pastels." Such a weird thing to say.

In the days before Bill arrived, Irwin bombarded me with a list of stipulations to ensure that the Sonny & Cher–loving public didn't find out our marriage was in trouble. We'd agreed not to publicize the news since we still had shows to finish, and at that point, I wanted to do them. I was informed that I could use the place in Malibu when I chose but was forbidden from being seen anywhere in public with a man. They tried to tell me I couldn't go out to restaurants or the movies, but I said that wasn't fair, so it was agreed that Paulette could pick me up and take me to the movies but not out to dinner.

I didn't care about any of that. I was free and had a bedroom of my own.

# 17

## *we can work it out*

J ust days after leaving Sonny, he and I returned to CBS and stood side by side onstage. He smiled and said, "It's good to see you're back."

"It's good to see my front too," I quipped, gesturing to my revealing gown.

Sonny shrugged and looked at my chest. "Same thing."

That show ended up running very late into the night, but we were on point and so funny because the hurt never entered our relationship when we were in that studio. I swear to God, we were the best we'd ever been that week, especially in our spoof of the Chiffon margarine commercials, in which Sonny played a man searching for the meaning of life. Chiffon's catchphrase was "It's not nice to fool Mother Nature," so Sonny was shown climbing to the top of a mountain, where I was sitting like a guru. When he asked, "What is the secret of life, Mother Nature?" I replied, "Go fuck yourself!" instead of my scripted line. Sonny collapsed in hysterics and then I did too. We laughed ourselves so silly that everyone had to wait until we'd calmed down. When Art suggested we go again, Sonny quipped, "Not without lawyers!" which set us off again, laughing so hard that everybody looked at us like we were nuts, which we were.

Sonny called my walking out on him my "Nagasaki moment" (for which he presented me with an eighteen-karat gold dog tag engraved with that and the date). There had been wild media speculation about our having a fight and his beating me up at the Sahara, but they could see from looking at me that Sonny hadn't hit me and by our demeanor that everything was fine.

Some people thought we must have been acting happy in the shows immediately after our split, but the rapport we still had onstage wasn't a lie. You can't fake that shit. We were always Sonny & Cher even when we weren't Cher and Sonny. I'd rib him mercilessly as I'd always done, and he'd become the natural clown that was hidden under all that El Primo bullshit. The zanier the sketch, the better we were. For those few hours in the spotlight, immersed in the work, we were having fun again.

As the weeks passed, I began to lead the kind of independent life I'd longed for. I felt vibrant and loved dressing how I liked without asking permission. I was a strange combination of sophisticated and naïve. I had traveled all over the world in a bubble. Now, everything was an adventure. I remember the first time I went to the market by myself, which I hadn't done in I don't know how long. I wandered the aisles oohing and ahhing at everything. I picked up whatever I felt like: Oreos, Snickers, Ruffles ("They have ridges"), and Dr Pepper (a staple). Beyond that, I had to get all the basic things: bread, milk, sugar, olive oil, all the things I tried to remember that I hadn't even thought of in years. It sounds stupid, but I had been busy working, and when we hadn't had any money, Sonny had done all the cooking. When I got to the checkout, the woman added up all my stuff and handed me my receipt. I signed it *all my love, Cher.* The lady picked it up and laughed. Pauli teases me about it to this day.

When I had free weekends, which wasn't that often because I was still working most days, Bill would fly in to see me and we'd stay at my place in Malibu. We talked for hours and really got to know each other. It was so nice to be with someone who asked what I thought and was interested in sharing experiences with me. Bill had a great sense of humor and was easy to be around and sex was like, I wanted to call the newspaper and say, "I found this amazing new thing!" In many ways Bill was the polar opposite of Sonny, and one way in particular was very fun for me: Bill loved to kiss. He was tall with a sweet smile and a Texas accent that reminded me of my family. (Mamaw had a Texas accent, Daddy had a Texas accent, I grew up with that accent.) I was a few years older than him, but in life experience I was younger. He would tell me about his life growing up and his brother Warren, who had a great voice and who I later hired as a background singer. There was no tension, no rules, and no pressure. For the first time in eleven years, I could wear perfume and listen to music. I didn't have to worry *Did I do the right thing? Did I say the right thing? Did I laugh too loud?* Once, we were planning to go to a movie and Bill asked me, "What do you want to see?" I broke down in tears. It was almost impossible for me to believe that question had made me cry, but Sonny had never asked me that before, and in all the years we were together I had only one good movie experience with him, *The Graduate,* and Billy Friedken had taken us.

Bill and I weren't supposed to go out in public together, but I broke the agreement for a very special cause. At my new place, I didn't have anything to play music on, which was fine because I didn't have any music, so Bill got the player and we went together to Tower Records on Sunset for cassettes. We started walking through the store and he went ahead of me. At some point he realized I wasn't behind him and he called out, "Where are you?!" When he found me I was lost in cassette land, picking up every tape on the shelf. I hadn't been in a music store in years. I spent $600 (over $4,000 in 2024 dollars). And we'd go back every couple of weeks whenever new albums came out. We had a chest at home where we'd keep the cassettes, and at the end of two months it was full. I remember buying the Beatles, James Taylor, the Doobie Brothers, and in particular, Stevie Wonder's *Talking Book*.

Bill and I didn't get to spend as much time together as we'd have liked because I was often at the studio and he was working wherever he could. I also tried to be home with Chas every night for her dinner and bath, so I only ended up seeing him once or twice a month. He had his own apartment in the Valley where he could stay when he wasn't with me in Malibu. I visited him there only once. I never really did drugs, but Bill sometimes would smoke weed, like most people I knew at that time, and I decided I would try some. I had one hit off his joint and felt pretty fine. He had to go pick up something, so I said I was okay to stay there by myself. While he was out, his roommate's girlfriend came in and lit a joint of her own. She offered it to me, and since I felt okay after the first hit, I took it from her and took maybe three more. Then I started to feel really funny, so I went into Bill's bathroom and took a hot bath. That's when I heard Sonny's voice say, "See, I told you something bad would happen if you left me. I hope you're satisfied." At that moment I was anything but satisfied.

Besides my weekends with Bill, I was still living in the big house with Sonny so I could be with Chas as much as possible, which worked out surprisingly well. The house was huge and we had two master bedrooms that were on opposite wings of the house. Sonny's assistant Connie moved in with us, which wasn't unusual, and the other assistant, Sharon Wixem, was staying in the house. Connie had a sweet girly voice and looked very unassuming. She'd wear her hair pulled back and dress in modest, kind of unattractive clothing. Chas and I both really liked her. It sounds odd, but when she went from Sonny's live-in assistant to his live-in girlfriend (and started dressing entirely differently) I still loved her. I'm sure she never thought we'd become friends, but strange as it seems, we all got along. There was plenty of room for all of us to have space in the 12,600-square-foot house. Sonny said he'd heard too much music in his lifetime and wouldn't even listen to classical, so Connie would run to my room, lock the door, light a cigarette, and listen to whatever I was playing. Chas would come in too sometimes, and we'd swear her to secrecy. What happened in the girls' room stayed in the girls' room.

Sonny and I were becoming friends again. One morning I came down to breakfast and he surprised me by saying, "You know, after you went off with Bill that night at the Sahara, I seriously thought about throwing you off our balcony." He laughed a little at that and so did I. It was crazy that he was telling me. He went on: "I figured I'd plead insanity like Spade Cooley and get seven years in jail before they released me. Then I'd get a book deal and my own show."

"Oh, you did, did you?" I replied. "Well, there would have been no need to push me because I was gonna jump!" Within seconds, we were howling. No one watching our response to what had been the darkest moment of our marriage would have understood. I didn't think for a minute that Sonny would have actually pushed me off the balcony, but I'm sure it crossed his mind, and he knew that jumping off had also crossed mine. What else could we do but laugh?

On the show, the writers came up with a new character for me that became one of my favorites. Her name was "Laverne," a raving bitch who was always at the laundromat. She became our audience's favorite too. Teri Garr played her friend Olivia brilliantly.

Bob Mackie and Ret Turner helped me pick out Larverne's look, choosing a tiger-print jumpsuit, diamanté cat-eye glasses, and an enormous ass. We decided her hair should be a bad version of Lucille Ball's character's in her show *I Love Lucy,* so a big red wig was made with a mess of curls and visible undyed roots. On my feet I wore horrible clear plastic heels with fake goldfish or some other cheap novelty embedded within. Bob also found some luminous plastic earrings the size of golf balls to clash with my tacky giant beads and bracelets and an awful stretch belt that went around my waist and accentuated the huge stomach and ass that he'd built into the costume. I put a pepperoni stick in Laverne's purse for her to pull out occasionally and nibble on.

My character was almost ready to face her public, but I still couldn't get her voice right, despite trying out several different accents. I always ended up as Edith Bunker from *All in the Family.* Standing in the wings before I went on for the first time, I saw one of the stagehands chewing bubblegum and said, "Hey, buddy, got any more?" I folded two pieces into my mouth and Laverne was brought to life. After examining myself in the mirror and declaring myself gorgeous, I was off. Everyone loved the character and she became a regular feature. "At the Launderette" was the only sketch we were able to shoot in front of the live audience because the set for it was small and there were only two characters, but it made the segment especially exciting for us and for the people watching. I could play Laverne so over the top, you could never go too far with her.

Now that I was a free woman, I got in touch with "Joe D" to invite him back into my life. I'd missed him terribly and wanted him to know his goddaughter Chastity better. Despite his ongoing legal battle against us after he was fired, Joe was thrilled to hear from me. He knew that Sonny and Irwin had lied to me and I hadn't been able to call him before.

Sonny and I were still "together" in the eyes of the public, so when he accepted an invitation to an election party hosted by Jack

Benny at his wife Mary's house, I went with him. The Republican president, Richard Nixon, was running against Senator George McGovern. Sonny and I were both for McGovern. I've always been a Democrat. My mother was a big traitor that year, putting up Nixon signs on her and Gilbert's front lawn, even though she never could have actually agreed with Nixon's policies given her social beliefs. Gilbert was a Republican, as most businesspeople are. I ripped the signs out of the grass and threw them in the big trash cans in the garage.

That season we'd had Ronald Reagan (then governor of California) on our show, which I hadn't been too happy about either. Sonny had presented him with "the coveted Bono award"—a mock-up of an Oscar with a huge nose and a mustache. "It's made up exactly in my image," Sonny told him proudly, to which I added, "It's even the same size." He was quite pleasant as a guest, but after all, he was an actor.

Jack Benny's election party was attended by Lucille Ball, Johnny Carson, and a host of other famous names. We sat in rows of seats set up in front of a large television set as we waited for the results. Listening to the pundits for what seemed like hours, I started thinking, *Fuck this. I don't want to be here.* Lucille was clearly bored too, because as the votes started coming in she began making wisecracks about the "windbags" giving commentary on what each update meant. She was being so funny and irreverent. If you knew Lucy, she was a balls-to-the-wall kick-ass chick, not taking anything from anybody. I had known her since I was little, but this night she got me in trouble. I couldn't help but giggle at her commentary. Knowing that I wasn't supposed to only cracked me up more, and as her snide comments continued, so did my laughing, which annoyed Sonny, especially since Johnny Carson was in the front room with the Ford sisters.

Before too long, Johnny Carson complained to Jack Benny's wife about the disturbance, and I was sure Lucy was going to be told off. Then I realized that nobody was going to say a word to her because she'd have neutered them. Everyone was terrified of Lucy. I, however, was a different thing altogether. Like a naughty child, I was banished to the den, so I wandered away and closed the door behind me as Lucy turned and gave me a wink. As I walked in the door, I saw Rosalind Russell sitting on the couch alone. It took my breath away. She was one of my heroes. She'd been one of my favorite actresses because she did everything, including *Auntie Mame*, which I think I've seen about five thousand times. Not actually, but you know what I mean. She played working women of all different walks of life: a judge, a lawyer, a newspaper woman, etc. She was a great role model and an amazing actress. At sixty-five, she was still beautiful. I said hello somewhat shyly and sat next to her on the sofa, wondering what we could talk about. Leaning in, she said one of the most memorable things anyone has ever said to me: "You know, Cher, I've watched your show, and you're funny and talented. I think you could be a good actress if you put your mind to it. I'd keep going with that if I were you." Just as with my acting coach Jeff Corey, this four-time Oscar nominee, winner of five Golden Globes, and Tony winner saw something in me, and I never forgot her words. I had a little repository in the back of my head where I kept my affirmations: first from my mom, then Jeff Corey, and now Auntie Mame.

That holiday season, Richard Avedon shot me for the cover of *Vogue* wearing eyelashes like tarantulas. It was my second *Vogue* cover that year. Richard had shot me in April modeling bathing suits by Eres. Using one of these pictures for the cover had defied all convention, and I was thrilled, only to find out later it was by default because "Doc," the man who picked the covers, didn't like anything else offered that month and decided to take a chance. A win is a win.

As I was growing into myself, Sonny started to change in small ways too. He no longer had the pressure of pretending to be a husband, and it put us back in an arrangement more like when we first met and were just friends. Without expectations, it was easier to enjoy each other's company. One morning he surprised me by asking, "Do you want to go to Paris for the weekend?" Now this is another thing that people won't understand. After all we were going through, I laughed and said, "Sure." I think we stayed in the Raphael, which was a cool hotel but not fancy. We went around visiting the sights, going to lunch and dinner and shopping. I remember I bought something at Kenzo. It wasn't exactly like the old days, but it was like a different version of his personality from the old days. He was funny and playful. Back at our hotel he took a bath while I sat on the floor with my back against the wall, my feet up on the bathtub, looking at him facing me.

"Girls these days won't put up with your shit," I told him. "You're going to have to change. You can't treat modern-day girls the way you treated me. They're not going to stand for being told where they can go and how to dress or if they can wear perfume or listen to music. They're not gonna take that shit from you like I did." But as it would turn out, they would take that shit from him. He just found young girls and gave them gifts to distract them. It was always the same: first, diamond studs; then a Porsche 914 if they stuck around; and if they became serious he'd upgrade the Porsche to a 911 Targa (very few made it long enough for the Targa).

Every time I try to explain that trip to someone, they say they can't understand how I did it or why I did it. It's not easily understandable, it doesn't make sense. The nuances are too convoluted, but at the time, it felt completely natural and normal. We were just two best friends having a good time. But whoa, did I have something coming.

In January 1973, the *Sonny & Cher Comedy Hour* was nominated for a Golden Globe for Best Musical or Comedy Series, and we were invited to the ceremony at the Century Plaza hotel in LA.

It was one event that I was more than happy to attend because of my love of movies and especially of the winning film, *The Godfather,* based on my favorite book of all time, brilliantly directed by our friend Francis Ford Coppola. We couldn't have been prouder. Sonny wore a tuxedo, and I wore a fox-fur coat over a multicolored skirt and matching crop top, with my belly button once again the focus of attention. As I said before, I wouldn't be seen dead in real fur now, but times were different then. We didn't win, but Marlon Brando won Best Actor, although he boycotted the ceremony and refused to accept it in protest of "US imperialism and racism." Other winners that night included *Cabaret,* starring Best Actress winner Liza Minnelli, and Diana Ross won New Star of the Year for her role as Billie Holiday in *Lady Sings the Blues.* I clapped so hard for my friends and fantasized about getting my chance to walk to that podium one day.

For a break from Los Angeles, Paulette and I flew to Hawaii, where Bill was meant to join us. O'ahu was really different back then from how it is now, with few high rises and not many houses built into the hill. The next time I went back I was shocked; there were so many houses you could barely even see the hill. Pauli and I had a great time together. Mostly we lay out on the beach and soaked up the sun. I remembered coming to Hawaii years before with Sonny to perform. We ran into an old couple—they seemed very old at the time, but in retrospect I'm not sure how old they really were. They were coming to our performance, and I had stopped to talk with them, which is a weird quirk of mine— sometimes I'll stop to talk with people I don't know. The husband told us, "My wife and I saved up money our whole marriage so we could come to Hawaii, and it's rained the entire time." It made me think, *You really need to do things while you're young.* Besides the rain ruining their trip, at their age they couldn't really run around the island or go swimming out in the water. It showed me something about waiting and I thought about it a lot. I was happy that they were excited about coming to see us, so they had at least one fun thing they could do. When Bill arrived, I was so happy to see him, but then he said he'd been thinking it over and what he really wanted was to get married and for me to move back to Texas with him. I told him, "I love you, but I'm not divorced and I have a child. I've been married my entire adult life and I don't think I want to get married again." He was really upset, and I couldn't do anything to fix it. Pauli had this friend, Barry Hilton, who had a yacht, so we got on it and sailed to Maui. I left Bill a letter. Years later somebody asked me if I left Sonny for another man, and I told them, "No. I left him for another woman. Me."

The second season of *The Sonny & Cher Comedy Hour* was ending that March, and Sonny was confident CBS would push us for season three, which would carry us until spring 1974. On our second-to-last episode we had one of our most impressive guests: Captain John "Spike" Nasmyth, a thirty-two-year-old American pilot who'd been held captive by the Vietcong for a hellish 2,355 days—over six years—during the Vietnam War, tortured and daily fearing for his life until he was freed. When he returned home, he asked his family for three things: the largest steak in California, updated clothes, and Sonny and Cher albums. We were truly honored.

He'd been released in February 1973, and a month later agreed to come on our show. Spike was gaunt with dark circles under his eyes but otherwise he seemed amazingly normal after his ordeal, and, humbled, I clung to his arm. Our audience gave him a standing ovation, and when he could finally speak, he told us that he and his fellow prisoners had often talked about Sonny and me in their "Hanoi Hilton" prison and often sang some of our songs to keep their spirits up.

We thanked Spike on behalf of America, and presented him with a gift-wrapped bundle of every album we'd recorded since he was captured. That was a special moment. At that time, Sonny and I had also been wearing what were known as POW/MIA bracelets—nickel bangles engraved with the names and service numbers of prisoners of war or those missing in action so that they'd not be forgotten. Mine had the details of Second Lieutenant Hayden Lockhart Jr., shot down in 1965. He eventually came on the show to get the bracelet from me. He was a young, sweet man whose name is forever engraved on my heart.

In March, we marked Chas's fourth birthday with a huge garden party, a celebration we both looked forward to, along with Halloween, when Chas wore costumes made by Ret. For her birthday there were pony rides and balloons and we hired a clown, laughing at the memory of the day Gee dressed as a clown for one of Chas's previous birthdays at St. Cloud, almost melting in the heat in her makeup and wig. There was the traditional frosted birthday cake from Ralphs, and Joe D came at my invitation. Pauli, Chas, and I were all thrilled. It was the first time he'd seen Sonny since they'd fallen out. I was relieved when everyone behaved politely and nobody died. Carol Burnett came with her four-year-old daughter, Erin, and all the other kids were agog because they thought of Carol as much more famous than we were.

Awards season continued with the 45th Academy Awards at the Dorothy Chandler Pavilion, which was as star-studded as ever, with presenters including Merle Oberon, Rock Hudson, Jack Lemmon, and Clint Eastwood. Liza won Best Actress for her amazing performance as Sally Bowles in *Cabaret*, and to our delight, our friend Francis Coppola won Best Adapted Screenplay for *The Godfather*, which also won Best Picture. Sonny and I were asked to present the Oscar for Best Original Song to the composer of "The Morning After" from the movie *The Poseidon Adventure*. This was the first time that the Oscars were broadcast internationally, so the eyes of the world were upon us. Dressed in a shimmering gold full-length beaded skirt and crop top that showed off my tan (still one of my all-time favorite outfits), I stood at the podium and complained that Sonny never took me out. In a carefully scripted reply, he said that was because I claimed I had nothing to wear. "That's right," I replied.

Looking me up and down, my midriff exposed, Sonny nodded and added, "And you're wearing it." The audience laughed.

Things weren't so simple at home. I was having trouble navigating our life. It was one thing to do it and another thing to understand it. Sonny suggested I see someone to talk about what I was feeling. He signed me up for sessions with a therapist in the Valley. I don't remember much about him, he was fairly generic, but I told him all about Sonny and our life together, hoping he could help. I explained how lonely I'd been and how I couldn't go anywhere or do anything without his permission. He had me delve deeper into the collateral damage of my childhood, too, which was just as hard to deal with as my marriage. It was only much later that I learned that the shrink was reporting everything I said back to Sonny. I remember when I found out I screamed at Sonny, "How could you do this?" and he didn't even have an answer. I still find that to be incredulous. Isn't that an extreme of betraying somebody's trust, having their therapist tell you everything they're saying? I was fucking furious. I felt violated, like I had been raped. It made me feel like I had before, as if there was no way to protect myself.

I soon learned that Sonny going behind my back had started much earlier in our relationship. Joe D admitted to me that throughout the time we were together, Sonny had been with dancers, actresses, waitresses, and even hookers in our home and on the road. He'd get an extra room he could enter by passing out a side door in our suite, through Joe D's and into a girl's, who would wait for him after I went to bed. After hearing this from Joe D, a couple of the women themselves started crawling out of the woodwork. They told me Sonny had said we were in an open marriage and that I knew. I think what shocked me the most was that, aside from the time I'd caught him in our house with a secretary, I'd never had the least bit of suspicion. I couldn't imagine where he found the time. In the coming years, as more people told me the truth, they'd say, "But you must have known. You had to! Everybody knew."

Well, I didn't.

In May, I recorded my second solo album, *Half-Breed,* with Snuff Garrett back producing. That fall, the title track would become my second number one hit as a solo artist. After I finished recording the album, Sonny and I went back on the road for a grueling summer tour of mainly one-night gigs.

Paulette and Ridgeway were part of our crew for this run, and I was happy to have my friend with me. I also started talking more with our pianist David Paich, who had been around for years. His father, Marty, was our orchestra leader, so I knew David even longer than the two years he'd been in the band. He was so sweet, and it was nice to have someone care about me again. We'd hang out and flirt with each other innocently. It was friendship that became physical and then became friendship again and only lasted for that tour.

One night we were all staying in a motel in a small town in Iowa, with a playground for kids out back. Paulette, David Paich, Jeff Porcaro, Steve Porcaro, David Hungate, Steve Lukather, and I wandered out to sit on the swings because it was still so early in the evening. We were talking and swinging, just hanging out like kids, some guys smoking weed, but not really doing anything, just bullshitting in plain sight. We'd done a good show and we were just relaxing and talking afterward. I can't emphasize enough how innocent this moment was. I went up to my room feeling good, but then Paulette came in telling me all hell had broken loose. I didn't know exactly what was going on, but she said Denis had gone down and taken the guys apart separately to threaten them. He'd become like Sonny's capo bastone. He told David that if he wasn't careful, he'd get his fingers broken and Jeffrey that he'd get his Porsche blown up. I fell asleep wondering what the hell was going on. Sonny was being very old-school Sicilian. In many ways old-school Sicilian is sexy. This wasn't one of them. The next morning I discovered that the band had all stopped talking to me under threat of being fired. More than that, Sonny had sent Chastity home with our nanny, Linda, so I wouldn't even have her for company. I'd thought that Sonny having control over me was over. With everyone ignoring me, I felt completely alone. The minute I had nobody to talk to, I started smoking, maybe because I needed something to do. I don't know, I just did it. I saw how quickly my freedom could be taken away, I had thought I was safe and then I wasn't. It was déjà vu all over again.

The only person to talk to me was David Brenner, our comedian and friend who spoke to me one time, saying, "I don't understand this, but I don't want to lose my job." That was it; nobody else talked to me for the entire tour.

Even Paulette didn't speak to me except for business. It took some time for me to forgive her. I was madder at her than anyone else who stopped talking to me because she was my best friend. In her defense, Pauli was too scared to defy Sonny, and she couldn't afford to lose her job. And she was dating a fellow employee who might have been fired too if she pissed Sonny off. It didn't help that Son had been coaching her on her troubled relationship with Ridgeway, imparting his skewed wisdom. He told her to play hard to get and not even have sex with him, moving her into our suite to be certain she was complying. His ploy worked—for a while— and Ridgeway realized what he was missing. When I challenged Paulette privately about shunning me, she said, "Cher, what do you want me to do? Everybody's terrified of Sonny. We have to do what he says, or we'll be out."

Seething quietly, I sometimes could no longer hide my anger, even in front of our fans. Once we were singing at a theater in the round and I just turned my back on Sonny and kept my back to him the entire time we performed "I Got You Babe." Like I said, I

*On the road with Chas.*

*Chas in the sandbox.*

*Keeping Chas entertained on the road. She loved clowns.*

*Chas and me after a swim at the St. Cloud house.*

*"Happy birthday Mom" in soap.*

*Chas conducting the orchestra.*

*Five generations of Sarkisians.*

*Chas and me working the Playboy Club.*

*On the floor at Muscle Shoals.*

*Chas's birthday with Joe D, Sonny, Gee as a clown, and me.*

*Pauli and me at the Met Gala, 1977.*

*Greeting fans at a music fair.*

*With Elton John, Bette Midler, and
Flip Wilson, during the taping of*
The Cher Show, *January 19, 1975.*

*With Rod Stewart and Dolly
Parton, for* Cher . . . Special,
*April 1978.*

*David Bowie and me.*

*With Bob Dylan singing "All I Really Want to Do" for David Geffen's birthday, Beverly Hills Hotel, 1974.*

*David in Aspen, making deals.*

*David and me. Aren't we cute?*

*Me, makeup bag in hand, leaving CBS.*

*Halston and me.*

*Me and my Dino, with Pauli.*

*Ange and me.*

*Gee and me.*

*Mom, Gee, and me on Thanksgiving.*

*Deb and me.*

*I love this photo of Gregory.*

*Gregory and me in Japan.*

*Pregnant, with Gregory in Hawaii.*

*With Gregory and Elijah, one day old.*

*Chas and Elijah meet Dr. Teeth of
The Muppets' Electric Mayhem Band.*

*Elijah and a furry friend.*

*My babies: Chas at seven years, Elijah at
four months.*

*Bathtime with Chas, 1974.*

*Elijah, Skeletor, He-Man, and me.*

can't fake it. And that night I didn't. I sang to the audience. Then everyone got mad at me. Paulette told me, "C'mon, Cher. That was dumb." They all thought I was being childish and should have been more professional. I felt so betrayed and thought, *Screw you guys. Sonny threatens to break someone's hands and blow up a Porsche, but me turning my back is out of line?*

I was so happy to get home from that horrible tour and be reunited with Chas, the love of my life. It was also a relief to return to CBS to prepare for season three, the first episode of which was airing mid-September. Back in Studio 31, I felt immediately at ease and grateful to be back.

As always with Sonny, once his anger subsided, everything went back to normal. As we started doing the show, everything was forgotten and Sonny was once again his funny over-the-top self, but I felt more uneasy from then on because I didn't understand what we'd done that had made him so angry. Sonny and I returned to the Sahara in Vegas with Chas and Linda, the whole gang. Our performances during those few weeks were recorded for posterity, as Sonny had cut a deal to release them as a live album. Sonny can be heard introducing the band. In a wistful mood, he went on to tell the audience that he and I had been together for a decade, and that when we started, we had very little. Then he spoke about our $85 piano and our old brass bed, adding, "We had this philosophy . . . that no matter how rough things got, as long as we had each other, everything would work out." There was a pause. "The philosophy became a song and then it became a record and then it became us. And we'd like to do it for you now." Cue "I Got You Babe."

Later he introduced "You Better Sit Down Kids," saying that the words always tugged at his heart because the lyrics were about a father who must tell his children that he and Mommy aren't going to be together anymore. Looking across at me, his eyes glistening, he said, "The toughest thing in the world would be to tell a little kid it's all over, because they don't understand, because they think you're perfect." I don't know if his words were calculated to make me feel guilty, but that's how I felt.

There were times when I could see in Sonny's face that he was nostalgic for how things were before, even though he was the one who'd caused it to end. He had had everything he wanted. I think he would eventually come to realize that I was the one who was always there for him, who loved him, and I think he loved me, just not enough to be faithful or kind. I still loved working with him, and I still loved parts of who he was, but I didn't know how to read him anymore. The truth is, I knew Sonny better than anyone, but sometimes I didn't know him at all.

# 18

## and then there was david . . . you raise me up

In December 1973, I was invited to the famous music producer Lou Adler's Christmas party. I told Sonny I was going to go, and he said, "No, you're not." I replied, "Yeah, and you can come with me or you can stay home but I'm going." So we went together to Lou's house, and I ended up on the floor talking to Goldie Hawn, who was sitting there in a onesie. People were coming and going, I don't remember exactly who, but the two of us were having a blast on our own. Then this man walked in and Goldie said, "David! Come sit with us." I recognized him because I'd seen him with Ahmet Ertegun at the Troubadour the year before. He'd been so deferential to Ahmet, I figured he was one of his promotion guys or a publicist. The three of us talked for a while, and I thought, *This guy is so great.* He was so smart and funny. Everyone was attracted to him, people kind of came over to where we were sitting and joined in. That's the first time I really met David Geffen. Two days later he called to see if I wanted to have dinner. Somehow he'd gotten my number. I don't remember how, but I said, "Sure." I was thinking, *This is great, everyone loves him, I can have a new friend.*

Driving to his house the next day, I read the directions he gave me for the first time and thought the name of the street was familiar. Then I realized that he lived three blocks from me on Copley Drive, which confused me. When I pulled up to a beautiful Spanish-style house, I was thinking, *How does a promotion man afford a house like this?* I rang the bell, and David opened the door wearing a plaid cotton shirt and jeans with a telephone receiver pressed to his ear, the phone in his other hand and the longest cord I'd ever seen trailing behind him. I would come to learn this was his go-to look. He said, "I didn't get a chance to take a shower." I thought that was funny, such random information.

He made a gesture welcoming me in. Then he hung up the phone and we walked through the living room into the dining room and there was Lou Adler. The boys sat at either end of the table and I was between them thinking, *This is kind of weird, but whatever.* I guess I'd assumed that when David invited me to dinner it was just going to be the two of us, but it was nice to see Lou, and even though I was kind of surprised, I didn't dwell on it. I don't remember the entire meal, but it started with this delicious cold avocado soup, which was something I'd never had before. After dinner we went into the living room to sit on the couch. We all talked for a while, then Lou excused himself and it was just David and me. He started telling me his life story, and I started telling him mine. We talked all night long. It felt so good to be myself without watching what I said.

When I finally found out what David did for a living, everything fell into place. I realized he wasn't one of Ahmet's promo guys, he was his protégé. David was a genius in business and had founded Asylum Records, which had recently merged to become Elektra/Asylum. He also managed, along with his partner Elliot Roberts, Crosby, Stills, Nash & Young, the Eagles, Jackson Browne, John David, Joni Mitchell, Elton John, and Linda Ronstadt. I was starting to realize what a huge titan he was in the industry. At one point while we were talking, Joni Mitchell let herself in the front door and passed through the living room on her way to bed. She was living with him while recording her latest album. David would go on to form Geffen Records and sign Guns N' Roses, John Lennon, Donna Summer, Peter Gabriel, Aerosmith, and myself. To this day I've never met someone who loved his business and artists the way David did. He was a new breed of record executive. He kind of treated them like his children.

By the early hours of the morning I felt like I'd known David my whole life. He was kind and giving and shy; he was my new best friend. David didn't want me to leave, but it was so late and I had to be at CBS in a few hours. I had just enough time to run home, take a shower, and go straight to the studio. David invited me to come with him to Robbie Robertson's house the following night. Bob Dylan and his wife, Sara, would also be there (as well as Libby Titus), and David was trying to sign Bob.

"Okay," I replied, feeling suddenly happy. He walked me out and kissed me goodbye on my cheek.

When I got to work, Sonny wasn't happy that I had been out all night, but I was my own person by then, or at least my own semi-person.

The following night David picked me up to drive me to Robbie's place by the ocean, talking the whole way. He was always the smartest one in the room, and I never met anyone who could outtalk him. We stopped to get gas, and while we were sitting there, he turned to me and said, "I told my psychiatrist today that I thought I was in love with you." I thought, *Oh fuck. This is going to ruin everything*, and scooted all the way over in my seat until the door handle was pretty much in my ribs. As if that was going to change anything.

I had thought I knew what things were going to be with David, that we would be friends who lived around the corner from each other, but he kept surprising me. I didn't immediately see him differently, but that dinner in Malibu changed my feelings at least a little. When we walked in, Robbie and his wife, Dominique, Libby, Bob, and Sara were seated around a wooden table that was covered in candles, so many that the flames lit the room and gave a warm glow to everyone in it. All David's friends were happy to see him, and they welcomed us to the table. It was like something out of a film. I remember looking at David across the table through the candles, with everyone talking affectionately to one another, and thinking, *You know, there's something special about him.* We went back to his house after and talked a bit, but unlike the night before, when I went to leave, I just looked at him like a deer in headlights and ran out the door without hugging him good night. I think David was kind of terrified because he thought I was going to kiss him, which was the last thing on my mind. The other night he'd had Lou there to protect him from me, which I thought was hysterical when I found out because I never made the first move with a guy in my entire life. I didn't see him for a few days after that because I was working. I really missed talking to him and being around him, and it made me realize, *Maybe I have to rethink this.*

We didn't start dating immediately; we kind of slipped into seeing each other more often until we became completely inseparable. We were crazy about each other. I was his first relationship. Within days he told his best friend Sandy Gallin, "I'm in love with Cher!" which Sandy couldn't believe. We didn't tell anyone else and still couldn't be seen out in public together, so mostly we spent time at his house.

David was an early riser and went to bed much sooner than I did. I'd stay until he fell asleep, then get up and head home. Usually my timing would be so perfect that Joni would be coming back from the studio as I was leaving, and once in a while she'd play me a demo of what she'd done that day. One night we were sitting on the couches across from each other and she said, "Cher, you have this beautiful green light around you like a gentle aura." She said it in a positive way like she was really digging it. I thought, *How cool.* When her album, *Court and Spark*, came out, it was so weird. The whole time she was making it, we were just hanging out and talking about life, then the album comes out and it's a huge hit, reaching number two on *Billboard.* It was second to Bob Dylan's *Planet Waves* and followed by Carly Simon's *Hotcakes* at number three, both of which were also released by David's record label. Joni had written one of the songs in her album, "Free Man in Paris," about David, and she really captured him in the evocative lyrics to that song.

She also wrote in that song that David dealt with "telephone screamers," which was true. He never had a temper with me, but he did when it came to business, in a genius way. He used to fight with entertainment lawyer David Braun, and I would hear them yelling. I don't know what they were yelling about, but David Geffen always won. I couldn't believe that kind, gentle man who always called me "sweetheart" could make so much noise.

Once Sonny realized who I was going to meet all the time, he became very uneasy because everyone in the industry knew who David Geffen was. Sonny didn't like that I was seeing someone so smart and powerful, much more powerful than himself. The strain started to show and Sonny began to change, even at work. Until David and I got together, Sonny and I had been getting along great and it had seemed like things were back to how they used to be, then all of a sudden the fun we'd been having on the show was gone. Maybe it didn't happen all at once. I don't really remember, but after David entered my life, Sonny wasn't the same fun, goofy presence he'd been on the show before.

David was the most loving boyfriend I'd ever had, and he took great care of me, because that's who he was. One evening, Tony Fantozzi came over to David's for dinner. Tony was the William Morris agent who'd handled Sonny & Cher and was so close with Sonny that they called themselves paisans. When Son and I first got picked up for that six-week trial show period, we'd celebrated with Tony at a restaurant and he'd taken a big marker and written on the paper tablecloth: *Here's to the beginning. The Sonny & Cher Show. Fantozzi.* Now, all these years later, he turned to me with a grin and said, "So, how does *The Cher Show* sound to you?"

My immediate reaction was outrage. I was so angry that I could hardly speak. It was the disloyalty that shocked me—this guy was supposed to be Sonny's close friend. It disgusted me and made me think, *Does anyone have any values anymore? Is it money over everything, is that it?* Truthfully I'd never considered my own show. I couldn't believe he had the nerve to come to David's house and propose that to me. It hadn't occurred to David either. He was livid and immediately asked Tony to leave. I never spoke to him again.

Besides Sandy Gallin, David's closest friends were Jack Nicholson, Anjelica Huston ("Toots"), and Warren Beatty, who was then dating the British actress Julie Christie. All of them seemed to understand that our relationship had to be kept quiet. The six of us had a lot of laughs together—especially with Jack, who's better known as "Johnnie" to his friends—although when I saw Warren again he was his own charming self. I told him, "It's okay, Warren. We don't have to do this again." And we both started laughing.

On February 14, I ran out to do some errands and a bit of shopping. I parked my car on Rodeo, and when I came back to it, I found a gift bag tied to my steering wheel. Settling into the driver's seat, I opened the bag and found a Cartier box with the most unbelievable diamond bracelet and a sweet note from David. I almost broke down and cried. It was the first Valentine's Day present I'd ever received, and sneaking it into my car as a surprise was so thoughtful. Like how he always made sure my car was filled with gas. Sonny and I had never celebrated Valentine's Day in all the years we'd been together, so I hadn't even noted the date. Sonny had given me expensive jewelry, but it always felt like a way to show other people the money he had, not something heartfelt for me. Sonny was loving and fun, but it wasn't really his nature to be romantic. David was, and he thought I was fabulous. I was the first person to share his bed and his life.

With CBS about to pick up the option for another season, one day David asked me about my contract and how I got paid. I told him I didn't know because I'd never read it. "It's about time you did," he replied, and somehow he got his hands on the document, I'm not sure how. He called me up after reading it and said, "Sweetheart, this contract is involuntary servitude. You work for Sonny. You have no rights, no vote, no money, nothing. You're an employee of something called 'Cher Enterprises' with a salary you were likely never paid and three weeks' vacation per year. He owns ninety-five percent of the company and the rest belongs to his lawyer, Irwin Spiegel." It turns out that's what Irwin had gotten for getting rid of Joe D.

"Wait a minute!" I cried. "That can't be right!"

"Cher, I'm right. I promise you. I'm sorry, sweetheart."

Then David started reading the contract to me, and sure enough, I couldn't even sign a check or withdraw any money without Sonny or Irwin's signature. I was an employee of Cher Enterprises with no ownership, so I couldn't access any of the money I earned for the company. Beyond that, I was signed to the company and could only work with Sonny's permission. That meant not only did I have no money, I had no way to make any money unless Sonny signed off on it. David told me the devastating contract had been created when Sonny and I were still together—it wasn't new. I remembered at some point Sonny had started having me sign pages that said "Cher Enterprises," but I didn't think anything of it at the time except that "Cher Enterprises" sounded cool. Everything David told me was a kick in the gut. I couldn't fathom that this was true. I could understand the words, I just couldn't understand the meaning—How did it happen? How could Sonny do that in good conscience? He'd been everything to me and for some time I had been everything to him. Then it got worse. David told me I was locked into Cher Enterprises for another two years.

I was more heartbroken than angry. I couldn't even cry. What good would tears do? Instead, I sat in a state of incomprehension until I finally said, "You mean I don't have any money? I don't own one of the houses? What am I going to do?"

"You don't have to worry about that now, sweetheart. We just need to get you out of this." Thank God I had David, because without him I would've had nothing. I wouldn't have been able to take care of myself or my family. Sonny would have left me with my car and my clothes. As it was, he left me with my car and my clothes, and I had to buy the big house from him. Well, I had no money to buy the house—David was going to buy it. It took several days for the full horror to sink in. I'd worked my whole life, yet apparently I had nothing to show for it. I'd never for a second imagined that I needed to protect myself from Sonny, of all people, yet the contracts he'd had me sign were secretly designed to strip me of my income and the rights to my own career.

All I could think was *What went through Sonny's mind the day he and Irwin drew up that contract?* And what did he do afterward, light a fucking cigar? In retrospect I wouldn't be surprised if it happened after I came back from being with Bill in Sausalito and told Sonny and Irwin that I didn't care what the consequences would be if I left the show. All I can do is guess, but I know that had really scared them because what can you do if someone has stopped caring? Sonny was undoubtedly responsible for making us who we were, but it took me a long time to accept that he could never have achieved that without my voice and comic talent. It's hard to understand, but I don't think Sonny thought he was doing anything that wrong. I don't think he saw it, I think he separated it from himself, and honest to God I think he preferred being the fun, goofy Sonny on our show to the cigar-smoking business tycoon. It had been like a self-fulfilling prophecy. He said he'd always thought I was going to leave him someday: "a butterfly to be loved by all." Then he made me leave. It's just my guess but it's an educated one. Sonny had his demons. There was something inside him that I could never understand, something that took him from being this fabulous funny guy to being someone who would take everything from me. For years, I've racked my brain for how he could have done what he did, and I still can't get over it to this day.

I called Lucille Ball to ask for her advice. I told her, "Lucy, I want to leave Sonny and you're the only one I know that's ever been in this same situation. What should I do?" Lucy and her husband had also become famous working together as stars on TV. And he was a huge womanizer too. Then Lucy had left him. She told me, "Fuck him, you're the one with the talent." David said I needed a lawyer, and I told him I had Irwin.

"No, no, no. He's Sonny's lawyer, you need your own lawyer," he said, and offered to pay for a good attorney. David called Joe D, who was actually about to start suing Sonny and me for his having been fired. David explained the situation and asked him to give me Mickey Rudin. Joe D agreed and was happy to do it. Mickey Rudin was one of the smartest attorneys in Los Angeles, the man who represented Frank Sinatra and who had also helped Lucy extricate herself from her marriage and TV show with Desi Arnaz. As part of their settlement, she bought out his stake in their company, Desilu, which she later sold for millions. Mickey advised me that the first thing I had to do to break my contract was to file for divorce. I couldn't bring myself to just have my lawyers send Sonny a petition for divorce. I wanted to speak to him first and look him in the eye.

Although it probably sounds bizarre, I was still locked into something inexplicable with Sonny. He was the father of my child, my onetime best friend and man I loved, father figure, big brother, crazy cousin, and just all-around partner in my life. Whatever he'd done, however mad I was at him, I felt I owed it to him to speak to him myself and see if we could work out a solution between us. David told me I needed to tell him I wouldn't do the show unless I was made an equal partner. At that point, I didn't want to do the show regardless. I was over it.

Flying on fumes, I couldn't face Sonny at home, so I asked for a meeting in his office. I walked in, sat down, lit a cigarette, and stared at his face. "Son, I've had someone look over my contract and it says that I'm your employee. That can't be right, can it? How can I be an employee? I'm your partner. Your wife. We created this whole thing together and neither of us had anything when we met, so tell me they're wrong."

Staring at me and lighting one of his stupid cigars, he didn't say a word.

"I want my half of the money, Son. I'm only asking for what's fair." I had worked my entire life from being a teenager to now and I had made nothing. I wanted what I'd earned. But his eyes were cold to me, there was none of the sparkle I'd once seen.

"You have to tear up that fucking contract, Sonny, and draw up a new one," I insisted. "I have to be your partner. Fifty-fifty."

To my surprise, Sonny shook his head and without any emotion said, "I'm not going to do that, Cher." I was genuinely shocked by his response. Reasoning with me in a way that sounded almost rehearsed, he told me I didn't know what I was talking about and asked who was advising me. I knew I had to fight for my rights. I had a daughter to raise and a sister and mother to worry about.

"If you don't agree to give me half the money and redo the contract, Sonny, I won't sign for another year with CBS. I won't do anything with you. I can't be working for nothing."

Sonny shrugged. "You'll get sued."

"I don't care."

"Well, CBS will renew any day, so let's see what you do then."

"I mean it, Son," I told him, standing up and stubbing out my cigarette. "I only want what's fair." He didn't think I'd ever throw away the show, but at that point, I couldn't go back no matter what. Sonny's face had always been jovial and his eyes always had a little twinkle in them. Even if we'd get in a fight, right after we'd be laughing again. This was a new version of him looking at me with no feeling, completely cold to me as if I was just anybody. I don't want to say he became a different person, but something about when he started smoking those cigars, he could look at me like I wasn't someone who loved him all these years. I left the room.

Sonny was convinced CBS wouldn't drop us and that I'd come back, so he simply ignored me. It took me a while to finally ask him how he could have taken all my money when we were together. He simply shrugged and replied, "I always knew you'd leave me." I told him that's not a real answer. Beyond taking my money, it was real cruelty to prevent me from making more. I never got an answer to what made him do that.

When Sonny had met me, he had given up on being a star, but we became Sonny & Cher together. Then we lost it all as Sonny & Cher together, but I never left during the bad times. I slogged it out. I've said time and again there would be no Cher without Sonny, but obviously there would be no Sonny without Cher either. It was the day he heard me singing in the bedroom that everything began to crystallize for him. So how could he do what he did to me?

When Sonny realized David had read the contract and was advising me, he got scared, and when he heard David had gotten me Mickey Rudin, Sonny knew he was in real trouble. He tried to push, coax, and reason with me, insisting he had always given me whatever I asked for—clothes, jewelry, Ferraris, and the houses of my dreams. He threatened to sue me along with CBS, but we both knew they couldn't sue me for anything if I didn't have a dime.

No longer able to trust Sonny, I decided to call Fred Silverman, the head of programming at CBS. David was pessimistic about this approach. He told me, "Sweetheart, people don't do things on your word. People do things by contract and they can't draw a contract with you until the show is let go." I knew that, but I had to try. I got Freddie on the phone and said, "Freddie, it's me. I'm calling to tell you something and I just need you to hear me out. I need you to not pick up the show." He was a little bit shocked—I'm sure that's the first time he'd heard that request in his life. Then I told him exactly what was happening. Nobody in their right mind would have broken up *The Sonny & Cher Comedy Hour* at that point, but I explained to Freddie that I couldn't go on as an employee of "Cher Enterprises" and promised him that I wouldn't go to another network. He said he'd think about it, and I think he believed me. He definitely liked me but had no real reason to trust me. Freddie barely knew me—he lived in New York and only once in a while visited the studio in LA to say hi.

In the meantime, Sonny and I still had our current season to finish. The first time I went back to CBS, I was nervous. I hadn't taken ten steps inside the building when I ran into Sonny. We stood facing each other in the corridor like gunslingers from *High Noon*. "Hello, Swifty," he said, pulling a funny face. He then started to laugh, so I did too. That's how bizarre our connection was. When he wasn't being a dick, Sonny Bono was so amusing I could almost love him.

We were so accustomed to continuing with the show no matter what was happening in our personal lives that we did exactly what was expected of us, and more. Although Sonny looked thinner and there were times when his smile didn't quite reach his eyes, he and I linked arms and sang "Will You Love Me Tomorrow." We managed to make it through the show before Sonny shook my hand with a formal "Thank you very much, bud."

Before we'd wrapped filming for the season, I got a call back from Freddie. He said, "I hear you're making a deal with NBC for *The Cher Show*." This was the first I'd heard of that.

"That's not true," I told him. It turned out that someone was spreading rumors I already had a deal going with NBC. All I could do was tell him the truth and hope he believed me. "I promise you, Freddie, if there ever is a 'Cher Show' I'll do it with CBS. It's my home and I don't want to go to the Valley." He laughed, and I think that made him trust I was being honest. I truly never would have done it with anybody else. Little did I know, David had been talking to Freddie as well. By some miracle, Freddie agreed, and CBS didn't renew the show. *The Sonny & Cher Comedy Hour* would end for good in March 1974. Season four, which had been due to start that fall, was dead in the water. I'd sacrificed the show to save myself.

Sonny and Irwin never thought I would do that. They lost their minds. "Do you know what you've done, Cher?" Sonny asked me in a voice that sounded unnatural to him: sad, angry, and powerless. Soon after, Sonny told me I had to move out of the big house. He wanted to sell it and said that for publicity reasons, our real estate agent couldn't show the house with both me and him living there. For some reason she had picked me as the one who would have to move out. I was starting to realize that the people Sonny and I worked with were loyal to him and not me. I would have much rather been the one to stay. He never wanted that house. It was my dream house and Chas's home.

The lease on the Malibu townhouse hadn't been renewed, so I had nowhere else to live and moved in with David for a little while.

It never occurred to me to refuse to leave the big house, because Sonny was so angry. I left without Chas, knowing she'd be safe with Linda. I drove away with a small bag of clothes.

When the press got hold of the news that CBS had canceled our show, they went crazy, and the coverage was brutal. Sonny was right—America wasn't happy. People were very disappointed. Those who blamed me didn't really know what it was like to be in my situation or how hard it had been. I don't know what I would have done without David, who was so loving and managed to take my mind off things. We went to dinners and to friends' houses, and he rented me a house out on Carbon Beach in Malibu. I think Dean Martin owned it at one time. It was behind a bicycle shop and had a fire pit on the beach, which was the backyard, so that was perfect for summer. That house was always full of people: Chas, Linda, Gee, Paulette. It was fun and lively, always noisy. David assured me that I was better off there away from the press and told me he'd take care of everything. He signed me up with his business manager Gil Siegel so that I had someone he trusted to run my affairs. He also persuaded me to stop smoking—well, at least cut back—by buying me a beautiful diamond chain mail ring like a mini Slinky that rotated on my finger. The idea was that I could play with it instead of reaching for a cigarette. It was beautiful and I still have it. When the gossip magazines got wind of his gift, they reported that we were engaged even though that thought wasn't in anybody's mind at that point.

On January 21, 1974, Sonny and I arrived together onstage to wrap up our final show, the sixty-seventh we had done together since 1972. It was to be aired a month later, on February 27, and then there'd be one last show already in the can that would be broadcast in early March. People lined up outside CBS for hours hoping to be part of the live audience for our final taping.

Before we came onstage, our producer Chris Bearde stepped out to speak to the three hundred fans in the studio, some of whom were already weeping. "I'm thinking exactly what you are," he told them. "It's sad about some of the things that have been happening. Everybody has problems and everybody deserves the chance to work them out. What about Sonny and Cher's? They're going to be out here in a minute, and you can decide for yourselves. You're going to see a lot of love on this stage. Thank you."

If I'd had my way, I'd have been open about our breakup with our millions of viewers and not just the live audience. I think it might have let America know that we still cared about each other, even if we couldn't stay married.

My mom and Gee came to the studio to support me and were both crying because it was all over—the marriage, and the show, and the music. That was a hard thing to face. They weren't the only ones in tears. The crew was in pieces. They'd become like family to us over the years. Within days it would all be wrapped up and the lovely, fun atmosphere we'd created together would be lost forever. Sonny and I were feeling the emotion, too, but we got through our opening song arm in arm. My solo was the last I'd ever record for *Comedy Hour* and—as always—Sonny stood behind the camera when I recorded it, singing "All in Love Is Fair" by Stevie Wonder. By the time that clip finished playing for our live audience, there wasn't a dry eye in the house.

On January 26, we were invited to attend the 31st Golden Globes. I'd been nominated for Best Actress in a Musical or Comedy Television Series, and *The Sonny & Cher Comedy Hour* was up for Best Musical or Comedy Series. Sonny and I decided not to attend. I stayed home and had my nails done instead. I wasn't in the mood to celebrate, and Carol Burnett had won the title several times before, so I was convinced she'd walk away with the award this time too. As I was explaining to my manicurist why I wasn't going to win, I heard the announcer read off my name. I was gob-smacked by the irony of it.

David's birthday was coming up in February, and I suggested

to some of his friends that they throw him a surprise party. So Louie Kemp, Bob Dylan's friend, arranged to rent the Grand Trianon room at the Beverly Wilshire Hotel. We had the room decorated to look like a carnival. It was amazing—we got a knife thrower, a unicyclist, two mimes, a fire eater, two wrestlers, a fortune teller, and strolling musicians. People came from all over the world. All the who's who of music and films were there, including Ahmet Ertegun, Warren Beatty, Jack Nicholson, and Ringo Starr to name a few. Mo Ostin was responsible for bringing David, and everyone cheered when he walked into the room. After the applause died down, I sang happy birthday and then Bob Dylan came on with me to sing the harmony for "All I Really Want to Do" with The Band playing backup. Rick Danko came up to sing "Mockingbird" with me, and our birthday set ended with Bob Dylan singing "Mr. Tambourine Man."

On Monday, February 18, Sonny filed for a divorce. That was a surprise. The news was splashed all over the press, and the lurid headlines about "the Battling Bonos" blasted every day, usually wildly inaccurate.

That Friday we flew to Houston to play as the closing number at the annual Livestock Show and Rodeo. Elvis and the Jackson 5 were also on the lineup that night. The facilities at the venue were, to put it kindly, basic, so my "dressing room" was a wooden booth that looked like an outhouse in the middle of the arena where they'd had calf roping and bull riding. It was a mess. It was great for cows and horses but not for female singers in beaded gowns. Paulette had come with me but was on an errand as I was struggling with my costume change mid-set. Because of the small space, my hair caught in the zipper on the back of my white jumpsuit. The more I struggled, the worse it got. Denis found me, and he couldn't do anything either.

Catching sight of myself in the mirror, my head yanked back by my trapped hair, I started laughing so hard that I couldn't stop, and hysteria took over. Denis went to get Sonny, who heard me but mistook my laughter for sobs. Throwing open the door, he saw me twisted into a human question mark and started laughing with me too. After everything that had just happened, I don't know how to make sense of it. Sonny started vamping to the audience on the mic, making cracks about what Denis and I were doing in there together. And it was so funny because I was in there forever. The audience was dying laughing, too. By the time Paulette came back, we were all in stitches with tears streaming down our cheeks. We eventually pulled ourselves together enough for Sonny to cut me free with scissors. My zipper was busted, so my ass was on full display and Pauli had to stuff tissue paper inside my pants—the show must go on.

Back in LA, Mickey Rudin filed divorce papers in which he claimed that Sonny had held me in "involuntary servitude," in direct violation of the US Constitution's Thirteenth Amendment, which abolished slavery. He also accused him of "unlawfully dominating and controlling" my business interests and career. This legal move drove Sonny crazy and led him to file a counterclaim, demanding the millions he estimated he'd lose when I split up our partnership. Sonny also filed a multimillion-dollar lawsuit against David, seeking a temporary restraining order and accusing him of interfering with our contractual relationship. David didn't respond, because that would have been beneath him, but I was sad that Sonny and I had reached a point of chiefly talking through our lawyers, although the crazy part was that we remained civil to each other on the phone when discussing Chas.

On March 2, David and I took a major step and arrived together at the Grammy Awards, held at the Hollywood Palladium. This was the first time I'd been seen with him in public, and the press went wild, dubbing us "the industry's hottest couple" as camera flashes dazzled us. I don't think David anticipated this level of scrutiny, and I could see it made him very uncomfortable, as he wasn't used to being judged in the public eye, so I never stopped holding his hand. He made it through.

A month after the Grammys I was asked to present the Academy Award for Best Original Dramatic Score to composer Marvin Hamlisch for the soundtrack to *The Way We Were.* I made a mess out of his name. I mean a complete mess. David accompanied me, and there were even more photographers this time. For some reason that year, they had a lot of presenters who were going to sit together backstage watching the monitor. There were maybe ten of us there waiting when a woman in a black Chinese-style pantsuit emerged from behind a curtain and walked right past me with a smile. "Hey, kid," she said as she passed. I froze. All I could think was *She spoke to me. She spoke to me!* It was Katharine Hepburn, a heroine of my youth, on her way to present an award.

Ms. Hepburn was such an outside woman, and by that, I mean someone who stood apart. She was tough, but never in a horrible way. She was just "Kate." I worshipped her, along with the other "Hepburn girl," Audrey, and I wrote to her a couple of times telling her how much I admired her work, like the fan I was. Years later, when she heard I was looking for a house, her assistant called to ask if I'd like to buy hers because she said Kate would like to see me in it since she knew I'd appreciate it. The property was in one of the great old sections of New York, but I didn't have enough money then. I'm still kicking myself that I didn't go see it and maybe get the chance to speak to her properly. I did see her one last time. I came across her sitting, legs crossed, on the desk in my doctor's office making a telephone call. She was wearing what looked like an outfit straight out of *On Golden Pond.* What a sassy, independent dame.

Trying to focus on my work, I returned to the studio to finish recording the rest of my next album, *Dark Lady,* with Snuff Garrett. The single of the same name flew straight to number one. It was another story song, so it wasn't my favorite, but people loved it and the album, so who am I to judge? Thanks to David, I was hanging out with amazing artists at the peak of their careers, all doing incredible things. Jack Nicholson, at thirty-six, had just starred in *Chinatown* and was about to start filming *One Flew Over the Cuckoo's Nest* (which would earn him his first Oscar). Anjelica Huston was a *Vogue* model at twenty-two; Warren Beatty, thirty-six, had been nominated for four Academy Awards and just produced a series of benefit concerts fundraising for McGovern's campaign; and Lou Adler, forty, was running the coolest club in town, had sold tens of millions of records on his label Ode Records, and had just won two Grammys for his work on Carole King's *Tapestry*, not to mention he was about to produce *The Rocky Horror Picture Show*. These were people at the top of their industries. Then there were all the hip musicians David knew, like the Eagles, Harry Nilsson, and Joni, who wrote their own material. I felt so inspired and wanted to be like them. I'd just had a number one hit, but I wanted to push myself and my work to a new level.

Knowing how I felt, David suggested I work with a songwriter like Jimmy Webb or a producer like Phillip Spector. I wasn't too sure about working with Phillip again, but I trusted David completely, so after I finished my album with Snuffy, I went to A&M Studios in Hollywood. Phillip was also producing John Lennon's latest album, *Rock 'n' Roll*, during that time and occasionally asked Harry Nilsson to step in and sing backup.

One day, Phillip asked both Harry and me to come and sing background together on John's album. By the time we got there, we heard a crash. Then John came storming out of the studio really angry as a chair sailed out after him. I could hear Phillip shouting. As John ran past us and out onto the street, he yelled, "I'm never gonna work with that madman again. He's fucking nuts!" When Phillip saw us, he stopped short and politely asked if we'd step in and lay down a guide vocal for an old Martha and the Vandellas number called "A Love Like Yours."

"John needs to hear the kind of thing I want, so if you wouldn't mind? Then when he comes back he can just listen and learn it." We did as he asked. It was the last time I laid down backing vocals for anyone. We didn't think anything of it until a few weeks later when our record companies called to tell Harry and me that he'd released the single illegally in Europe, in violation of each of our contracts.

Furious, I asked Paulette to drive me to Phillip's house. It was dark and spooky when we got there, so I hesitated for a moment before the gates opened and we drove up the driveway, to be met by security guards. Determined to confront Phillip, I marched up to the front door while Paulette waited in the car. A member of his staff let me in. The house was cold with tall ceilings—it felt kind of like an old haunted house or like I was walking into a scene from *Sunset Boulevard.* I was led to a room where Phillip was standing next to a pool table. I went in and gave him a hug, then told him, "Phillip, you know you can't do this. Harry's on one label, I'm on another, and you put it out under yours. What were you thinking?"

Then he started to act weird. He became agitated and got kind of smart with me—a little too smart, like he was trying to intimidate me. He told me he could do whatever he wanted. He said our record companies could sue him if they didn't like it. Then he picked up a revolver that I hadn't previously noticed lying on the green felt. Staring at him in fury as he twirled it around his fingers, I said, "Don't fuck with me, Phillip! You can't pull that shit on me, you asshole. This is me, Cher, okay? You've known me since I was sixteen and you're going to try to do this with me? Put that fucking gun down and promise me you'll never do anything like this shit with my music again, okay?" Walking out as he apologized, I hurried back to the car and told Paulette to get us the hell out of there.

I didn't believe Phillip would have used that gun on me and was sure he was playing with it for show, but I was still pissed off. "Hell, it probably wasn't even loaded," I told Pauli on the way home, but there was something about him that night that troubled me.

When John Lennon charged out of Phillip's studio, it wasn't the last I saw of him. Not long afterward, David and I walked into Dan Tana's restaurant, and there was John at the bar with Harry Nilsson. The pair had been friends for years and years. When Harry spotted me, he asked if I could take them to Hugh Hefner's house for movie night. "John's dying to see the Playboy Mansion," Harry pleaded. Hef held parties all the time, many of which became notorious as drunken orgies with some of the Playmates, but his Sunday movie nights were casual affairs for friends to enjoy cocktails and dinner before watching a new release. They were very calm events. I didn't have anything else going on that night, so I agreed to drive them to Hef's. There were about fifty of the usual hangers-on when we arrived, people I didn't much like because they only ever went for the free drinks and food. John and Harry were acting fine until we got inside the house, which is when I realized they must have been drunker than I'd thought. Just as the movie was about to start, the two of them put on aristocratic English accents and started chanting, "Hef! Hef! Hef!" except with the accents it sounded like "Huff! Huff! Huff!"

I was mortified and could tell Hef was starting to get pissed off. I told them, "Stop that! Come with me." It was like I became the mother and they were two fourteen-year-old boys. I took them outside while David went to apologize to Hef. Giggling and falling over each other, John and Harry staggered out into the grounds. I sat them down inside the infamous Grotto—it was like a huge cave that one end of the swimming pool went into. I left them on some benches that looked like rocks while I went to find them something to drink. When I came back, they were standing in the middle of the Grotto naked, inside the water, thank God. But they started to come out, and I said, "Guys, do not come out. This is not pretty what I'm seeing. Please do not come out." The whole time they were giggling and naked. I was trying not to laugh, but it was impossible not to. They kept threatening to wander around the mansion naked. David thought they were being ridiculous. We were exasperated with them, but they were hysterical. It took me ages to get them back in their clothes. It was like herding drunks.

I continued to live at the beach house in Malibu as my lawyers negotiated my divorce, which involved the division of an estimated $28 million worth of property and assets, which would be $175 million in 2024. I couldn't have done any of it without David. He was always on the phone with Mickey Rudin making sure I was being taken care of. Paulette was still working as my assistant, but she and Ridgeway had split up for good, so she moved in with me briefly and then with Gee at her funky little property in Laurel Canyon. At twenty-two, my sister was acting in commercials and doing bit parts in shows like *Happy Days* but hadn't yet had her big break on *General Hospital.*

On March 21, 1974, Gee and I found out that our father John Southall, the only man I'd ever called Daddy, was very sick. He was fifty-two. On April 13 Gee and I were heading home from New York when David, knowing how important a visit would be, arranged a private plane to fly us to Texas so we could see Daddy. We walked in the room and his skin so yellow, like the color of a banana. He was almost unrecognizable as the handsome father I remembered as he lay in bed in a veterans' hospital not far from Burleson, dying of liver failure. When he saw me and Gee, his face lit up. He looked so happy to see us there. This was the man who'd rescued me from babysitters to be with him and Mom. The one who'd taken me for ice cream when Gee was born and who taught me how to drive. We stayed with him about an hour and a half. Although we'd kept in touch off and on, the Daddy I'd missed with a physical pain after he and my mother separated had a whole new life with Jane and their three children in Texas, so our paths rarely crossed.

There was so much I wanted to say to him, but I kept quiet. After all, he was Gee's biological father, and I thought her feelings should take priority over mine. Knowing it was the last time we'd ever be together, Daddy began to cry. He died less than a week after our visit. His wife, Jane, later told us that he'd been in and out of consciousness, but after we left he was talking about Gee and me to her, saying that he was so glad he'd gotten to see us one last time. I felt so lucky that David had made our visit possible and that I had him to come home to.

Although David never stopped working, he could also be spontaneous and fun. We often traveled to New York together or spent time with Chas on the beach in Malibu. Chas and David got along surprisingly well. I have some great photos of the three of us playing together. At first, Chas loved David so much. One night she was so excited to talk with him, she ran into the bathroom while he was taking a bubble bath and went right up to the edge of the tub, swishing her hand in the water while she was kind of mindlessly telling her story. I had to pick her up and tell her, "Baby, come and talk to David from here," because David was kind of freaking out. But then one day her attitude toward him abruptly changed and she took on Sonny's feelings toward David. It was horrible and made me so mad. David didn't have much experience with kids and didn't know how to deal with Chas's change of heart. After that, Sonny and I agreed that we would never say anything bad about each other or the people we were dating to Chas because all it did was hurt her. We really stuck to that and I was proud of us.

Then Sonny did something that shattered me. Changing tack in the divorce proceedings, he applied for full custody of Chas and accused me of being an unfit mother. His case hinged on the fact that, one afternoon, I'd taken Chas to Hef's to see his pet monkeys and play in his pool. Our little girl had known and loved Hef her whole life. In fact, his house was like heaven for her, a place where she could have ice cream served to her by a waiter in the Grotto. Sonny's lawyer Irwin Spiegel spun it into me taking Chas to a "house of fornication." The day in question was entirely innocent.

The only person we saw was Pam Grier. I never would have taken her there if something inappropriate was going on.

The thought of losing custody of Chas or only having her on the weekends filled me with anxiety. I didn't understand how Sonny could contemplate taking our daughter away from me. He and she had their own special bond, but I was her mother.

In May, Sonny and I were summoned to the Santa Monica courthouse to give evidence about this new aspect of our divorce. Paulette sat beside me as we watched Mickey Rudin do his best to destroy Sonny's accusations. We heard the judge tell Irwin Spiegel that he was getting into deep water, and if he didn't stop, there could be a lawsuit in his future for defamation of my character. This was the same judge who in a previous hearing had given me a stern talking to, telling me, "In this country, Mrs. Bono, contracts are meaningful." What he hadn't understood then was how could I go and sing "I Got You Babe" and perform with Sonny when we weren't married? I just couldn't bring myself to do it. I was relieved that he seemed to be on my side regarding this custody question, but he postponed his final decision, so we left the courtroom unsettled. When we walked outside we were greeted by a mass of reporters and photographers shouting questions like "Do you still love Cher, Sonny?" or "Cher, what was it like being Sonny's servant?" I guess after a life led in the public eye, we couldn't expect our divorce to remain private. I stood silently beside Sonny, waiting for him to respond for us both as he always had. I was caught completely off guard when he flung me backward, grabbed hold of my face, and stuck his tongue down my throat. By the time he'd released me while cameras flashed, he was laughing so hard that the only thing I could do was laugh too, even though I wanted to be mad at him. It was another example of his insane sense of humor, which could almost always make me laugh, even in the middle of all that mess. Thankfully, the judge finally ruled in my favor and ended up allocating Sonny even less time with Chas. Shocked,

Sonny asked me, "Are you really going to stick to that?" to which I replied, "Of course not, dummy. You can see her whenever you like." The last thing I was going to do was keep our child from seeing her best friend.

The financial negotiations dragged on and I was missing living in the big house. Then one day David asked Mickey Rudin what we could do, and Mickey said all I had to do was walk in the front door and stay. David and I drove over on a weekday morning. I was nervous because I didn't know what to expect. I was so relieved to find that Sonny wasn't home when we arrived. Connie was, and even though we'd become friends, she immediately called Sonny at his office. Incredibly, he did nothing at all. Connie left, and a few days later Sonny sent someone to collect their things and bring all their stuff to the St. Cloud house, which they moved into once he'd made me sign it over to him.

I was so happy to be back in my dream home and was excited to share the big house with David, who moved in with me, promising to throw the kinds of dinners and parties I'd always dreamed of hosting and bringing his German butler Klaus and his cook Ida. I was especially delighted about Ida because she made that delicious chilled avocado soup I loved.

My happiness was tragically interrupted in July 1974, when we heard that our friend Cass Elliot had died in London at the age of thirty-two. Having recently sold out the London Palladium for the first time as a solo artist, she had spent the evening about town, first at Mick Jagger's birthday party and then at a couple of other events, before returning to Harry Nilsson's Mayfair apartment. After drinking some champagne, she called her friend and fellow band member Michelle Phillips. That night, she died in her sleep from a heart attack. The day of her funeral, Michelle turned up at my door with Cass's seven-year-old daughter, Owen, and asked me if I could watch her until the service. As she walked into our home, the child I barely knew looked up at me with sad eyes and said,

"My mom's dead," so I gave her a hug and comforted her. I was a mom, I knew what to do. She and Chas played quietly together for a while until it was time to leave for Mount Sinai Cemetery and a service attended by everyone from Carol Burnett to Robert Redford. Sonny and Connie were also there. It was a sad day, but as Michelle said, at least Cass died peaceful and happy.

It seemed like I'd just been with her driving along Mulholland in her Mini Cooper. Cass had just about killed me going so fast on the winding road, trying to prove to me how the car wouldn't turn over. I was like, "Cass, maybe we don't have to learn that now." Then we went back to her house and she lay down because she'd hurt her back. She ate a meatloaf sandwich with mashed potatoes and put her cigarette out in the potatoes. I told her, "Cass, this is just wrong."

I can't recall where I was when I heard that Sonny had signed on with ABC to host a new solo show, *The Sonny Comedy Revue.* Our friends at CBS had passed on the option even though Art Fisher would direct and several of our show's veterans, including Teri Garr, Billy Van, and Freeman King, were on board. It had everything from Sonny's monologues to his solo skits, and ABC liked that it would be a near copy of our show and planned to invite different female celebrities to take my place. In promotional interviews, Sonny joked that the only difference would be that when he looked left, there "wouldn't be an Indian standing there." Guests lined up for the first season included Glen Campbell, Smokey Robinson, the Jackson 5, the Hudson Brothers, and Frankie Avalon.

I didn't want Sonny to fail, but I didn't know what would happen to me if he succeeded. With our own show over, I wasn't sure if I'd ever work in television again. I had little to my own name and was living in a house I couldn't afford, wondering what was to become of me. David kept telling me, "Don't worry, I'm going to fix it."

I've always thought that whether you get a break or not is purely down to luck. There are a million people more talented than me who struggle to make it and will never be famous. Talent counts, but if you're not lucky, no one will see it. I sometimes wonder what would have happened if I hadn't been in Aldo's coffee shop the day I met Sonny or hadn't been singing while making the bed that day, or if Darlene hadn't been late into the studio one morning. These were the key moments that changed my luck.

David must have sensed my restlessness, because he set aside his empire momentarily to negotiate with CBS on my behalf and secure me my own show, to be simply called *Cher*. I didn't know how he did it or whether I'd have to pay Sonny half of what I earned, but he and Mickey Rudin kept my career—and my spirits—alive. I was excited and scared and enormously grateful to David for brokering the deal.

I met with Bob Mackie to discuss how I would look on the new show now that I was single and told him, "I don't want to look like a housewife in an evening gown, okay?"

Bob threw back his head and laughed. "Oh, Cher, my dear, we will never have to worry about that!"

With some time on my hands until I had to start work in the new year, David and I were home playing backgammon (a game I taught him) when he announced that if he lost, I could ask him for anything. Thinking how much I wanted a vacation, I said I'd like a trip to Europe for me, Pauli, and Gee. You can imagine my delight when I beat him that night—although, being a man, he insisted, "Sweetheart, I lost on purpose." Whatever. Thrilled and excited, the girls and I planned a grand adventure in late September 1974, starting with first-class fights to Paris.

A week before we were due to fly out, *The Sonny Comedy Revue* premiered on ABC. It was up against *Kojak* and the family favorite *The Wonderful World of Disney*, which was a pity for Sonny. Those were hard acts to beat. They should have put him on a night when he could have built up an audience and then moved his slot—everyone knew that. It was kind of a bullshit thing to do. When he bounced onto the stage, the audience went wild as he told them, "Thank you! Thank you! You'd think I was Robert Redford or Paul Newman, but it's just me, Sonny Bono . . . a combination of both." I watched the rest of his first solo attempt and there was a lot about it that I liked. If our show had never existed, it might have been a hit, because Sonny was truly funny. I took Chas and some of her friends to see him backstage and give him moral support, because it took a lot of guts for him to go out there on his own.

The following day, CBS announced the *Cher* show, which was set to air on Sunday nights at 8 p.m., going head-to-head with Sonny's. The scheduling decision seemed unnecessarily cruel to us both, as if they wanted a face-off. As things went, we didn't end up competing, since Sonny's show ended up canceled before mine began.

A night after that I went with Gee and Paulette to the Troubadour to see the last US gig of a Scottish funk group called the Average White Band (David was tied up in meetings). My sister had a crush on the singer and guitarist, Hamish Stuart (whom she later dated). After the gig, all three of us went backstage and were invited to a party out in the Hollywood Hills. Gee and Paulette went home to pack but I decided to be a big girl that night and go on my own. And I was going to do drugs.

I didn't know the host, a Wall Street dropout in his thirties named Ken Moss who'd set up—and lost—a budget airline, but almost as soon as I arrived at his house, he offered me something off a piece of tin foil. I assumed it was cocaine, the hot new drug. For a fleeting moment, I thought, *I'm such a square. Everybody else takes drugs all the time. Maybe I should try this.* Then I remembered how bad stimulants always made me feel and came to my senses. "Nah, thanks," I told him, so Moss took some himself and then offered the band some white powder from a different stash stored in a small glass vial. I watched drummer Robbie McIntosh take a few hits and didn't think anything of it.

As everybody around me started to get high, I lit a cigarette and went to get myself a drink.

I was talking with the band's guitarist Alan Gorrie in the kitchen when he suddenly started sweating and his skin turned bluey-white. He told me he felt nauseous.

"Why don't we go outside for some fresh air?" I suggested. Out in the yard he felt better for about ten minutes, before doubling over and throwing up violently. "Okay, okay," I said, patting his back. "Let me get you a wet cloth." When I went back inside, it was like something from a Hieronymus Bosch painting. You could feel the panic, as people were vomiting everywhere. Hamish then came running up to me and told me, "Robbie's real sick upstairs in the bathroom, Cher. Can you help us?" When I said Alan was sick too, he told me they'd taken the same drug.

I have always been cool in a crisis. Hamish and I were the only ones who hadn't done any drugs, so we went around trying to take care of everybody. Taking a breath, I told him, "Let me go check on Alan first." I found him still retching but seemingly a little better, so I left him and ran upstairs. Robbie was out cold, lying in about six inches of water in the bathtub. There were random people standing around, and Ken Moss was half blocking the doorway. Shocked, I screamed, "God, he looks terrible!"

That's when I noticed that Robbie's fingernails had gone blue. I panicked. After Bill Bixby's wife had committed suicide, they shaved off her fingernail and it was black and blue. My manicurist, who also worked for Bixby's wife, had told me this and that it meant the person wasn't getting enough oxygen. No one seemed to take me seriously when I said we should call for help, so I ran downstairs to find a telephone and call my doctor. This was before the days of 911. My doctor didn't pick up, so I tried my gynecologist, and I couldn't even get him. I ended up talking to the brand-new gynecologist who had just started in their office. Breathlessly, I told him, "I'm at this party and everyone is throwing up. They took some kind of drugs but I don't know which kind. Someone is lying unconscious in a bath with his fingernails turning blue."

"All right," he said, his voice steady. "Take him to the emergency room right away. You can just drop him off, nobody will arrest you, and they'll take care of him. You should take him right away, any breath could be his last. And the guy you're taking care of who keeps puking, just keep him up until he's stopped dry heaving for an hour."

After hanging up, I repeated everything he'd said to Hamish, who said, "OK." Then I helped Alan into my car and drove him back to my house. After I left, Ken Moss told everyone that I was being "an alarmist" and that Robbie would just have an awful hangover in the morning, but he'd be fine, so nobody took him to the hospital. In my kitchen I gave Alan some ice packs and forced him to walk around until he stopped retching. Then I took him to the bathroom, where he lay on the floor looking like death. I sat with him for a long time until he was no longer dry heaving, and he eventually fell asleep.

The next day he woke early feeling horrible and, after taking a shower, called to see how Robbie was. The band said he was having a bad time after being driven back to their motel but seemed like he was going to be fine, so everyone hoped he'd dodged a bullet. Then they called back a few hours later and told Alan that Robbie had died. He broke down when he heard, and so did I. These guys weren't druggies; they were just young musicians from Scotland celebrating the last night of their gig. It had been a hugely successful night for them, everybody had showed up. Going out afterward was a special occasion, and they'd trusted the drugs Moss had given them were safe. It turned out the powder was a mixture of morphine and heroin. Robbie was twenty-four and left behind a wife and young son. All those who got sick had been given the drug by Moss. Although I couldn't have done more than I did, I felt so bad for not forcing them to get Robbie to the hospital while there was still time.

Alan left to be with his grieving bandmates, and when David came home and found me crying, he insisted on calling the police. Two detectives arrived to take my statement because I was a key witness to a potential crime. They told us that all weekend people were dying from this mixture of drugs and that Moss had fled the country. They also told me that they'd spoken with other people from the party and nobody had mentioned that I was there, which I thought was amazing. The investigation started a chain of events that would eventually lead to my testifying to a grand jury that convicted Moss of involuntary manslaughter for handing out high doses of heroin to his guests. Upon his return to the United States, Moss was arrested and went to prison.

The press jumped all over my accidental connection to Robbie's death and ran all kinds of false stories and lurid headlines, which mortified me. I was used to having horrible things written about me, but David was not. He felt thrown in the deep end. I had to explain that part of the package with me was a giant spotlight on every aspect of my life. But this time, the attention felt intense and it was untrue. The truth is all I did was save one man's life and try to save another's, but the implication was that I'd taken part in a seedy drug party and was an unfit mother after all. Sonny was furious. Everyone in my life wanted to know why I'd gone to that party by myself. Truthfully, it's very simple: I wanted to. I didn't want to have a chaperone. I just wanted to go to a party on my own.

# 19

----

## *both sides now*

W hen Paulette, Gee, and I flew to Paris, we packed a ridiculous twenty-two suitcases between us. I was so happy to be on a trip with two of my favorite people. When we checked into the Hôtel de Crillon, we were starving and jet-lagged. We had Paulette dial room service because she was the only one who spoke French. I had learned French when I was pregnant, but I had nobody to practice with, so I could only speak it a little, like a child. Gee had had a French boyfriend but forgot most of what she learned after they broke up. Paulette was the only one who could really speak it fluently, but her accent was frightening. We'd laugh so hard every time she needed to say something.

After dinner, we showered and changed and then I started on the girls' makeup. I was the official makeup artist for our trip. I had a lot of practice, since I did my own makeup while we toured and for the show. It was always a moment of calm for me, almost meditative. With the girls, it took us about three hours to all get ready, so we would always leave at about midnight, but we thought we looked like a million dollars, or like hookers. We went downstairs and walked through the lobby together. I wore an exquisite purple felted cape designed by Bob Mackie, and the girls wore beautiful coats they'd borrowed from me. Hearing an argument, we spotted two Frenchwomen in a corner pointing at us and talking animatedly. One of the women hurried over to me and said, "Madame, I am so angry! That woman thought you were hookers and said you shouldn't be allowed in a hotel like this, but I told her, *Non, non, non,* that woman is Cher, a famous American TV star! You should show some respect, *je m'excuse.*" I went back to the girls and told them, "That chick thought we looked like hookers, too." And we all became hysterical. It wouldn't be the last time, but it was probably the most memorable. We had a fabulous night out, and the next evening we did it again.

We soon discovered that we couldn't afford to blow David's vacation budget on such an expensive hotel, so we moved to the Hôtel Raphael near the Arc de Triomphe. My priority was to find the best dance club in the city, even though my sister hated to dance. The girl who'd had her nose in a book for most of her childhood usually sat things out whenever Pauli and I went dancing, but not in Paris. At some point we heard the American musician Johnny Rivers was in town, and it started a running joke for us. Everywhere we went out we'd tell people, "We're looking for Johnny Rivers, have you seen him?" It didn't mean anything to anyone but us, but sometimes a person would respond, "Oh, I just saw Johnny Rivers performing at so and so club." It really made us laugh, and we kept it up the whole trip, but the truth was we really did want to see him! Dani's was the hottest club with the coolest people, best ambience, and a great dance floor. The Parisians knew who I was, but they didn't mob me the way people did in America. Although we were still attracting attention, I like to think it was more for our moves on the dance floor than for my fame.

One night, though, everyone stopped dancing and turned their heads in the same direction, to a statuesque young blonde in a black fishnet catsuit that left ~~little~~ nothing to the imagination under the disco lights. It was the Texan model Jerry Hall, eighteen years old with a body to die for and no inhibitions whatsoever, flinging her long blond hair about as the cameras popped. Paulette also got a lot of attention while we were in France, and guys were always trying to take her out. She met the French writer-director Pierre Billon, who immediately took a liking to her. He was so infatuated that one night Paulette, Gee, and I were having dinner in a kind of Western-looking restaurant, and he drove his motorcycle literally inside the restaurant and up to the bar trying to find her.

Their romance lasted maybe a day and, regardless, soon we were off to Amsterdam. Instead of us staying in another five-star hotel, I said to Pauli that we needed to find someplace where college students would go. The "boutique" place she found for us turned out to be at the top of a five-story walk-up. Gee and Pauli would hardly talk to me after we had to lug every single piece of luggage—now more than fifteen, because I'd purchased Louis Vuitton suitcases in Paris. (A waiter in Paris would later tell me on this same trip that only hookers carry Louis Vuitton suitcases. Again with the hooker accusations.) After we'd settled in, Pauli took us to a nightclub where we could dance. It smelled a bit strange when we walked in, but I didn't think much of it. The music was great, and I went crazy dancing. Taking a break to catch my breath, I sat down and pulled out a container of mints. When the guy sitting next to me saw me pop one in my mouth, he asked if he could have one. "Sure," I said, but ten minutes later he asked for another. Finally, he turned to me and said, "When is this acid going to kick in?" I almost did a spit take. Minutes later, the police burst in and arrested three people right in front of us on the dance floor for heroin. It turned out the place was a hash den, which explained the smell. I asked Pauli, "Why are we here again? What am I missing?" Clearly, it was time to leave that club.

Outside, we couldn't find a cab but met some American boys who were driving around Europe in a Volkswagen van, and they offered to drive us back to our hotel. Giddy with spontaneity, we piled in, but they were so high and were making dumb jokes. We humored them, thinking, *Can you please just get us to our hotel?* Then one of the guys, who was really high, turned to Pauli to ask her to make a sacrifice for the free ride but made a Freudian slip and accidentally asked, "Can't you just make a sacrifuck?" and we just died laughing. That expression still cracks us up to this day.

Back in Paris a few days later, Paulette met up with Johnny Hallyday, France's most famous rock-and-roll singer and bad boy. Pierre was yesterday's news. Then we all flew to London, where we stayed at what must be one of the smallest hotels in the city. It was like a doll hotel. The baggage man must have been ninety-seven years old and couldn't lift any of the luggage we'd brought. Between that and the elevator being so small that only two people could fit in at once, it took about forty minutes to get all our bags up to our suite, which turned out to be the size of a postage stamp. If one person was walking around, the other two had to sit down. It was ridiculous. Lew Grade had gotten us tickets to the play *John, Paul, George, Ringo . . . and Bert* and sent a limo to bring us to the show. It was a great play that was later named Best Musical of 1974 by the Evening Standard Theatre Awards and London Critics' Awards. When we came back, I sat on the edge of the glass coffee table to give Paulette space to cross the room and the table broke right underneath me. I said, "I'm out of here." We were trying to figure out where we could go, and called all the hotels we could think of in London. None of them wanted to give us a room at that hour, as it was already past 10 p.m. They didn't care that we had money or that I was Cher. My sister and Pauli were so pissed, so we packed up all our stuff without knowing where we were going and left the hotel. I suggested we go to the Playboy Club, but when we called them they also said there wasn't any space. I told them, "I bet if Hugh Hefner called you'd let us in." The guy on the phone laughed and said, "Of course." So I called Joe D, who coincidentally was at Hef's house. He told us, "Go to the hotel. Hef's taken care of it. They're expecting you." Relieved and excited, we went to the Playboy Club, where they welcomed us in. We crammed all our bags into the lobby, then they brought us up the elevator and to a huge suite, which they said was their best, but when they opened the doors, the place was a mess. There were old takeout chicken boxes lying around with leftover pieces of chicken in them and old pizza all over the place. We went back to the lobby exhausted and disappointed. It was almost three in the morning and we didn't have a place to sleep. We sat on our mountain of luggage and I called Joe D, telling him that the suite was disgusting and asking where else we could go. He reassured me that Hef had a friend, Bernie Cornfeld, with a big house and told me the address. So, off we went again with one taxi for us and an extra for our luggage. For some reason I got confused about the exact address, so when we pulled up to what seemed like the correct house, we sent Paulette to the door. After ringing the bell for about five minutes, some poor woman came down in curlers, bunny house slippers, and a babydoll nightgown. This was clearly not Bernie Cornfeld. It turned out Hef's friend's house was the one next door, so we rang the bell and a small man answered, standing in shadow, wearing only a kimono. He let us into the house, and in the full light of the foyer we realized his kimono was so short that when he walked you could see just your old-fashioned penis. As we followed him I kept trying not to look. He showed me to my room and gave me two hand towels. I was getting ready to take a shower when he made a surprise visit back to my room. I was only holding one hand towel, and I didn't know what to cover, my top or my bottom—it was like a slideshow. Not sure what else to do, I jumped into bed. Bernie followed and sat on the edge of the mattress making conversation as if it were all very normal. He'd put my sister and Pauli in a basement room, which they said was like an old musty boat. They didn't last down there long and came up to stay with me, finding Bernie still chatting away cheerfully in his minuscule little robe. He finally left the room and all three of us squeezed into my double bed. I slept with their feet on either side of my head. The next day we packed our bags again and got in another taxi (with another extra taxi for our luggage) to go to a regular hotel that would finally let us in now that it was daylight and our request for a room seemed more respectable. I remember I took a bath and we all sat together in bed watching a documentary. We were so happy just to be by ourselves.

David had missed me terribly while I was gone, and almost as soon as we got back, he told me we were going to Aspen to join Lou, Jack, Toots, Warren, and some other friends. It was my first trip to Aspen, and I was excited. I'd missed David so much. We flew to Colorado in a private jet with Anjelica, the actress and model Britt Ekland, my friend Ara Gallant from *Vogue,* and the models Apollonia van Ravenstein and Ingrid Boulting, who'd become the face of Biba, my favorite London store. Some of them stayed at Art Garfunkel's place, but David and I checked into the Caribou, a private members' club at the bottom of Ajax Mountain that was so great, I wanted David to buy one of their condos.

Aspen in the seventies was different than it is now—it was a real town. The people who worked there could actually afford to live there, and it was all independent stores, no chains. David and I used to walk around the town just looking at all the shops. There was a great place called Poppycock's, where you could buy crêpes; a Tom's Market, actually run by a man named Tom; and a shop that sold the best hot chocolate in the world. There was an opera house and an old hotel, a toy store, and a restaurant that had been the Ute City Bank. I fell in love with the whole vibe of the place and its energy. I had a ball learning to ski and would dance all night. I loved that you could just bum around town without having to worry about how you looked because it didn't make any difference. One night David suggested again that we should get married once my divorce was finalized, and I didn't disagree.

After we flew back to Los Angeles, David kept talking about marriage, but when I reminded him that he hadn't formally proposed, he did it properly in the library of the big house on Carolwood after a game of backgammon. "Will you marry me, sweetheart?" he asked, taking my hand. I smiled and said, "Yes, Dave." Excited to set a date, he suggested the following summer since my divorce would be done by then, but I said I wanted to wait until the winter so we could get married in Aspen. It was too much to grasp at one time for me. I wasn't even divorced.

In November 1974, I was invited to New York for the Met Gala. Diana Vreeland had been brought on as a special consultant for the Costume Institute after leaving *Vogue* in 1971. She turned the gala into a one-of-a-kind party and was the one who introduced hosting it at the Metropolitan Museum of Art, which was genius. Before Diana, it had been a midnight dinner held at places like the Waldorf Astoria, Central Park, and the Rainbow Room. She also had the idea to embrace pop culture and include celebrities on the guest list alongside high-society people and politicians. In 1999 Anna Wintour would take over as chair and bring her personal power and artistry as well as the resources from *Vogue*, which were tremendous. Through the efforts of these two women, a dinner party costing $50 a head transformed into the global phenomenon it is today. It had been many years since Diana had told me "You have a pointed head. You're beautiful" at the party thrown for Jacqueline Kennedy. She was the first person to see beauty in a different kind of woman and make her beautiful in the eyes of her readers, and the first person who thought that I could be in the pages of *Vogue*. I was Hollywood and she made me fashion. She was a breed apart.

It was Diana's idea to set an annual theme for the gala, and that year she'd made it "Romantic and Glamorous Hollywood Design." No wonder I aced it, but being naked helps. When I asked Bob Mackie to take me, he asked what I wanted to wear. I knew immediately. "The souffle dress," I replied. It was a dress he'd made for my most recent *Vogue* layout that was called "Fashion from the 20s to the 70s." The dress had white feathers woven into the beading and was made of "souffle" material, which Bob told me was actually banned in the United States because it was so flammable. Marlene Dietrich had brought it in from France a long time before for Bob to make her a dress. If it catches a match, it goes up like magician's paper, so you have to be extra careful around candles or anyone smoking, which of course at the Met Gala everyone was.

The dress transformed into something truly enchanting when Bob sprayed it with water and patted it onto my skin so it just looked like my bare body was covered in beads and feathers. It didn't occur to me how naked I looked until one of the guests came up to me and asked, "How does it feel to be naked?" I told him it felt great. To this day the magic of Bob's dress has never been duplicated, though just about everyone in the universe has tried.

Bob's dress was the talk of the town. Richard Avedon's photograph of me in what became known as "the naked dress" was chosen for the cover of *Time* in March 1975. That magazine sold out everywhere but was banned in several states. Some people in the South were so offended by the controversial image, which they claimed overstepped the bounds of common decency, that they ripped off the cover. After that, Bob and I only ever referred to it as "the dress."

The Met Gala was a triumph, and I had a blast with Pauli, Bob, and Bob's partner, Ray Aghayan, who was also a brilliant, sought-after fashion designer and would go on to be Oscar-nominated three times, for his costume design on *Lady Sings the Blues*, *Funny Lady*, and *Gaily, Gaily*. There were many spectacular people there, like Liza Minnelli, Andy Warhol, Gloria Vanderbilt, Lauren Hutton, Twiggy, Jackie Kennedy, and Peggy Rockefeller. Diana had set up displays of costumes from various movies. A few of my costumes were included in the display as well, even though I'd only been on TV and not in a film. Bob's designs were that spectacular. They also displayed a few of Carol Burnett's costumes designed by Bob, but hers were more comedic and mine were gowns, which better fit the theme.

While in New York for the gala, I agreed to my first interview with Andy Warhol for his *Interview* magazine. Ara Gallant styled me beautifully for the December cover, weaving Christmas tree lights into my hair and making braids that were nailed to a board behind me. It was an incredible look. David came with me to the interview at the Pierre Hotel. Andy Warhol's interviews were not like regular interviews. He wouldn't say much. He just sat there and got me talking while he kept the recorder on. It was more like a "happening" (old-school). In this interview he asked me about everything that went down with Sonny, and then he asked me if I did my own fingernails. He had that way about him.

Back in LA for Christmas, David decided to throw the biggest party Carolwood had ever seen and invited enough stars to light the entire house. Before the party, David asked Paulette to suggest something I might like as a gift. She knew better than to surprise me, so she came to me right away. I knew exactly what I wanted. Van Cleef & Arpels was running a full-page ad in the December issue of *Vogue* for a beautiful diamond necklace. It was long and dipped low between the model's breasts. I loved it. "Well, that's easy," Pauli said, ripping out the page. When she told him, David ordered the necklace from the store. He presented it to me early so that I could wear it at the party, and I excitedly tore open the wrapping, lifting the lid of the box only to find a necklace that was half the size. It turned out the photo in the magazine showed two necklaces styled together, not just one. I'll never forgive you for the false advertising, Van Cleef & Arpels! It was the greatest injustice in modern history. But of course I loved the necklace and Dave for being so sweet.

The party itself was perfect. It was the epitome of the "event of the year," and people talked about it forever. Paulette and Gee were in charge of the guest list, which meant they went through every hot guy from every band they could think of and sent them invitations. All of them came. There were a ton of people, and the house and the event tent were both overflowing with guests. It was really windy and cold that night, so we had to bring in heaters and needed so many that we sourced them from all over California. Sonny and I had never thrown a party in that house (or any house, actually), so this was especially exciting for me. Paulette was trying her best to get time with all the guys she and Gee had invited, but every time someone would arrive, they'd say something like "Oh, the house is so beautiful," and David would respond, "Pauli will show you around!" and bring them to her. She spent all night showing people around our house while Gee was talking to the guys. Pauli was rolling her eyes like she was ten the entire time. David didn't realize how he was ruining the party for Paulette. She and I still laugh about it.

With the new year came my new show. On January 6 at 8:45 p.m. I walked onstage alone for the first time. Even though I was surrounded by people I loved, with Art Fisher directing, Bob and Ret putting on my costumes, Renate doing my hair, the Hammer (George Schlatter) producing, and Paulette, Gee, and my mother backstage for support, I was still petrified. If I'd known stage fright before, it was nothing compared to the sheer terror I felt that night. I knew I'd be all right doing all the songs and sketches with guests, but the opening monologue had me quaking in my size

7.5 stilettos. All kinds of things were going through my mind at that moment. I thought of being alone, no Sonny to turn to and say under my breath, "How am I doing, Son?" Standing in the dark, the song started with just the piano. Hearing the first notes of "Let Me Entertain You," I was so nervous I didn't know if my voice would come out. Then the full track came up and suddenly I felt good, real good. I sang in a solo spotlight, then after a musical cue I threw off my cape, revealing a nude tulle rhinestone dress that was so gorgeous and otherworldly you could hear people gasp. I went strutting down the runway in high heels as the stage shot out farther and farther into the audience. It was no mean feat—the platform was narrow and moving really fast as I was strutting on it. It was terrifying and exhilarating. We had to try to create something that would be as exciting as Sonny and me coming out together. After the applause died down, I said, "Can I hear a little commotion for the dress?" as I wiggled my hips. Turning and lifting my hair, I said, "Okay, now let's hear it for the back of the dress."

My palms sweaty, I stood in the spotlight and began my monologue by saying that people may have noticed I'd been gone for a little while, but I was so thrilled to be back. "My name is Cher," I added, staring straight into the camera. "I am twenty-eight years old, five feet seven and a half inches tall, have black hair and brown eyes, weigh a hundred and four pounds when I'm happy, and a hundred and eight when I'm miserable. I'm a hundred and six now, and my fate is in your hands." Then they rolled the tape.

Thank God for David, because my first guest was Elton John, and the others were Flip Wilson and Bette Midler. It was usually hard to get really successful musicians to appear as TV guests, but because David was such a powerhouse, he seemed to be able to get anybody. Elton and I sang "Lucy in the Sky with Diamonds" on a silvery set studded with stars, and then my old friend Laverne emerged from the laundromat to do a fun sketch with Flip Wilson, who played Geraldine, which was a popular character he'd created for *The Flip Wilson Show.* The two of them were great together re-creating a high school reunion between rivals.

Bette Midler joined me for a "trashy ladies" medley set in a bordello. We wore suspenders, stockings, and lacy corsets as we sang about brassy dames in history, from Mame to Sweet Georgia Brown. Then it was Elton and me again, this time having fun singing "Benny and the Jets" before what was one of the funniest sketches that I have ever been in. Entitled "The Final Curtain," it had me, Elton, Bette, and Flip as decrepit retirees living in an old folks' home in the year 2025, reflecting on our former showbiz lives. Bob Mackie pulled out all the stops with our madcap costumes. As Elton whizzed around in a glittery wheelchair decked out Harley-Davidson style, I wore the beanbag boobs Bob had first perfected for Carol Burnett, and Bette sported breasts the size of footballs and mammoth butt cheeks.

For my show's grand finale, Bette, Elton, and I did a medley of songs, including "Mockingbird," "Proud Mary," and "Ain't No Mountain High Enough." Bob outdid himself with our costumes and we were all decked out in silver and white, singing on an ethereal set with balloons everywhere that looked like huge bubbles. I knew the premiere would be a smash, and I couldn't have done it without my guests, David, Bob, and everybody on my team. The question was, could I keep up the momentum? The answer turned out to be yes. My show had an estimated twenty-one million viewers for its premiere and ended up being a bigger hit than *The Sonny & Cher Comedy Hour.* It beat out *The Wonderful World of Disney* for viewers in the 8 p.m. Sunday slot, which was crazy. No studio had ever been able to do it, and CBS had been trying to knock down Disney forever, literally. I remember being ten when they were building Disneyland and I couldn't wait to watch that show every week. I was shocked and delighted at the ratings. Everybody was congratulating me, and I was so grateful. I have to give credit to David for everything:

for getting me out of my contract, being such a loving boyfriend, and taking over my life that was such a mess. I would have gone running into the night screaming if I'd been him.

I wasn't fully prepared for how different it would be performing as a single woman from a married one. Even though my new dresses were no more revealing than the ones from *The Sonny & Cher Show* and the dialogue was no more provocative, I now had two censors on set monitoring everything I wore and did. All the things I had gotten away with when I was with Sonny, I wasn't getting away with anymore as a single woman. Somehow everything I wore was too low-cut or revealed too much. Were they living in a cave the whole time *The Sonny & Cher Show* was on? Sometimes it became ridiculous. One night I was recording a solo in a set that was made to look like an artist's loft. Bobby Kelly was a genius and made it with huge windows that had water streaming down the outside to look like rain. I was standing in a long flowing gown that fit the mood and singing when one of my censors came up and said I looked like a French prostitute. I said, "Are you kidding? This is beautiful." The censors had a way of interpreting everything as being about sex. Bob started arguing with them, and I went out into the hall to calm down because I was so upset, which is where I saw Norman Lear and grabbed him. I told him, "Norman you've got to come up and help me. They're telling me I can't do this song because I look like a prostitute." He went in and ripped the two censors a new asshole, telling them to get their minds out of the gutter.

When Raquel Welch came on the show, I told her about how bad the censors were, but I don't think she believed me. Bob made us matching cutaway dresses for our duet "I'm a Woman," which went fine, but when it was time for her solo she wore a satin slip dress to perform "Feel Like Makin' Love." The dress was gorgeous, and she looked like a million bucks. When she got into the song, she ran her hands along her body, and I guess they thought she looked too sexy because they cut her song and it never saw the light of day. That's how bad the censors were.

By mid-January, I'd come to the reluctant decision that I couldn't marry David after all. No matter how much I loved him, I wasn't sure I was ready so soon on the heels of divorcing Sonny. David moved out to live at the Beverly Hills Hotel for a while, but we still hung out constantly and he told the producers that he would still help with the first season. David was always taking care of me. I think he thought I would change my mind and maybe I would have. I wasn't sure of the decision. I wasn't sure about lots of the decisions I was making, because I still had no practice making them.

Needing some female company, I asked Paulette if she wanted to move in with me and Chas. She jumped at the chance. Without husbands or boyfriends, she and I went around town on weekends shopping and dancing as much as we liked. We were like a couple of teenagers. One day my Ferrari was low on gas and Pauli said she'd fill it up. But when we were leaving the studio later, we stalled out smack in the middle lane of Santa Monica Boulevard. "How could you forget to put gas in the car, Paul?" I asked, frustrated, as the people behind us honked like crazy. "Oops!" she responded. I was annoyed but forgiving—until, I kid you not, the same thing happened a week later! And then it was pretty much *What is your problem, Paul?*

Another time Paulette thought it would be fun to get stoned before we did some errands, so she pulled over on Sunset and lit a joint. Even though I'd hated weed back when I was with Bill, I felt like I was a different person now. Besides, I'd only done it three times and the one time I hadn't known what too much was. I had a few hits with Paulette and it felt fine. We went to North Beach leather to get my clothes fitted, but when I got up to the salesman, it started to hit me and I just handed him my clothes and walked out. A few minutes later Pauli spotted a police car and she was overcome with paranoia. She made me swallow half our baggie of dope and I was sick for hours. That, my friends, was the last time I ever did drugs (well, except for maybe one time in Aspen).

Paulette loved going to concerts, but I never got to go to many because first I'd been with Sonny and then I was always working. She had seen the Allman Brothers at the Forum in November and she wouldn't stop talking about them, so when I was driving home one day and saw Gregg Allman's name on the marquee at the Troubadour as opening for Etta James, I went home and told her. She said, "Cher, don't be ridiculous, why would Gregg Allman be playing a tiny venue like the Troubadour? You don't go from the Forum to the Troubadour. And opening for Etta James?"

"Pauli, I can read the sign. English is my first language." I didn't have any knowledge of the Allman Brothers, but Pauli filled me in. From Florida and Georgia, they were considered pioneers of the Southern rock sound. Gregory LeNoir Allman was the younger brother of Duane Allman, the band's leader, who'd been killed in a motorcycle accident three years earlier at the age of twenty-four. Their bassist died in a similar crash a year later, so the band re-formed and released two successful albums featuring iconic numbers such as "Jessica" and "Ramblin' Man." Gregory and the band's guitarist Dickey Betts were the most popular in the group and people always came to see them.

When it turned out I was right about the show, Paulette was very excited and said we had to go, so we all went: me, David, Gee, Paulette, and Tatum O'Neal, who was the token twelve-year-old who'd been staying with us. The Troubadour was an intimate venue and already packed when we arrived. Etta James had an incredible history, having first found fame touring with Little Richard. She'd dated B. B. King, she'd sung duets with Elvis Presley, and she was a friend of Jackie Wilson. Seeing two great performers in one show doesn't happen that often, but when it does, it's amazing.

Before Gregg Allman started playing that night, the crowd was noisy with people yelling over one another. Then the lights went out and everyone was still talking, but you could see a figure making his way through the room. He sat at the piano and began playing. Within seconds you could hear a pin drop. Then the lights came up on him. He was so beautiful with long blond hair to his shoulders and big blue eyes. He had a calm personality, but his face said everything. He was completely mesmerizing.

Gregory finished his set and the room got dark again while the crew broke down his equipment and started setting up Etta's. Gee and I were talking during the lull when the person I would come to know as Gregory's right-hand man, Chank, came up and handed me a note, which I put in my pocket. Gee asked me what it said, but I told her casually, "I don't know, Gee. I didn't read it." Ignoring my disinterest, she suggested we go over to the cigarette machine, where there was more light to read by, so we did. When I unfolded the slip of paper and read what was written, I couldn't help but smile. It was so flowery. It began, *Dear enchanting lady . . .* He said it was his last night, but if I'd come back the following night, he would "deem it an honor" to play for me. And then he wrote down his telephone number and signed it "Gregg Allman." Intrigued, I thought, *Well, that's nice,* and put it back in my pocket. A few days later I called Gregory and told him that he could take me to dinner instead.

That night, I had no idea what to wear. "What do you think Gregory will be wearing?" I asked Pauli, looking at the heap of clothes I'd thrown across my bed.

"A hand-tooled North Beach leather jacket with matching pants," she replied confidently. North Beach was the coolest label in LA and San Francisco at the time. "Put on some jeans, heels, a hot little top, and a jacket and you'll be good to go."

Sure enough, when Gregory arrived, he was wearing exactly what Pauli predicted. I was still getting ready, so Pauli offered him a drink while he waited. He was so nervous he asked for a Coke before changing his mind twice just to end up back at a Coke. As I came down the stairs, I spotted him checking himself in the mirror. "You look okay to me," I said, laughing. He smiled and handed me a gift: a tiny wooden octagonal box decorated with an enamel moon and stars (it was very '70s). I slid the little lid open to reveal a tuft of cotton. Seeing only white contents in a small container, Pauli exclaimed, "She doesn't do cocaine!"

"Relax, Paul," I said, pulling out the cotton to show her. It was protecting the teeniest elephant you ever saw, carved out of pink stone. I still have it today.

And then Gregory and I went out for what turned out to be one of the worst nights of my dating life. I've had some shitty dates in my time, but this topped the list. He first took me to Dino's restaurant on Sunset, named after Dean Martin, with its dark wood paneling and leatherette booths. Sliding into one in the dim light, we sat looking at each other, but neither of us could think what to say. Trying a line on me, he said he'd fly me to Hawaii for the weekend. "Does that work on other girls?" I asked, knowing the answer was yes.

From there we went to a party in a suite at the Continental Hyatt hotel on Sunset. I said hi to Judy Carne, the comic actress from *Rowan & Martin's Laugh-In*, and Gregory introduced me to Edgar Winter, another long-haired blond musician I didn't know. The party was full of way too many drugged-out people, and as the only sober person there, I felt like an alien. When Gregory tried to kiss me, I told him to stop. "Whoa, dude," I said. "You know what, why don't you just take me home?" As I got out of his car, he leaned over and said, "Tell your secretary I said hello," meaning Paulette. *Asshole.* The whole night was a big disappointment.

The following evening, I was at CBS being fitted for my costumes when I burst into tears thinking how horrible the evening had been. I'd never had to date Sonny, I'd just moved in, and my relationship with David started with dinner at his house, so that was the sum of my dating experience in the previous twelve years.

Sobbing, I told Paulette, "Last night was terrible. I'll never be good at this."

When Gregory called the next day I told him, "That was the worst date I ever had."

"I know. Me too. Can we try that again?"

All I could do was laugh. "Why would we want to?" I asked, but eventually agreed. This time he took me to the Candy Store nightclub in Beverly Hills, where we danced until our hair was wet. Afterward we sat and talked, and Gregory was completely different. No longer trying to impress me, he was just himself. For the next few days, we became inseparable, though he soon went back home to Macon, a rural town in Georgia. Then he was touring with his band, so we could see each other only in between our busy schedules. It was hard not to be together, but we talked on the phone a lot and fell for each other pretty quickly. I'd never been with a bad boy, and he had a reputation as one quintessential bad boy.

Inevitably, word got out that we were dating, and *Esquire* magazine ran a cover story that asked the question "Who's man enough for this woman?" as news of "Cher's new love" was splashed all over the newspapers. Some were the same publications that had claimed I was dating Elvis and Robert Redford, two men I'd never even met, although they'd have made great bookends (insert tongue in cheek).

David couldn't believe that I'd gone from him to an Allman Brother. He called me up and told me, "If we're walking on the street and I'm on one side, cross over to the other." That was really hard for me to hear, because I still loved him.

Gregory and I really started to fall in love when he came back to visit me during a break from touring and we could be together again in person. We were crazy in love and so attracted to each other. Though he had that bad boy image, he was soft-spoken, kind, and very very Southern in the way Mamaw and Pa were. Southern people have a special way about them. I called him "Gui

Gui" and he called me "Chooch," which he said meant "eloquently funky." I thought he was so beautiful. He had thick long blond hair, pale skin, and rosy cheeks. Sometimes I'd look at him and his face would almost glow. He was at his softest when he'd lean back in bed with his guitar in the middle of the night and play me songs, singing along. His voice was so beautiful.

Any time I wasn't working, I'd spend with Gregory. We'd go out for dinner, or listen to music and hang out at home. One night he and I came home from a party and lit a candle while we were getting ready for bed. We fell asleep with it still lit and I woke up to a loud licking sound. I looked over to see the macrame lampshade next to my bed had caught on fire. Worse, the fabric under the lamp had also caught fire, and worst of all, the wall by my bed, which was covered in fabric, had also gone up in flames. My hair looked like it would be next: it was curled from the party and splayed out from sleeping so it was about an inch from the fire. Gregory got up and ran to the bathroom in like a second, grabbing towels, wetting them in the bathtub, and bringing them back. The next day I went out shopping with Ronnie Wilson and redid the whole bedroom by that afternoon. We designed it in a modern Balinese style, and it looked amazing. The rest of the house was all designed with antiques, and I wanted something new, so the fire was a blessing in disguise.

People warned me early on that Gregory was doing drugs, but I didn't want to hear it. He didn't drink very much and he was easy to be around. I think they were trying to be helpful, but I didn't want to be warned. I didn't care what people thought. I noticed that he wore long-sleeve shirts all the time, even to bed, but he told me it was because he sweats a lot, and I believed him. I thought maybe he was doing something, but I didn't suspect the extent. At one point, someone told me, "If you're doing heroin, then you're not having sex." So I thought, *Then he's definitely not doing heroin!*

On one of my weekends off, Gregory flew me to his home in

Macon. He picked me up from the airport, and when we got back to his house, there were two women there cooking barbecue in his backyard. You could see the woods all around. The ladies, Inez Hill and Louise Hudson, were so kind, and their food was incredible. They had a famous restaurant in town called H&H Soul Food. Gregory's best friend was there too—Hewell "Chank" Middleton, the skinny Black dude who'd handed me the note in the Troubadour. I think he spent more time at Gregory's house than at his own. Everybody loved Chank, including me, especially when he referred to me as "Ms. Allman" (which he did till the day he died). Chank was always in good spirits—that's just who he was—and was like a surrogate big brother to Gregory.

I also met the rest of the band on this visit, but I didn't like them as much as Chank. As I got to know them, it seemed like some of them were jealous of Gregory, and frequently undermined his confidence, until I reminded him that he was the only Allman in the band. The only one who was nice to me was the singer-songwriter and guitarist Dickey Betts, one of the founding members and the man who wrote "Jessica" and "Ramblin' Man." Dickey welcomed me to the "family" and told me about the band's support for their Democratic governor, Jimmy Carter, a peanut farmer who grew up not far from Macon and shared the same values on civil rights. They'd raised the money that had started his campaign. He was an honest-to-goodness civil servant, the polar opposite of some politicians who would sell their souls to keep their jobs. It was a long shot for him to reach the Oval Office, as America hadn't elected a president from the Deep South since before the Civil War, but the band admired him and he'd become their friend.

Gregory waited a few visits for me to finally meet his mother, Alice, who everyone called "Mama A." She'd had a tough life. When I went to her house, she brought out a scrapbook and showed me pictures and newspaper clippings from when her whole family had been together and happy. It hadn't lasted long.

Her husband, Willis, had been murdered in Virginia at thirty-one, when Gregory was just two years old and his brother, Duane, was three. A lieutenant in the army, Willis was shot dead by a hitchhiker he and another friend stopped to help. He'd robbed them of five dollars before telling them to lie facedown in the dirt. While his friend fled, Willis grabbed for the barrel of the gun but was killed in the struggle. Mama A never recovered from the shock, and when she lost her eldest boy two decades later, she started to drink. Who could blame her? The scrapbook of photos and newspaper clippings ended at Duane's death. Confused, I asked, "But, Mama A, the book stops in 1971. What about the years since?" She told me, "There was no reason for me to keep a scrapbook after Duane died." I don't think she said it to be mean. I think she was caught off guard and just told me the truth. I don't think she even realized Gregory was in the room and could hear her. I could see in his eyes that it hurt him.

Gregory loved driving me through the streets of his adopted town in his Corvette. He'd had such a difficult life, losing his father in a senseless crime and then his brother who, he told me, always protected him. Duane had been the one to persuade Gregory to join his band, the Allman Brothers. Gregory had been accepted to medical school to train as a dental surgeon, but his brother called him and said, "Come home." He chose music because of Duane. A surrogate father and the best big brother one could hope for, Duane was Gregory's rock until he was killed three months into their meteoric rise. As Gregory said, Duane had two speeds on his bike—a hundred miles per hour and park. When a truck pulled out in front of him, he didn't stand a chance.

The more Gregory opened up to me, the more I grew to love him. We had a soulful connection far deeper than anything I'd ever had before, perhaps because he was also wounded and needed help. He was also such a great artist, and I'd never been with anyone like that before. Our unique connection was hard for others to understand, and the fans hated that a hard-core rocker like him was dating someone as commercial and mainstream as me. On my last night with him in Macon, I was half-asleep when Gregory woke me up at 6 a.m., took me in his arms, and confessed, "I'm a heroin addict, Chooch." I didn't know what to do with this information. What I did know was that confessing to me was a breakthrough, and I hoped it meant that he was ready to get some help. He wanted to get straight, he told me, and I didn't know how to respond. I called my mom, who had married my father, Johnnie, who'd become a heroin addict. After hearing me out, she asked me, "Do you love him?"

"Yes, I do," I replied, crying.

"Then bring him home."

# 20

## all in love is fair

Paulette and I decided we'd dry Gregory out ourselves. I was doing *The Flip Wilson Show*, so Pauli stayed with him during the day and I stayed during the night and just didn't get any sleep. After a week or ten days, it worked.

The decision to stand by Gregory no matter how hard that might be or how much it damaged my reputation didn't come easy. The backlash was worse than I expected. Some of the media had already questioned whether I was a drug user after the Ken Moss party, and that rumor gained credibility once I was with a rock star. Many friends asked me why I stayed with Gregory once I found out about his addiction, but I thought I could get him sober.

Whenever he was off the drugs, he was such a kind, sweet human being. He came to my rehearsals and was adorable with Chas, who took to him right away. What he didn't expect was the tidal wave of publicity that came with us being together. Much of the coverage was negative, and I longed for America to know him for who he was, not who they thought he was. When I told George Schlatter that I wanted to have Gregory on my show as a guest, I could tell he wasn't happy. No one was. An Allman Brother wasn't the kind of person anyone wanted on a prime-time family show, especially not when America was deciding whether to hate me or not and millions were still hoping I'd get back with Sonny. Even though I thought Gregg Allman was one of the greatest singers in America, I knew in my heart that he didn't really fit into what my show was about. But I insisted. It was important to me that he be included in that part of my life, and after a lot of discussion, CBS agreed. I was totally wrong. It wasn't good for either one of us. His fans hated it and so did mine. It was a lose-lose.

I'd go see Gregory perform whenever I could and was shocked at how brazen and persistent some of his fans were, even when I was next to him. I could be standing right beside him backstage and a girl would run up to kiss him and hand him her telephone number. He'd tell them, "I'm talking to my wife!" but they acted like I wasn't even there. (We weren't married yet, but he said it to let them know to respect me.) I felt like screaming, "I'm Cher, motherfucker!"

In March the two of us were invited to a party thrown by Paul McCartney and Wings to launch their new album *Venus and Mars* on the *Queen Mary* cruise liner moored at Long Beach. Gregory flew in for the event, and we went with Gee and Paulette, who brought Mark Hudson, who she was currently going out with, and his brother Brett Hudson; the brothers had done a really funny summer replacement for *The Sonny & Cher Comedy Hour*. We have stayed friends to this day.

Among the two hundred or so guests piped aboard by naval cadets were George Harrison, David Cassidy, Marvin Gaye, and the Faces, and friends like Bob and Sara Dylan, Joni Mitchell,

Carole King, and, of course, my old friend Tony Curtis. The week before the party, the Jackson 5 had been my show guests and made it the Jackson 6 when they insisted that I learn their dance steps and perform with them. Michael was at the party, too, so he and I spent some time on the dance floor together. Naturally shy, he'd grown up so quickly from the sweet kid who'd been on *Comedy Hour* with Sonny and me. It was a night to remember.

The only party I enjoyed more that year was my twenty-ninth birthday, which Joe D threw for me at his nightclub PIPS on Robertson Boulevard, which he'd opened with backing from Hef and Stan Herman. It had quickly become a celebrity hangout. Everyone from Mick Jagger to Lucille Ball would come to have dinner and then play backgammon or dance. Pauli helped organize the party and she still has the original guest list, which included Joni, Tatum, the Hudson Brothers, Carole King, and too many others to name. Paulette was dating Ryan O'Neal by then, and I invited Sonny, who arrived with a new girlfriend. The sun wouldn't have set if he didn't. We figured that Paulette, Gee, and Chas's nanny, Linda, were the only women in our circle Sonny hadn't slept with. (Pauli was actually a little offended that she was the only assistant he never slept with—"What's wrong with me?" she joked.)

My divorce from Sonny was finalized on Friday, June 27, 1975, and it had taken so long and been so convoluted that I felt relief when it was over. I had my own life, and Sonny and I were friendly.

I didn't know whether my relationship with Gregory would last or not. I was living each day as it came. Then I found out I was pregnant, and we decided to get married. Everything was arranged within a few days. I told Paulette and Gee by walking up to them tanning by the pool and saying, "Okay, guys. Get dressed. Gregory and I are getting married." Both girls jumped up and looked at me as if I'd gone into an alternate universe, but I said,

"Come on, let's just do this." Joe D arranged a Learjet owned by Harrah's Hotel and Casino to fly us all to Las Vegas.

I pulled on the powder-blue two-piece with white lace trim that I'd worn when I'd introduced Gregory on my show. Without doing my makeup or hair, I grabbed a floppy straw hat, jumped in the car with Gregory and the girls, and drove to Burbank Airport. Whatever their private thoughts, neither of them said a word.

I just kept putting one foot in front of the other. The future is never written in stone. I did what I thought was the right thing to do. I was thinking that no matter what happens, if I was having a baby, then I wanted to be married. Joe was waiting for us in Vegas and took us straight to Caesars Palace, where he and Mickey cleverly started a rumor that Frank Sinatra was marrying his girlfriend Barbara Marx that day, but at a different venue, so that the press would be too busy chasing that story to notice us. In Mickey's suite, District Court Judge James Brennan was waiting to officiate, and a posy of white flowers was waiting for me, the conflicted bride who could have jumped ship at any moment, even though I was the one who'd launched it. I was smiling and trying to be happy, but inside I was thinking, *Cher, what is your plan?* With Gee and Pauli as my bridesmaids and Joe as our best man, the ceremony was over in minutes. Then we posed for the camera and flew straight back home. I was no longer Cher Bono but Cher Allman, Gregory's third wife.

There was little about our wedding day that was romantic. There would be no honeymoon.

I knew Gregory had to get back to work, and I had to get back to CBS to start rehearsals for season two.

Separating made us both sad.

The next morning I woke up and he was gone. I didn't have the energy to fight for him. I don't think he had it either. I'm not sure I even saw a future with him at that point. It was depressing. I went into his bathroom and noticed that he had forgotten his

Dopp kit. I don't know why I went through it, but in the inside pocket there was a plastic bag full of white powder. I think when something like that happens, it tests the strength of a relationship and ours was not strong. Usually I had the will to help him and he had the willingness to let me try, but this time, neither of us had either.

I couldn't wonder about it for too long, though. I still had my pregnancy to think about. I made an appointment to see my doctor for a checkup. He'd taken care of me since we first moved to St. Cloud. Since then, he'd helped me with two miscarriages and had delivered Chas, so he knew me well and we'd become friends. While examining me, he discovered I had some ovarian cysts and told me, "I can go ahead and take care of these." I'd known him for so long, if they'd been dangerous he would have said, "You have cysts. I have to take them out." I pretty much knew what he meant when he offered it as a choice. I was thinking about how I'd had to be on bed rest when I was pregnant with Chas and couldn't go in a car for four months except for checkup appointments. I needed to be at work on Monday. I needed to be singing and dancing. I had a child, mother, and sister to take care of. I knew I had to make a choice, and I knew what it was. It made it harder that I didn't have Gregory to talk to about it, but I made my decision and I was so grateful to my doctor's compassion for giving me one.

A day or so later, I was sitting at the studio around six o'clock in the morning doing my makeup when my press agent Richard Grant, who was my friend, called me. He said, "Cher, do you know Gregg is divorcing you?"

"No. Hum a few bars." Humor is sometimes how I deal with devastation. In fact, I was hilarious on set that day—it was like spinning pain into gold.

I'd actually heard this news a few days earlier from Dickey, who'd seen Gregory filing papers for divorce in his lawyer's office, but when I'd asked Gregory about it, he'd lied and denied it. Obviously it was true, because now it was happening. The following morning, nine days after our wedding, I filed for divorce myself, citing "irreconcilable differences."

The press coverage about Gregory and me was wilder than ever after we both filed for divorce, and there was no escaping the reporters. When cornered by one, I said that after years of having decisions made for me by Sonny, I was making my own but was bound to get it wrong sometimes. I was making mistakes that you might make when you're eighteen, and I was having to do it as one of the most famous women in America. In Macon, Gregory told reporters there'd been a misunderstanding and that our divorce wouldn't go ahead, but I had no idea why he thought that. The next thing I heard he was in Buffalo, New York, seeking help from two psychiatrists who specialized in addiction, but it was too late as far as I was concerned.

Reaching out to Sonny, I asked if he could come over so we could talk. Despite all we'd gone through, he was still someone I could reach out to in a crisis. He came right away and did what he always did, telling me what he thought I should do and how to handle the press. Later that July he was scheduled to appear on *The Tonight Show*, hosted that week by the actor George Segal.

"Hey, why don't you show up as a surprise guest when I've finished my interview? That might put a stop to the feeding frenzy." I wasn't sure at first, but he convinced me, so I walked on set that night as he suggested. It was the first time Sonny and I had been seen together in public since I'd married Gregory, but we fell straight back into our usual banter. George Segal asked me what was up, and I replied, "Oh, nothing new has been happening with me," as the audience howled with laughter. Then I added, "The sad part of my life is that I don't have to do anything to have people think that I'm doing too much."

"Well, I'd like to ask you some questions," George continued. Giving him my best straight face, I asked him, "Are they any of your business?" And so it went on. After that I also appeared with Elton John and a pregnant Diana Ross on the Rock Music Awards, having been carried in on a bier by half-naked men (just another Friday afternoon) and the media interest in my personal life died down a little.

Then one day I received a call from Gregory's doctors in Buffalo telling me that they'd never seen anyone more determined to kick the habit. They said it was important for his recovery that I come see him. Sonny agreed I should go and said he could keep Chas while I was away, so I went to stay with Gregory in rehab. When I met the people running the program, they seemed very well-meaning, but I don't think they were good enough to be treating him, a hard-core addict with circumstances that were beyond his control. I went to some therapy sessions with Gregory where he told me he felt too much pressure to be "Mr. Cher." He said he found it impossible to be all that he thought I wanted him to be. I really didn't want him to be anything but sober. He also hated the fact that wherever we went, the paparazzi were lying in wait. He couldn't stand all the attention. In between trying to reconcile our differences, he and I walked, talked, and picked apples from an orchard in the grounds. Sharing his room, we lay in bed watching soppy movies together, either crying or laughing depending on the movie. It was a peaceful interlude for us, and the therapy seemed to help him for the month or so that he was there. Gregory thought that once he got everything off his chest, things between us would be great. I was happy that he did it, but I'm not sure how I felt after. It's not that I didn't trust him, but it was only a matter of time before he'd go back to work again, where not all the guys in the band were always supportive and other people would be getting high. Gregory was an amazing performer. He could go onstage and hold the audience in the palm of his hand, but for some reason, he could never feel confidence in that. He did his art in spite of his fear (and I know so many artists like that, myself included). Gregory was super sensitive, which made him vulnerable.

Despite my mixed feelings, I dropped the divorce proceedings and decided to give him another chance.

I went home soon after, and Gregory suggested we next meet in Jamaica for a belated honeymoon. As we were preparing to leave, I saw him pack a small metal box that was locked with a key. I said, "What's in the box?"

"Methadone," he told me. "But I don't need to take it if I don't want to." He opened the box and dumped all the little bottles in the toilet.

I was a little confused because it seemed like what was inside this box must be important if it was locked up, but I was happy that he was seeming to be more responsible for his sobriety. I wasn't really sure what methadone was. If I'd known that he really needed it, I would have said, *Don't be ridiculous, take it with you.* It turned out that he was shooting himself in the foot.

The small beach resort of Negril had become popular with musicians and was known for its pretty cottages on the edge of some of the most beautiful white coral beaches in the world. Gregory and I arrived in paradise.

We had an idyllic few days in that beautiful place. An older woman who lived in a little house next door fed and cared for us while I swam and sunned myself on the beach. Gregory was calm to begin with, but then he became restless, which made me nervous because I knew the signs. When I came in from the beach late one afternoon, I found two strangers in our living room with Gregory drinking. He didn't even bother to introduce me, so I figured they weren't people he wanted me to know. He had a bottle of rum that was nearly empty, and I was thinking maybe it was a mistake for him to have poured the methadone down the toilet.

I walked into the kitchen to find the lady who'd been helping us chopping fruit. A few minutes later, Gregory came bursting in, all puffed up, overpowering, and loud. He was a tall man, and although he didn't have a violent bone in his body, he looked menacing. The old woman must have thought so too, because she pulled a knife from the drawer and told him, "If you touch the little lady, I'll use this!" Gregory calmed right down, probably because he could see that even though she was tiny, she meant business. He staggered back out to the living room, and she and I immediately left the cottage. It was the strangest of evenings, because outside her place, which was a tiny house on the beach, dozens of huge green and yellow crabs were running across the sand away from men chasing after them with gunnysacks and torches.

Once we felt it was safe to return to my cottage, certain that he'd have gone looking for more drugs, I went in and grabbed my belongings as she kept watch. I hastily packed my suitcase, and my savior arranged for a man to drive me to a hotel at Montego Bay. I was scared to be driven on the terrible roads in the dark with a complete stranger. That surreal night took another bizarre turn when I was dropped off at the hotel where I'd stay before my morning flight and the waiter who brought me a chocolate malt grabbed hold of me and kissed me. I thought, *Could this night get any worse?* I mean, what did he think was gonna happen? What a nightmare.

The next morning, I flew to Atlanta, where I was meeting Paulette. We were going to fly right back to LA together, but unexpectedly the band's roadies showed up at the airport. They'd known I was flying in since I'd called Chank saying I was worried about Gregory. We ended up going with them to a campaign event for Jimmy Carter, where they were performing, including Gregory, who met us from Jamaica, where he'd managed to get himself beaten up going into a bad part of Kingston looking for drugs. After the event, we all flew back to LA. The trip ended up being the opportunity Dickey needed to finally convince Paulette to go out with him, and the two started dating.

Back in LA, I returned to the studio to shoot season two of my show. During the summer hiatus between seasons one and two, CBS filled my time slot with a show called *Joey and Dad*, because my show was expensive to shoot, so replacing it for the summer saved them money in the short term. The replacement did so badly that people switched to watch *The Six Million Dollar Man* instead, which was on at the same time and rose from the bottom of the ratings to number one by the time I came back. There was no audience left over; that show was a phenomenon. *Joey and Dad* had taken my time slot from a 23.3 rating at the end of my first season to a 7 by the end of their summer replacement. There was nothing I could do about that. It's a bitch, but it happens.

That season they tried to increase security measures at CBS. Everyone always entered the studio from the loading dock; nobody walked in the front. I'd come and go at least a few times a day, because we loved to run out to the Farmers Market if we ever had free time. Then one day I was walking up and one of the security guards stopped me, saying, "You need to show an ID to get in." I said, "What do you mean? You know who I am." He replied, "I know, Cher, but it's a rule now, so I can't let you in without one." The next day I walked up with an eight-by-ten publicity photo pinned to my chest. The guard laughed, and so did everyone else by the loading dock because they all knew me, too, and I knew them. That's part of why I loved working at CBS—it was like a team. Sometimes the guys who worked around the studio would come watch us shoot. Everyone was friendly and pulling for one another. The guard let me in, and they never mentioned needing an ID to me again. I bet Carol Burnett didn't need one either.

By season two David had left the show. Losing his influence and support seemed to be a catastrophe. George was more than a competent producer and a close friend of mine, but without David and now up against *The Six Million Dollar Man,* we couldn't get the same A-list artists. My old friend Teri Garr came on as a guest a few times and we filled slots with appearances by Chas, as well as me answering questions from the audience, and ran blooper reels. But you can't fight numbers, and trying to crawl back from *Joey and Dad,* up against the unbelievable popularity of *The Six Million Dollar Man*, was close to an impossible task.

Though we no longer got every guest we wanted, we still managed to have on a handful of really amazing guest stars. When Ray Charles arrived to perform on my show, I was incredibly nervous and told him so. He sweetly said that he was worried about meeting me, too. I told him that I'd cried when watching him sing "Georgia on My Mind" on television as a child. Soon afterward I could hardly believe I was standing at his piano singing that very song with him.

Bob kept up his work with designing gorgeous gowns for the show and also many hilarious costumes for our sketches. When I had Carol Burnett on, he made us these insane matching chicken sweatshirts that even had the red crest on the top, the wattle underneath, and some beaded decoration. We wore them for a skit that had the whole floor in tears of laughter. From then on, Carol and I had a chicken joke between us that got completely out of hand. I had fifty buckets of Colonel Sanders chicken delivered to her dressing room one day, and in retaliation, she sent me a clutch of live hens. We had loose chickens walking all over the set. The studio wasn't thrilled, but we were having a great time. Lord only knows what happened to them.

I fought with George and the team about inviting David Bowie, a British artist who fascinated me. When the twenty-nine-year-old singer known as "the Thin White Duke" arrived for rehearsals, the first thing I noticed was that one of his eyes was blue and one was brown, after a teenage fistfight over a girl. That wasn't only mesmerizing but sexy as hell. Chatting in the dressing room, he told me he was heading to the Sears department store after rehearsals to buy a suit to wear for the show. Imagining that someone like him would shop somewhere more upscale, I said, "Okay, David, but why Sears?"

"I heard about it back in England, so that's where I want to go." He returned an hour or so later with a weird crunchy purple polyester jacket that I'd never have chosen for him, but he was one of those people who looked good in anything. After he was on the show, I became a lifelong fan.

Tina Turner came on the show twice with her then-husband. Ike. Tina was a breathtaking performer and became a friend. One of the days we were shooting, she came to my room before we went on asking if I had some cover-up. She had a bruise on her arm she didn't want showing on camera. I told her I had something that would work. She sat down while I looked for it and then quietly said, very straightforward, "Tell me how you left him." I looked at her and told her, "I just walked out and kept going." In retrospect, that reminds me of me going to Lucy.

When we were rehearsing onstage after, Tina and I were up on a riser and Ike was on the ground. As he played, he made no facial expression at all, like a shark. He didn't smile one time; he just played the guitar without any emotion. I just knew that whatever he was feeling wasn't good.

Despite my best efforts, my ratings slid and I was finding it increasingly hard to balance my schedule, my child, my marriage, and my life. I didn't have a lot of time to worry about Gregory. One day in the midst of all of this, I ran smack into David Geffen at our business manager's office in Beverly Hills. He was walking one way and I was walking the other. I thought, *Oh no*, but he said, "Sweetheart!" and I said, "Dave." He gave me a hug and a kiss, then told me that he'd just returned from an incredible self-actualization workshop that helped him free himself of his past and cleanse his mind of bad thoughts. Since then, he'd forgiven everyone for everything. "The program's called est," he added. "You should try it. It's transformational."

I did some digging and discovered *est* was an acronym for "Erhard Seminars Training," run by Werner Erhard. Werner had gone from a car salesman to a guru. I think not. But David had clearly gotten a lot out of the sessions, so I paid the $600 fee and persuaded Gregory to accompany me for a sixty-hour workshop spread over two weekends at a building like a huge ballroom on the outskirts of town. As soon as we arrived, we were handed a set of ground rules, which included removing our watches, fasting for much of each fifteen-hour day, remaining silent until spoken to, and having no bathroom breaks unless we asked for bathroom privileges, which I immediately requested.

We sat in a room full of at least a hundred other people, all of them strangers. It was uncomfortable just being there; everyone kept looking at me and Gregory because we were famous. Then the program started, and we listened to hour after hour of people being singled out and publicly criticized. I guess the idea was that you're put down the first weekend and built back up the second. I have no idea. I didn't come back for the second. If I wanted to be put down, I could go to a good friend. I was glad that Dave had gotten something out of this, but to me these guys seemed like a bunch of pompous a-holes. When Gregory started fidgeting on his hard metal chair, I knew he'd never stick around for two days. I was surprised he even stayed the night, but he did, and we had sex for the first time in ages. Maybe there was something in the est philosophy after all. I woke to find him gone and had no idea when I'd see him again.

I'm not sure what made me go back into the session that second morning, because my heart was heavy that day. I should have run away like Gregory, because things were about to get worse. Soon after the session began, a man who was about my age stood up to say he had something to get off his chest. "When my wife and I were young," he began, "we had enough money for two eight tracks." At "eight track," I knew I was in trouble. He went on,

"Herb Alpert and the Tijuana Brass and Sonny and Cher. When she left Sonny, my wife left me, and what I want to know is, what is *she* doing here!" As he said "she," he turned around and pointed his finger at me. I was two tables back and a little over, but he didn't have to search around; he knew exactly where I was sitting. Then he started to sob.

I promptly got up and went to the bathroom. Thank God I had asked for bathroom privileges. I suddenly became aware of something powerful and unexpected. I just knew it. I knew I was pregnant again. It reminded me of something that would happen to my great-grandmother or my grandmother: out of nowhere you just know something. Fanning my hands over my belly, I took a deep breath and said, "If you're coming, you've got to get here on your own. I don't have time to stop." I knew I wouldn't be able to stop working to help this child get here. As soon as I could, I went to see my doctor, even though I already knew.

It was all coming down on me: Gregory, the baby, not having David. The ceiling was falling in. I turned to the one person who'd understand. I called Sonny and asked him to come over. It's a wonder to me now that I could go to him. Actually, it's a wonder that I didn't kill him. Instead, I did the opposite. I threw him a lifeline. Sitting together in our old bedroom, I confessed, "It's hard for me at CBS, Son. I don't like fighting the network and the censors, and I can't recover from *Joey and Dad*. I don't want to do it by myself anymore." I paused. "So you wanna work with me again?" He laughed and instantaneously said yes. Sonny had loved our show even more than I had.

Jumping into action, Sonny arranged a meeting with Fred Silverman and other senior CBS executives and explained what we proposed. They liked the idea, and a deal was arranged between my lawyers and Sonny's that effectively did away with our existing divorce settlement and allowed me to repay him by way of the new show plus dozens of Sonny & Cher gigs on the road. When everything was agreed in principle at a final meeting, Sonny drove me back to the house all full of excitement. That was the moment I should have told him about my pregnancy, but it didn't feel right, and I couldn't get myself to bring him down on such a happy day. But the following morning, I found the courage and asked him to come over again. Sitting him down on the couch in the library, I took a breath and then blurted, "Son, I have to tell you something. I'm pregnant."

Dropping his head into his hands like he always did, he said, "Sheesh, Cher!" sucking the air through his teeth. His face had a pained expression, as if I'd physically wounded him.

"I know, I know. I'm really sorry I didn't tell you before," I said. "I was going to, but I wanted to find out if a new show was possible and then see if I could even hang on to this baby. Nobody else knows. Nobody. Not even Gregory. So I'm telling you now."

"They're not going to let us come back on air. Not with you pregnant. And definitely not pregnant by Gregg Allman." Despite being shocked by my confession, he never once lost his temper or tried to make me feel guilty. Actually, after he processed it, he thought it was kind of funny. He told me, "Cher, only you." By this time, nothing really surprised either one of us about the other, and Sonny went into fix-it mode with one mission—how do we solve this? His first task was to square everything away with CBS. I don't know how he did it, but he did. It was a gargantuan and historic deal for them to bring us back. I mean, showing my belly button had been the biggest thing to have happened in the history of TV in twenty years. For me to be coming back to star in a show with my ex-husband, while impregnated by my new husband, who was also a heroin addict and had divorced me once and was otherwise out of my life . . . nothing like that had ever happened in the history of the universe. For another couple, it would have been a recipe for disaster, but we were when the moon was in the seventh house and Jupiter was aligned with Mars. The new *Sonny & Cher*

*Show* would be announced in December and start airing in February 1976.

We'd worked out that the baby would be due three months after our first season ended in April. That was doable, because—apart from my boobs—I hadn't gotten too big when pregnant with Chas, and Bob Mackie could be trusted to make me something wonderful to de-emphasize my bump. I was going to give the censors heart attacks. They wanted to be censors. I was their punishment.

When I called Gregory to tell him I was pregnant, he didn't believe me. "Why would I lie about something like that?" I replied. He came back to Los Angeles for a while, but I didn't see him. Gregory was upset that the tabloids were seizing upon the new show with Sonny, creating a juicy love triangle where there was none. I thought he wanted to be a tortured soul, but I realized he was a heroin addict. Of course he was already a tortured soul.

He ultimately couldn't take it, and I found a note from him that read: *Chooch, I have two choices—go back to Macon and be heartbroken and lonely, or stay here and be made a fool of, the latter of which I just can't do because I'm a man, and a damn good one. I almost wish I could live with being a fool, for then I could live with you. Your happiness still rates number one. My God, I love you, Gregory.*

With that, he was gone.

Sonny and I went to a press conference at the Beverly Wilshire about our new show and we fended off questions like blows: "Are you just doing this for the money?" and "Are you still Sonny's servant, Cher?" and "What if your public hates you?" I didn't really give a damn what these people were saying. Getting to do *The Sonny & Cher Comedy Hour* again was a gift from heaven. What I cared about was if our audience would like us and if Sonny and I would still have fun. Nothing else mattered. I'd made up my mind, and once that happens, I'm balls to the wall. Sonny did most of the talking, as usual, speaking of our honesty and openness, as I sat there happy to say very little.

Sonny and I opened our show on February 1, 1976, by running onstage to the announcement: "Ladies and gentlemen, together again for the first time, it's Sonny and Cher!" Behind us was a huge new Sonny & Cher motif in lightbulbs with two crossed fingers in place of the ampersand. We got a lengthy standing ovation, and once our excited audience finally sat back down, Sonny circled me, staring at my belly, before saying that when I did something, I did it real good. He went on to tell everyone how great it was to be there, adding, "When I was working alone, there weren't many laughs," to which I replied, "I know, Sonny, I saw your show." And with that, we were back. Our viewers loved it when we sang "Love Will Keep Us Together," and the ratings indicated that they couldn't wait to watch the next episode. That first episode would become one of the most watched programs in American television history (right up there with the "Who Shot JR?" episode of *Dallas*).

Looking back at those shows, I'm amazed at how funny we still were even though we were divorced. Maybe because we were. Our comedy was sharper and more relevant once we lost the mother-in-law jokes. The public had always wanted us back, so even if they couldn't have us exactly the way they hoped, we were still Sonny & Cher, and they could see we were still having a good time. Sonny even persuaded Harold Battiste to return as our musical director, and there were a lot of preshow discussions about which songs we could get away with now that we were divorced. Everyone agreed that "I Got You Babe" would always be our signature number, and besides, its message still rang true. Sonny and I did still have each other as support systems. That part of our relationship never changed.

We had some terrific guests that first season, but perhaps our most memorable moment came when Sonny screwed up his introduction to the actor Raymond Burr, who starred in *Ironside,* the popular show about a wheelchair-bound detective. Filming at the end of a long day when we were tired and eager to get home, Sonny kept messing up and then bursting into fits of uncontrollable laughter, which set me off. After many takes, he half pushed me out of the frame and I lost it completely, walking in circles behind him and telling the crew through tears of laughter, "I can't work like this!" A few seconds later, his shoulders started shaking once more, and three months pregnant in a black strapless gown, I had to exit stage left in hysterics. Our bloopers were so ridiculous that we ended up running the reel in its entirety for both our live audience and the viewers at home. That clip has since been seen by millions of people and perfectly sums up who Sonny and I were. The strength of our show was our relationship. No matter what happened between us, we never lost that childlike sense of fun.

The fun and games continued for Chas's seventh birthday party that March, which was a blast as always. She'd asked for a monster theme, so everyone dressed up and we screened *Young Frankenstein*. Chas was in love with Gene Wilder, who starred in the film. Well, in her mind, she was in love with Willy Wonka, which is the first role she'd seen him in. During the Willy Wonka phase years before, I'd seen Gene at a pâtisserie in Beverly Hills with Teri Garr, who was going with him at the time. I told Gene, "Chas is in love with you. Please, please, please will you say hello to her or something? It doesn't matter what, she'll love it." When Chas walked in with David a few moments later, Gene went up and said hi to her. When she realized who he was, she just looked up into his face and stared. She didn't even move. If I'd seen Elvis at her age, I would have done the same thing. Gene spoke to her with such a gentle voice, then he leaned down and kissed her cheek and they walked out the door together. We didn't see them for twenty minutes; they just went around Beverly Hills together. She was so entranced, I think she would have walked with him to Egypt. For her monster-themed party, Chas dressed as a boy as she often liked to do, and I noticed for the first time that day that she'd also developed Sonny's long, lumbering walk. Talk about a chip off the old block. I was so proud of Chas for surviving our divorce, my marriage to Gregory, my pregnancy, and the press through all of it. I knew it couldn't have been easy, and I also knew that, because of my punishing work schedule, I wasn't around as much as I wanted to help guide her through all that. The good news was that she was excited about the baby and was really happy that Sonny and I were working together again. I think she maybe hoped we'd end up back together properly, like any child would.

Under the deal David Geffen had made with Warner Bros., I was committed to completing another album that year. My previous one, *Stars,* produced by Jimmy Webb, hadn't fared well, although I'd loved making it and enjoyed being back in the studio again. Jimmy was a great producer and fun to work with, especially on my favorite track of the album, "Geronimo's Cadillac." *I'd Rather Believe in You,* which took six months to record because I was so busy, was destined to bomb too. I honestly don't remember much about the album, because I didn't connect to the music I was making. You never like it when an album does badly, but all I knew was that I had to earn a living and hope that some of the better songs would be hits. I didn't do it just to cash a check, though. Singing was my first love and the thing I first learned how to do. I just never kidded myself that what I did was great or rose to my own expectations. I didn't have much respect for my ability as a singer back then. I never thought, *Oh, my albums are so good,* or *I'm proud of this one.* I didn't like my voice that much until years later I worked with my singing teacher Adrienne Angel, who totally transformed my voice. You have to know your limitations and then either rise above them or make peace with the fact that you're never going to.

By the time we got to shooting the last episode of our first season, I was six months pregnant. We had Diahann Carroll as a guest and she and I were going to perform a tap routine together dressed as sailors, so that last night before our show's hiatus, she and I were tap dancing until two o'clock in the morning trying to nail the routine. I just kept thinking, *Tomorrow I get to go to Hawaii.*

I was so relieved to get on that plane. I'd rented a house in Kahala and brought Chas and Ange, who was my trainer and became my friend. I'd finally figured out that I needed to keep moving for my physical and mental well-being. It had taken me years, but I was happy I was able to keep up, even in my condition.

Chas and I had a great time playing on the beach and flying kites, even if every man for miles felt the need to show us how to do it. We'd be looking up at our kite high in the sky with Chas holding the string, then a man would come up and try to show us what to do. So many men tried to do this, I was thinking, *These men are such idiots. I'm not letting them anywhere near our kite.* So finally if I saw one walking up to us I'd just say, "No, we're flying our kite just fine, thank you." I really wanted to say, "Go fly your own fucking kite!" It was like something out of Tom Sawyer, except it was flying a kite instead of painting a fence. Then Chas and I would walk to a little outdoor food stand that was part of the Kahala Hilton for lunch and sit out on the beach eating and watching the ocean. It was our ritual and really fun to have that time with her. Walking back with her to our hotel one day, I heard wolf whistles from behind. Laughing, I turned so that the men hitting on me could see how pregnant I was. I couldn't help but grin as I watched their faces fall and they sputtered their apologies.

A while before heading to Hawaii, I'd given Gregory another ultimatum. I'd told him not to call me unless it was from the rehab facility at the Silver Hill psychiatric hospital in New Canaan, Connecticut, by a certain date in June. I don't remember what date I'd chosen exactly. It was something arbitrary. I had had it with us repeating the same pattern again and again, and had told him over the phone, "I'm just so tired of doing this, Gregory. I'm so tired of going to rehab with you." He was quiet on the other end of the line. "But I keep going," he said softly. His answer stopped me in my tracks, because it was true. He kept going to rehab, kept trying to get clean, kept making an effort despite failing in the past. In that moment, instead of thinking of my own exhaustion, I empathized with him. "Okay, Gui," I said. "But if you don't call me from the clinic at three o'clock that day, then don't ever call me again." As the date drew closer, I became increasingly anxious.

The hour Gregory was due to call me from rehab came about a week into our trip. I was home with Chas and Ange sitting on a twin bed watching TV and needlepointing. If I want to keep my mind clear, I need at least two other things to think about. Then the phone rang, and it was him. I was so excited the whole time we were talking. After I hung up, Ange wanted to hear the blow-by-blow girl version: What'd he say? How'd he sound? How do you feel? Are you going to see him? If a girl tells a story, it's always better than when a guy tells it, because girls never forget any detail. Finally, I had to stop her and say, "Ange, something is wrong." I felt really nervous. First I thought it was an adrenaline rush, but it turned out that wasn't it, because then I felt a contraction. No doubt my reaction to the telephone call had caused this premature labor. Thank God Ange was there. I called my doctor in LA and he told me, "Pour yourself half a glass of scotch."

"I don't have any," I responded.

"Okay it doesn't make any difference. Bourbon, something."

I said, "We don't have any alcohol at all."

"Well, do you know your neighbors? Ask them to give you a drink."

So I went next door and they gave me half a glass of scotch. I got back on the phone with my doctor and said, "I'm a bit nervous." He told me, "You can sip it, but I want you to drink it."

With my drink in the back seat, Ange drove me to Queen Kapiʻolani Hospital, where the doctors told me they were putting an alcohol drip in my arm. I started crying again and told them, "I don't drink and just had half a glass. What's this going to do to me?" They told me I'd be fine and that it works as a uteran relaxant. Then they hooked me up to the drip. Ange called everyone to let them know what was happening. When she reached Sonny, he immediately offered to be by my side. That was so typical of him, and I appreciated it so much. She also called my sister, Pauli, and Gregory, who said he was on his way. I felt conflicted about that, since it meant he was leaving rehab.

It was all so stressful, but I do have a funny memory of Ange using one of those big tin trash cans as an improvised salon sink to wash my hair in the hospital room because my hair was so long. She really helped me out, and just a few weeks before, we'd only really known each other through our workouts. By the time Gregory arrived, my contractions had calmed down, and I was allowed out of the hospital with some medication I had to take every four hours to stop me from having more contractions. We went back to the rented house right on the ocean with nothing around us and spent the next five weeks together in that idyllic place, enjoying probably the best days of our marriage. He took such good care of Chas and me that I fell for him all over again, praying that he'd finally won his battle with addiction.

Once I was allowed out of bed, I spent my days sunbathing and wading in the ocean with Chas, who liked to play in the water. Happy in each other's company, Gregory and I only went out twice during the whole time we were there. At a restaurant one night I went to the bathroom, and when I was washing my hands, a woman came in and said, "We don't need people like you here." I thought I must have misheard her at first, but then realized I hadn't. A week later, we went to the movies, and as Gregory was getting his keys out of his pants, a guy came up and asked him a question. While Gregory was responding, with his hands still in his pockets, the guy punched him right in the face and said, "That'll teach you to go with our women." I was so brown, and my hair was down to my butt, so he thought I was an islander. That did it for us. I said, "This isn't working. Let's just go home." We rarely went out again. Gregory joined in Chas and my ritual of getting food from the little outdoor stand and sitting on the beach watching the water.

Paulette and Gee hung around for a bit too but didn't stay long. Dickey had given Paulette the ultimatum that she had to move to Sarasota or they were through. She told me, "I don't want to leave you, Cher, but I love him and I'm going to try to make a life for myself there. Please try to understand." With that, she resigned as my assistant. We didn't speak for two years.

When it was time for Gregory, Chas, and me to fly home, my gynecologist Dr. Heldfond came out and met us in Hawaii so he could be on the flight with us. He was wonderful and had agreed to deliver my baby as his last before he retired. Back in LA, I rested and waited, but my due date came and went. I was several centimeters dilated, but the baby stayed put. First he was coming too soon, and then he refused to come at all! Before he was even born, he was so Elijah. But his delay bought me time to do something that had somehow slipped my mind: finish the nursery. Beyond painting the walls, I'd forgotten to buy the things a baby actually needs. I heaved my belly into a fancy French baby boutique on San Vicente and made a beeline for a pair of saleswomen standing by the register. "Hi, I need a crib, a changing table, and a baby bathtub and I'm five centimeters dilated!" I said hurriedly. Their mouths fell open in disbelief. "But—but should you even be here right now?" one asked. They helped me as quickly as they could—they were scared I would give birth on the sales floor.

I was finally induced on July 10. Gregory remained by my side throughout the short labor and had tears in his eyes as he helped deliver our beautiful son, Elijah Skye Blue. He picked the name Elijah and I chose the rest because when I was in that Hawaiian hospital fighting to keep him, all I could see out of the window was blue sky.

Our son was a healthy boy weighing seven pounds, six ounces, with all his fingers and toes, blond eyelashes and hair—pure Gregory. There wasn't a stitch of me evident. Gregory and I were so happy that day, and when my album came out later that year, I dedicated it to my son, thanking him for waiting until I'd finished recording.

Those first few weeks back at the big house with our new baby and his doting big sister were blissful. One night I left my room and spotted Chas at the end of the hallway. Elijah was in her arms and she was strolling down the long hall. It wasn't as long as a football field, but it seemed that way. My heart stopped, and so as not to scare her, I tried to sound casual as I told her, "Chas, I . . . maybe we shouldn't hold the baby by ourselves. He's really teeny." My seven-year-old rolled her eyes at me and said, "Mom, I've been doing it since he came home." Unbeknownst to me, for a week she'd been toting him around and saw nothing wrong with it. I just said, "Okay, but why don't we do it together next time?"

# 21

## changes

January 1977, Jimmy Carter, the peanut farmer from Georgia, had won the election and become the thirty-ninth president of the United States. After the inauguration, Gregory and I were invited to the first cocktail party Jimmy held at 1600 Pennsylvania Avenue to thank the supporters he'd dubbed "the Georgia Peanut Brigade."

As the party was ending, I asked one of the staff if it might be possible to see the Mary Todd Lincoln table setting. This was the dinner service Abraham Lincoln's wife commissioned when disappointed by the mismatched china in the White House. The French porcelain set was displayed in a glass-fronted cabinet in the East Wing and didn't disappoint. With purple and gold scalloped edges, each dish featured an American eagle holding an olive branch and an arrow above a shield of stars and stripes. Lincoln had fascinated me since my school days and I'd read several books about him, so to see the dishes he'd eaten from gave me a thrill. We were also shown things that belonged to other first ladies as well as the "Nixon piano," which was upstairs in the hallway of the private residence, before being taken to meet "Miss Lillian," Jimmy Carter's seventy-eight-year-old mother. We met her in the Lincoln Bedroom, which was once used as the sixteenth president's office and the place where he signed the Emancipation Proclamation in 1863. The bed was very narrow and very high, coming right up to my ribs. It must have been like sleeping on a rail.

Caught up in the moment, I threw myself on the bed and then danced around the room as the others laughed. It was a mad, irreverent act, but when was I going to be in the Lincoln Bedroom again? Miss Lillian knew Gregory from Georgia, so he went to talk to her while I used the bathroom, with its wicker seat and cistern. Next to it was a bottle of Wild Turkey bourbon, and when I asked Miss Lillian about it, she explained that she'd brought it from Georgia as a precaution, adding, "Well, who knows what kind of liquor they have up here?"

Just then, President Carter's nine-year-old daughter, Amy, came running in and said, "Mama wants y'all to stay for dinner." It was an invitation we couldn't refuse. We ate in the dining room of the private quarters with Jimmy and his wife, Rosalynn; Amy; her nanny, Mary; and Miss Lillian, who sat next to me. She was a pistol. I loved her spirit. I also loved Jimmy, who was far too honest to be a politician. He was so excited as he told us about his plans to find the American people work. We had such hopes for him that night as we'd had with JFK. A member of the White House security staff took a photo of us with the family's Brownie camera and confided to me that the staff already loved them because they put on no airs and told the chef that they'd eat whatever everyone else ate. That night we had smothered chicken, black-eyed peas, and corn bread, which were all delicious.

After dinner, Jimmy suggested that we all take pictures together. There was Rosalynn, Miss Lillian, Mary, Rosalynn's hairdresser, Gregory, Joe D, me, and the president. Knowing a bit about Joe D's past, I remember thinking, *God, I brought a felon into the White House.* Then Jimmy explained that when Mary was young, she'd been unjustly charged with a crime she didn't commit. She was serving a prison term but was able to come out every once in a while to see Jimmy and his family as part of a program he was piloting that was designed to rehabilitate inmates. Mary was ultimately found completely innocent, which Rosalynn always knew in her heart. It made me feel less strange about bringing Joe D.

Leaving the White House that night, Gregory was thrilled because he felt like he'd played a part in getting Jimmy elected, which is true. President Carter even said publicly, "It was the Allman Brothers that put me in the White House, raising money when I didn't have any." Of course I was extremely proud—my husband had helped elect the president of the United States.

Life returned to normal, as Gregory went back on the road and I went back to the studio. We'd sold the big house a few months after Elijah's birth and were living in a three-bedroom Spanish-style house with a swimming pool on Linden Drive in an area of Beverly Hills known as the Flats. It had everything we needed and was beautiful. The market was down when I sold the big house fully furnished to a carpet baron for a million dollars. Later someone told me the original wood paneling alone was worth at least that much. As we were driving away from my dream house, which had Chas's over-the-top pink bedroom, she turned to me and said, "Mom, I have to tell you something . . . I hate pink."

In March 1977, Sonny and I gave what we suspected would be our last performances together on *The Sonny & Cher Comedy Hour.* For one of our final shows the writers came up with the idea of dressing us as we'd looked in 1964. We wore our bobcat vests and bell-bottom pants. Both of us wore wigs—Sonny in his

Prince Valiant and me with bangs and little side bits cut shorter. Harold Battiste sat at a grand piano, while I sat on top, and Son stood next to us explaining how he was fooling around on our old upright when he came up with a three-chord riff for what turned into "Baby Don't Go." "I wrote it for Cher," he told the audience. "But—believe it or not, folks—in those days, Cher was shy." They laughed even harder when he told them I was so afraid to sing it alone that he had to join in with me. Cue the first song Sonny & Cher ever recorded together. That was quite a moment.

When the season ended, we embarked on our reunion tour, during which we promoted our latest single, the aptly named "You're Not Right for Me." We were still on the road when we heard that CBS wasn't renewing our TV option. We weren't thrilled, but we were proud of the work we'd done. We'd created a show that was unlike anything that had been on the air. Fred Silverman would later call what we made "a monumental hit that did so much for the image of CBS . . . we never approached that with another show."

That summer Sonny and I went back on the road and took the kids with us. Much like Chas in her early years, Elijah first learned to crawl in a hotel hallway as Sonny took pictures. He was always great with both Chas and Elijah.

After touring, Sonny moved to Palm Springs. I'd go out there occasionally with Chas. Sonny would throw barbecues, and it was a great time. He never sat down and ate. He just tasted and watched everyone else eat. He went through numerous new girlfriends but cheated on most of them; he couldn't help himself. One time a girlfriend of his found out and ended things. He never expected that. He showed up on my doorstep in tears. Sitting in my kitchen, he said to me, "I'm sorry for what I did to you. I was dishonest and I had all those women, and I didn't think how it might affect our relationship. I realize now that I've lost Sarah because I just kept doing the same thing I've always done, even though you warned me not to. I hurt you both and I apologize."

I never thought I'd hear that apology from him. It couldn't change anything, but it felt good to know deep down inside that he'd realized for the first time how hurtful what he'd done was and was genuinely sorry. Eventually, he and Sarah got back together and married, with Chas as a bridesmaid.

Gregory had been back in Macon or on tour for much of 1977 with his new band, the Gregg Allman Band, which he'd formed after the Allman Brothers broke up in 1976, right before Elijah was born. Gregory and I had also made our own album that year, called *Two the Hard Way* by "Allman and Woman." It was my idea to drop my name because I wanted people to focus on the music. I loved working with Gregory in the studio. Making music together felt easy. My favorite track is "Do What You Gotta Do," because the lyrics described our relationship. The finished record wasn't as good as I'd hoped, though, because his voice was so much better than mine.

Later that summer, Gregory, Chas, and I went to Osaka, Japan, where Gregory was touring, leaving Elijah with Alicia and Benito, my longtime live-in housekeepers. Gregory was the tallest person everywhere we went, and we completely stood out when we were walking around. One day while I was going down the street a stranger came up to me and offered $500 to buy my jeans. I wouldn't have parted with them for any amount of money. I'd just gotten them patched and was looking hot. The people there were so kind. I even left a camera on the bullet train, and when I went back to look for it, it was still there, untouched. I was shocked. Chas wanted to buy a camera for herself while we were there, so I gave her maybe $300 and she came back with about $2,000 worth of equipment, maybe more. I said, "Da, where did you get that?" She said, "A really nice man gave it to me." She had all kinds of stuff, lenses, paper, flashes, a carrying case. Her tutor said the salesman just lost his mind over her and gave her the extra stuff. I'd go to Gregory's shows wearing little or no makeup and in plain clothes like a T-shirt and jeans, hoping to blend in. Occasionally I'd sing some background or harmonies for him but not at every show.

After Japan we went to Europe. While we were in Germany, I found out that Gregory was drinking and hiding it from me. I packed up and flew home.

A few weeks or so later, Sonny and I flew to Hawaii for our last-ever mini tour of hotels and theaters, with a few days of rehearsals. The first day of rehearsals, Ange and I started up the stairs to the studio. We could see people's feet and legs before anything else. When we got to the top of the stairs, I saw the back of a man's head and started to say "That guy," about to finish with "looks like Bill," when the man turned and I realized it was him, standing there with his guitar slung over his shoulder. It was the first time I'd seen Bill since I left from Oahu on Barry Hilton's yacht. I thought, *Goddamn, Son, really? This is too much, but I'm so not surprised.* The Machiavellian character I'd been married to had told Denis Pregnolato to ask Bill to join us to mess with me somehow. That was Sonny in a nutshell.

Ange and I didn't know whether to gasp or fall on the floor and couldn't wait to be alone to talk about it. Why did Sonny do that? What was his motivation? What did he think would happen? Why did Bill say yes? Only Sonny could plan this and make the effort to do so. And like with all the other ridiculous things he did, I could only laugh because it was absurd. But then the joke was on him, because even though Bill wouldn't talk to me at first, by the time we finished the first show, we'd reconnected. Amazing, I know, but I still had a soft spot in my heart for him, and throughout these years, I was growing up on the fly. I still hadn't completely matured, even now that I was in my early thirties. This isn't a cop-out. I just didn't know how to do it, and I'm also a strange combo of naïve and astute. Some things I'm really good at—work and (now) judging people's character—but it doesn't mean I'm not going to make mistakes. I only learn the lesson by making the mistake. I don't know—I perplex even myself.

Being back with my sweet Texan for a while wasn't what either of us expected and certainly wasn't what Sonny planned, but man, it felt good, although it ended when the gigs did. My last performance with Sonny as Bill played guitar was on New Year's Eve 1977 at the Hilton Hawaiian Village in Honolulu. Our closing number was "I Got You Babe."

At eighteen months, baby Elijah was an old pro at walking, and Chas was great with him, which was a relief, as he was already quite a handful. The two of them made me laugh, though, and we had a lot of fun by the pool and at the beach as I tried to re-create some of the best times of my own childhood with Daddy and my mom's lovely friends. Gregory would visit when he could. He had a long period of sobriety while he stayed with us at the Linden house, and he was so good with Elijah there. There was a piano downstairs, and he used to put Elijah between his legs and play the piano while Elijah used all his fingers on both hands to hit the keys, instead of just picking with one finger like kids normally do. Gregory took credit for it and rightly so. I told him, he didn't get it from me. The house was always full with Chas's friends running around: Ricky and Hayden and Mia and Nicky. It was a joyful time, but then Chas told me one day that after Gregory had picked her up from school, he brought her to a bar. I was furious, but relieved she'd told me and that she was safe. I hid my anger from her and simply said, "Don't worry, babe."

Looking back, I can see that I was a little crazy with Gregory. I kept doing the same thing and hoping for different results, and therein insanity lies. I am stubborn and hardheaded, which can be a good quality, because I won't give up—but that can work against me, too. It got me where I am today, but sometimes you gotta know when to quit. That point came soon after, when Gregory had a paranoid breakdown one night and insisted he saw men with guns in the backyard. *This is the last straw,* I thought. *Whatever he is now, it's not safe for kids.* It only happened once, but I couldn't risk it. Like all of us, Gregory was traumatized and hard to decipher. He was complicated. For the right reasons and the wrong, I loved him. We went our separate ways and divorced at the beginning of 1978.

I was soon busy filming a new special that would air in April on ABC. Art Fisher directed, and I was a cowriter and coproducer, flexing new muscles. I made a cameo as Laverne and my guests included the Tubes, a topless Rod Stewart doing a great "Hot Legs" sketch, and Dolly Parton, whom I'd met that year.

I'd been at a party at my manager's house when I spotted an extraordinary-looking woman with a mass of blond curls in a white pantsuit with what seemed like thousands of multicolored buttons covering the bust of her top.

Giving my manager the side eye, I asked, "Who is that?"

He laughed. "Don't make your mind up based on appearance. You're going to love her. She's a fabulous country singer. Her name is Dolly Parton." He was right, and she is still my friend to this day. When we were looking for someone to play the embodiment of "good" across from the Tubes' "evil" for my special, I knew she was just the woman.

Since I was a teenager, I'd wanted to play all the parts in *West Side Story*. When I was fourteen and everybody left the house, I'd do the whole play by myself in my living room. The Jets would have the couch, the Sharks would have the table—everyone had a place so I could jump to the right location as I performed each character. I was a great director even then. I didn't think I'd ever actually get a chance to do it, but then when we were looking for a piece to put in the special, I brought the idea to Art and he said, "Let's do it." It was kind of a slog: ten characters all done in chroma-key. It's wonderful to fulfill a dream you've had since you were young. When I was a kid, it seemed so beyond my grasp. To do it in real life was magical, like I hadn't given up on it. Now I was doing it for real, on TV for an ABC special as Cher. Art was a genius with chroma-key: I played Maria looking at myself in the mirror, then they panned over and up to a staircase and I was Anita singing, then both of us were singing together. When I played the Jets, there was a line of different versions of me doing synchronized choreography together. At one point all the versions of me ran toward the camera and past it. Then it panned over to big steps and Bernardo (also me) was sitting with a red shirt and black pants, his hair falling just over his forehead. I actually wish I'd waited, because I could have done it better just some years later.

I even managed to get Mom and the kids involved with my special. We re-created scenes from my childhood in which my mother's voice was heard chastising the little-girl version of me for messing up her record collection. Chas and Lijah helped close the show, with my nine-year-old scolding me for messing up her record collection and my two-year-old sitting on my lap as I sang "A Dream Is a Wish Your Heart Makes." At one point, Lijah was supposed to smell a flower I handed him and go "Mmmm" like it was pleasant, but he made a horrible face and went "Ugh!"

One night Neil Bogart, the head of my record label, invited me to his house for a reception he was holding for Gerald Ford. I said, "I'll come for you. I'm not a Republican, but I'll come." He was pleasant; it was a gig for him. I was sitting at Neil's table when someone asked me if I'd like to meet Gene Simmons, to which I replied, "Oh God, yes! I'm a huge fan. I've seen all her movies," mistaking the fire-breathing, tongue-waggling, ghoulish bass player for Jean Simmons, the British actress. It was an embarrassing mistake, but one I quickly rectified by asking Gene to sign something for my rock-loving daughter, who I knew would be thrilled.

When he was onstage, Gene wore black leather and his signature black and white makeup, and was known by his fans as "the Demon." In the real world, he looked like a pretty regular guy, but when he spoke, his voice was a deep rumble, like he was trying to be sexy. I laughed and asked him, "Is that your real voice or do you just always talk that way?" which embarrassed him. I didn't say it to be mean—it was a real question. After that, he started speaking normally and turned out to be very nice and surprisingly polite, albeit with a rock god ego. An Israeli-born former sixth-grade teacher—he told me he realized he didn't really want to be a teacher, he'd just wanted to be up in front of the class—he was four years younger than me and an only child devoted to his mother, who'd survived a Nazi concentration camp. Best of all, he was stone-cold sober and had never had a drink in his life. By the end of the evening, I was impressed.

"How about I take you home?" he suggested. On the drive to my house, he told me he would drop me off, then go to his hotel so he could pick up some things for Chas and bring them back after. I said okay, and he came back with like five thousand pieces of Kiss merch. I think Chas thought she'd died and gone to heaven, first, because she had the swag, and, second, because he was in the living room. She said, "Mom, I just asked for his autograph. This is the greatest thing ever!"

Gene suggested we go out on a date the following night to a Tubes gig. At that point, I'd never even heard of the San Francisco band and asked if I could bring my close friend, the actress Kate Jackson. The Tubes show blew my mind. They were so good they scared me, but Gene spent the entire night flirting with me *and* Kate. When he left, we looked at each other and both chimed, "What an asshole," so I figured that was that. He called the next day to apologize, but I told him neither Kate nor I liked him.

Soon after, he left to play the Budokan in Japan but called me while he was away. We talked so long on the phone he ended up with a $2,800 telephone bill. That's when he blurted out that he loved me. We hadn't even kissed. We'd only been out once before he left. *What is it with these men?* I remember he told me that coming home from that trip he'd walked right offstage to the airport with his clothes and makeup still on and boarded the plane that way, taking it off during the flight. We began what turned out to be a surprisingly nice relationship.

I'd decided to invest in a plot of land and build myself something new. I don't know what possessed me, but home was the only place where I had any privacy, and that had become so important to me. I went looking for the perfect place for me, Chas, and Lijah to live in peace and found a four-acre plot in Benedict Canyon, north of Holmby Hills, the only land I could afford, as it wasn't yet a hip area. The property belonged to a man who painted the celluloid sheets, known as "cels," used in cartoons for Walt Disney. He and his wife lived in a tiny house he'd built there without permits. It was so insubstantial you could almost have blown it down. I had a clear idea in my mind of what kind of house I wanted to build. I'd always been fascinated by the Egyptians with their unusual eye makeup and hairstyles, as well as their dancing, music, perfume, and architecture.

The six-bedroom property that would be known as "the Egyptian house" was a copy of an authentic whitewashed home in North Africa that remained unchanged since biblical times. Among its unusual features was a giant front door that slid into the wall with wrought-iron asps in the metalwork. It was the kind of unconventional house everybody wants now, but it wasn't easily understood then. What I didn't know was that my new home would take almost as long to build as the Great Pyramid and cost twice as much. The architect, Ted Grenzbach, thought I was crazy—everyone did—likely because he had never designed anything like it before. I hadn't realized Ted only designed traditional houses. I don't know why he didn't step away as soon as he saw my plans, but maybe he wanted to break out and do something interesting. This was certainly that. He was patient with me as I showed him sketches of homes in a souvenir book from the Zeffirelli series *Jesus of Nazareth*. When I told him I needed a vast glass roof that opened electronically over a central courtyard to expose the sky, as well as massive floor-to-ceiling windows that were narrow at the top and wide at the bottom, he warned me that if the glass broke, I'd have to take out the whole wall in order to extract the rest of the broken window from its frame. I told him I didn't care. Bit by bit, the layout started to take shape as the footprint rose from the ground.

So that he could see me more often, Gene got a bungalow at the Beverly Hills Hotel where he could stay while he was in town from New York. We didn't do so much as kiss at first, because I didn't want to yet. I've always felt that I don't want to sleep with someone until I'm sure I'll be happy to wake up next to them the next morning. I don't want to wake up next to someone I can't talk to or, worse, who I don't like. So Gene and I got to know each other; we talked and we walked. I even took him jogging on the beach. He called me "Puppy" and surprised me for my birthday with "I Love You Cher" written in the sky above the Beverly Hills Hotel, before a full choir and a marching band marched into our bungalow, through our hotel room, and back out. If that weren't enough, he rented an army tank; filled it with my favorite chocolate bars, Snickers; and had us driven down Sunset Boulevard to Le Dome restaurant, where friends, family, and circus acts were waiting.

My children also loved having "Genie" around. He was kind of like a big kid. He was an excellent businessman and had created an incredible and successful image as "the Demon" and built a massive merch empire. Years later he'd built an entire extra building to hold all their merch, much of which he'd also designed himself. He was very proud of what he'd made: when he immigrated to this country, he still spoke with an accent, and with hard work he and his bandmate Paul Stanley created a massively successful business behind their band. But you create something and then you're the prisoner of it. Being around kids, he could just be the kid he was inside. He took Chas to the movies, gave Elijah his first guitar, taught him how to swim, and gave him piggyback rides all over the place. Chas was already a huge Kiss fan, so when Gene asked if she'd like to contribute to his solo single "Living in Sin" with me, she almost died of happiness. We became a merry band of travelers, especially after Gene set my sister up with Paul Stanley and they started dating.

Gene enjoyed his time in Los Angeles, but it wasn't really his scene. There was press everywhere in this city and especially everywhere I was. The makeup and clothes that make Kiss so recognizable also allowed them to have separation between when they were "on" as celebrities and when they were leading private lives. Dating me blurred the line, because he'd want to go out with me as regular Gene, but then the press would be there. He didn't want to put on his persona when we went on dates, but he didn't want to appear to the public as his private self. They'd all wear bandannas over their faces like cowboys when they went out without makeup. Gene was so sweet, it was interesting to watch how he changed when he put on his Kiss costume. One night he told me, "Puppy, when I'm in my costume I might get crazy and not treat you the same." I asked him what he meant, and he said, "Well, then I become the Demon."

"O-kay," I said, wondering what that meant. When he emerged from his dressing room all dressed up and marched across the room to loom over me like a monster and growl, I gave him a proper slap across the face and cried, "Genie! What are you doing?"

"Nothing, Puppy," he replied, shrinking back.

"Good, 'cause I'm not going to put up with it!"

When Gene recorded an album in England, he invited me to come out with the kids to visit. We stayed for a week or two. The recording studio was in the countryside, which was gorgeous, and there were two dogs that were so huge Elijah could ride on them. Gene was so loving with both Chas and Elijah, and the three of them would play soccer together. He even stopped some recording sessions while we were in town so he could play with them and got them their own bodyguard named Eddie Balandas. Elijah would call him "Eddie Bananas," and he'd get on the field and play with them, too. It was so cute to see these large men like Gene and Eddie running around the field with little Chas and Elijah and the dogs.

In 1978, I wanted to record a rock album, branching out into the kind of music I liked to listen to. But Neil Bogart, who'd launched the careers of Donna Summer and the Village People, said it would be better if they broke me out as a disco artist first. "Everybody's doing disco these days," he assured me. "Even the Rolling Stones." Although I loved to dance, I didn't think I was going to be a disco queen. I also worried that since I'd never done anything in the disco world, I wouldn't be welcomed into that community. I'd been searching for a place where I fit with my music, but I wasn't sure if my exploring would come off to people as a kind of "flavor of the month." So I said, "No fucking way!" Well, I might have said it in my mind, but I didn't say it to Neil. I liked him, and I trusted his judgment. He was a smart businessman and he loved music—that's the best combination. Also, this was my first song with Casablanca Records, and Neil and I had a good relationship, so I wanted to be a team player and do this for him. I went along with his suggestion and recorded the album *Take Me Home,* produced by Bob Esty. Once I recorded the title track, I felt good about it. We played the song back in the studio and everybody liked it. You kind of know when you have a hit because there's a feeling in the room. Sometimes the people in the room have the right instinct and sometimes not. In this case we were right. The album reached number eight on the *Billboard* charts and stayed there for five months.

Gene came up with the concept for the album's cover: a photo of me in a gold bikini with large gold wings attached—complete with gold nipples—arm cuffs, and a headdress under a pleated gold cape. I looked like a barmaid from Valhalla.

At this time, I was also financially supporting my mother. She vacillated between being full of pride that I was living her dream and being frustrated that my work kept me so busy. She often told me she didn't want to rely on me, what she really wanted was for me to set her up in business. So, at the age of forty-eight, she opened a store called Granny's Cabbage Patch in Brentwood selling patchwork quilts and old brass beds. It was there that she met Craig Spencer, who was one year younger than me. She'd initially thought Craig would be a good match for Gee, who was single and had just left *General Hospital* in the hopes of getting bigger roles. I went out of town for a few days, and when I came back Gee said, "Mom's going with Craig." And I said, "Where are they going?" And she said, "No, she's going out *with* Craig." And I thought, *Whoa! Go, Mom!*

She soon made Craig her business partner. It was nice to see her happy and in a loving relationship. Craig and I didn't get along in the beginning, but as the years went by, we became good friends and still are. Mom's store attracted a lot of press attention, but it was never solvent and soon began to lose money. As my business manager put it, "Georgia's independence is killing you."

My own independence felt good. Gene and I saw each other off and on, but most of my focus was on my career and my children. Elijah, Chas, and I moved out of the Linden house and to a small house in the Malibu Colony, which is a group of homes that dates back to the Golden Age of Hollywood. We had a double lot with a swimming pool and a tennis court where Elijah would ride his tricycle. Chas and Elijah each had their own rooms done the way they wanted. Elijah had a Mimi London bunk bed that was made of logs. We were really happy in that house.

Elijah looked up to his big sister more than anyone else and called her "Da," because when he was little we tried to get him to say "Chastity" by breaking it down to him slowly in syllables: "Cha-sti-ty" and he'd say back "Da-dee-da." It was hilarious, and Chas has been "Da" ever since. Elijah got the nickname "General Fatface" because he was born so chubby, but the moment he started walking, he started running and he became like a string bean. If he ever did something naughty or got into trouble (which was near constant), he'd always hightail it to Chas for refuge. They were so close and I was happy they had each other, because like all working mothers, I worried about having to focus so much on my career. As it turned out, though, they loved being part of my career, especially going on tour.

Elijah was always rambunctious. When he was just nine months old, we rented a house in Hawaii and I watched him crawl across the backyard over to a drain cover filled with leaves and mud. Unfazed, Lijah thrust his hands into the gunk and started splashing it everywhere. I rushed over, told him to stop, and wiped his hands. Two minutes later, that kid was right back there, plunging his hands in deeper. "No, Lijah!" I cried. "It's dirty!" I added, *"Sucio!"* because he had a Spanish nanny. "There are bugs. Don't play with that, okay?" I cleaned him up and moved him away again. Hardly a second went by, and that boy crawled directly back to the gunk, turned to face me, looked me straight in the eye, and put his hands behind his back to grab some more slime. Now I was annoyed, so I snatched him up and popped his behind. Furious, he glared at me, his big green eyes filling with tears. I set him down near me, but as soon as his knees touched the ground, he crawled off at a speed Chas and I couldn't believe. We were trying our best not to laugh when he got to the gate, opened it, and crawled away. Chas and I were staring after him, thinking, *Is this child kidding?!* Just like me as a kid, he'd decided he'd learned all he could from adults and was ready to set out on his own. *Oh, boy.* My mom used to tell me, "I hope you have a child who is just like you," and he was. She wished him on me. Elijah was sweet, too, though. He just marched to his own drummer. At maybe two years old, he sat down at the nail salon table next to me, put his hands out, and picked out a red polish he wanted for his fingernails. Truly his mother's child.

Chas was always an angel and very mature for her age. She was a tomboy, preferring to wear only jeans and T-shirts and rejecting anything too "girly." I didn't care what she wore as long as it looked nice enough. She was always level-headed and responsible, so I was surprised when I was called into school one day by her principal, who told me my daughter was having emotional problems that were causing her to do poorly in school and suggested I bring her to a psychiatrist. Her words shattered me with their cruelty, and I wondered if they might be true. Thank goodness for Betsy Glaser, Chas's teacher, who'd been at the meeting and waited until we were out of earshot to tell me, "It's not true. I'm Chas's teacher. I know." Furious, she said, "This woman doesn't know Chas and she doesn't have a degree in child psychology. You've got to get Chas tested right away."

"For what?"

"A learning disability. That's what I think this is." And sure enough, the specialists diagnosed her as dyslexic and she was sent to a special school (that she hated). When I read some of the literature they sent me about dyslexia, I thought, *Oh shit. That's me.* Dyslexia testing didn't exist when I was a child and I'd never even heard the word until Chas's diagnosis, but it explained so much. The difference was that there were systems in place to help Chas that were never available to me. It felt like an old mystery had finally been solved, left over from my childhood.

There was something else from my childhood that had never gone away—my first love, acting. My Dumbo dreams, my Cinderella hopes. Though I was performing on *Sonny & Cher,* I knew that wouldn't add up to people thinking I could be taken seriously as an actress. (I was right.) I might have had an Emmy, but my friends had Oscars. Still, I remembered what my acting coach Jeff Corey had told me when I was a teenager about having talent. Being me, I had competing thoughts about it—I could do it and be one rotten tomato, or I could do it and be great.

For five years I quietly tried everything I knew to break into legitimate acting roles, but I couldn't even get an agent to represent me for theatrical work. That was devastating for someone who'd been on the cover of *Time* magazine. All of my peers were at the top of their game, and I didn't want to beg. You can't ask people you're going to dinner with for a job. If we were hanging out socially with agents or producers, I'd listen and gently express interest and ask what they were working on to see if there were any parts I could audition for, but there were never any openings. I wasn't even really saying that I wanted to be an actress out loud. And when I eventually asked David for his help, he told me, "Sweetheart, I don't have a way right now and you don't want to make anyone uncomfortable or seem desperate." I didn't want to compromise him at all, but it's hard when people see you in a certain light and don't think you can do anything beyond that. I was used to that my whole life, but it didn't make it any less painful.

Jack Nicholson did agree to help me meet Mike Nichols, who was directing him and Warren Beatty in the upcoming movie *The Fortune*. Jack made the introduction and I went to Mike's office. Mike wasn't mean, but he said, "There are two kinds of women, and you're not the kind I need for this character." He was gentle but blunt. There was no follow-up comment like, "If there's another part for you in the future, Cher, I'll call," nothing like that. It was a flat turndown. I was angry and upset and I don't know where I got the balls, because in a moment of my brazen self triumphing over my shy self, I stood up and told him, "I'm really talented, and one day you're gonna be sorry." Yes, I said that to Mike Nichols, an Academy Award–winning director. Then I turned on my heel and walked out.

The next meeting I was able to get was with the producer Jon Peters about his upcoming movie, a remake of the classic film *A Star Is Born*, which Sandy Gallin had told me was rewritten using some stories from my relationship with Gregory that he was familiar with from being my manager at that time. Jon sat in his office smoking pot, and when I got there, I realized he may have had an ulterior motive in agreeing to see me. And it was also a waste of my time because in the end his girlfriend, Barbra Streisand, coproduced the movie and got the role. She did a great job, by the way. Then I was called in to see Ray Stark, a major producer and another champion of Streisand. Stark was in his sixties and married to the daughter of the late, great comic actress Fanny Brice. The meeting was at his house, and the second I sat in my seat, Mr. Stark said, "Do you know why a taco is shaped like a pussy?" I immediately lost my hearing, which happens to me when I go into shock. He was a major producer, but everything in me screamed, *You've got to get out of here.* I jumped up and said, "Oh, God, I'm so sorry. I was ill this morning, but I wanted to have the meeting with you so badly that I came anyway. But I have to go, I don't want to get sick on your furniture." As he was wishing me better, I got the fuck out of there. Years later, Jane Seymour revealed that he'd sexually assaulted her, and sadly, I wasn't the least surprised.

With no one offering me any roles, I had no choice but to return to what I knew, and that meant going back on the road, an idea that truly frightened me because it would be my first time without Sonny. Knowing this show had to be a spectacle beyond what anybody had ever seen, we got to work creating it in Los Angeles. We hired Joe Layton, who came with the whole show already imagined as well as all the people needed to pull it off. It was genius. All we had to do was learn it. He had this idea to have male performers impersonating me, Bette Midler, and Diana Ross; Bette and Diana recorded their voices beforehand, so you'd hear Bette's voice saying, "Cher, I'm on my way out!" or Diana calling out, "Hi, girlfriend, I'm coming onstage." Then the impersonators walked out. J. C. Gaynor, who played Diana, and Kenny Sacha, who played Bette, were so incredible that friends of Bette and Diana would ask to come backstage after the show to say hello. Even they were fooled. I found my impersonator, Elgin Kenna, while watching an afternoon TV show and immediately made a call saying, "I need that boy." He was the most talented female impersonator I've ever seen; sometimes I'd look over during the show and think I was looking in a mirror. You really couldn't tell who was who; it was frightening.

My debut performance was set for the Sahara in Reno in the summer of 1979. As I was getting ready backstage to perform to a sellout crowd, my old enemy, stage fright, crept into my head, and there was no one there to shove me on. Looking in the mirror as I did my own makeup, I thought, *This is insane, Cher. You're never going to be able to do this. What were you thinking?* Which is what I think lots of times before I go onstage, but there's no crying in show business.

I'd recently hired a new assistant, a young woman from Ohio who'd been a dental hygienist, named Deb Paull. Deb's sister Monica (who we call "Mons") had worked for Sonny and me on the road and then continued working for just Sonny after. Knowing I was looking for someone, Mons had told me, "I have a sister who can be your assistant." When Deb finally arrived, Monica handed her the phone book, said "Good luck," and left. This kid with frizzy brown hair didn't know anything. Driving to California from Ohio, she'd packed her vinyl records under the rear window in direct sunlight and they all melted. But she was game and she loved show business. Her first day on the job, she caught a glimpse of Genie in a pink bathrobe lumbering down the stairs and hid in the kitchen. Luckily, Deb was eager and fun, and we spent a lot of time together. It was Deb who was with me on my opening night, and despite having no previous experience with show business, she did a great job at keeping me from running off screaming. God only knows what Deb thought of this scared woman shivering in the dark as if she'd never stepped into a spotlight before. What she didn't realize, and few people really know, is how sensitive and nervous I've always been. It's a case of closing my eyes and jumping. Deb is still with me forty-five years later, so I guess she's got me figured out by now.

I can't recall whose idea it was for me to surprise the crowd by coming out as Laverne, but it was genius. Everyone was expecting Cher to appear in the spotlight in some amazing gown, but instead I came tottering through the crowd in my ridiculous heels, muttering to myself in that scratchy Brooklyn voice, which immediately broke the ice. Laverne was a familiar presence for this audience. Hiding my nerves behind her character and giggling to myself about the pepperoni Deb had put in Laverne's purse for Italian good luck, I gave a short monologue and then whipped backstage for a quick costume change before emerging as they'd expected in a glamorous Bob Mackie triumph. Just as I started singing, though, the fire alarm went off, drowning out my voice. Giving the audience a grimace, I quipped, "I know I'm hot, but this is crazy." Someone managed to stop the bell from ringing and the show went on, but then my goddamn mic cut out. When the sound eventually came back on, I told the crowd, "I knew Sonny was going to come here and screw this up!" The laughter I'd missed filled the auditorium, and that's when I knew that I'd be just fine.

That show was such a success that I agreed to my first residency at Caesars Palace in Vegas and Lake Tahoe, as part of a four-year deal. I also agreed to go to Atlantic City; Washington, DC; and a bunch of other places. Some of my critics scoffed, but all I knew was that this act paid the bills and also people loved it.

I broke Frank Sinatra's attendance record my first month playing Vegas on my own. My show was different from anything audiences had seen. Whether the people on my end of the industry thought I was a sellout or untalented, I didn't care. There was one critic who every year would write that I was on my way out. I finally told him, "You know I'll still be here even after you're gone." I was right.

To help plug my records and the upcoming gigs, I booked *The Dinah Shore Show,* where I told the woman I'd first watched on TV as a kid that the older I got, the less nervous I was about failing in the eyes of the public. I was referring to playing the long game and how I'd developed a thick skin to some extent, with all the changes in my personal life and the attention I'd attracted. Having weathered countless storms over the years, emotional and financial, I never knew what was going to happen next. But I did know I'd survived and discovered that nothing could break me (unless something happened to my health or to my kids). I'd also come to appreciate that whenever I did something new, my fans might not like it and might wish I'd do something else, but they still liked me in the end. When Dinah inquired about the men in my life, I admitted that I picked "strange people," but added that they were all special and unique. She couldn't help but agree.

Then it was back on the road to debut the show in Las Vegas—one night after Frank Sinatra occupied the same stage, which seemed surreal. Even though I'd toured before with Sonny, this tour was an entirely new experience. With Sonny, I'd throw on my outfit each night and go onstage, then straight back to my hotel room after. Now I was learning right along with Deb all the things that went into a touring show, and it was so much fun. Deb and I would ride from LA to Vegas in the back of a limousine together. We'd wedge our Louis Vuitton trunks between the bench seats, throw some blankets and pillows on top, and sleep on it like a big limo bed.

There was a pie place about an hour from Vegas and we'd stop, usually after dark, to have a slice of apple pie and a glass of milk. Then a guy named Angelo would meet us at the back door of Caesars, and after all the luggage was unloaded, he'd sneak us in to see Sinatra do his last number. There was a specific way we had to be brought in, because Sinatra didn't like any light to come into the theater while he was performing (he found it distracting).

I didn't yet love Vegas, although it was the town that proved to be the one constant in my life for decades. Things were changing there, too, as the era of the Rat Pack and the old-school Mafia faded. Innovative new buildings were sprouting along the Strip. I found myself in good company, with friends like Diana Ross playing at Caesars, and the Eagles and Tina Turner performing nearby, too. Johnny Cash and Willie Nelson were also in town, so the whole place had a different vibe.

My *Take Me Home* show had the brilliant comic Michael Keaton opening for us, who was one of the funniest people I have ever met. We also had five dancers, three backup singers, spectacular Bob Mackie costumes, all kinds of wild props, like a bucking bronco and a huge red shoe with a slide down the toe, as well as, of course, our impersonators, who allowed the impression of instantaneous costume changes in addition to their skill as dancers and overall performers. I changed into one incredible costume after another, sticking to my rule of never being in the same outfit for more than ten minutes. We used Sonny's home movies of Chas and Elijah as a backdrop and broadcast a tape of my mother's voice saying, "She always did want to be naked," as slides rolled of me scantily clad as a kid. Each night, we did the first show at 8 p.m. and the second at midnight. (I would fall asleep between them and wake up thinking, *My God, how the hell am I going to do it all again?*) After the second show, the cast and crew would go somewhere to unwind. Sometimes it was Cleopatra's Barge, which we called "The D Cup" in honor of the waitresses' breastplate uniforms. Deb would go early to scout the scene beforehand and use their staff-only red telephone to report back. Other times it was to an all-night club to dance, in which case we'd have to remind one another to bring sunglasses for when we'd finally emerge hours later into the blinding morning sunlight.

Even though everyone made fun of me—thank God there was no social media back then—our record-breaking show was one of the hottest tickets in town. Mamaw came once to see it and asked for a little brandy to enjoy while she watched. She kept having more and more brandy until she was plastered. We took her up to her room, but she wanted to go down and gamble, so I said, "Deb, take her shoes," so she couldn't leave. She got so angry and yelled at Deb, "Deborah, I want my shoes!" Deb said no, and Mamaw started whacking her with her purse.

Our crew and I became so emotionally attached that they felt like family, and many of them remained with me for years and years. That made it all the more heartbreaking when AIDS came along later and claimed the lives of Kenny Sacha and so many lovely friends, including my dancers Michael Perea, Peter Tramm, and Randy Wander. They were all in their thirties when they died. I went to so many bedside farewells, it nearly killed me.

After my Vegas run, we played the Kennedy Center Opera House in Washington, DC, which turned out to be interesting for the wrong reasons. At rehearsal, I noticed a lot of security guards hanging around, and although we were in the political heart of America, I thought that was strange for a Cher gig and asked my new agent about it. Billy Sammeth was a junior agent and was known by all as "Bumper." He shrugged and said, "Oh, you know, this is how they work. They like to give people extra security at the Kennedy Center."

The gig began, and as often happens, a teenage boy ran up and tried to jump onto the stage. Within seconds there were armed police and FBI agents around him like a swarm of bees. They pulled him off so violently that I shouted at them, "He's just a kid!" It seemed like such an extreme reaction. After the gig, the FBI continued to follow me around, going everywhere I went. Nervous, I asked Bumper what was going on, but he brushed me off again. Wanting to do my own thing, I told him I was going to get some ice cream, but the agents still followed me. They finally lost me when I made a left down a street that had a dress shop I liked. When I got back to the hotel, shopping bags in hand, everyone was very anxious. Bumper finally had to explain that someone had contacted the Kennedy Center before my gig and told them that he was going to shoot me. Well, I guess they missed their chance.

That Christmas I went to Aspen with Pauli, Gee, Chas, and Lijah, who was three by then. To begin with, we rented a condo, but later I bought our beloved peeled-log cabin with its huge fireplace. Going to the cabin for the holidays would become a tradition. I'd make all the food and we'd all decorate the place, and each year we'd have a Christmas cookie competition that I'd always win. The cabin had a high peaked roof, so I was able to make a room above the kitchen for my sister. It was really nice, but there was no staircase, so I put in a ladder that would extend down from the room for her to go up and down. Sometimes I'd lock her up there and she'd get so mad. We had fun taking the children to the movies or their favorite restaurant, the Shaft, which was all decked out like the inside of a mine with coal trucks, tools, and plates that were like the pans they used to pan for gold. When Elijah walked out into a blizzard and saw snow for the first time, he frowned, looked up at me, and said, "What is this? What the hell is this?" I lied about his age to send him for ski lessons, because I figured they really only cared whether he was potty trained or not. Plus, he was tall so they couldn't tell the difference. He became a fearless skier, like Chas before him.

Back at work at the start of 1980, I took my show to Europe and then all over the world. To fill my time, I started needlepointing again. Gene was still in my life, but we were rarely in the same city at the same time, so he asked me to consider moving to New York with the kids. We went house-hunting together and Gene picked an older building at Fifth Avenue and Sixty-Fourth Street opposite the Central Park Zoo. When he went back on tour, my architect was flown in from LA to create the perfect home, and I helped Ronnie Wilson do the interior design, but Gene's and my relationship was over by the time the apartment was finished. Our friendship, however, lasted for years.

Life went on and I was finally able to move into my Egyptian house in LA, which cost a fortune to build. It had actually sucked up my money faster than I could make it, on top of the $1.4 million I had to pay Sonny in settlement for not fulfilling all of my performing contract I'd signed before we split up. When I'd broken the contract, we were on such bad terms—he was trying to take Chas and prove I was an "unfit mother"—I couldn't imagine performing with him again. I didn't see any option besides backing out. With all that money leaving my bank account, I found myself at the kitchen table looking down at Chapter 11 papers, not wanting to sign them. I didn't care how much "better it was than bankruptcy," supposedly. While staring at the papers, my mom walked in to say, "I found a great house and put an offer in."

"Well, you'd better hope they don't accept it, because I don't have the money," I told her. I'd thought I was doing well. I didn't understand how I'd overspent so much. That's when Joe D told me, "There's something wrong. Your managers are making more money than you are." I thought to myself, *So I didn't miscalculate*, and quickly got rid of them. But that's not what saved me from Chapter 11. Just as I was about to sign the papers, my new business manager called me. "Cher, you must be the luckiest person in the world," he told me. In a time when I'd had money for investments, I'd been advised to buy apartment buildings, but I'd since sold them to a man who was paying me by installments. Out of the blue, he suddenly decided he'd get a better tax break if he paid me in full, and that's what saved me. *Thank you, God.* I vowed never to overextend myself like that again. (Not that it stuck—I've been overextending myself in a million ways my whole life!)

The house was worth all the anxiety it caused. I was very happy there and threw a barbecue every Sunday for all our friends. I'd make a lot of different food. Often, I'd make this fabulous dish that Jake taught me: tomatoes, olives, cubed potato, mayonnaise, celery, a few other things, and a salty seasoning called Beau Monde. Another favorite was shredded purple cabbage with sour cream and Beau Monde. All the boys would barbecue, because that's what boys do, they barbecue. And who wants to do that anyway?

One night while I was living there, my close friend Kate Jackson and I were having dinner in a Japanese restaurant off Mulholland and we got into an argument about something, though I couldn't tell you what. I was getting myself worked up, really giving Kate a piece of my mind, and punctuating each brilliant point I made with a shot of sake. It was the first time I'd ever had sake. "And another thing!" I'd say, knocking one back. The sake didn't seem to do a thing to Kate, but when I woke up the next day, I wished I hadn't. I'd never been hungover before, and it was beyond excruciating. Head pounding, I called my doctor. "Arnie," I cried, "can you die from a hangover?" Apparently not, but you could've fooled me.

The kids loved the new house, too. Elijah was still small, getting into mischief left and right. He was thrilled when Santa gave him one of those drivable electric cars for Christmas, and I explicitly told everyone at the house that he couldn't take it on our long driveway at all. One day when he was zooming around, he saw me arriving home in my Jeep and excitedly drove to greet me, but there was no one there to stop him. He picked up too much speed coming down the hill and was heading straight for the Jeep. I very nearly ran over him and swerved at the last second, but he disappeared from view and I was sure he'd gone under the car. I could hardly get out of the car; I was so scared and not sure whether he was alive or dead. I was afraid I'd cut his head off. He wasn't making a sound. I found him unharmed, having crashed into the wheel instead, which was my intention with turning the wheels once I'd realized we were going to collide. I lost my mind. I stormed inside yelling at my staff, firing everyone within eyesight on the spot for not watching him. Shaking, I went upstairs, got into a hot bath, and started sobbing. That night we were all supposed to go see the movie *Mommie Dearest*. Oops. And, yes, later that afternoon I rehired everybody.

When I wasn't home, I'd bring the kids on tour with me. In Vegas, they'd have a great time hanging out with the crew, eating in the coffee shops, being by the swimming pool all day, and staying up late. Being there made them feel like grown-ups, and wherever they went my team and the staff at Caesars knew to keep an eye out for them. When I went on tour to places like Australia and South Africa, I'd go in the summertime so they could come along too. If we went in the winter I'd still bring them, but I'd also take a tutor with us. It was an unconventional life, but it was the life that Lijah and Chas knew.

During a break from touring the show, I went on a mini tour for my rock album *Black Rose* and dated Les Dudek, who played guitar in the band. He was kind with a great sense of humor and a highly respected guitar player. He played for the Allman Brothers, helped Dickey write their song "Jessica," and also played with the Steve Miller Band, Boz Scaggs, Mike Finnigan, and Stevie Nicks. I remember he had a black Porsche with a license plate that said "EFlat," and before I knew him I'd seen it and asked around, "Who's the guy with the Porsche that says 'EFlat'?" Everybody knew, *Oh yeah, that's Les Dudek*. I had so much fun with him.

My life was exciting and full. I had my two children I loved, my house I'd designed, a heap of success from three different TV shows and multiple world tours, my family of crew on the road, and for the first time I was doing it with nobody to hold my hand and no net. Yet as much as I loved California and my life there, I had this yearning for something more. I still wanted to pursue my dream of acting.

With my show in Vegas, I was making money and making people happy. I was proud of that. When people asked the cab drivers what they should do, they'd always say, "Go to the Cher show," but I wanted my dream. I wanted to move people, to touch them, not just with my voice but with my skills as an actress. I'd never stopped wanting to see if Jeff Corey and Rosalind Russell were right. Experience so far had shown me that no one would take me seriously. I felt stuck.

Then I was just walking offstage one night, still blind from the bright lights, when I heard a voice cry, "Cher!" I couldn't see who it was at first, but blinking, I finally saw it was Francis (Ford Coppola). I was so happy to see the old friend who used to come to Sonny's and my house in Encino to play cards and have clam-eating contests. With four Oscars under his belt after both *Godfather* movies and *Apocalypse Now*, he was a major player in Hollywood and I couldn't have been prouder of him. A year earlier, I'd visited him at his Zoetrope Studios, described as "the forerunner to DreamWorks" because of its innovative idea to have writers, cinematographers, and directors working together under the same roof. We had such a magical couple of days, and he was so funny, taking me and his son Gio for a bike ride around the old ten-acre Hollywood General Studios lot on the corner of Santa Monica Boulevard and Las Palmas Avenue. Francis knew everyone's names, and as we rode he played tour guide, pointing to different places and explaining what they were going to build there. He showed Gio and me the unbelievable set built on a soundstage for his movie *One from the Heart,* starring Nastassja Kinski and my friend Teri Garr. Then we went back to his bungalow on the lot and Francis had a meeting with Gene Kelly, so Gio and I sat in one of the back bedrooms just hanging out and talking. Gio showed me the new Walkman that Francis had gotten in Japan. After the meeting, we talked a bit longer before I had to go.

Sitting together in my dressing room at Caesars Palace, Francis and I reminisced. He told me how much he'd enjoyed my show and then, after a brief pause, added, "Why aren't you making movies?"

I almost burst into tears and thought, *How are you seeing something in me that no one else does?* Instead, I told him about the rejections I'd had for being too old, too ethnic, too tall, or too typecast. I was "Cher, of Sonny & Cher"—made a punch line for my complicated personal life. I explained how producers and directors insisted I could only ever do TV comedy, never anything serious or real.

Francis was sympathetic but added, "The problem is that until you do something, nobody will believe you can. The worst that can happen is that you fail, but at least you'll have tried." I told him his advice reminded me of something Shelley Winters once said to me: "If you're really serious about acting, Cher, then stop fucking around and go to New York."

Francis smiled. "Okay, then," he said. "So what are you waiting for?"

# acknowledgments

Writing this book was like jumping off a cliff, but I didn't do it alone.

My thanks to fellow travelers:

Roger Davies—maestro and manager

Lindsay Scott—bonzer and manager

Wendy Holden—for listening and interpreting

Julia Leatham—for getting me to the finish line with grace, talent, and so much dedication

Hillary Matthews—for endurance

Liz Rosenberg—protection

The entire HarperCollins US and UK team

Carrie Thornton—publisher, with perseverance

Katya Shipster—UK editor

Liate Stehlik, Heidi Richter, Allison Carney, Ben Steinberg, Rachel Meyers, Jennifer Eck, Renata De Oliveira, Mark Robinson, Melanie Bedor, Tracey Menzies, Susan Kosko—Dey Street Books

Alan Nevins—for utmost patience

Janet Zand—always a call away

Joe D Carlo

Sonny—& Cher

Gregory—Chooch

David—sweetheart

Paulette Howell, Angie Best, Joanna Staudinger, and Deb Paull—four amazing women

Jen—miracle worker

Alexander & Slash—Cherish

Mom, Georganne and Ebar, Chaz and Elijah—forever